The Financial Numbers Game

Detecting Creative Accounting Practices

ONE WEEK L

Charles W. Mulford
and
Eugene E. Comiskey

WILEY

JOHN WILEY & SONS, INC.

To Debby Mulford:
Her strength and courage
are an inspiration for us all.

Library of Congress Cataloging-in-Publication Data

Mulford, Charles W., 1951–
 The financial numbers game : detecting creative accounting practices / Charles W. Mulford and Eugene E. Comiskey.
  p. cm.
 Includes bibliographical references.
 ISBN-10 0-471-77073-6 (pbk. : alk. paper)
 ISBB-13 978-0-471-77073-2
 1. Financial statements—United States. I. Comiskey, Eugene E. II. Title.
HF5681.B2 .M75 2002
657'.3—dc21   2001045648
Printed in the United States of America.
10 9 8 7 6 5 4

Foreword

It has only been a few short years since publication of *The Financial Numbers Game: Detecting Creative Accounting Practices*. While much has happened since then, the techniques advocated for detecting creative accounting practices continue to be effective.

We wrote the book at a time when there was less of a stigma attached to earnings management. In fact, the activity was arguably quite widespread and was viewed by many as a responsibility of management for the purpose of reaching forecast targets. In a speech given in the late 1990s, the chairman of the Securities and Exchange Commission (SEC) noted that earnings management, which includes aggressive accounting actions both within the boundaries of generally accepted accounting principles (GAAP) and that extend beyond those boundaries, had become a game of sorts as managers took all manner of steps to report earnings at or slightly above expectations.

In writing the book that we will refer to here simply as *The Financial Numbers Game,* we surveyed financial professionals to get their perspective on the subject of earnings management. It is interesting now to look back at their views and marvel at how those views have changed. For example, the following observation regarding earnings management is representative of many we received at the time: "It helps companies who manipulate earnings for the purpose of maintaining stability in their stock price by smoothing earnings over time, rather than sending volatile earnings reports to the market." These are exactly the kinds of steps that managers at Fannie Mae and American International Group, Inc. (AIG) were taking in order to report a smoother, less risky earnings stream. We suspect that fewer financial professionals would view earnings management as this benign today.

The Enron Corp. fraud was uncovered around the time the book was published. It was followed in short succession by the discovery of fraud at World-Com, Inc. Both frauds resulted in dramatic bankruptcies that wiped out billions of dollars in shareholder funds. Suddenly, the perception took hold that while earnings management may begin small, it can often grow and become harmful to investors. Congress responded and passed in short order the Sarbanes-Oxley Act of 2002. The financial-reporting landscape in the United States was changed dramatically as new requirements were put in place for managers, their firms, and auditors.

America wanted to see the perpetrators of the alleged crimes dealt with harshly. Prosecutors responded and a series of high-profile court cases, including trials of managers at Enron Corp., World-Com, Inc., Tyco, Inc., Dynegy, Inc., and Health-South Corp., among many others, took place.

Today, even as we continue to feel the fallout from Sarbanes-Oxley, investors are understandably interested in whether financial statements can be trusted. Are the frauds over? Has the financial numbers game stopped or has it changed into something new?

While Sarbanes-Oxley cannot stop financial fraud, it can make it more difficult and costly, and, in the process, theoretically, reduce the number of frauds and their size. However, such assurances are of little consolation when fraud is discovered in a firm in which one has an investment position.

The Financial Numbers Game is designed to help investors and creditors uncover earnings management and fraud in financial statements. The methods advocated are as effective today as when we wrote the book.

In this Foreword, we look back at the financial reporting landscape at the time the book was written. We trace developments in financial reporting since then and highlight the changes. Finally, we address how *The Financial Numbers Game* can help investors today just as it did when the book was first written.

THE CHAIRMAN MAKES HIS PLEA

At the time we wrote *The Financial Numbers Game* we felt that it was crucial to stress the seriousness of what we considered to be an important and growing problem—one of using aggressive, or what we referred to as creative, accounting practices in an effort to mislead investors and creditors. It seemed to us that it was too easy for managers to employ many tricks in an effort to achieve desired earnings targets.

For example, revenue might be recognized even as a secret side agreement introduced as contingencies that effectively negated the sale. Or, charges might be taken and reserves established for merger-related costs or restructuring activities. Later, these reserves could be reversed and used to boost income. Similarly, useful lives of depreciable assets might be manipulated to achieve desired results. Sometimes these actions were within the boundaries of GAAP, and sometimes they extended beyond those boundaries. In all cases, however, the impressions of investors and creditors regarding financial performance were affected.

As early as 1998, Arthur Levitt, then chairman of the Securities and Exchange Commission, was also vocal about the developing problem. In a speech, which we cite in the book's introduction, he warned those in attendance at a gathering of the New York University Center for Law and Business of a "widespread, but too little-challenged custom: earnings management."[1] He noted that the process had evolved into what he characterized as "a game." He continued, noting that, if not addressed soon, the game would "have adverse consequences."

In hindsight, the speech is alarmingly prescient. It is probably more accurate than even the Chairman could have foreseen. One could reasonably question why the Chairman did not do more to stop the problem if he was so sure that adverse consequences would be the end result. However, he did try to effect change. In fact, some of the action steps he proposed, which were designed to address the problems with financial reporting that he felt existed at the time, actually found their way into the Sarbanes-Oxley Act that became effective several years later.

The Chairman identified five accounting practices that he thought were being abused. He devoted SEC time and resources to uncovering instances of their use and effecting change. These five practices, which we look at more carefully in Chapter 4, were the heart and soul of aggressive earnings management. They consisted of the use of big-bath charges, such as those taken in a restructuring, which were designed to reduce current earnings but to boost future earnings. In addition, according to the Chairman, creative acquisition accounting provided a means for writing off much of the cost of an acquisition, typically in the form of purchased in-process research and development. Cookie jar reserves were accruals for any number of ordinary operating expenses that are expensed in advance of payment and carried as a liability. Subsequently, these reserves could be reversed, thus providing a means to absorb and reduce future operating expenses. He identified a problem with the application of materiality rules, where individual items may not be material, but collectively they breach normal materiality thresholds. Finally, he noted problems with revenue recognition, where companies were recording revenue before a sale was made and delivery had taken place.

The Chairman laid out an action plan that was designed to return reliability and transparency to financial reporting in the United States. The plan was divided into four broad categories. The first, improving the accounting framework, was focused on rectifying the five accounting practices that he thought were being abused. In the second, enhancing outside auditing, he asked auditors to review the way audits were being performed and determine if changes were needed. In the third action step, strengthening the audit committee process, he called for a blue-ribbon panel to develop recommendations to strengthen audit committees. Finally, in the fourth step, pursuing cultural change, he called on corporate management and Wall Street to examine the reporting environment and find ways to reward open and transparent reporting and punish abusive practices.

While on target, the Chairman's plan was probably both too little and too late to head off the firestorm that was emerging. The year 1998 was at the height of the last great bull market. Corporate managers, rich with stock options, Wall Street, feasting on fees derived from investment banking and mergers and acquisitions, individual and professional investors, rich and giddy with double-digit annual returns generated over several years, were not interested in change. As many in these groups likely thought at the time, if earnings management helps to keep the party going, why should we change?

A SURVEY OF FINANCIAL PROFESSIONALS

A survey of financial professionals, which we completed during 2001, did not provide an unequivocal view that earnings management was necessarily bad. Some results suggested that earnings management was not a problem while others viewed it with growing concern. For example, some survey respondents viewed earnings management as harmful if it gave the appearance of greater stability than was the case, or if it kept negative items temporarily hidden. Others saw benefits from the smoothing of earnings that might have a beneficial effect on share prices. If done within the GAAP boundaries, earnings management was also seen as helpful since it could help firms to meet or beat analyst estimates of earnings.

The dramatic accounting-related turmoil that exploded in late 2001 and early 2002 has no doubt affected some of the relatively benign attitudes toward earnings management that existed when the survey was conducted. For example, survey respondents rated earnings management achieved through the use of "real" actions as midway between (1) within the flexibility afforded by GAAP and (2) at the outer limits of the flexibility afforded by GAAP. The real actions included in the survey included adjusting advertising expenditures, increasing production, relaxing credit standards, announcing next-year price increases in the fourth quarter of the current year, delaying year-end shipments, and selling investments in order to book a gain.

The real actions above that involved the relaxation of credit standards and the announcement of price increases in the fourth quarter—to take effect in the next year—could be seen as part of a "channel-stuffing" strategy. In recent years firms that have engaged in channel-stuffing activities have become targets of the SEC. Those affected have included, among others, such prominent firms as Bristol-Myers Squibb Co. and The Coca-Cola Co.

In a SEC Accounting and Auditing Enforcement Release, Bristol-Myers Squibb was charged with, among other actions, "stuffing its distributions channels with excess inventory."[2] A $100 million civil penalty and a $50 million shareholder fund were required as part of the settlement. Bristol-Myers Squibb was found to have engaged in channel stuffing "near the end of every quarter in amounts sufficient to meet sales and earnings targets set by officers."[3]

In the case of Coca-Cola, the focus of the SEC Accounting and Auditing Enforcement Release was also on channel stuffing. With Coca-Cola, the practice was referred to as "gallon stuffing."[4] Coca Cola (Japan) Company, Ltd. offered extended payment terms to bottlers at or near the end of reporting periods. "The income generated by gallon pushing in Japan was the difference between Coca-Cola meeting or missing analysts' consensus or modified consensus estimates for 8 out of 12 quarters from 1997 through 1999."[5] Unlike Bristol-Myers Squibb, the Coca-Cola Company avoided any fines. However, it did agree to a cease-and-desist order and to institute a range of "remedial efforts" to avoid a repeat of its "channel-stuffing" adventures.

In the case of both Bristol-Myers Squibb and Coca-Cola, a central theme of the SEC actions was that the channel stuffing was not disclosed and that the implications for future profits were not highlighted. A reasonable inference might be that, if disclosed, the channel-stuffing activities of both firms would not have been considered to be a violation of either GAAP or SEC regulations. However, if these activities had been disclosed it seems clear that the analyst community would not have considered, for example, the earnings targets of the channel-stuffing firms to have been met. That is, increases in earnings from channel stuffing are inherently unsustainable. They would be removed from reported earnings in the process of revising reported earnings so that these revised numbers could then be compared to the forecasts.

A reasonable conclusion about the use of real actions in efforts to manage earnings is that their use should be expected to be somewhat reduced in the post-2002 era because of the active and aggressive SEC action that is taking place. In addition, it is clear from the SEC action in the cases of Bristol-Myers Squibb and Coca-Cola that channel-stuffing activities and their effects on earnings must be disclosed. However, if disclosed they will lose much of their effectiveness as earnings-management tools.

Beyond earnings management involving real actions, the 2001 survey respondents would probably view the exploitation of the inherent flexibility in GAAP in a more negative manner today. Moreover, if the disclosure requirements, discussed in connection with the cases of Bristol-Myers Squibb and Coca-Cola, for real actions are extended to other earnings-management actions, then a reduction in the use of GAAP flexibility should be the result. The combination of increased SEC scrutiny, new reporting requirements, and the severe penalties being levied against company officers, make going to the edge with GAAP flexibility less likely in the future than in the environment of 2001.

THE ONE-TWO PUNCH THAT SHOOK THE INVESTMENT WORLD

In an environment where there were equivocal views about the problems posed by the use of creative accounting practices, it was difficult for the SEC to get much traction in the Chairman's crusade to foster transparent financial reporting and punish abusive practices. There was little agreement about whether a problem existed, much less on how to deal with it.

However, much like the manner in which an unexpected explosion can turn all eyes in the same direction, toward the blast, the events of 2001 and 2002 changed everything. The discovery of the frauds at Enron Corp. and WorldCom, Inc. fostered the consensus view that something must be done.

It was 2001 when news of the elaborate fraud we now know as Enron captured the nation's attention.

That fall, the company filed for bankruptcy. The average American felt empathy for Enron's employees as television stories carried video clips of them leaving their offices for the last time with boxes of personal effects. As details of the fraud became available, we learned that the company's profits were illusory and liabilities were kept off of the balance sheet. The firm effectively transacted with itself through unconsolidated special-purpose entities, recognizing gains on transactions that had no real economic substance. While rules were in place to force consolidation of special-purpose entities, Enron illegally skirted those rules. Analysts who focused on cash flow as a means of confirming the company's earnings were jarred as it became clear that much of its cash flow from operations was actually borrowed and funneled through the same special-purpose entities. Loans were reported as deferred revenue instead of borrowings, enabling the company to report the proceeds received as operating instead of financing cash flow.

For several months Enron was viewed as an outlier, an isolated event and not a reason to effect wholesale changes in financial reporting in the United States. Then, in the summer of 2002, the WorldCom, Inc. fraud was uncovered. At WorldCom, billions of dollars of operating expenses, costs for connecting long-distance phone calls, were capitalized and kept off of the income statement. They were reported instead as property, plant and equipment. It was a relatively simple fraud to commit, devoid of the accounting complexity and nuance that was part and parcel of the Enron fraud. Yet, analysts were misled because the company's capital expenditures, which included these capitalized operating expenses, were kept in line with company-provided projections.

Like Enron, bankruptcy followed the WorldCom fraud. Once again, investors lost billions and employees lost jobs. Congress, feeling a need from constituents to do something about accounting fraud in the United States, responded with the Sarbanes-Oxley Act of 2002.

SARBANES-OXLEY

The Sarbanes-Oxley Act was signed into law on July 30, 2002, only weeks after the WorldCom fraud was uncovered. In hindsight, it is truly remarkable that such sweeping legislation was enacted so quickly. The Act contained many provisions, all of which were focused on the financial reporting system in the United States.

Accounting Oversight Board

Recognizing that auditors may have been deficient in their discovery of fraudulent accounting, Sarbanes-Oxley created the Public Company Accounting Oversight Board (PCAOB). PCAOB is a government-sponsored entity given authority to set standards for auditing, quality control, and ethics, to inspect the work of registered accounting firms, and to conduct investigations and take disciplinary actions. As a check on its power, PCAOB is subject to SEC review and oversight.

The concept for regular review of the work of audit firms was not a new one. For years, the work of accounting firms was subjected to peer review, where audit firms would review each other's work. However, the results of these reviews were not publicly disclosed and sanctions for shoddy efforts were virtually nonexistent. Sarbanes-Oxley brought important changes, as the results of PCAOB audits would now be made public.

In August 2004 the PCAOB published the results of a limited investigation of the Big Four public accounting firms, Deloitte & Touch, LLP, Ernst & Young, LLP, KPMG, LLP, and PricewaterhouseCoopers, LLP. If the accounting firms held the belief that the work of the PCAOB would be anything but in-depth and hard hitting, these first reports surely changed that view. The investigations were very detailed and looked at the procedures followed at selected audit engagements as well as firmwide policies and procedures. For example, across all four firms the PCAOB found instances where (1) GAAP violations were not identified or addressed, (2) departures occurred from PCAOB or firm-specified quality control policies, and (3) documentation was lacking of audit steps performed. We suspect that the threat of PCAOB review will keep auditors much more focused on audit quality.

Auditor Independence

Concern that audit firms may not be sufficiently independent of the companies they audit led to provisions for stricter independence rules. Auditors would be limited in the scope of non-audit services they could provide their clients. For example, auditors would not be allowed to consult on the design of a financial reporting system or conduct internal audits of firms where they were also the external auditor of record. In effect, auditors would not be permitted to audit themselves.

Corporate Governance and Responsibility

The Act contains provisions that are designed to stiffen the resolve and oversight of auditors by audit committees. Members of audit committees must be independent of company management and directly responsible for the appointment, compensation, and oversight of the company's auditors. At least one member of a company's audit committee must be a financial expert. The Act made it clear that the primary duty of auditors is to the public company's board of directors and the investing public, not to its managers.

As a deterrent to corporate misconduct, the Act contains a number of new provisions. For example, for the first time, CEOs and CFOs must certify that company financial statements fairly present the company's financial condition. Also, the Act prohibits any company officer or director from attempting to mislead or coerce an auditor.

Issuer and Management Disclosure

The Act imposes a range of new corporate disclosure requirements including all off-balance-sheet transactions and management conflicts of interest. The Act also requires that all pro-forma disclosures must be made in a manner that is not misleading and must be reconciled with GAAP-based measures.

Provisions in the Act require management to assess the effectiveness of its company's internal controls and make a statement in its annual filings with the SEC that it is responsible for creating and maintaining adequate internal controls and assessing the effectiveness of those controls. The company's auditors must review management's assessment of internal controls and identify the nature of any material weaknesses uncovered.

Fraud and Criminal Penalties

Sarbanes-Oxley imposes a range of tough new criminal penalties for financial fraud. For example, top corporate executives that certify the financial statements of a company knowing they are false can be subjected to fines of up to $5 million or 20 years in prison, or both.

As we go to press, the trial of Richard Scrushy, former CEO of HealthSouth Corp., is continuing. For Sarbanes-Oxley, this is an important trial as it is the first that included charges against an officer for violations of the Sarbanes-Oxley Act.

Will It Be Effective?

Whether Sarbanes-Oxley will be effective in reducing financial reporting fraud is an open question. Notice that we did not posit whether the Act would eliminate such fraud. We know that it will not. Human nature being what it is, given the right motivation, opportunity, and attitude, managers will succumb to temptation. What Sarbanes-Oxley did was to reduce the opportunity and increase the penalties for fraud on the premise that such moves will be effective. While naysayers abound, including those who question the Act's cost and its potential to limit the appeal of publicly raised capital, we remain optimistic that Sarbanes-Oxley will be effective in at least reducing the number and size of financial reporting frauds committed in the United States.

THROW THE BUMS OUT

As this foreword is being written, some trials have been completed and many are continuing of executives at several of the companies at which frauds were allegedly conducted. While prosecutors have not always been successful, and many verdicts are not in, some defendants have been found guilty. Their sentences have not been light. Consider the following examples of several high-profile cases.

Enron Corp.

Kenneth Lay, the former Chairman and CEO of Enron Corp., and Jeffrey Skilling, also a former CEO of the company, face numerous criminal and civil charges related to the company's fraud. Both men await trial. A former finance chief at the company, Andrew Fastow, pleaded guilty to fraud and admitted to conspiracy in inflating the company's profits, in return for a 10-year sentence.

WorldCom, Inc.

In a very high-profile case, Bernard Ebbers, former chairman and CEO of WorldCom, Inc., was found guilty on all counts of securities fraud, conspiracy, and causing the company to make false filings with securities regulators. In his trial, the defendants maintained that he relied on his officers and did not know that the fraud was taking place. In a sobering development for other defendants who may use a similar defense tactic, the jury was not swayed by his contentions. Scott Sullivan, the company's former CFO, pleaded guilty to orchestrating the fraud and testified against Mr. Ebbers.

Tyco International, Ltd.

L. Dennis Kozlowski, Tyco's former CEO, and Mark Swartz, the company's former CFO, were accused of looting approximately $600 million from the company in unauthorized compensation and illicit stock sales, and using questionable accounting practices to hide their misdeeds. The trials of both men ended without the jury reaching a verdict. At present, a retrial of Mr. Kozlowski is ongoing while Mr. Swartz awaits a retrial.

HealthSouth Corp.

The trial of Richard Scrushy, former chairman and CEO of HealthSouth Corp., is continuing. The officer is accused of knowingly issuing fraudulent financial statements. More than a dozen officers at the company, including five former CFOs, have pleaded guilty in the case. Yet, Mr. Scrushy maintains that he was a victim of the fraud and did not know that it was taking place.

Cendant Corp.

Jurors failed to reach a verdict in the fraud trial of Walter Forbes, former chairman of CUC International Inc., the company that merged with HFS, Inc. to form Cendant Corp. A retrial is scheduled. However, a former vice chairman at the firm, E. Kirk Shelton, was found guilty of inflating the company's revenue by more than $500 million, among other charges. He faces a prison sentence of up to 40 years.

Dynegy, Inc.

Jamie Olis, a former vice president of finance and attorney for Dynegy, Inc., was sentenced to 24 years in prison for his role in an accounting fraud at the company. Interestingly, two of his former colleagues reached plea agreements with prosecutors that included no more than five years in prison.

Adelphia Communications Corp.

John Rigas, the founder of Adelphia Communications Corp., and one of his sons, Timothy Rigas, were found guilty of looting the cable company of more than $100 million. Their sentence is pending, but the more serious of their charges carries a maximum sentence of 25 years in prison. A jury was unable to reach a verdict in the trial of a second Rigas son, Michael. A retrial will be conducted.

Rite Aid Corp.

In 2004, Martin Grass, the former CEO of Rite Aid Corp., was sentenced to eight years in prison for his role in the accounting fraud at the drugstore chain. Five other executives were also found guilty.

IN SUMMARY

Much has happened since *The Financial Numbers Game: Detecting Creative Accounting Practices* was published. The requirement that corporate officers attest to the effectiveness of their company's internal controls and certify to the accuracy of their financial statements has increased their responsibility for the quality of their company's financial reports. A heightened threat of civil and now criminal proceedings against them has increased the penalties they may receive for accounting malfeasance. Audit committees have been strengthened, made more independent, and afforded more oversight of the audit process and more responsibility for audit failures. Accounting firms have refocused their attention on audits of their clients' financial statements and less on providing non-audit consulting services. Awareness of the PCAOB's oversight of their work has them exercising more care in the audit services they provide. The staff at the SEC has been increased markedly and is more focused on pursuing and effecting change in accounting practices that they consider to be questionable.

These important changes notwithstanding, however, earnings management and, in some cases, financial reporting fraud will continue. Investors and creditors must be ever diligent in carefully reviewing financial reports for questionable results. In this regard, *The Financial Numbers Game: Detecting Creative Accounting Practices* continues to provide much needed assistance and guidance.

NOTES

[1] A. Levitt, The "Numbers Game," remarks to New York University Center for Law and Business, September 28, 1998, para. 4. Available at: www.sec.gov/news/speeches/spch220.txt.
[2] Accounting and Auditing Enforcement Release No. 2075, Securities and Exchange Commission v. Bristol-Myers Squibb Co. (Washington, DC: Securities and Exchange Commission, August 4, 2004).
[3] Ibid.
[4] Accounting and Auditing Enforcement Release No. 2232, In the Matter of The Coca-Cola Co. (Washington, DC: Securities and Exchange Commission, April 18, 2005).
[5] Ibid.

About the Authors

Charles W. Mulford is the Invesco Chair and Professor of Accounting and Eugene E. Comiskey is the Callaway Chair and Professor of Accounting in the DuPree College of Management at the Georgia Institute of Technology in Atlanta. Both professors have doctorates in accounting and are professionally qualified as certified public accountants. In addition to their work at Georgia Tech, they actively consult with lenders at commercial banks in the United States and abroad. Professors Mulford and Comiskey have published articles on financial reporting and analysis issues in leading academic journals in the accounting and finance fields as well as in such widely read professional journals as the *Commercial Lending Review* and the *Financial Analysts' Journal*.

This is the authors' third book. Their first, *Financial Warnings*, published in 1996, identifies the warning signs of future corporate earnings difficulties. Their second, *Guide to Financial Reporting and Analysis*, seeks to simplify the complexities of current-day generally accepted accounting principles as an aid to practicing financial analysts and other users of financial statements.

Preface

With a certain mind-numbing frequency, users of financial statements—investors and creditors—find themselves buffeted with announcements of accounting irregularities. These irregularities are called many things, including aggressive accounting, earnings management, income smoothing, and fraudulent financial reporting. While they may vary in the degree to which they misreport financial results, they have similar effects—financial statements that serve as a foundation for important investment and credit decisions are incorrect, improper, and worse, misleading.

Companies of all sizes and types, from the start-up to the venerable, from those traded on the "Bulletin Board" to the "Big Board," are susceptible to the problems we refer to here collectively as creative accounting practices. When these acts are discovered, adjustments are needed. Often, prior-year financial statements must be restated, sometimes more than once. Unfortunately, many learn of these accounting problems only after it is too late—after assessments of earning power have been reduced and share prices have fallen precipitously.

Aware that the proper functioning of our capital markets is dependent on the reliability and transparency of financial statements, the Securities and Exchange Commission (SEC) has taken important steps in recent years to rein in the problem. Calling the problem a "numbers game," a former chairman of the SEC increased the enforcement actions taken by the Commission against accounting practices it considered to be errant. As an example of the SEC's newly found diligence, during one month the agency instituted action against 68 individuals at 15 different companies.

Some would say the SEC has gone too far and has begun to question financial reporting practices that are well within the flexibility afforded by generally accepted accounting principles (GAAP). This appears to be a minority view. Moreover, attesting to a need for the SEC's diligence, the problem of companies employing creative accounting practices in their financial reporting is continuing. And the problem will continue as long as there are measurable rewards, including positive effects on share prices, borrowing costs, bonus plans, and corporate regulations, to be gained by those who seek to play this financial numbers game.

The Financial Numbers Game: Detecting Creative Accounting Practices was written, first and foremost, to help readers of financial statements avoid being misled by financial results that have been altered with creative accounting practices. Key chapters conclude with checklists designed to help the reader discern when creative accounting practices have been employed. These checklists, and the text that supports them, were developed with examples of hundreds of companies that were caught in the act of playing the financial numbers game.

Beyond its primary objective, the book provides a sense of perspective. It looks at the embedded flexibility within generally accepted accounting principles, why it is there, and how companies might use it to their advantage—sometimes pushing their financial reporting within that flexibility and other times pushing it well beyond. It looks at the role of the SEC in enforcing the securities laws and identifies the specific statutes used to prosecute those it considers to have pushed beyond the flexibility inherent in GAAP. It provides the results of a survey of important financial professionals, including equity analysts, lenders, and chief financial officers, among others, on their views of the propriety of many financial reporting practices and on the steps they use to detect creative accounting practices. The results of the survey are not always predictable and show disagreement not only between the groups but also within the groups as to which practices are appropriate and within GAAP boundaries, which ones go beyond them, and which ones actually constitute fraud.

The Financial Numbers Game: Detecting Creative Accounting Practices was written for serious readers of financial statements, whether equity analysts or investors, credit analysts or the credit professionals they serve, serious individual investors, or any parties whose interest in financial statements goes beyond the casual read. The steps outlined here should become a standard component of financial analysis and an important future reference, ultimately helping to answer the question: Do the numbers make sense?

A Special Note to Our Readers

As we went to press, the details of the accounting and reporting shortcomings at Enron Corp. that facilitated the company's demise were only beginning to come to light. Unfortunately, their investors and creditors had not fully discounted the risk associated with the firm's trading activities, its off-balance sheet liabilities, and its related-party transactions. Given our publication deadline, we were unable to incorporate a full accounting of the events that took place at the company. However, we do believe that careful attention to all the steps outlined in the checklists that conclude Chapter 8, "Misreported Assets and Liabilities," and Chapter 11, "Problems with Cash-Flow Reporting," would have provided an early alert to the possibility of developing problems.

Contents

Contents

CHAPTER ONE

Financial Numbers Game

I'd like to talk to you about another widespread, but too little-challenged custom: earnings management. This process has evolved over the years into what can best be characterized as a game among market participants. A game that, if not addressed soon, will have adverse consequences . . .[1]

With an all-too-frequent occurrence, users of financial statements are shaken with disclosures by corporate managements that certain "accounting irregularities" have been discovered and, as a result, current- and prior-year financial results will need to be revised downward. Consider these examples:

Sybase's shares dropped an additional 20% when the company reported improper practices at the Japanese subsidiary, which Sybase said included booking revenue for purported sales that were accompanied by side letters allowing customers to return software later without penalty.[2]

Bausch & Lomb oversupplied distributors with contact lenses and sunglasses at the end of 1993 through an aggressive marketing plan. . . . The company said yesterday that in the fourth quarter of 1993 it "inappropriately recorded as sales" some of the product it sent to distributors.[3]

Nine West Group Inc. said its revenue-booking practices and policies are under investigation by the Securities and Exchange Commission. The company's shares plunged 18% on the news.[4]

MicroStrategy Inc., the high-flying software company . . . announced it would significantly reduce its reported revenue and earnings for the past two years. . . . Shares of MicroStrategy plummeted 62%, slicing about $11 billion off its market value.[5]

In a long-awaited restatement, Sunbeam Corp. slashed its reported earnings for 1997 by 65%. . . . Sunbeam said the robust profit reported for 1997 resulted largely from an overly large restructuring charge in 1996, premature booking of revenue, and a variety of other accounting moves that have been reversed.[6]

California Micro Devices Corp., a highflying chip maker, disclosed that it was writing off half of its accounts receivable, mostly because of product returns. Its stock plunged 40%

1

after the announcement on August 4, 1994, and shareholders filed suit alleging financial shenanigans.[7]

Waste Management Inc., undoing years of aggressive and tangled accounting, took $3.54 billion of pretax charges and write-downs, and said more conservative bookkeeping going forward would significantly crimp its earnings.[8]

The once-highflying stock of Cendant Corp. plunged 46.5%, knocking $14 billion off the company's market value, after the marketing and franchising concern said accounting problems would require it to reduce last year's earnings and would hurt this year's results.[9]

Aurora Foods Inc.'s chief executive and three other top officers resigned as the company disclosed an investigation into its accounting practices that it said could entirely wipe out 1999 profit.[10]

Baker Hughes Inc. said it discovered accounting problems at a business unit that will result in pretax charges of $40 million to $50 million, a disclosure that sent its stock falling 15% and revived Wall Street's questions about the company's performance.[11]

Every one of the above examples entails, in one form or another, participation in the financial numbers game. The game itself has many different names and takes on many different forms. Common labels, which depend on the scope of the tactics employed, are summarized in Exhibit 1.1.

While the financial numbers game may have many different labels, participation in it has a singular ultimate objective—creating an altered impression of a firm's business performance. By altering financial statement users' impressions of a firm's business performance, managements that play the financial numbers game seek certain desired real outcomes.

REWARDS OF THE GAME

Expected rewards earned by those who play the financial numbers game may be many and varied. Often the desired reward is an upward move in a firm's share price. For others, the incentive may be a desire to improve debt ratings and reduce interest costs on borrowed amounts or create additional slack and reduce restrictions from debt covenants. An interest in boosting a profit-based bonus may drive some. Finally, for high-profile firms,, the motivation may be lower political costs, including avoiding more regulation or higher taxes. These rewards are summarized in Exhibit 1.2 and discussed below.

Share Price Effects

Investors seek out and ultimately pay higher prices for corporate earning power—a company's ability to generate a sustainable and likely growing stream of earnings that provides cash flow. That cash flow either must be provided currently, or there must be an expectation among investors that it will be provided in future years.

Firms that communicate higher earning power to investors will tend to see a favorable effect on their share prices. For the firm, a higher share price increases market valuation and reduces its cost of capital. For managers of the firm with outright equity stakes or options on equity stakes, a higher share price increases personal wealth. Playing the finan-

---

Exhibit 1.1   Common Labels for the Financial Numbers Game

Label	Definition[a]
Aggressive accounting	A forceful and intentional choice and application of accounting principles done in an effort to achieve desired results, typically higher current earnings, whether the practices followed are in accordance with GAAP or not
Earnings management	The active manipulation of earnings toward a predetermined target, which may be set by management, a forecast made by analysts, or an amount that is consistent with a smoother, more sustainable earnings stream
Income smoothing	A form of earnings management designed to remove peaks and valleys from a normal earnings series, including steps to reduce and "store" profits during good years for use during slower years
Fraudulent financial reporting	Intentional misstatements or omissions of amounts or disclosures in financial statements, done to deceive financial statement users, that are determined to be fraudulent by an administrative, civil, or criminal proceeding
Creative accounting practices	Any and all steps used to play the financial numbers game, including the aggressive choice and application of accounting principles, fraudulent financial reporting, and any steps taken toward earnings management or income smoothing

[a]Refer also to the glossary at the end of this Chapter and to Chapter 2 for additional elaboration.

---

cial numbers game may be one way to communicate to investors that a firm has higher earning power, helping to foster a higher share price.

Strong earning power and higher earnings were expected from Centennial Technologies, Inc., in the quarters and months leading up to a peak share price of $58.25 on December 30, 1996. However, playing a role in the company's supposedly bright future were many creative and fictitious accounting practices that boosted the company's prospects. Among the accounting practices employed were the overstatement of revenue and such assets as accounts receivable, inventory, and investments. As the company's true financial position came to light over a two-month period following its share-price peak, investors bid the share price down 95%.[12]

During 1997 and early 1998, Twinlab Corp. saw a dramatic increase in its share price. From just under $12 per share at the beginning of 1997, the company's share price increased to the high $40s per share in July 1998. However, during that time

---

Exhibit 1.2   Rewards of the Game

Category	Rewards
Share-price effects	Higher share prices
	Reduced share-price volatility
	Increased corporate valuation
	Lower cost of equity capital
	Increased value of stock options
Borrowing cost effects	Improved credit quality
	Higher debt rating
	Lower borrowing costs
	Less stringent financial covenants
Bonus plan effects	Increased profit-based bonuses
Political cost effects	Decreased regulations
	Avoidance of higher taxes

---

period, the stellar results that investors grew to expect from the company were not entirely real. The company later announced that it would restate its results for 1997 and for the first three quarters of 1998 because "some sales orders were booked but not 'completely shipped' in the same quarter."[13] By the end of 1998, the company's share price had declined back to $12.

In 1997 Sylvan Learning Systems, Inc., received a $28.5 million breakup fee when it was outbid for National Education Corp. The company established two not-for-profit organizations with the proceeds of the breakup fee to avoid paying income taxes on it. That is, the taxable income associated with the proceeds was offset with a contribution to the newly established not-for-profits. The not-for-profits, however, had a link to Sylvan Learning. They contributed to marketing efforts of Sylvan Learning, doing advertising for the company and promoting Sylvan's software training and licensing programs. Had these promotional costs been borne by Sylvan Learning, they would have been reported as expenses on Sylvan's income statement. Under the current arrangement, however, Sylvan was able to keep the marketing and promotion costs off of its income statement, boosting pretax income.[14]

Between January and July 1998, Sylvan Learning's share price rose from the low $20s per share to the high $30s per share. The unusual reporting scheme may have played a role in this share price rise. However, when knowledge of the arrangements made with the not-for-profits became widely known, the company's share price declined rather abruptly to around $20 per share.

The financial numbers game was being played, although to different degrees, at Centennial Technologies, Inc., Twinlab Corp., and Sylvan Learning Systems, Inc. While the game was being played, and before it became evident, all three companies enjoyed higher and rising share prices. Those higher share-price rises may be attributed, at least in part, to the higher earning power implied by the financial results reported by the companies. An interesting aside from the examples provided is just how punishing the markets can be when news of accounting gimmickry becomes widely known.

Investors also seek and ultimately pay higher prices for the shares of firms whose earnings are less volatile. Reduced volatility implies less uncertainty about the direction of earnings, fostering an impression of reduced risk. The financial numbers game can be used to reduce earnings volatility and, in the process, encourage a higher share price.

Borrowing Cost Effects

Higher reported earnings, and the higher assets, lower liabilities, and higher shareholders' equity amounts that accompany higher earnings, can convey an impression of improved credit quality and a higher debt rating to a lender or bond investor. As a result, the use of creative accounting practices to improve reported financial measures may lead to lower corporate borrowing costs.

Sales at Miniscribe Corp. grew from just over $5 million in 1982 to approximately $114 million in its fiscal year ended in 1985. Profits, however, were elusive as the company continued to report losses from operations. In 1986 the company's financial fortunes changed for the better as sales grew to $185 million and the company reported a profit from operations of $24 million. The timing was perfect as the company was able to use the strength of its latest financial statements to successfully issue $98 million in bonds.

Unfortunately for bond investors, the improved financial results of the company were mostly fabricated, including fictitious shipments to boost revenue and manipulated reserves to reduce expenses. Reported net income for 1986 of $22.7 million was later restated to a greatly reduced $12.2 million. Without the altered financial results, it is unlikely that the company would have been able to sell its bonds as successfully as it did, if at all. Unable to recover from the debacle, the company sought bankruptcy protection and sold its assets in 1990.

Miniscribe Corp. was a public company issuing publicly traded debt. The temporary benefit derived from its use of creative accounting practices, including an ability to secure lower interest rates on the debt issued, was clearly evident from the example. Another potential benefit for borrowers derived from playing the financial numbers game is less stringent financial covenants. This benefit can accrue to borrowers whether they are public companies or privately held.

Debt agreements typically carry loan covenants—express stipulations included in the loan agreement, which are designed to monitor corporate performance and restrict corporate acts—that afford added protection to the lender. Positive loan covenants typically express minimum and maximum financial measures that must be met. For example, a positive loan covenant might call for a minimum current ratio (current assets divided by current liabilities) of 2, or a maximum total liabilities to equity ratio of 1, or a times-interest-earned ratio (typically, earnings before interest, taxes, depreciation, and amortization divided by interest) of 5. Failure on the part of a borrower to meet these covenants is a covenant violation. Such violations may be cured with a simple waiver, either temporary or permanent, from the lender. However, they also may give the lender the opportunity to increase the loan's interest rate, to seek loan security or guarantees, or even in extreme cases, to call the loan due.

Negative loan covenants are designed to limit corporate behavior in favor of the lender. For example, a negative covenant might restrict a company's ability to borrow additional amounts, pay cash dividends, or make acquisitions.

Creative accounting practices can play a very direct role in relaxing the restrictive nature of financial covenants. Steps taken to boost revenue will increase earnings, current assets, and shareholders' equity and, in some instances, reduce liabilities. Such changes in a company's financial results and position improve its ability to meet or exceed financial ratios such as the current ratio, liabilities-to-equity ratio, and times interest earned ratio mentioned above. Steps taken to reduce expenses have a similar effect. As creative accounting is used to improve a company's apparent financial position and build a cushion above its existing financial covenants, those covenants become less restrictive.

Bonus Plan Effects

Incentive compensation plans for corporate officers and key employees are typically stock option and/or stock appreciation rights plans. With such plans, employees receive stock or the right to obtain stock, or cash, tied to the company's share price. When properly structured, such plans successfully link the officers' and employees' interests with those of other shareholders'. Occasionally companies use a measure of earnings—for example, pretax income—in calculating a cash or stock bonus. When such bonus schemes are tied to reported earnings, officers and employees have an incentive to employ creative accounting practices in an effort to maximize the bonuses received.

Few bonus plans were as lucrative as the plan in place for Lawrence Coss, chairman of Green Tree Financial Corp., a subprime lender. Mr. Coss's bonus was calculated at 2.5% of Green Tree's pretax profit—a significant amount being paid to a single person. The bonus was paid in shares of stock as opposed to cash. However, helping to increase the amount of the payout, the price used in determining the number of shares of stock to issue to Mr. Coss was set at a much lower, and fixed, historical amount of approximately $3 per share. For example, during 1996, Green Tree's shares traded between the low $20s and low $40s per share. That year, a $3,000 bonus would effectively buy 1,000 shares of Green Tree stock at the fixed price of $3 per share. If the stock were selling at $30 per share, that $3,000 bonus actually would be worth $30,000 (1,000 shares times the current market value of $30 per share).

In the years ended 1994, 1995, and 1996, Green Tree Financial's pretax earnings were $302,131,000, $409,628,000, and $497,961,000, respectively. A bonus computed at 2.5% of this amount would be $7,553,000, $10,241,000, and $12,449,000, respectively, for that three-year period. Yet Mr. Coss received an annual bonus in stock worth $28.5 million in 1994, $65.1 million in 1995, and $102.0 million in 1996. Clearly, with amounts such as these involved, there is considerable motivation to use creative accounting practices in an effort to boost the company's pretax earnings.

Green Tree's business was to make consumer loans, package them into investment pools, and sell interests in the pooled loans to investors in the form of asset-backed securities. The company would receive funds for the securities sold and pay an agreed interest amount to investors in those securities. When its loan-backed securities were sold, the company immediately recorded as profit an amount based on the estimated interest income it was scheduled to receive on the loans underlying the securities over and above the interest the company had agreed to pay the investors in those securities. The estimate of the amount of interest to be received from the underlying loans was very sensitive to assumptions on such factors as changing interest rates, loan prepayments, and loan charge-offs. Green Tree was aggressive in the assumptions it used, thus increasing the amount of operating profit reported on sales of the loan-backed securities.

In 1997 the company adopted less aggressive assumptions on the repayment of its consumer loans. The company restated its 1996 net income downward to $184.7 million from the previously reported $308.7 million. As a result, Mr. Coss returned a substantial portion of the bonus shares he received for that year.

Another bonus plan that was tied to reported profits and offered a motivation to its management to engage in creative accounting practices was the plan in place at Leslie Fay Companies, Inc. In 1991 the company's plan paid a bonus to certain key officers of the company if net income exceeded $16 million. No bonus was paid if net income fell short of that amount.

Whether it was the bonus plan that encouraged questionable behavior on the part of the company's management is not clear. What is clear in hindsight is that earnings reported by the company in 1991 and 1992 were largely fictitious. Until the company's fictitious profit scheme was uncovered, Leslie Fay's management enjoyed higher bonuses than they would have if the altered amounts had not been reported.

Political Cost Effects

Large and high-profile firms may have the motivation to manage their earnings downward in an effort to be less conspicuous to regulators. Few readers old enough to have experienced firsthand a strong Organization of Petroleum Exporting Countries (OPEC) and the price effects of the oil embargoes of the 1970s will forget the term *obscene profits* as it was applied to the earnings of the oil companies during that period. The earnings of those companies were viewed as sufficiently high that Congress enacted a special "windfall profits tax" in an effort to rein them in. Oil prices moved so quickly during that period that likely there was very little these companies could have done to mitigate the positive earnings effect. Given time, however, they might have been encouraged to take steps, such as deferring revenue or accelerating expenses, in an effort to lower reported income.

A company that has been very clearly in the spotlight of regulators in recent years is Microsoft Corp. Although it has a market share of as much as 90% of the personal computer operating systems market, the company has unsuccessfully argued in federal court that it does not have monopoly power. Like the oil companies in the 1970s, reporting lower profits could actually be in Microsoft's interest. A review of the company's accounting policies does show instances where it has taken a very conservative stance.

Consider, for example, its accounting for software development costs. As is detailed more carefully later, accounting principles for software development costs call for capitalization of these costs as opposed to expensing them once technological feasibility—that the software can be produced to meet its design specifications—is reached. Interestingly, the company expenses 100% of its software development costs, capitalizing none. This approach is taken even though research and development (R&D) at the company, primarily software development, totaled $1.8 billion, $2.6 billion, and $3.0 billion, or 28%, 29%, and 23%, respectively, in 1997, 1998, and 1999, of operating income before R&D expense. By expensing all of these costs as incurred, the company's earnings are reduced, helping it to appear to be less profitable and, it is hoped, less of a regulatory target.

Microsoft also has taken a conservative approach in the determination of unearned revenue, or the portion of revenue that, while collected, is not yet recognized in earnings. Instead, such unearned revenue is reported as a current liability on the company's balance sheet. The company describes its policy for determining the unearned portion of its software revenue in this way:

> A portion of Microsoft's revenue is earned ratably over the product life cycle or, in the case of subscriptions, over the period of the license agreement. End users receive certain elements of the Company's products over a period of time. These elements include browser technologies and technical support. Consequently, Microsoft's earned revenue reflects the recognition of the fair value of these elements over the product's life cycle.[15]

Under this accounting policy, Microsoft correctly defers or postpones recognition at the time of sale of a portion of the revenue associated with services to be provided over an extended license period. The amount deferred is a function of the value assigned to these undelivered elements. Under this policy, the higher the value assigned to the undelivered elements, the greater the amount of revenue deferred at the time of sale.

Microsoft has deferred significant amounts of revenue under this policy. Unearned revenue reported on the company's balance sheet grew from $1.4 billion in 1997 to $2.9 billion in 1998 and $4.2 billion in 1999. However, late in 1999 the company adopted a new accounting principle and altered how it calculated the amount of revenue to be deferred. Here is how the company described its adoption of the new principle:

> Upon adoption of SOP 98-9 during the fourth quarter of fiscal 1999, the Company was required to change the methodology of attributing the fair value to undelivered elements. The percentages of undelivered elements in relation to the total arrangement decreased, reducing the amount of Windows and Office revenue treated as unearned, and increasing the amount of revenue recognized upon shipment.[16]

Whether the company, before adoption of this new principle, was being overly conservative in its revenue recognition practices cannot be known. However, what is known is that the company was being more conservative than what accounting regulators deemed appropriate.

CLASSIFYING CREATIVE ACCOUNTING PRACTICES

Using creative accounting practices, managements can alter impressions about their firms' business performance. Assessments of corporate earning power can be rendered inaccurate, leading to inappropriate prices for debt and equity securities. When resulting misstatements are discovered, the markets can be unforgiving, causing precipitous declines in debt and equity prices. The objective of this book is to enable the financial statement reader to better detect the use of creative accounting practices. As a result, the reader will be better able to assess corporate earning power and avoid equity-investment and credit-granting mistakes.

A practical classification scheme is especially valuable in determining whether one or more creative accounting practices are being employed. Such a scheme provides order and helps the financial statement reader to become more focused in his or her search for items that may indicate that earning power may not be what is implied by a cursory read.

The classification scheme that is used here begins with groups based on the measurement of revenue and expense and assets and liabilities: Recognizing Premature or Fictitious Revenue, Aggressive Capitalization and Extended Amortization Policies, and Misreported Assets and Liabilities. Additional classes are added for creativity employed in the preparation of the income statement and cash flow statement. These classes are known as Getting Creative with the Income Statement and Problems with Cash Flow Reporting.

These five categories will provide the detail needed to represent the kinds of creative accounting practices employed in contemporary financial statements. They are applied as labels to the accounting practices employed, whether those practices are the result of aggressive policies, both within or beyond the boundaries of generally accepted accounting principles (GAAP), or whether they are the result of fraudulent financial reporting. The classification scheme is summarized in Exhibit 1.3 and explained further below.

Recognizing Premature or Fictitious Revenue

Given the prominence of revenue on the income statement and its direct impact on earnings, it is not surprising that creative accounting practices often begin with revenue recognition. In fact, premature or fictitious revenue recognition is an almost indispensable component of the financial numbers game. This should be clear from the examples already cited because many of them involved some form of premature or fictitious revenue recognition. In those cases, reported revenue was boosted, at least in the near term, positively impacting earnings and communicating higher earning power.

Premature revenue recognition refers to recognizing revenue for a legitimate sale in a period prior to that called for by generally accepted accounting principles. In contrast, fictitious revenue recognition entails the recording of revenue for a nonexistent sale.

Exhibit 1.3   Classification of Creative Accounting Practices

Recognizing Premature or Fictitious Revenue

Aggressive Capitalization and Extended Amortization Policies

Misreported Assets and Liabilities

Getting Creative with the Income Statement

Problems with Cash-flow Reporting

Much like the gray area that exists between the aggressive application of accounting principles and fraudulent financial reporting, however, it is often difficult to distinguish between premature and fictitious revenue recognition. It is a matter of degree.

Revenue for ordered goods that have not left the shipping dock might be recognized as though the goods had already been shipped. Such an act would entail premature revenue recognition. More aggressively, product might be shipped and revenue recognized in advance of an expected order. Given the lack of an order, such an act would, in our view, entail fictitious revenue recognition. However, many financial statement users would reserve the derogatory term, fictitious revenue recognition, for cases of even more blatant abuse of revenue recognition principles. Examples would include recording sales for shipments for which orders are not expected, or worse, recording sales for nonexistent shipments.

For purposes of analysis, a careful demarcation between premature and fictitious revenue recognition is less important than determining that, in both cases, revenue has been reported on the income statement that does not belong. Expectations about earning power will have been influenced accordingly.

In its 1994 annual report, Midisoft Corp. described its accounting policy for revenue recognition in this way: "Revenue from sales to distributors, other resellers and end users is recognized when products are shipped."[17] While the policy, as expressed, and subject to a proper accounting for estimated returns, is consistent with GAAP, the company was recognizing revenue improperly in two ways. First, in an act of premature revenue recognition, the company recognized revenue on goods that were not shipped until after the end of its fiscal year. Second, in an act of fictitious revenue recognition, the company recognized revenue on transactions for which products were shipped on a timely basis, but for which, at the time of shipment, the company had no reasonable expectation that the customer would accept and pay for the products shipped. These shipments were eventually returned to the company as sales returns. However, at the time of shipment, an insufficient provision for returns had been recorded. As a result of these actions, the company overstated revenue for 1994 by approximately $811,000, or 16%.[18]

For firms receiving up-front fees that are earned over an extended period, recognition might be accelerated to the time of receipt. For years prior to 1998, The Vesta Insurance Group, Inc., recognized revenue for reinsurance premiums in the year in which the related reinsurance agreements were contracted. This policy was followed even though the terms of those contracts bridged two years, calling for those premiums to be recognized ratably over the contract period. As a result, over the period from 1995 through the first quarter of 1998, the company had overstated earnings and shareholders' equity by a cumulative $75,200,000.[19]

Premature or fictitious revenue recognition will appear often in examples of the aggressive application of accounting principles and fraudulent financial reporting. As such, the revenue recognition group is an important category of creative accounting practices.

Aggressive Capitalization and Extended Amortization Policies

Rather than taking steps to boost revenue, or in some cases, in addition to taking steps to boost revenue, some firms will increase reported earnings by minimizing expenses. In this category, Aggressive Capitalization and Extended Amortization Policies, companies will minimize expenses by aggressively capitalizing expenditures that should have been expensed or by amortizing capitalized amounts over extended periods.

In many cases, determining the portion of an expenditure to capitalize is straightforward. For example, amounts paid to purchase equipment and prepare it for use are capitalized into the equipment account and amortized, or depreciated, over the equipment's useful life. Often, however, the items involved are a bit more esoteric, including such items as direct-response advertising, software development, and landfill site acquisition and development costs, entailing judgment in determining whether capitalization is appropriate or not.

When capitalized, an expenditure creates an asset that is amortized over some predetermined useful life. When contrasted with the more conservative expensing option, near-term earnings are increased, implying higher earning power.

American Software, Inc., has historically capitalized software development costs. The practice is consistent with GAAP, which permit capitalization of software development costs, including such costs as software coding, testing, and production, after technological feasibility is reached. As noted earlier, technological feasibility occurs when it is determined that the software can be produced to meet its design specifications.[20] However, the proportion of these costs that was being capitalized by the company was somewhat aggressive. Using figures available in its annual report, for the years ended April 30, 1997, 1998, and 1999, the company capitalized $7,363,000, $12,112,000, and $11,511,000, respectively, of software development costs incurred. During those same years, the company amortized software development costs that had been capitalized previously in the amounts of $4,700,000, $6,706,000, and $6,104,000, respectively. The difference between these amounts each year, the amounts capitalized and the amounts amortized, or $2,663,000 in 1997, $5,406,000 in 1998, and $5,407,000 in 1999, boosted the company's pretax income in each of those years. However, in the year ended April 30, 1999, the company wrote off $24,152,000 in capitalized software development costs, as a result of "ongoing evaluations of the recoverability of its capitalized software projects."[21] The company apparently had capitalized more software development costs than could be realized through operations, and it therefore became necessary for the company to write those costs off. In the intervening years leading up to the write-off, however, the company's capitalization policy had boosted its reported earnings and its apparent earning power.

Before its acquisition, Chambers Development Company, Inc., was in the business of collecting, hauling, and disposing solid waste and of building and operating solid waste sanitary landfills and related operations. During the period 1989 to 1990, the company capitalized significant amounts of landfill development costs. Generally accepted accounting principles permit capitalization where future realization of the costs through anticipated revenue is given careful consideration. In the case of Chambers, however, future realization was not considered in determining the amounts to be capitalized. Instead, Chambers calculated expenses and determined amounts to be capitalized based on targeted profit margins determined in advance. As a result, the company appeared to be more profitable, indicating higher earning power, than it otherwise would have been. In fact, the company's capitalization policy converted it from a loss to a profitable operation. Using amounts provided by the Securities and Exchange Commission, the company originally reported pretax income of $27.1 million and $34.4 million in 1989 and 1990, respectively. Revised amounts, restated to correct for improperly capitalized landfill development costs, were pretax losses of $16.5 million and $40.6 million, respectively.[22]

Another practice used to reduce expenses and boost earnings is to lengthen amortization periods for costs that have been capitalized previously. This practice might be used for such assets as property, plant, and equipment, or any of the assets, including capitalized software development and capitalized landfill development costs, mentioned above.

In an example provided earlier in this chapter, Waste Management, Inc., took a special charge of $3.54 billion to, among other things, write-down fixed assets that had not been depreciated quickly enough. The company adopted new, more conservative accounting practices that included shorter useful lives for fixed assets. Examples such as Waste Management, and others, where earnings have been boosted through aggressive cost capitalization or through extended amortization periods, are grouped in this category of creative accounting practices.

Misreported Assets and Liabilities

In the category of misreported assets and liabilities, we include assets that are not subject to annual amortization, such as accounts receivable, inventory, and investments. Expenses and losses can be minimized through an overvaluation of such assets. For example, by overestimating the collectibility of accounts receivable, the provision for doubtful accounts, an operating expense, is reduced. Similarly, a loss can be postponed by neglecting to write-down slow-moving inventory or an investment whose value has declined and is not expected to recover. An example noted earlier was that of Centennial Technologies, Inc. The company's fraudulent acts to misreport its earning power included overstatements of all three assets, accounts receivable, inventory, and investments.

Also included in this category are steps taken to boost earnings by understating liabilities. While the example entailed an error and was apparently not deliberate, the direct link between accounts payable and cost of goods sold was apparent in the case of Micro Warehouse, Inc. The company understated inventory purchases and accounts payable, understating cost of goods sold and overstating its operating income by a cumulative amount of $47.3 million.[23] Other liabilities that might be understated, boosting reported earnings, include accrued expenses payable, environmental claims, and derivatives-related losses. All of these liabilities, in addition to assets that are not subject to amortization, such as accounts receivable, inventory, and investments, are included in this group of creative accounting practices.

Getting Creative with the Income Statement

Getting creative with the income statement includes steps taken to communicate a different level of earning power using the format of the income statement rather than through the manner in which transactions are recorded. Companies may report a nonrecurring gain as "other revenue," a recurring revenue caption, or a recurring expense might be labeled as nonrecurring. Such practices result in higher apparent levels of recurring earnings without altering total net income. One example is that of International Business Machines

Corp. (IBM), which in a 1999 interim report netted $4 billion in gains on an investment against selling, general and administrative expense.[24] As a result, the company imparted an impression that recurring operating expenses were being reduced.

Problems with Cash Flow Reporting

A company can communicate higher earning power not only by reporting higher earnings but by reporting higher and more sustainable cash flow. The statement of cash flow divides the total change in cash into three components: cash flow provided or used by operating activities, investing activities, and financing activities. Given the potential recurring quality of operating cash flow, the higher the apparent level of that cash flow statement subtotal, the greater will be a company's apparent earning power.

In order to boost operating cash flow, a company might classify an operating expenditure as an investing or financing item. Similarly, an investing or financing inflow might be classified as an operating item. Such steps will not alter the total change in cash.

Companies that capitalize software development costs will, in most instances, report the amount capitalized as an investing cash outflow, keeping it out of the operating section. Accordingly, a company that capitalizes a greater portion of its software development costs, as American Software did, will report higher amounts of operating cash flow than companies that expense all or most of their software development expenditures. Interestingly, if a company, such as American Software, later writes down its capitalized software development costs, the resulting noncash charge does not penalize operating cash flow.

Certain accounting guidelines for cash flow reporting may result in reported operating cash flow amounts that are misunderstood. For example, cash provided by operating activities includes nonrecurring cash flow arising from the operating income component of discontinued operations. Also, all income taxes are reported as operating cash flow, including taxes related to items properly classified as investing and financing actions.

Accounting rules for cash flow reporting that may be misunderstood combined with steps taken by some managements to boost apparent operating cash flow may result in cash flow amounts that yield misleading signals. All such items that may render operating cash flow a less effective tool in evaluating financial performance are referred to here as problems with cash flow reporting.

PLAN OF THIS BOOK

As noted, the objective of this book is to equip the financial statement reader to better detect the use of creative accounting practices and avoid equity-investment and credit-granting mistakes. This objective is achieved with the chapters detailed below.

In Chapter 2, "How the Game Is Played," we look at the flexibility that is available to those preparing financial statements and how that flexibility can be used, and often stretched, sometimes to the point of fraud, in an effort to achieve desired results. By better understanding this reporting flexibility, the reader will be more prepared to see how it might be used to mislead. Chapter 3, "Earnings Management: A Closer Look," provides an in-depth look at the use of earnings management and income smoothing techniques, a subset of creative accounting practices. In Chapter 4, "The SEC Responds," we describe how the SEC has become more diligent in recent years in pursuing creative accounting practices. However, even though the commission is more actively pursuing the use of creative accounting practices, it cannot eliminate them. The financial statement reader will need to remain on guard. In Chapter 5, "Financial Professionals Speak Out," we report the findings of a survey of many different groups of financial professionals, including financial analysts, chief financial officers, commercial bankers, certified public accountants, and accounting academics, on their views regarding the detection of creative accounting practices. The objective is to supplement our knowledge on the subject with information gleaned from professionals who prepare, use, and instruct others on the use of financial statements.

In Chapters 6 through 11 we detail our recommendations for detecting creative accounting practices. In Chapter 6, "Recognizing Premature or Fictitious Revenue," we detail certain likely signs that revenue may have been recorded in a premature or fictitious manner. Expenses and losses become the focus in Chapters 7 and 8. In Chapter 7, "Aggressive Capitalization and Extended Amortization Policies," attention is directed to assets that are subject to periodic amortization. In Chapter 8, "Misreported Assets and Liabilities," the focus is directed to assets that are not subject to periodic amortization and to liabilities.

Creative financial statement presentation is the subject for the last three chapters of the book. In Chapter 9, "Getting Creative with the Income Statement: Classification and Disclosure," and Chapter 10, "Getting Creative with the Income Statement: Pro-Forma Measures of Earnings," the focus is on the reporting of earnings, both in accordance with the guidelines of generally accepted accounting principles and in pro-forma reports, where such formal guidelines do not presently exist. The book concludes with Chapter 11, "Problems with Cash Flow Reporting." Even when total cash flow is reported accurately, the manner in which those cash flows are reported can alter a reader's impression of recurring cash flow. Collectively, the final three chapters look at the creative use of reporting formats to alter impressions of earning power.

SUMMARY

This chapter establishes an organization for the entire book. Key points raised include the following:

- Examples of creative accounting practices, attributable to managements engaged in the financial numbers game, occur often in contemporary financial statements.
- Potential rewards for playing the financial numbers game can be substantial. Included among them are positive share-price effects, lower borrowing costs and less-stringent financial covenants, boosted profit-based bonuses, and reduced political costs.
- Markets can be very unforgiving when news of accounting gimmickry becomes widely known.

- Given the various creative accounting practices that can be used to play the financial numbers game, a classification scheme was devised to facilitate their discovery. The scheme has five categories:
  1. Recognizing premature or fictitious revenue
  2. Aggressive capitalization and extended amortization policies
  3. Misreported assets and liabilities
  4. Getting creative with the income statement
  5. Problems with cash flow reporting

  Separate book chapters are devoted to each of these categories of creative accounting practices.

GLOSSARY

Accounting Errors   Unintentional mistakes in financial statements. Accounted for by restating the prior-year financial statements that are in error.

Accounting Irregularities   Intentional misstatements or omissions of amounts or disclosures in financial statements done to deceive financial statement users. The term is used interchangeably with *fraudulent financial reporting*.

Aggressive Accounting   A forceful and intentional choice and application of accounting principles done in an effort to achieve desired results, typically higher current earnings, whether the practices followed are in accordance with generally accepted accounting principles or not. Aggressive accounting practices are not alleged to be fraudulent until an administrative, civil, or criminal proceeding takes that step and alleges, in particular, that an intentional, material misstatement has taken place in an effort to deceive financial statement readers.

Aggressive Capitalization Policies   Capitalizing and reporting as assets significant portions of expenditures, the realization of which require unduly optimistic assumptions.

Big Bath   A wholesale write-down of assets and accrual of liabilities in an effort to make the balance sheet particularly conservative so that there will be fewer expenses to serve as a drag on future earnings.

Bill and Hold Practices   Products that have been sold with an explicit agreement that delivery will occur at a later, often yet-to-be-determined, date.

Capitalize   To report an expenditure or accrual as an asset as opposed to expensing it and charging it against earnings currently.

Creative Accounting Practices   Any and all steps used to play the financial numbers game, including the aggressive choice and application of accounting principles, both within and beyond the boundaries of generally accepted accounting principles, and fraudulent financial reporting. Also included are steps taken toward earnings management and income smoothing. See *Financial Numbers Game*.

Earning Power   A company's ability to generate a sustainable, and likely growing, stream of earnings that provide cash flow.

Earnings Management   The active manipulation of earnings toward a predetermined target. That target may be one set by management, a forecast made by analysts, or an amount that is consistent with a smoother, more sustainable earnings stream. Often, although not always, earnings management entails taking steps to reduce and "store" profits during good years for use during slower years. This more limited form of earnings management is known as income smoothing.

Extended Amortization Periods   Amortizing capitalized expenditures over estimated useful lives that are unduly optimistic.

Fictitious Revenue   Revenue recognized on a nonexistent sale or service transaction.

Financial Numbers Game   The use of creative accounting practices to alter a financial statement reader's impression of a firm's business performance.

Fraudulent Financial Reporting   Intentional misstatements or omissions of amounts or disclosures in financial statements done to deceive financial statement users. The term is used interchangeably with *accounting irregularities*. A technical difference exists in that with fraud, it must be shown that a reader of financial statements that contain intentional and material misstatements must have used those financial statements to his or her detriment. In this book, accounting practices are not alleged to be fraudulent until done so by an administrative, civil, or criminal proceeding, such as that of the Securities and Exchange Commission, or a court.

Generally Accepted Accounting Principles (GAAP)   A common set of standards and procedures for the preparation of general-purpose financial statements that either have been established by an authoritative accounting rule-making body, such as the Financial Accounting Standards Board (FASB), or over time have become accepted practice because of their universal application.

Income Smoothing   A form of earnings management designed to remove peaks and valleys from a normal earnings series. The practice includes taking steps to reduce and "store" profits during good years for use during slower years.

LIFO   The last-in, first-out method of inventory cost determination. Assumes that cost of goods sold is comprised of newer goods, the last goods purchased or manufactured by the firm.

Loan Covenants   Express stipulations included in loan agreements that are designed to monitor corporate performance and restrict corporate acts, affording added protection to the lender.

Negative Loan Covenants   Loan covenants designed to limit a corporate borrower's behavior in favor of the lender.

Political Costs   The costs of additional regulation, including higher taxes, borne by large and high-profile firms.

Positive Loan Covenants   Loan covenants expressing minimum and maximum financial measures that must be met by a borrower.

Premature Revenue   Revenue recognized for a confirmed sale or service transaction in a period prior to that called for by generally accepted accounting principles.

Securities and Exchange Commission (SEC)   A federal agency that administers securities legislation, including the Securities Acts of 1933 and 1934. Public companies in the United States must register their securities with the SEC and file with the agency quarterly and annual financial reports.

NOTES

1. A. Levitt, The "Numbers Game," remarks to New York University Center for Law and Business, September 28, 1998, para. 4. Available at: www.sec.gov/news/speeches/spch220.txt.
2. *The Wall Street Journal*, February 26, 1998, p. R3.
3. Ibid., January 26, 1995, p. A4.

4. Ibid., May 7, 1997, p. A4.

5. Ibid., March 21, 2000, p. B1.

6. Ibid., October 21, 1998, p. B6.

7. Ibid., January 6, 2000, p. A1.

8. Ibid., February 25, 1998, p. A4.

9. Ibid., April 17, 1998, p. A3.

10. Ibid., February 22, 2000, p. A3.

11. Ibid., December 10, 1999, p. A4.

12. Accounting and Auditing Enforcement Release No. 883, *Securities and Exchange Commission v. Emanual Pinez* (Washington, DC: Securities and Exchange Commission, February 14, 1997).

13. *The Wall Street Journal*, February 25, 1999, p. B9.

14. Refer to *The Wall Street Journal*, December 22, 1998, p. C2.

15. Microsoft Corp., Form 10-K annual report to the Securities and Exchange Commission, June 1999, Exhibit 13.4.

16. Ibid. SOP 98-9 refers to Statement of Position 98-9, *Modification of SOP 97-2, Software Revenue Recognition with Respect to Certain Transactions* (New York: American Institute of CPAs, 1998).

17. Midisoft Corp., annual report, December 1994. Information obtained from Disclosure, Inc., *Compact D/SEC: Corporate Information on Public Companies Filing with the SEC* (Bethesda, MD: Disclosure, Inc., December 1995).

18. Accounting and Auditing Enforcement Release No. 848, *In the Matter of Alan G. Lewis, Respondent* (Washington, DC: Securities and Exchange Commission, October 28, 1996).

19. The Vesta Insurance Group, Inc., Form 10-K annual report to the Securities and Exchange Commission, December 1998, pp. 20–21.

20. SFAS No. 86, *Accounting for the Costs of Computer Software to Be Sold, Leased, or Otherwise Marketed* (Norwalk, CT: Financial Accounting Standards Board, August 1985).

21. American Software, Inc., Form 10-K annual report to the Securities and Exchange Commission, April 1999, p. 35.

22. Accounting and Auditing Enforcement Release No. 767, *In the Matter of John M. Goldberger, CPA and C. Kirk French, CPA, Respondents* (Washington, DC: Securities and Exchange Commission, March 5, 1996).

23. Micro Warehouse, Inc., Form 10-K annual report to the Securities and Exchange Commission, December 1996, Exhibit 11.

24. *The Wall Street Journal*, November 24, 1999, p. C1.

CHAPTER TWO

How the Game Is Played

First Union Corp. managed to meet Wall Street's forecasts for its third-quarter profit, in part because of a one-time gain the bank didn't disclose in its initial report on the quarterly results. . . .[1]

The principal adjustments to net income are the result of improper capitalization of overhead expenses, improper charges to acquisition reserves and recognition of certain income in periods prior to earning such income.[2]

. . . it appears to have been simple. . . . People just made things up.[3]

The financial numbers game is played by actively altering reported financial results (i.e., the income statement and statement of cash flows) or reported financial position (i.e., the balance sheet) in some desired amount and/or some desired direction. A company can achieve this end through accounting policy choice, accounting policy application, or outright fraudulent financial reporting.

ACCOUNTING POLICY CHOICE AND APPLICATION

One way that the financial numbers game is played is through a firm's selection of the accounting policies it employs in the preparation of its financial statements or in the manner in which those accounting policies are applied. The companies involved are simply using available flexibility in accounting principles.

Consider MicroStrategy, Inc., discussed in Chapter 1. The company's problems arose from its revenue recognition practices. Historically, the company had separated the revenue earned from large, complex contracts into elements, recognizing some elements up front while deferring others. On the surface, there was nothing wrong with such a practice provided the company could demonstrate that the up-front revenue had been earned at the time it was recognized. In early 2000 the company admitted to the difficulty of demonstrating that certain portions of contract revenue had been earned up front and decided to begin deferring entire contract amounts, recognizing the related revenue over the lifetimes of the related contracts. The company's former practice had seemed innocent enough. However, with the new policy in place, the company's results for 1999 were restated to a per-share loss from what had been an earnings-per-share amount of $.15.

As noted in Chapter 1, Baker Hughes, Inc., was also employing flexibility in accounting principles. The extent of the company's problems, however, leads one to question whether it had sufficient internal controls and accounting oversight at certain foreign subsidiaries. The company's consolidated 1999 results were misstated by $31.0 million, net of taxes, due to miscalculations in the collectibility of accounts receivable and of inventory shortages, asset impairments, and in the amounts of certain current liabilities.[4]

Flexibility in Financial Reporting

The selection and application of generally accepted accounting principles (GAAP) is flexible, leaving much room for judgment in certain areas. As a result, through their choice and application of accounting policies, companies in similar circumstances may report dissimilar results. Consider the flexibility available in three areas common to modern financial reports: inventory cost determination, software revenue recognition, and goodwill amortization periods.

Inventory Cost Determination

One of the more common examples of flexibility in the selection and application of accounting policies and the impact that flexibility can have on amounts reported in the financial statements is the selection of the method used to determine inventory cost. Companies have many inventory methods from which to choose. The more likely candidates are either the first-in, first-out (FIFO) method; the last-in, first-out (LIFO) method; or the average cost method. Data on the popularity of each of these methods taken from a survey of 600 companies conducted by the American Institute of Certified Public Accountants is provided in Exhibit 2.1. Companies are actively using the different methods available to them, with FIFO being the more popular and LIFO following closely behind.

When inventory costs are changing, each inventory cost method will result in a different earnings amount on the income statement and different amounts for inventory and shareholder's equity on the balance sheet. Longview Fibre Co. uses the LIFO method of inventory cost determination for all of its inventories except supplies. Exhibit 2.2 provides the company's inventory amounts taken from its 1999 annual report.

In the exhibit, Longview Fibre Co. discloses a LIFO reserve. For inventories carried on the LIFO method, the LIFO reserve measures the difference between inventories measured at LIFO cost and those same inventories measured at replacement cost— roughly FIFO cost. It is a SEC requirement that public companies using LIFO disclose the excess of replacement cost, generally approximated by FIFO, over LIFO cost.[5]

Exhibit 2.1 Inventory Cost Determination

	Number of Companies		
	1997	1998	1999
Methods			
First-in first-out (FIFO)	415	409	404
Last-in first-out (LIFO)	326	319	301
Average cost	188	176	176
Others	32	40	34

Source: American Institute of Certified Public Accountants, *Accounting Trends and Techniques*, 54th ed. (New York: 2000), p. 201.

Note: Columns total more than 600 because many firms report the use of more than one inventory method.

As can be seen from the exhibit, there is a substantial difference between the company's inventories measured at LIFO cost and FIFO cost. That difference totaled $42,151,000 in 1997, $47,999,000 in 1998, and $40,450,000 in 1999. Had the company used the FIFO method of inventory for those inventories for which it used the LIFO method, its reported inventories would have been higher by 50%, 57%, and 51%, respectively, in 1997, 1998, and 1999. The company's shareholders' equity also would

Exhibit 2.2 Inventory Cost Disclosures: Longview Fibre Co., October 31, 1997, 1998, and 1999 (thousands of dollars)

	1997	1998	1999
Finished goods	$ 43,571	$ 35,645	$ 36,248
Goods in process	28,881	32,730	30,768
Raw materials	11,879	20,676	13,200
Supplies (at average cost)	42,322	42,907	39,797
	126,653	131,958	120,013
LIFO reserve	(42,151)	(47,999)	(40,450)
	$ 84,502	$ 83,959	$ 79,563

Source: Longview Fibre Co. annual report, October 31, 1999. Information obtained from Disclosure, Inc., *Compact D/SEC: Corporate Information on Public Companies Filing with the SEC* (Bethesda, MD: Disclosure, Inc., March 2000).

have been affected. Under the FIFO method, and assuming a combined federal and state income tax rate of 40%, shareholders' equity would have increased by $25,291,000, or 6%, in 1997, $28,799,000, or 7%, in 1998, and $24,270,000, or 6%, in 1999.

Under the FIFO method the company's pretax earnings also would have differed from the amounts reported under LIFO. In 1998, had the company employed the FIFO method, its reported pretax loss of $14,152,000 would have been lower by $5,848,000, calculated as the increase in the LIFO reserve ($47,999,000 minus $42,151,000). In 1999 the company's pretax earnings of $31,484,000 would have been lower under the FIFO method by $7,549,000, calculated as the decrease in the LIFO reserve ($47,999,000 minus $40,450,000).

Under GAAP, companies are relatively free to choose the inventory methods they wish. The decision is a function of whether inventory costs are rising or falling, tax consequences, and the desired direction for reported earnings to shareholders. There are also other regulatory constraints on the decision. A company that elects the LIFO method for tax purposes also must use the LIFO method for financial reporting purposes. Also, while a company generally can discontinue use of the LIFO method when it chooses to do so, Internal Revenue Service guidelines prevent that company from returning to LIFO once again for 10 years.[6] Subject to these constraints, however, the choice of inventory cost method offers firms much flexibility and room for judgment in deciding how their financial results and position are reported.

Software Revenue Recognition

One example of flexibility in the application of accounting principles that has recently been tightened significantly by accounting regulators is in the area of software revenue recognition. The Microsoft example provided in Chapter 1 illustrated how changes in accounting standards have forced the company to accelerate the recognition of its software revenue. Additional sweeping changes in software revenue recognition have affected many other software firms.[7]

As an example of how software revenue recognition practices have changed, consider the following revenue recognition practices taken from the footnotes to the annual reports of four software companies in early 1991 and 1992.

From the annual report of BMC Software, Inc.:

Revenue from the licensing of software is recognized upon the receipt and acceptance of a signed contract or order.[8]

From the annual report of American Software, Inc.:

Upon entering into a licensing agreement for standard proprietary software, the company recognized eighty percent (80%) of the licensing fee upon delivery of the software documentation (system and user manuals), ten percent (10%) upon delivery of the software (computer tapes with source code), and ten percent (10%) upon installation.[9]

From the annual report of Autodesk, Inc.:

Revenue from sales to distributors and dealers is recognized when the products are shipped.[10]

From the annual report of Computer Associates International, Inc.:

Product license fee revenue is recognized after both acceptance by the client and delivery of the product.[11]

At the time, all four companies were following their interpretation of existing accounting rules for revenue recognition—generally, that software revenue, like revenue in other transactions, was recognized when earned and collectible. However, the flexibility that existed in that general rule was great and led to significant differences in accounting policies for companies even in the same industry.

BMC Software recognized software revenue upon receipt and acceptance of an order. At that point, the company likely had not shipped the software. By recognizing revenue at this early stage, the company was able to boost reported earnings. Any amounts recognized, however, were at risk of order cancellation. American Software recognized the bulk of its revenue at the time the user manuals were shipped, even if that shipment time was before shipment of the software product itself. With this policy, a shipment of manuals at the end of an accounting period could result in an increase in revenue recognized. In contrast, Autodesk waited until its software products had been shipped before recognizing revenue. In this more conservative stance, the earning process was linked to actual shipments.

As noted, accounting principles for software revenue recognition have been tightened in recent years. Today, at a minimum, software companies must have shipped their software products before recognizing revenue. All of the companies identified here now abide by that rule. However, when greater flexibility existed, they used it.

That is not to say that no flexibility remains in GAAP for software revenue recognition. For example, while shipment remains the primary trigger for revenue recognition in the software industry, Computer Associates continues to be more conservative, waiting until its software products have been not only shipped but accepted by their customers before recognizing revenue. Further, using the example provided in Chapter 1, Microsoft accelerated recognition of revenue for software elements earned over an extended license period. This was done to be consistent with new accounting principles. However, that change notwithstanding, flexibility and judgment continue to play a significant role in its revenue timing. As noted by the company in the footnotes to its 1999 annual report:

The percentage of revenue recognized ratably decreased from a range of 20% to 35% to a range of approximately 15% to 25% of Windows desktop operating systems. For desktop applications, the percentage decreased from approximately 20% to a range of approximately 10% to 20%.[12]

With such broad ranges of up-front software fees being deferred and recognized over more extended license periods, the company continues to have flexibility in its recognition of revenue.

Goodwill Amortization Periods

Another example of flexibility in the application of accounting principles is in the choice of amortization periods, that is, an estimate of the useful lives of assets. Consider the following amortization periods for goodwill taken from the footnotes to the 1999 annual reports of three medical products companies.

From the annual report of Matria Healthcare, Inc.:

Intangible assets consist of goodwill and other intangible assets, primarily resulting from the company's acquisitions. . . . Goodwill is being amortized using the straight-line method over periods ranging from 5 to 15 years.[13]

From the annual report of Allergan, Inc.:

Goodwill represents the excess of acquisition costs over the fair value of net assets of purchased businesses and is being amortized on a straight-line basis over periods from 7 to 30 years.[14]

From the annual report of C. R. Bard, Inc.:

Goodwill is amortized straight-line over periods of 15–40 years as appropriate.[15]

All three companies share the same general industry group, yet all three have chosen amortization periods for goodwill that differ. The periods range from as little as five years to as many as 40. At the time of this writing, generally accepted accounting practices require amortization of goodwill but permit companies to choose the amortization period. The only requirement is that the amortization period cannot exceed 40 years. The longer the amortization period, the lower the annual charge to expense. As a result, different companies can report different earnings amounts for no other reason than their choice of amortization period. The accounting standard requiring amortization of goodwill is, however, changing. For fiscal years beginning in the second half of 2001 or later, goodwill will no longer be amortized but will be reviewed periodically to determine if it is value impaired.[16] Thus, the accounting flexibility derived from the choice of amortization period will no longer exist.

Collection of Estimates

The goodwill amortization example demonstrates clearly that estimates must be employed in the application of accounting principles. To a significant extent, financial statements are a collection of estimates. As can be seen from the following note taken from the Citigroup, Inc., 1999 annual report, the use of estimates adds to the flexibility inherent in the preparation of financial statements:

As a result of these processes and procedures, the reserves carried for environmental and asbestos claims at December 31, 1999 are the company's best estimate of ultimate claims and claim adjustment expenses, based upon known facts and current law. However, the conditions surrounding the final resolution of these claims continue to change. Currently, it is not possible to predict changes in the legal and legislative environment and their impact on the future development of asbestos and environmental claims. Such development will be impacted by future court decisions and interpretations as well as changes in legislation applicable to such claims. Because of these future unknowns, additional liabilities may arise for amounts in excess of the current reserves.[17]

The Citigroup, Inc., note makes it clear that the company must use estimates in determining its liabilities for environmental and asbestos claims. There is ample room for the company to use inherent flexibility in the estimates employed and sway its financial reporting if it were so inclined.

Why Does Flexibility Exist?

Inventory cost determination, software revenue recognition, and goodwill amortization periods are only three examples among a multitude of accounting policy-choice and estimation decisions that offer companies flexibility in the recording of transactions and the preparation of financial statements. It is through the presence of this flexibility that managements can get creative in the preparation of financial statements and play the financial numbers game.

Of course, the natural question is, why does flexibility exist? Why do accounting regulators—for example, the Financial Accounting Standards Board and the Securities and Exchange Commission—permit companies to have such flexibility? Would it not make sense for regulators to require all companies to report their financial transactions in the same way?

Unfortunately, it is not that simple. Financial transactions and the economic conditions surrounding them are not sufficiently similar to warrant use of identical accounting practices, even by companies within the same industry.

Consider the determination of inventory cost. Even if the focus is on the financial statements exclusively, ignoring the benefits of LIFO for tax purposes, there are valid reasons for some companies to use the LIFO method and others to use the FIFO method. The LIFO method uses more current inventory costs—amounts closer to replacement cost—in the calculation of cost of goods sold. As a result, with LIFO, the income statement provides a more realistic and meaningful measure of operating performance. For companies with large inventories, especially when inventory costs are rising dramatically, LIFO is a likely choice. However, LIFO uses older, more out of date costs in the valuation of inventory for the balance sheet. Accordingly, with LIFO, the balance sheet is less useful in determining a current valuation for inventory on hand. Thus, depending on the materiality of inventory and the direction of inventory costs, companies have valid reasons to gravitate to one extreme or the other for inventory cost determination. Adding to these financial reporting considerations are income tax considerations. When inventory costs are rising sufficiently fast that LIFO provides tax advantages not available under the FIFO method, companies have additional reasons to select the LIFO method.

Requiring all companies to use one inventory method or the other would ignore and assume away the varying economic conditions that brought the different methods into existence in the first place. Such an act, even in the name of consistency, would not benefit financial reporting.

In the case of software revenue recognition, accounting regulators have considered it necessary to better define the earning process for software revenue. However, flexibility has not been eliminated. Subject to the new standards, the software companies themselves are best equipped to determine when software revenue is earned.

In the goodwill amortization example, there are valid reasons for varying amortization periods. Goodwill arises in an acquisition when an acquiring company pays a premium over the fair market value of the acquired firm's net assets—its assets less its liabilities. In the opinion of the acquiring company, the acquired firm as a whole is worth more than the sum of its parts.

Goodwill might arise for many reasons, including a well-recognized brand name, a particularly loyal customer base, an efficient distribution system, or even adept manufacturing practices. The acquiring firm anticipates earning above-average returns from its acquisition over some predetermined future period. It is over that period that the acquiring firm's management should amortize the acquired goodwill.

The periods over which above-average returns from acquisitions can be realized will certainly vary across acquired firms. Thus, requiring identical amortization periods would not result in more meaningful financial reporting. Here again, reporting flexibility is appropriate.

For valid reasons, flexibility in financial reporting exists. It will and should remain as long as circumstances and conditions across companies and industries vary. The existence of flexibility in the choice and application of accounting policies, however, should not result in misleading financial statements. Rather than using that flexibility to mislead financial statement users, companies should employ it to provide a fair presentation of their financial results and financial position. In the vast majority of financial reports, this does take place.

For example, Longview Fibre Co.'s use of the LIFO method of inventory cost determination is not done to mislead. Rather, in the company's opinion, that inventory method gives a fairer view of its financial performance. Similarly, using judgment to select the timing of software revenue recognition or an amortization period for goodwill does not, on the surface, indicate use of creative accounting practices. The examples cited of software revenue recognition, after being tightened by accounting regulators, and goodwill amortization periods are of normal applications of accounting flexibility done to achieve a fair presentation.

Aggressive Application of Accounting Principles

When the financial numbers game is played, however, rather than using reporting flexibility for fair presentation, companies select accounting principles and apply them in an aggressive manner. They push the envelope and stretch the flexibility of GAAP, sometimes beyond its intended limits. The purpose of this aggressive application of accounting principles is to alter their financial results and financial position in order to create a potentially misleading impression of their firms' business performance. The ultimate objective is to achieve some of the game's rewards that may accrue to them.

Referring again to some of the examples in Chapter 1, consider the case of Sybase, Inc. In its 1998 annual report, the company describes its revenue recognition policy in this way:

> The company licenses software under noncancellable license agreements. License fee revenues are recognized when a noncancellable license agreement is in force, the product has been shipped, the license fee is fixed or determinable, and collectibility is reasonably assured.[18]

As described, the policy is well within generally accepted accounting principles for software revenue recognition. It links recognition to shipment and collectibility of the amounts due. It was determined, however, that the company's Japanese subsidiary was recording revenue "for purported sales that were accompanied by side letters allowing customers to return software later without penalty."[19] Such open return policies, especially considering the use of side letters and the lack of sufficient estimates of returns recorded in the accounts, clearly pushed the company's practices beyond the intended limits of GAAP.

In its annual report for 1996, Sunbeam Corporation described the following corporate restructuring:

> On November 12, 1996, the company announced the details of its restructuring and growth plan for the future. The cost reduction phase of the plan includes the consolidation of administrative functions within the company, the rationalization of manufacturing and warehouse facilities, the centralization of the company's procurement function, and reduction of the company's product offerings and stock keeping units ("SKU's"). The company also announced plans to divest several lines of business which it determined are not core for Sunbeam. . . . In conjunction with the implementation of the restructuring and growth plan, the company recorded a pre-tax special charge to earnings of approximately $337.6 million in the fourth quarter of 1996.[20]

Undertaking a corporate restructuring can be a positive event. To the extent that it is successful in streamlining operations and controlling costs, such a restructuring can bode well for a company's future. The act of recording a restructuring charge does not, in and of itself, denote the aggressive application of accounting principles. According to GAAP, the charge should be recorded in the year of the restructuring and should incorporate all anticipated costs of its implementation. On the surface, that is precisely what Sunbeam was doing. However, the company intentionally overestimated the costs of its restructuring, leading to understated results for 1996 and higher results for future years. In so doing, Sunbeam was applying accounting principles aggressively.[21]

By recording unusually high restructuring costs, the company was able to effectively move future-year expenses into its 1996 results. For example, among the costs included in the restructuring charge were write-downs of inventory and fixed assets. Such write-downs reduce future-year expenses for cost of goods sold and depreciation. Also included in the company's restructuring charge were reserves or liabilities for future environmental and litigation costs. To the extent that these costs were normal operating expenses of future years, they should not have been included in a charge taken in 1996.

Thus, by recording an overly large restructuring charge in 1996, the company was able to boost its results for 1997 and beyond.

The restructuring charge was not the only instance where Sunbeam applied accounting principles aggressively. The company was also aggressive in its policy of revenue recognition. Sunbeam boosted 1997 revenue through "bill and hold" practices, where it sold products to customers with an agreement that it would deliver them later. In addition, the company recorded as revenue what were effectively consignment sales given the liberal return policies that were instituted. These practices were apparently put in place for the first time during 1997.

In 1996, including the effects of the restructuring charge, Sunbeam reported a pretax operating loss of $285.2 million. In 1997, before restatement, the company reported pretax operating income of $199.4 million. So proud was the company of its supposed turnaround in 1997 that its then-chairman and chief executive officer, Albert Dunlap, opened his letter to shareholders with the following self-congratulatory note:

> We had an amazing year in 1997! During the past 12 months we set new records in almost every facet of the company's operations. We experienced significant sales growth and concurrently increased margins and earnings. Most importantly, however, we improved the underlying operations of the business.[22]

Once results for the year were restated to remove the effects of the overly large restructuring charge and to adjust for aggressive revenue recognition practices, Sunbeam's pretax operating profit for 1997 was reduced to $104.1 million.[23]

A quotation from Waste Management, Inc., in Chapter 1, noted that the company took $3.54 billion of pretax charges and write-downs as it made its accounting practices more conservative. Interestingly, much of the company's financial reporting problems arose from an aggressive stance taken in its selection of useful lives and residual values for property and equipment. One would not normally expect that accounting practices as innocuous as fixed asset useful lives and residual values could have such material effects on the financial statements. But that is the case for companies with heavy investments in capital assets.

Property and equipment, excluding land and construction in progress, are depreciated to their estimated residual values over their useful lives. Residual value or salvage value is the estimated fair value of an asset at the time it is expected to be removed from service. The useful life of an asset is its service life—the time period over which the asset is expected to be used in operations. It is up to management to determine appropriate useful lives and residual values for property and equipment. When managements use this flexibility in an aggressive manner to artificially boost earnings, by selecting either useful lives that are too long or residual values that are too high, periodic charges for depreciation and amortization expense will be understated. As a result, current earnings will be overstated, as will the book values of the assets in question. If later it is determined that those book value amounts are higher than the undiscounted net cash flows to be realized through their use, a write-down may be in order. Waste Management's practices resulted in such write-downs.

In its 1997 annual report, Waste Management described its change to more conservative accounting:

> As a result of a comprehensive review begun in the third quarter of 1997, the company determined that certain items of expense were incorrectly reported in previously issued financial statements. These principally relate to vehicle, equipment and container depreciation expense, capitalized interest and income taxes. With respect to depreciation, the company determined that incorrect vehicle and container salvage values had been used, and errors had been made in the expense calculations.[24]

In a subsequent section of its report, the company described the actual changes in the useful lives of certain assets:

> Effective October 1, 1997, the Board of Directors approved a management recommendation to revise the company's North American collection fleet management policy. Front-end loaders will be replaced after 8 years, and rear-end loaders and rolloff trucks after 10 years. The previous policy was to not replace front-end loaders before they were a minimum of 10 years old and other heavy collection vehicles before they were a minimum of 12 years old. . . . Depreciable lives have been adjusted commencing in the fourth quarter of 1997 to reflect the new policy. Also effective October 1, 1997, the company reduced depreciable lives on containers from between 15 and 20 years to 12 years, and ceased assigning salvage value in computing depreciation on North American collection vehicles or containers. . . . Also effective October 1, 1997, the company changed its process for estimating landfill lives. The company now amortizes landfill costs over estimated landfill capacity which includes permitted landfill airspace plus expansions which are probable of being obtained in the next five years.[25]

Historically, Waste Management had played the financial numbers game and artificially boosted earnings with extended useful lives and inappropriately high residual values. With these disclosures, the company was announcing that in the future, it would be less aggressive in its application of accounting principles for depreciation and amortization and reduce the useful lives and residual values of its property, plant, and equipment.

In the fourth quarter of its 1993 fiscal year, Bausch & Lomb, Inc., used aggressive revenue recognition practices in order to boost near-term profitability. The company's policy was to recognize revenue at the time of shipment. However, during that period in 1993, the company oversupplied distributors with contact lenses and sunglasses through "an aggressive marketing plan."[26] When customer demand did not meet expectations, the company was forced to buy back significant amounts of inventory.

Bausch & Lomb was abiding by its policy of recognizing revenue at the time of shipment. The company's aggressive act was to overship product and stuff its distribution channels while providing insufficiently for likely returns.[27]

Aurora Foods, Inc., built itself by buying brand products from established food companies. These brands, including such well-known names as Duncan Hines, Aunt Jemima, and Lender's, had not been sufficiently promoted by their previous owners. Aurora's strategy was to acquire the brands and rebuild customer loyalty by lavishing higher amounts of advertising on them.

The company's earnings seemed to indicate that its strategy was working. The company reported pretax operating profit of $17,186,000, $23,395,000, and $44,762,000 in 1996, 1997, and 1998, respectively.[28] The year 1999 was also proceeding particularly well, with pretax operating profit reported at $92,865,000 for the first nine months of that year.

In early 2000, however, the company announced that it was restating its results for the last two quarters of 1998 and three quarters of 1999, wiping out $81,562,000 of pretax earnings for the two years. Operating profit for the year ended 1998 was restated to $6,492,000 from $44,762,000, and to $49,573,000 from $92,865,000 for the first nine months of 1999. The primary culprit was the company's method of accounting for promotional expenses paid to retailers. The company's revenue recognition practices and amounts recorded for cost of goods sold and brokerage and distribution expense were also part of the restatement, but to a much lesser extent.

Food companies compensate retailers for shelf space and supermarket displays. Aurora was apparently recognizing promotion expense not at the time it shipped product to the food retailers but rather when the retailers later sold that product. As such, Aurora was postponing expense recognition. In its 1999 annual report, the company described the impact of its improper practices:

> Upon further investigation, it was determined that liabilities that existed for certain trade promotion and marketing activities and other expenses (primarily sales returns and allowances, distribution and consumer marketing) were not properly recognized as liabilities and that certain assets were overstated (primarily accounts receivable, inventories and fixed assets). In addition, certain activities were improperly recognized as sales.[29]

Even after the elimination of significant amounts of the company's operating profit for 1998 and 1999, the company announced that "Sales of the company's premium branded food products remain strong." Still, one must reconsider whether earlier assessments of earning power were not overly optimistic given recent disclosures of its accounting practices. The markets agreed. The company's share price was bid down to a low of $3 in early 2000 from a high of near $20 in 1999.

Special Case of Earnings Management

Earnings management is a special form of the financial numbers game. With earnings management, the flexibility of GAAP is employed to guide reported earnings toward a predetermined target. Often that target is a sustained, long-term growth rate in earnings, absent the kinds of dips and peaks that might ordinarily be considered representative of normal economic processes.

Storing Earnings for Future Years

A company's management might consider a compound growth rate of 15% in corporate earnings to be a worthy long-term target. In particularly good years, that management might use more conservative assumptions about the collectibility of accounts receivable, about expected future warranty claims, or about fixed asset useful lives and residual values to increase expenses and "manage" earnings downward. More conservative revenue recognition practices also might be employed in order to defer more revenue and reduce current earnings. In the process, through this use of so-called cookie jar reserves, the company is able to store earnings for future, slower years when, without help, earnings may be projected to come in below the target rate of growth.

In that slower year, the allowance for uncollectible accounts receivable or the liability for expected warranty claims might be reduced, or fixed asset useful lives might be extended, or residual values might be increased, in order to reduce expenses and increase earnings. Similarly, a reduction in deferred revenue would boost revenue and increase earnings.

From the preceding examples, it can be seen readily why earnings management is also known as income or profit smoothing. It is because the practice of earnings management often is designed to produce a smoother earnings stream, one that suggests a lower level of earnings uncertainty and risk.

Earnings at General Electric Co. (GE) have grown steadily for decades. So predictable are the company's earnings that *The Value Line Investment Survey*, a respected analyst-report service, gives the company its highest ranking for earnings predictability, a score of 100.[30] Drawn on a page, a temporal line of the company's annual earnings is remarkably straight, inexorably upward.

One would not expect such a smooth and growing earnings stream from a company whose business segments include such diverse and often cyclical products and services as aircraft engines, appliances, industrial lighting, locomotives, medical systems, and financial services. Certainly the diverse nature of the company's product and service mix provides a diversification effect that yields a more stable earnings stream. Beyond its product and service diversification, however, the company has in the past demonstrated a willingness to take steps that appear to manage its earnings to a smoother series. Martin Sankey, an equity analyst, noted that GE is "certainly a relatively aggressive practitioner of earnings management."[31]

Some of the actions the company has taken include offsetting one-time gains on asset sales with restructuring charges and timing the sales of equity stakes to produce gains when needed. For example, in 1997 the company recorded a gain on its disposition of an investment in Lockheed Martin. The company described the transaction as follows:

> Included in the "Other items" caption is a gain of $1,538 million related to a tax-free exchange between GE and Lockheed Martin Corporation (Lockheed Martin) in the fourth quarter of 1997. In exchange for its investment in Lockheed Martin Series A preferred stock, GE acquired a Lockheed Martin subsidiary containing two businesses, an equity interest and cash to the extent necessary to equalize the value of the exchange, a portion of which was subsequently loaned to Lockheed Martin.[32]

Without the nonrecurring gain from the tax-free exchange, pretax income for 1997 would have fallen 10.8% below that reported for 1996. With the gain, however, pretax income was up 3.5% in 1997 over 1996. Another step taken in 1997 was for the company to reduce its effective tax rate. It was reduced to 26.6% in 1997 from 32.6% in 1996. The tax-free nature of the exchange with Lockheed Martin Corp. was a primary contributor to the decline in the effective tax rate. However, an item described only as "All other—net" also played a role.[33] Once the reduced effective tax rate was factored in, the company's net income increased 12.7% in 1997 from 1996—maintaining the company's continued growth streak.

Understandably, GE takes exception to the observation that it manages earnings. When asked whether steps taken by the company to offset one-time gains with one-time charges could be considered earnings management, Dennis Dammerman, GE's chief financial officer, said, "I've never looked at it in that manner."[34]

In most instances, as with General Electric, earnings management is effected within the boundaries of GAAP. During good years, the companies involved employ more conservative accounting practices and loosen them slightly during leaner times. The steps taken are within the limits of normal accounting judgment. Interestingly, during the good times, regulators may on occasion view the accounting practices employed as being too conservative.

Consider, for example, SunTrust Banks, Inc. The company is known for its conservative accounting practices, pristine balance sheet, and steady earnings growth, which in recent years has approximated 12.5% on a compound annual basis.[35] In 1998, at the request of the Securities and Exchange Commission, the company agreed to restate its results *upward* for the three years ended December 1996. The SEC had determined that the company's allowance for loan losses was too conservative given its loan profile. As a result, the company restated its provision and related allowance for loan losses, reducing them by a cumulative amount of $100 million and increasing cumulative pretax income by the same amount.

In its 1998 annual report, the company provided the following disclosure of the restatement:

> In connection with the review by the Staff of the Securities and Exchange Commission of documents related to SunTrust's acquisition of Crestar Financial Corporation and the Staff's comments thereon, SunTrust lowered its provision for loan losses in 1996, 1995 and 1994 by $40 million, $35 million and $25 million, respectively. The effect of this action was to increase net income in these years by $24.4 million, $21.4 million and $15.3 million, respectively. As of December 31, 1997, the Allowance for Loan losses was decreased by a total of $100 million and shareholder's equity was increased by a total of $61.1 million.[36]

It is the exception, not the rule, where the SEC considers earnings to be reported too conservatively. However, given its actions toward SunTrust, it is clear that it does happen.

Sears Roebuck & Co. reported an increase in pretax income of 17.5% in 1995 and 21.8% in 1996, accompanied by an increase in the company's share price. At least one analyst, however, did not consider the company's improved fortunes to be real. David Poneman argued that the company had, in previous years, increased unduly its reserve for credit card losses. Now the company was able to use that balance sheet account to help absorb credit card losses while minimizing new charges to expense. As noted by Mr. Poneman, "Sears is using its superabundant balance sheet to smooth out its earnings. . . . the big addition to reserves 'moved income out of 1992 and 1993 and into 1995 and 1996.' "[37]

Big Bath

More flagrant applications of earnings management stretch the boundaries of GAAP. For example, in a bad year a company may decide to write-down assets in a wholesale fashion. It is a bad year anyway. Earnings expectations have not been met. The implicit view is that there will be no additional penalties for making the year even worse. By writing down assets now, taking a "big bath," as it is called—the balance sheet can be cleaned up and made particularly conservative. As such, there will be fewer expenses to serve as a drag on earnings in future years.

For example, the large reserve for credit card losses carried on Sears' balance sheet arose as part of a particularly large restructuring charge in the amount of $2.7 billion that the company took in 1992. That year the company reported a pretax operating loss of $4.3 billion. The restructuring charge, which helped set the stage for higher earnings in later years, was described as follows:

> The Merchandise Group recorded a pretax charge in the fourth quarter of 1992 of $2.65 billion related to discontinuing its domestic catalog operations, offering a voluntary early retirement program to certain salaried associates, closing unprofitable retail department and specialty stores, streamlining or discontinuing various unprofitable merchandise lines and the writedown of underutilized assets to market value. Corporate also recorded a $24 million pretax charge related to offering termination and early retirement programs to certain associates.
>
> During the first quarter of 1992, the Merchandise Group recorded a $106 million pretax charge for severance costs related to cost reduction programs for commission sales and headquarters staff in domestic merchandising.[38]

Special Charges

Restructuring charges, even in the absence of a big bath, provide a convenient way to manage earnings. Analysts tend to focus on earnings excluding such charges. Thus, when used inappropriately, the charges can be used to absorb what might otherwise be considered operating expenses. That was the case at W.R. Grace & Co. In an administrative and cease and desist proceeding against the company dated June 30, 1999, the SEC found that Grace, through members of its senior management, misled investors from 1991 to 1995. This was done, according to the SEC, through the use of excess reserves that were not established or maintained in conformity with GAAP. The ultimate objective of the procedure was to bring the company's earnings into line with previously set targets.[39]

Special charges also are often taken in conjunction with corporate acquisitions. Business combinations are supposed to create certain synergies. As the thinking goes, it is these synergies, derived from combining such activities as production, distribution, and administration, that increase postcombination shareholder value. At the time of an acquisition, a combined entity often will record a special charge in order to effect the combination and begin to achieve the projected synergies. Included in the charge might be estimated severance costs, lease termination expenses, and losses associated with anticipated asset disposals. In recording estimated expenses at the time of the acquisition, liabilities or reserves are recorded against which actual future payments and realized losses are charged. Investors tend to ignore these acquisition-related charges and focus instead on postcombination earnings.

In an effort to foster higher future earnings, companies may use creative acquisition accounting and get aggressive in the size of their acquisition-related charges. By recording higher charges at the time of the business combination, future expenses can be reduced. Some companies may go even further and in future years charge operating expenses against their acquisition-related reserves. Such action is clearly beyond the boundaries of GAAP.

Fine Host Corp., an operator of food concessions for companies, sports facilities, hospitals, and other institutional customers, gave an impression of higher postacquisition earnings by charging improper items against acquisition-related reserves.[40] This technique was also used at CUC International, Inc., one of the predecessor companies of Cendant Corp.[41]

Purchased In-Process Research and Development

A common charge seen at the time of the combination of technology firms is a charge for purchased in-process research and development. As the name suggests, purchased in-process R&D is an unfinished R&D effort that is acquired from another firm. It might be an unfinished clinical study on the efficacy of a new drug or an unfinished prototype of a new electronics product.

Under current generally accepted accounting principles, if the acquired R&D has an alternative future use beyond a current research and development project, the expended amount should be capitalized. Capitalization also would be appropriate for purchased in-process software development, a form of R&D, if the software project has reached technological feasibility—in effect, when it has been shown that the software will meet its design specifications. However, if acquired in-process research and development can be used only in a current R&D project, or for software, if technological feasibility has not been reached, it should be expensed at the time of purchase. This accounting treatment is the same as the treatment afforded internal research and development. It is expensed as incurred.[42]

When a technology firm is acquired, undoubtedly there is research and development that is being conducted. Accordingly, a portion of the price paid for the acquired firm is properly allocated to this in-process activity. Not knowing whether the acquired R&D will have alternative future uses, expensing currently the amount paid for it is proper. In an effort to stretch the rules, however, some companies will allocate an overly large amount of the purchase price to in-process R&D, permitting them to charge off a significant amount of the purchase price at the time of acquisition. This accounting procedure enables them to minimize the portion of the purchase price that must be allocated to goodwill. Goodwill must be carried on the balance sheet and written down when evidence indicates its value is impaired, necessitating a change to earnings. The greater the portion of an acquisition price that can be allocated to in-process research and development, the smaller the amount attributed to goodwill, eliminating the risk of future charges to earnings.[43] Moreover, paying for research and development suggests more strategic opportunities and higher future returns than paying for goodwill. It just sounds better.

One company that has used acquisitions as part of its growth strategy is Cisco Systems, Inc. Given that its acquisitions are of technology firms, it is common to see purchased in-process R&D reported on its income statement. For example, for its fiscal years ended July 1997, 1998, and 1999, the company reported purchased in-process R&D in the amounts of $508 million, $594 million, and $471 million, respectively. These were in addition to expenses reported for its own internal R&D of $702 million, $1,026 million, and $1,594 million, respectively, for that same three-year period.

In its 1999 report, Cisco Systems described its accounting policy for purchased in-process R&D:

> The amounts allocated to purchased research and development were determined through established valuation techniques in the high-technology communications industry and were expensed upon acquisition because technology feasibility had not been established and no future alternative uses existed.[44]

The policy gives a glimpse of the judgment that is involved in determining what portion of an acquisition price should be allocated to in-process R&D as opposed to other assets acquired, including goodwill.

The significant portion of acquisition prices allocated to purchased in-process research and development by the company is made clear in Exhibit 2.3, taken from the company's 1999 annual report.

The exhibit shows for each acquisition completed during 1999, the total consideration paid and the portion of that consideration allocated to purchased in-process research and development. While not presented in the company's display of its acquisitions, on average, purchased in-process research and development comprised 63% of the total acquisition prices paid by the company during fiscal 1999. That is a significant portion of the price paid, though it is down from 86% in 1997 and 1998.

Other companies reporting significant amounts of purchased in-process research and development include National Semiconductor Corp. and MCI WorldCom, Inc. In 1997 and 1998 National Semiconductor expensed $72.6 million and $102.9 million, respectively, in purchased in-process research and development. That was enough to push the company into reporting a pretax operating loss of $7.7 million and $146.9 million, in each of those two years, respectively.

During 1998, WorldCom, Inc. paid approximately $40 billion for MCI Communications Corp. The company had originally intended to allocate between $6 billion and $7 billion of the acquisition price to purchase in-process research and development. However, the SEC convinced the company to reduce that amount. This statement was given in a filing made with the SEC in September 1998:

> MCI WorldCom has completed asset valuation studies of MCI's tangible and identifiable intangible assets, including in-process research and development projects ("R&D"). The preliminary estimate of the one-time charge for purchased in-process R&D projects of MCI, was $6–$7 billion.
>
> The Securities and Exchange Commission (the "SEC") recently issued new guidance to the AICPA SEC Regulations Committee with respect to allocations of in-process R&D. Consistent with this guidance, the final analysis reflects the views of the SEC in that the

---

Exhibit 2.3   Allocation of Acquisition Price to Purchased Research and Development: Cisco Systems, Inc., Year Ended July 31, 1999 (millions of dollars)

Acquired Companies	Consideration	Date	Purchased R&D
Fiscal 1999			
American Internet Corporation	$ 58	Oct. 1998	$41
Summa Four, Inc.	$129	Nov. 1998	$64
Clarity Wireless, Inc.	$153	Nov. 1998	$94
Selsius Systems, Inc.	$134	Nov. 1998	$92
PipeLinks, Inc.	$118	Dec. 1998	$99
Amteva Technologies, Inc.	$159	June 1999	$81

Source: Cisco Systems, Inc., annual report, July 1999, p. 42.

---

value allocated to MCI's in-process R&D considered factors such as status of completion, technological uncertainties, costs incurred and projected costs to complete.

As a result of the preliminary allocation of the MCI purchase price, approximately $3.1 billion will be immediately expensed as in-process R&D and approximately $26 billion will be recorded as the excess of purchase price over the fair value of identifiable net assets, also known as goodwill, which will be amortized on a straight-line basis over 40 years.[45]

Concern over potential abuse of the purchased in-process research and development caption led the SEC to become more diligent in investigating the accounting treatment afforded amounts paid in acquisitions. As a result, the agency convinced MCI World-Com to reduce the amount of the planned charge for purchased in-process research and development from $6 to $7 billion to $3.1 billion. The amount of the charge was still a sizable sum.

Accounting Errors

It is possible that there is no premeditated intent to mislead when financial statement amounts are reported outside the boundaries of GAAP. In the absence of intent, such misstated financial statement amounts are simply considered to be in error. When errors are discovered, adjustments to correct the financial statements call for restatements of prior-period amounts.

For example, in 1998 Neoware Systems, Inc., announced that it was restating results for its first and second quarters, "revising them from profits to losses because of accounting errors."[46] Little in the way of detail was provided regarding the errors committed. However, because the errors were identified early, before year-end results had been published, corrections entailed restating prior-quarter results only.

Bigger errors, extending over longer time periods, were committed at Micro Warehouse, Inc. In 1996 the company announced that "accounting errors make the company 'likely to restate its financial results for 1994 and 1995.' "[47] Ultimately it was determined that the errors discovered were more pervasive and affected more years than originally thought. In its 1996 annual report, the company made this statement:

> In late September 1996, an internal review led to the discovery of certain errors in Micro Warehouse's accounting records. A Task Force comprised of company representatives and members of its outside accounting firm, KPMG Peat Marwick LLP, was immediately organized to determine the extent, causes and implications of these errors and appropriate corrective action. Simultaneously, the Audit Committee of the Board of Directors engaged outside counsel and independent auditing advisors to examine these matters.
>
> Over the course of the next several months, the Task Force and Audit Committee examined these issues in detail. Ultimately, the company determined that the errors primarily impacted accrued inventory liabilities and trade payables since 1992. Inaccuracies in these accounts totaled approximately $47.3 million before tax. The 1992 through 1995 restated financial statements reflect aggregate net pre-tax adjustments of $41.9 million, net of the recovery of $2.2 million of incentive bonus payments for 1995 made to certain senior executives. The balance of $3.2 million in pre-tax adjustments were made to the company's first quarter 1996 results and were reflected in its Form 10-Q for the third quarter ending September 30, 1996.[48]

At Micro Warehouse, the identified errors entailed understated amounts for inventory purchases and accounts payable. As a result, cost of goods sold was understated and gross profit and operating profit were overstated for a cumulative amount of $47.3 million before tax for the period 1992 to 1996.

While misstatements such as those reported by Neoware Systems and Micro Warehouse were the result of errors and were not deliberate, adjustments to correct the financial statements still can have a material effect. Moreover, expectations about earning power, formulated on financial amounts that were reported in error, will be overly optimistic and will need to be adjusted downward.

One final error example involves the financial statements of Union Carbide Corp. In 1999 the company stated that it had "miscalculated earlier earnings after employees made a bookkeeping error during the transition to a new accounting computer system."[49] As a result of the error, first- and second-quarter earnings for 1999 had been understated by a cumulative amount of $13 million. In addition, the fourth-quarter's earnings for 1998 had been understated by $2 million.

Creative Classifications within the Financial Statements

In some instances, the financial numbers game is played in the manner in which amounts are presented in financial statements themselves rather than in how transactions are recorded. Companies that seek to communicate higher earning power might classify a nonrecurring gain in such as way as to make it sound recurring. For example, a nonrecurring gain on sale of land might be labeled "other revenue" and reported in the revenue section of the income statement. Similarly, an expense or loss, the occurrence of which could reasonably be expected to recur, might be classified as nonrecurring, implying the amount should be discounted in assessing earning power.

For its nine months ended September 1999, IBM reported a 53% increase in operating income on revenue growth of just 12%. To the casual observer, the results suggest the company was being very diligent in controlling expenses, helping to fuel its growth in operating income. Upon closer examination, it was learned that IBM netted $4 billion in gains from the sale of its Global Network to AT&T Corp. against its selling, general, and administrative expenses (SG&A). The reporting practice does not alter net income. However, it may alter how readers of its financial statements perceive its business performance. By netting the nonrecurring gains against SG&A, which are recurring expenses, the impression is made that the recurring expenses are lower. As a result, operating income, which should be reported before nonrecurring gains, is higher. When asked about the practice, one analyst noted that IBM should be "roundly criticized for its policy of bundling one-time gains and other nonoperating activities into operating income."[50]

When First Union Corp. released results for its third quarter of 1999, the company was able to meet Wall Street's forecasts. It was not until the company filed its financial statements for the quarter with the SEC that it became known that its quarterly results had been helped with a nonrecurring gain. As reported at the time and quoted earlier, "First Union Corp. managed to meet Wall Street's forecasts for its third-quarter profit, in part because of a one-time gain the bank didn't disclose in its initial report on the quarterly results."[51] In the absence of the one-time gain, the company's earnings would have disappointed Wall Street, falling two cents per share short of analysts' forecasts.

In some instances, in an effort to communicate an enhanced ability to generate recurring cash flow, companies will get creative in the presentation of information on the cash flow statement. The idea here is to boost the amount of cash flow reported as being provided by operating activities. As operating cash flow is increased, cash disbursements in the investing or financing section also might be raised, resulting in no change in total cash flow.

For example, the classification of an investing item as an operating item, or vice versa, is one way to boost cash flow provided by operating activities without changing total cash flow. For its fiscal year ended February 2000, Helen of Troy, Ltd., reported the proceeds from sales of marketable securities, $21,530,000, as a component of cash provided by operating activities. The item, which is more appropriately classified with investing activities, was the primary factor behind the company's growth in cash provided by operating activities to $28,630,000 in 2000 from $11,677,000 in 1999.

As another example, when software development costs are expensed as incurred, the associated cash disbursement is reported in the operating section of the cash flow statement. However, when software development costs are capitalized, the cash disbursement typically is reported as an investing item. Thus, a company that capitalizes software development costs will report higher operating cash flow than a company that does not capitalize such costs.

Often financial analysts, dismayed by the general misdeeds conducted in the measurement and reporting of earnings, will turn to cash flow for a truer picture of a company's performance. Unfortunately, even when total cash flow is not altered, operating cash flow, a key metric in the valuation models used by many analysts, still can be swayed in one direction or another.

FRAUDULENT FINANCIAL REPORTING

In the majority of cases in which the financial numbers game is played, accounting policy choice and application simply fall within the range of flexibility inherent in GAAP. While the point can be argued, the manner in which accounting policies is employed is largely a function of management judgment. In most cases, this judgment results in the biasing of reported financial results and position in one direction or another. It is aggressive accounting. It presses the envelope of what is permitted under GAAP, although it remains within the GAAP boundaries. It is not fraudulent financial reporting.

At some point, a line is crossed and the accounting practices being employed move beyond the boundaries of GAAP. Often this is known only in hindsight. Once the line is crossed, the financial statements that result are not considered to provide a fair presentation of a subject company's financial results and position. Adjustments become necessary.

Fine Host Corp., mentioned earlier, had for years capitalized the costs incurred in obtaining new food-service contracts. These capitalized amounts were reported as assets and amortized over time. In its 1996 annual report, the company described its accounting policy for these contract rights:

> Contract Rights—Certain directly attributable costs, primarily direct payments to clients to acquire contracts and the cost of licenses and permits, incurred by the company in obtaining contracts with clients are recorded as contract rights and are amortized over the contract life of each such contract without consideration of future renewals. The costs of licenses and permits are amortized over the shorter of the related contract life or the term of the license or permit.[52]

The company capitalized these costs as opposed to expensing them on the premise that the costs incurred would benefit future periods. As such, under the matching principle, by amortizing the capitalized costs over those future periods, the company was properly matching the costs with the revenue they helped to generate. Such a practice does appear to fit within the flexibility offered by GAAP.

In the beginning, the amounts involved were small. In 1994, according to its statement of cash flows, the company capitalized $234,000 in contract rights. Over time, however, the amounts involved increased substantially. In 1995 the company capitalized $3,446,000 in contract rights, and in 1996 $6,277,000 were capitalized.

Had the company gone beyond the boundaries of generally accepted accounting principles? Certainly as of the date of its latest audited financial statements, 1996, it had not, because the company's statements had been audited and the company's auditors agreed with its reporting practices.

However, the amounts involved continued to grow. For the nine months ended September 1997, the company capitalized $13,798,000 in contract rights. By then the balance in contract rights reported on the company's balance sheet, including capitalized amounts and amounts obtained through acquisitions, had grown to $48,036,000, or 22% of total assets and 42% of shareholders' equity.

At this point, in fact in December 1997, the company announced that it had discovered, "certain errors in the company's accounting practices and procedures."[53] Things began to unravel quickly from there. Within a short period of time, the company terminated its chairman and CEO, the Nasdaq stock market took steps to delist the company, and the SEC began an informal investigation.

In February 1998 the company announced that it would restate its results for the years 1994 to 1996 and for the first nine months of 1997. What had been reported as income before tax of $3.3 million in 1994, $3.8 million in 1995, and $6.5 million in 1996 was restated to losses of $1.6 million, $4.3 million, and $6.3 million, respectively, for those same years. Pretax income for the first nine months of 1997, originally reported at $8.8 million, was restated to a loss of $11.4 million. The culprit was primarily the company's accounting policy for capitalized contract rights, but there were also other problems, as noted in this announcement:

> The principal adjustments to net income are the result of improper capitalization of overhead expenses, improper charges to acquisition reserves and recognition of certain income in periods prior to earning such income.[54]

What had started as an accounting policy choice within the boundaries of GAAP grew into more. In addition to capitalizing costs incurred for contract rights, the company was improperly charging unrelated items against reserves set up in conjunction with its numerous acquisitions. The company was also recognizing revenue prematurely. The company clearly had moved beyond the boundaries of GAAP.

Still, before the label of fraudulent financial reporting can be applied, there must be a demonstration of intent. Specifically, fraudulent financial reporting entails a premeditated intent to deceive in a material way.[55]

KnowledgeWare, Inc., an Atlanta-based software firm, was accused by the SEC of having fraudulently reported revenue. The company gave some customers extended payment periods that called into question the collectibility of large portions of its sales. These sales were nonetheless recorded as revenue. The SEC alleged that in recording these sales, and in other acts committed by the company, such as side letters designed to remove the responsibility of customers to pay, KnowledgeWare had a predetermined intent to deceive readers of its financial statements.[56]

In more flagrant cases of fraudulent financial reporting, realism is totally suspended as fictitious amounts get recorded in the accounts. In such instances, a fraud team of a few individuals within an organization collude to dupe the auditors and investors with fabricated numbers unhinged from the real world.

The financial fraud at Comptronix Corp. began in 1989, around the time the company lost a sizable customer. Rather than report disappointing results, management instituted a profit-increasing scheme that entailed collusion among several members of the management team. Management took steps to boost gross profit by recording an adjustment to inventory and cost of goods sold. Basically, inventory was increased and cost of goods sold was reduced for a fictitious amount, boosting current assets and gross profit.

This adjustment, for varying amounts, was recorded on a regular basis, typically monthly. To hide the adjustment from analysts, portions of the bogus inventory were moved to the equipment account, as it was easier to hide the overstated amounts there. Fake invoices were prepared to support the increases to equipment, making it appear that actual purchases of equipment had been made. Inventory was also reduced through the recording of fictitious sales. These sales also increased the company's reported profits. As a result of the fictitious sales, phony accounts receivable were recorded. To show collections of these accounts receivable that did not really occur, the company wrote checks to vendors supposedly in payment for its equipment purchases. These checks, which were not endorsed by the bogus equipment-vendor payees, were then deposited in the company's own bank account, resulting in a simultaneous increase and decrease to its cash account. While not changing the cash balance, the complicated arrangement gave the appearance of cash activity, of collection of accounts receivable and payment of amounts due. This last step required participation by the company's bank. A bank spokesperson said the deposit arrangement was put in place "to accomplish a legitimate business purpose" when one of the company's customers was also a vendor.[57] Thus the bank appeared to be an unwitting accomplice in the company's scheme.

The alleged financial fraud at Comptronix Corp. may have begun small. By the time it was uncovered, however, it had grown to immense proportions and involved many individuals. In this example, given the scope of the fraud, including the amounts and people involved, it is easy to see fraudulent intent.[58]

During the period 1990 to 1992, an alleged financial fraud was being conducted at the Leslie Fay Companies, Inc. As the facts of the case have become known, it was determined that management personnel of the company were falsifying revenue, including the reporting of sales for shipments made after the end of an accounting period and for shipments made to a company-controlled storage site. The company also reported borrowings and the proceeds from the sale of a corporate division as sales revenue. Other steps taken included the overstatement of inventory and accounts receivable with fictitious amounts and the understatement of cost of goods sold.[59]

Like the Comptronix example, the Leslie Fay financial fraud may have started small. Here again, however, given the pervasive nature of the deceitful steps taken, fraudulent intent is quite evident.

Labeling Financial Reporting as Fraudulent

Fraudulent financial reporting carries a more negative stigma and connotes much greater deceit than what is implied by accounting actions considered only to be aggressive. However, identifying the point beyond which aggressive accounting becomes fraudulent is difficult. While it is easy to see fraudulent intent in the cases of Comptronix and Leslie Fay, it is much more difficult in an example such as KnowledgeWare.

What starts as an aggressive application of accounting principles may later become known as fraudulent financial reporting if it is continued over an extended period and is found to entail material amounts. But when does that happen? Certainly it is a matter of the extent to which aggressive accounting policies have been employed and the supposed intent on the part of management. However, even with these guidelines, determining the point at which aggressive accounting practices become fraudulent is more art than science.

In the United States, public companies fall under the jurisdiction of the Securities and Exchange Commission. Accordingly, it is up to that regulatory body to determine, subject to due process, whether the antifraud provisions of the securities laws have been broken. When, after a hearing, either presided over by an administrative law judge or through a civil action filed with a U.S. District Court, it is determined that the antifraud provisions have been broken, then the label fraudulent financial reporting can be applied.

Often in cases of alleged fraudulent financial reporting facing the SEC, a hearing will not be held. Rather, the defendant will make an offer of settlement, without admitting or denying the allegations. The settlement will contain any number of penalties, from a cease-and-desist order to more serious sanctions, all of which are discussed at greater length in Chapter 4. The SEC can accept the settlement or decide that a formal hearing is needed. If the settlement is accepted, technically the case of alleged fraudulent financial reporting remains just that, an alleged case, although the penalties, administered as if the case had been prosecuted successfully, remain.

The Division of Enforcement within the SEC investigates potential violations of securities laws. Financial reporting that is deemed to be a misrepresentation or omission of important information would fall within the matters investigated by the division. The division identifies cases for investigation from many sources, including its own surveillance activities, other divisions of the SEC, self-regulatory organizations, the financial press, and investor complaints. The Division of Enforcement makes recommendations to the SEC as to when alleged violations should be pursued and whether, depending on such factors as the seriousness of the alleged wrongdoing and its technical nature, an administrative or federal civil action should be pursued. The division also can negotiate settlements on behalf of the SEC with or without administrative or civil hearings.

The actions of the SEC are civil, not criminal and, as such, do not involve incarceration. However, in more egregious cases of fraudulent financial reporting, federal prosecutors will monitor the SEC's civil probes to determine whether separate criminal actions are warranted. This may occur, for example, when revenue is not recognized simply in a premature fashion but fictitiously—without regard to whether a sale actually has occurred. Other examples would include the pure fabrication of assets, such as accounts receivable or inventory.

Criminal fraud charges were brought against Bernard Bradstreet, former president and co-chief executive officer of Kurzweil Applied Intelligence, Inc. Under Bradstreet's direction, Kurzweil recorded millions of dollars in phony sales during a two-year period surrounding its initial public offering in 1993. While products were supposedly sold and shipped to customers, they were instead shipped to a company-controlled warehouse.[60] Criminal charges also were brought against Barry Minkow of ZZZZ Best company. Minkow's carpet-cleaning company reported revenue growth from next to nothing to $50 million over the period 1984 to 1987. During that same time period, net income surged from $200,000 to over $5 million. Unfortunately for investors, virtually all of the numbers were fabricated.[61] As noted by author Mark Stevens, "In reality, the carpet-cleaning wizard had masterminded a complex Ponzi scheme, raising millions of dollars from unsuspecting lenders and investors only to shuffle the money among a series of dummy companies controlled by Minkow . . ."[62] It is clear that the acts taken by Bradstreet and Minkow went well beyond aggressive accounting. The sheer scale and bravado of the acts committed by them likely encouraged prosecutors to seek criminal indictments.

Given the strong negative stigma attached to the term *fraudulent financial reporting*, it should not be used lightly. In addition, because of the need to demonstrate a premeditated intent to deceive in a material way before financial reporting can be referred to as fraudulent, the label should not be applied unilaterally. Management of the reporting company should have an opportunity to be heard and defend its actions. Accordingly, the term "fraudulent financial reporting" is reserved here for cases where a regulator with proper jurisdiction, such as the SEC, or a court, has alleged a fraudulent misdeed. Often, especially with financial fraud cases involving the SEC, a settlement is reached with the defendant neither admitting nor denying the allegations. For this reason, care will be taken to note that the supposed fraudulent acts are alleged.

It is important to note that when the financial numbers game is played, whether through aggressive accounting practices within the boundaries of GAAP, through aggressive accounting practices beyond the boundaries of GAAP that are not determined to be fraudulent, as a result of errors, or through fraudulent financial reporting, reported financial results and position are potentially misleading. The numbers have been biased in one direction or another, though, depending on the cause, to differing degrees, and may give an altered impression of a company's financial health. Reliance on those reported amounts can lead to erroneous decisions and financial losses. Regardless of the reason, it is important to determine when financial statements are potentially misleading in order to limit the likelihood of such decisions.

Two examples identified in Chapter 1 that were found to entail alleged fraudulent financial reporting are the cases of California Micro Devices Corp. and Cendant Corp. During its fiscal year ended in 1994, rather brazen revenue recognition practices were being followed at California Micro Devices Corp. Fraudulent acts included the recording of revenue for shipments of product before customers had placed an order, for shipments on consignment, and for shipments with unlimited rights of return to distributors who were paid handling fees to accept them. The company also failed to reverse sales for returned goods. As the fraud developed, revenue was even recorded for sales to fake companies for product that did not exist. In testimony at a criminal trial of certain management personnel it was learned that "clerks compiled memos titled 'delayed shipment,' which became a euphemism for fake sales. Soon, even low-level workers were 'joking about' the fraud."[63] So pervasive did the fraudulent revenue recognition practices become that as much as one-third of the company's annual revenue for fiscal 1994 and up to 70% of quarterly revenue during the summer of 1994 were determined to be spurious. The company wrote off as much as one-half of its accounts receivable in August 1994.[64]

As seen in the following announcement made by the company, revenue for 1994 had been overstated by 50% and instead of a previously reported net income of $5.1 million for 1994, on a restated basis the company reported a net loss of $15.2 million:

In October 1994, the company's Board of Directors appointed a Special Committee of independent directors to conduct an investigation into possible revenue recognition and other accounting irregularities. The ensuing investigation resulted in the termination of the company's former Chairman and CEO, Chan M. Desaigoudar, and several other key management employees.

In January 1995, the company reported that an investigation conducted by the Special Committee of the Board of Directors and Ernst & Young LLP had found widespread accounting and other irregularities in the company's financial results for the fiscal year ended June 30, 1994. On February 6, 1995, the company filed a Report on Form 10-K/A restating its results for the fiscal year ended June 30, 1994. Upon restatement, the company reported a net loss of $15.2 million, or a loss of $1.88 per share, on total revenues of $30.1 million. The company previously had reported earnings of $5.1 million, or $0.62 per share, on revenues of $45.3 million.[65]

Aggressive accounting practices had led to losses at CUC International, Inc., years before its merger with HFS, Inc., in 1997 to form Cendant Corp. As early as 1989, an effort to clean up previously aggressive policies for the capitalization of membership acquisition costs and their expensing over extended amortization periods had led to an accumulated charge to operations of $58.9 million. In early 1998, only months after Cendant Corp. was created, a significant accounting fraud was uncovered at CUC International that had extended back several years. Commenting on the fraud, Cendant investigators said, "it appears to have been simple . . . People just made things up."[66]

An important part of the fraud was fictitious revenue recognition. One approach followed involved the acceleration of revenue recognition from membership sales. In an effort to recognize this revenue at the time of sale rather than over an extended membership period, sales of memberships were entered as sales made by the company's credit-report service, because such sales of credit reports could be recorded at the time of sale. However, at least these membership sales did involve a customer and led to a collection. Much of the company's other revenue was totally fictitious, including bogus amounts of $100 million in 1995, $150 million in 1996, and $250 million or more in 1997, according to an audit investigation.

The fraud extended, however, beyond fraudulent revenue recognition practices. What were termed "consolidation entries" involved not only recording fictitious revenue but also false entries to trim expenses, leading to increased profitability. Operating expenses also were reduced by charging them to unrelated acquisition reserves. The fraud became so pervasive that it eventually encompassed the results reported by "the majority of the CUC business units."[67]

Cendant officials later concluded that the fraud began after "CUC no longer could increase the profitability of its membership business through legitimate operations."[68] Once restated, net income (loss) for Cendant Corp. was reported at $229.8 million, $330.0 million, and ($217.2) for 1995, 1996, and 1997, respectively, from amounts originally reported as $302.8 million, $423.6 million, and $55.4 million, respectively. Certainly investors, including HFS, Inc., were misled by the accounting practices at CUC.[69]

CLEANING UP AFTER THE GAME

At some point, after reported financial results and position have been pushed to the boundaries of GAAP, or beyond, by either the aggressive application of accounting principles or, worse, through fraudulent financial reporting, one or more of several potential catalysts draw attention to the fact that the financial statements require adjustment. The catalyst that ultimately results in adjustment depends on the size of the misstatement, whether the financial statements are considered to be presented in accordance with generally accepted accounting principles, or whether the misstatement entails what regulators might ultimately consider to involve fraud.

When accounting principles have been applied in an aggressive fashion, but short of what might be considered financial fraud, it is likely that top management within the company will have knowledge of the practices being followed. Depending on the materiality of any single item, top management and the auditors may even have discussed the matter, possibly at the time of each audit and review. If they do have knowledge of it, the auditors may consider the practices being followed to be aggressive, but they may determine that, taken as a whole, the financial statements do not misstate the subject company's financial results and position. However, any one of several potential catalysts might change the views of either management or the auditors. Likely candidates include declining economic fundamentals, a change in management, an increase in the underlying materiality of an item leading to a change in the auditors' stance toward a company's policies, or a change in the company's auditors. Other possible catalysts include a change in accounting standards affecting the company or, in instances where material misstatement or possible fraudulent financial reporting is suspected, an investigation by a regulatory body such as the Securities and Exchange Commission. These potential catalysts for change are summarized in Exhibit 2.4.

A company may have been aggressive in its choice and application of accounting principles anticipating that amounts reported as assets will be realized or amounts recorded as liabilities will be sufficient. For example, companies that capitalize significant amounts of software development expenditures, or that capitalize costs incurred in developing landfill sites, or that choose unusually high asset residual values do so with the expectation that the amounts reported as assets will be realized through operations. These companies may apply optimistic assumptions about those future operations. Similarly, companies that minimize accruals for such liabilities as warranty claims or liabilities for an environmental cleanup do so with the expectation that amounts accrued will

---

Exhibit 2.4 Catalysts for Changes of Management's or Auditor's View of Reporting Practices

Declining economic fundamentals

Change in management

Change in auditor's position toward policies used

Change in auditors

Change in accounting standards by standard-setting body such as the FASB

Investigation by regulatory body such as the SEC

be sufficient to cover future payments. Here again, optimistic assumptions may have been used. In the absence of fraudulent intent, these are judgment calls. Because the preparation of financial statements requires a collection of estimates, management has a degree of discretion.

Any one of the previously mentioned catalysts may lead to a revision in judgment. Economic fundamentals may deteriorate and demonstrate that amounts carried as assets will not be realized. Similarly, declining product quality or higher than anticipated environmental cleanup costs may expose the inadequacy of the liabilities accrued. A new management may decide that new, more conservative accounting policies should be employed. Alternatively, the auditors may have been uncomfortable with a company's accounting policies in the past but they may have agreed with them given what they perceived to be a lack of materiality. As amounts involved increased, however, the auditors may have decided to seek a change. Another possibility is that the company may have new auditors who consider the old accounting judgment to be beyond the boundaries of GAAP and unacceptable. Given that judgment is involved, different auditors may have different views of what is acceptable. Occasionally, accounting standards are changed, leading to more conservative accounting practices. Finally, the SEC, which constantly reviews the financial statements filed with it in search of what it considers to be inappropriate accounting treatments, may influence a change in a company's policy.

When management reassesses its judgment as to estimates involved in the determination of assets or liabilities, a revision in measurement is effected. That revision is known as a change in estimate. Such a change is handled prospectively with a charge or credit to earnings across the current and future years affected by the item in question.[70] For example, a decrease in the perceived realizability of capitalized software development costs or of landfill development costs would be handled with an immediate write-down and charge to current earnings. An increase in product warranty claims also would result in a current charge to earnings, although with an accompanying increase in a liability account.

The next example, taken from the 1999 annual report of Kimberly Clark Corp., demonstrates the accounting for a change in estimate:

> In 1998, the carrying amounts of trademarks and unamortized goodwill of certain European businesses were determined to be impaired and written down. These write-downs, which were charged to general expense, reduced 1998 operating profit $70.2 million and net income $57.1 million. In addition, the Corporation began depreciating the cost of all newly acquired personal computers ("PCs") over two years. In recognition of the change in estimated useful lives, PC assets with a remaining net book value of $16.6 million became subject to accelerated depreciation charges.[71]

The company determined that its estimates as to the realizability of amounts carried as assets for trademarks and goodwill were overly optimistic, necessitating a write-down and current charge to earnings. In addition, useful lives for its personal computers were reduced to two years from previously estimated longer time periods. As a result, future depreciation charges will be increased.

A change in accounting principle—for example, from capitalizing expenditures to expensing them—in the absence of evidence that would indicate that the financial statements are in error, would be handled as a cumulative-effect adjustment.[72] That is, the cumulative prior-year effects of the change in principle would be reported after tax as a single line item on the income statement.

An example of a change in accounting principle for membership fee income is provided from the 1999 annual report of Costco Wholesale Corp. (dollars, except per-share amounts, in thousands):

> Effective with the first quarter of fiscal 1999, the company will change its method of accounting for membership fee income from a "cash basis", which historically has been consistent with generally accepted accounting principles and industry practice, to a "deferred basis" . . . The company has decided to make this change in anticipation of the issuance of a new Securities and Exchange Commission (SEC) Staff Accounting Bulletin regarding the recognition of membership fee income. . . . The change to the deferred method of accounting for membership fees will result in a one-time, non-cash, pre-tax charge of approximately $196,705 ($118,023 after-tax, or $.50 per share) to reflect the cumulative effect of the accounting change as of the beginning of fiscal 1999 and assuming that membership fee income is recognized ratably over the one year life of the membership.[73]

Historically, Costco Wholesale had recognized membership fee income at the time of receipt. In the future, the company will defer that membership income and recognize it over the membership period. The after-tax, prior-year, cumulative effect of the change was $118,023,000, and was reported in calculating net income for 1999.

When one of the aforementioned catalysts helps to focus attention on the fact that the financial statements are no longer in accordance with generally accepted accounting principles, a restatement of prior-year financial statements is in order. In effect, those prior-year statements are considered to be in error. In addition, there will be an adjustment to the current-year financial statements for any current-year misstatement. The adjustments, a restatement of prior years and a current-year adjustment for the year in progress, will be the same whether the financial statements are in error due to what later may be determined to have entailed fraudulent financial reporting.

Many examples of the accounting treatment for prior-year and current-year financial statements considered to be in error have been provided in this chapter. Fine Host Corp. is representative. The company's announcement in 1997 was that it had discovered "certain errors in the company's accounting practices and procedures."[74] It became necessary for the company to restate its results for the years 1994 to 1996 and for the first nine months of 1997. Because the annual financial statements for 1997 had not been released at the time of the discovery of the errors, corrections for the full year were handled as a current-year charge.

Exhibit 2.5 summarizes the various adjustments needed to clean up after the financial numbers game. As seen in the exhibit, the appropriate adjustment depends on whether a change in accounting estimate or principle is needed or whether prior-year financial statements are considered to be in error.

Exhibit 2.5   Accounting for Changes in Estimates, Principles, and for Errors

Nature of Change and Examples	Method of Accounting
Change in Estimate	**Prospectively**
Decline in estimated asset realizability	Decrease asset with current charge to earnings.
Increase in estimated liability claim	Increase liability with current charge to earnings.
Decline in estimated asset useful lives	Decrease asset book value more rapidly with increase in current-year and future-year amortization expense.
Change in Principle[a]	**Cumulative-Effect Adjustment**
Change from capitalizing to expensing costs incurred	Change made as of beginning of year of change. Costs incurred are henceforth expensed when incurred. Cumulative amounts capitalized in prior years are reported after tax as separate expense line item in net income.
Change from recognition to deferral of fees collected	Change made as of beginning of year of change. Amounts collected are henceforth deferred and recognized as revenue over time as earned. Cumulative amounts recognized in prior years that are now considered unearned are reported after-tax as a separate expense line item in net income.
Error	**Restatement**
Expenditures capitalized in error	Change made as of beginning of year error is discovered. Prior-year financial statements are restated to remove effects of improperly capitalized amounts from net income.
Revenue recognized in error	Change made as of beginning of year error is discovered. Prior-year financial statements are restated to remove effects of improperly recognized amounts from net income.

[a]A limited set of other changes in accounting principle, including changes from the LIFO method of accounting for inventory and in the method used to account for long-term contracts, is accounted for as a restatement of prior-year financial statements.

CLARIFYING TERMINOLOGY

Several terms were used in this chapter and in Chapter 1 to describe what a financial statement reader might like to think of simply as objectionable accounting practices. This section is designed to help clarify the terminology being used.

The term *aggressive accounting* is used here to refer to the choice and application of accounting principles in a forceful and intentional fashion, in an effort to achieve desired results, typically higher current earnings, whether the practices followed are in accordance with generally accepted accounting principles or not. Aggressive accounting practices are labeled as *fraudulent financial reporting* when fraudulent intent, a preconceived intent to mislead in a material way, has been alleged in an administrative, civil, or criminal proceeding.

Like aggressive accounting, *earnings management* entails an intentional effort to manipulate earnings. However, the term *earnings management* typically refers to steps taken to move earnings toward a predetermined target, such as one set by management, a forecast made by analysts, or an amount that is consistent with a smoother, more sustainable earnings stream. As such, earnings management may result in lower current earnings in an effort to "store" them for future years. *Income smoothing* is a subset of earnings management targeted at removing peaks and valleys from a normal earnings series in order to impart an impression of a less risky earnings stream.

The term *creative accounting practices* is used here in a broad sense, encompassing any and all practices that might be used to adjust reported financial results and position to alter perceived business performance. As such, aggressive accounting, both within and beyond the boundaries of generally accepted accounting principles, is considered to be included within the collection of actions known here as creative accounting practices. Also included are actions referred to as earnings management and income smoothing. Fraudulent financial reporting is also part of the creative accounting label. However, while the term *creative accounting practices* implies something less egregious and troubling than fraudulent financial reporting, that is not the intent. An encompassing term was needed to describe all such acts, whether ultimately determined to be fraudulent or not. Creative accounting fits the bill.

The *financial numbers game* refers to the use of creative accounting practices to alter a financial statement reader's impression of a firm's business performance.

A term that is often seen in conjunction with creative accounting practices is *accounting irregularities*. The term was defined in Statement of Auditing Standards (SAS) No. 53, *The Auditor's Responsibility to Detect and Report Errors and Irregularities*.[75] Accounting irregularities are intentional misstatements or omissions of amounts or disclosures in financial statements done to deceive financial statement users. SAS 53 was superseded by SAS No. 82, *Consideration of Fraud in a Financial Statement Audit*.[76] In SAS 82, use of the term *accounting irregularities* is replaced with the term *fraudulent financial reporting*. Today the two terms, *accounting irregularities* and *fraudulent financial reporting*, tend to be used interchangeably.

Occasionally the term *accounting errors* is used in conjunction with financial reporting. Accounting errors result in unintentional misstatements of financial statements.

SUMMARY

This chapter summarizes how the financial numbers game is played. Key points raised include the following:

- The financial numbers game often is played by exploiting normal reporting flexibility within generally accepted accounting principles.
- Reporting flexibility exists and should remain as long as circumstances and conditions across companies and industries vary.
- Some managements move beyond the inherent and intended flexibility in accepted accounting practice and play the financial numbers game by reporting financial results and positions that exceed the boundaries of generally accepted accounting principles.
- Fraudulent financial reporting is used to describe aggressive accounting practices only after a regulatory body, such as the Securities and Exchange Commission or a court, alleges fraudulent intent in an administrative, civil, or criminal hearing.
- Financial statements that are misstated due to the aggressive application of accounting principles, earnings management, error, or fraudulent financial reporting are likely misleading. Care should be taken in using them.
- The manner in which financial statements are revised after discovery of problems associated with the financial numbers game depends on when the accounting problems are discovered. Changes made in the current year that are due to inaccurate judgment calls and do not result in errors in prior-year financial statements are treated as changes in estimate and adjusted to earnings of current and future years. Changes in accounting principle, in the absence of errors, are handled as cumulative-effect adjustments. Misstatements that render prior-year financial statements to be in error are handled with restatements of those prior-year financial statements.

GLOSSARY

Accounting Errors   Unintentional mistakes in financial statements. Accounted for by restating the prior-year financial statements that are in error.

Accounting Irregularities   Intentional misstatements or omissions of amounts or disclosures in financial statements done to deceive financial statement users. The term is used interchangeably with fraudulent financial reporting.

Aggressive Accounting   A forceful and intentional choice and application of accounting principles done in an effort to achieve desired results, typically higher current earnings, whether or not the practices followed are in accordance with generally accepted accounting principles. Aggressive accounting practices are not alleged to be fraudulent until an administrative, civil, or criminal proceeding takes that step and alleges, in particular, that an intentional, material misstatement has taken place in an effort to deceive financial statement readers.

Aggressive Capitalization Policies   Capitalizing and reporting as assets significant portions of expenditures, the realization of which require unduly optimistic assumptions.

Big Bath   A wholesale write-down of assets and accrual of liabilities in an effort to make the balance sheet particularly conservative so that there will be fewer expenses to serve as a drag on earnings in future years.

Bill and Hold Practices   Products that have been sold with an explicit agreement that delivery will occur at a later, often yet-to-be-determined, date.

Capitalize   To report an expenditure or accrual as an asset as opposed to expensing it and charging it against earnings currently.

Change in Accounting Estimate   A change in accounting that occurs as the result of new information or as additional experience is acquired—for example, a change in the residual values or useful lives of fixed assets. A change in accounting estimate is accounted for prospectively, over the current and future accounting periods affected by the change.

Change in Accounting Principle   A change from one generally accepted accounting principle to another generally accepted accounting principle—for example, a change from capitalizing expenditures to expensing them. A change in accounting principle is accounted for in most instances as a cumulative-effect–type adjustment.

Cookie Jar Reserves   An overly aggressive accrual of operating expenses and the creation of liability accounts done in an effort to reduce future-year operating expenses.

Creative Accounting Practices   Any and all steps used to play the financial numbers game, including the aggressive choice and application of accounting principles, both within and beyond the boundaries of generally accepted accounting principles, and fraudulent financial reporting. Also included are steps taken toward earnings management and income smoothing. See *Financial Numbers Game*.

Creative Acquisition Accounting   The allocation to expense of a greater portion of the price paid for another company in an acquisition in an effort to reduce acquisition-year earnings and boost future-year earnings. Acquisition-year expense charges include purchased in-process research and development and an overly aggressive accrual of costs required to effect the acquisition.

Cumulative-Effect Adjustment   The cumulative, after-tax, prior-year effect of a change in accounting principle. It is reported as a single line item on the income statement in the year of the change in accounting principle. The cumulative-effect-type adjustment is the most common accounting treatment afforded changes in accounting principle.

Division of Enforcement   A department within the Securities and Exchange Commission that investigates violations of securities laws.

Earnings Management   The active manipulation of earnings toward a predetermined target. That target may be one set by management, a forecast made by analysts, or an amount that is consistent with a smoother, more sustainable earnings stream. Often, although not always, earnings management entails taking steps to reduce and "store" profits during good years for use during slower years. This more limited form of earnings management is known as income smoothing.

Extended Amortization Periods   Amortizing capitalized expenditures over estimated useful lives that are unduly optimistic.

FIFO   The first-in, first-out method of inventory cost determination. Assumes that cost of goods sold is comprised of older goods, first purchased or manufactured by the firm.

Financial Accounting Standards Board (FASB)   The primary body for establishing accounting principles that guide accounting practice in the United States. The FASB has the full support of the Securities and Exchange Commission (SEC). The SEC has indicated that financial statements conforming to standards set by the FASB will be presumed to have substantial authoritative support.

Financial Numbers Game   The use of creative accounting practices to alter a financial statement reader's impression of a firm's business performance.

Fraudulent Financial Reporting   Intentional misstatements or omissions of amounts or disclosures in financial statements done to deceive financial statement users. The term is used interchangeably with *accounting irregularities*. A technical difference exists in that with fraud, it must be shown that a reader of financial statements that contain intentional and material misstatements has used those financial statements to his or her detriment. In this book, accounting practices are not alleged to be fraudulent until done so by an administrative, civil, or criminal proceeding, such as that of the Securities and Exchange Commission, or a court.

Generally Accepted Accounting Principles (GAAP)   A common set of standards and procedures for the preparation of general-purpose financial statements that have either been established by an authoritative accounting rule-making body, such as the Financial Accounting Standards Board (FASB), or over time have become accepted practice because of their universal application.

Goodwill   The excess of the purchase price paid for an acquired firm in excess of the fair market value of the acquired firm's identifiable net assets.

Income Smoothing   A form of earnings management designed to remove peaks and valleys from a normal earnings series. The practice includes taking steps to reduce and "store" profits during good years for use during slower years.

LIFO   The last-in, first-out method of inventory cost determination. Assumes that cost of goods sold is comprised of newer goods, the last goods purchased or manufactured by the firm.

Purchased In-Process Research and Development   An unfinished research and development effort that is acquired from another firm.

Restatement of Prior-Year Financial Statements   A recasting of prior-year financial statements to remove the effects of an error or other adjustment and report them on a new basis.

Restructuring Charges   Costs associated with restructuring activities, including the consolidation and/or relocation of operations or the disposition or abandonment of operations or productive assets. Such charges may be incurred in connection with a business combination, a change in an enterprise's strategic plan, or a managerial response to declines in demand, increasing costs, or other environmental factors.

Securities and Exchange Commission (SEC)   A federal agency that administers securities legislation, including the Securities Acts of 1933 and 1934. Public companies in the United States must register their securities with the SEC and file with the agency quarterly and annual financial reports.

Special Charges   Nonrecurring losses or expenses resulting from transactions or events which, in the view of management, are not representative of normal business activities of the period and which affect comparability of earnings.

Technological Feasibility   A point in the development of software when it is determined that the software can be produced to meet its design specifications.

NOTES

1. *The Wall Street Journal*, November 22, 1999, p. A4.
2. Fine Host Corp., Form 8-K report to the Securities and Exchange Commission, February 6, 1998, Exhibit 99-1.
3. *The Wall Street Journal,* August 13, 1998, p. A1.

4. Ibid., December 10, 1999, p. A4.

5. Securities and Exchange Commission, Regulation S-X, Rule 5-02.6.

6. Internal Revenue Service Revenue Procedure 88-15. For a more complete treatment of the topic of inventory accounting, the reader is referred to E. Comiskey and C. Mulford, *Guide to Financial Reporting and Analysis* (New York: John Wiley & Sons, 2000).

7. Statement of Position 91-1, *Software Revenue Recognition* (New York: American Institute of Certified Public Accountants, December 1991), was the first accounting principle to tighten the revenue recognition practices of software companies. That principle was superseded by Statement of Position 97-2, *Software Revenue Recognition* (New York: American Institute of Certified Public Accountants, October 1997), Statement of Position 98-4, *Deferral of the Effective Date of a Provision of SOP 97-2, Software Revenue Recognition* (New York: American Institute of Certified Public Accountants, March 1998), and Statement of Position 98-9, *Modification of SOP 97-2, Software Revenue Recognition with Respect to Certain Transactions* (New York: American Institute of Certified Public Accountants, December 1998).

8. BMC Software, Inc., annual report, March 1991, p. 42.

9. American Software, Inc., annual report, April 1991, p. 39.

10. Autodesk, Inc., annual report, January 1992, p. 28.

11. Computer Associates International, Inc., annual report, March 1992, p. 20.

12. Microsoft Corp., Form 10-K annual report to the Securities and Exchange Commission, June 1999, Exhibit 13.4.

13. Matria Healthcare, Inc., Form 10-K annual report to the Securities and Exchange Commission, December 1999, p. F9.

14. Allergan, Inc., Form Def. 14A report to the Securities and Exchange Commission, December 1999, p. A22.

15. C. R. Bard, Inc., annual report, December 1999, p. 22.

16. SFAS No 142, *Goodwill and Other Intangible Assets* (Norwalk, CT: FASB, June 2001).

17. Citigroup, Inc., Form 10-K annual report to the Securities and Exchange Commission, December 1999, p. 28.

18. Sybase, Inc., annual report, December 1998. Information obtained from Disclosure, Inc. *Compact D/SEC: Corporate Information on Public Companies Filing with the SEC* (Bethesda, MD: Disclosure, Inc., March, 2000).

19. *The Wall Street Journal*, February 26, 1998, p. R3.

20. Sunbeam Corp., annual report, December 1996. Information obtained from Disclosure, Inc., *Compact D/SEC: Corporate Information on Public Companies Filing with the SEC* (Bethesda, MD: Disclosure, Inc., September 1997).

21. A summary of the restatement to the financial statements of Sunbeam Corp. provides details of the income effects of the bill and hold practices and of the overstated restructuring charge. Refer to Sunbeam Corp., Form 10-K/A amended annual report to the Securities and Exchange Commission, December 1997, p. F31.

22. Sunbeam Corp., annual report, December 1997, pp. i–ii.

23. Sunbeam Corp., Form 10-K annual report to the Securities and Exchange Commission, December 1998, p. F5.

24. Waste Management, Inc., annual report, December 1997. Information obtained from Disclosure, Inc., *Compact D/SEC: Corporate Information on Public Companies Filing with the SEC* (Bethesda, MD: Disclosure, Inc., December 1998).

25. Ibid.

26. *The Wall Street Journal*, January 26, 1995, p. A4.

27. Refer to Accounting and Auditing Enforcement Release No. 987, *In the Matter of Bausch & Lomb, Incorporated, Harold O. Johnson, Ermin Ianacone, and Kurt Matsumoto, Respondents* (Washington, DC: Securities and Exchange Commission, November 17, 1997), and Accounting and Auditing Enforcement Release No. 988, *Securities and Exchange Commission v. John Logan, United States District Court for the District of Columbia, Civil Action No. 97CV02718* (Washington, DC: Securities and Exchange Commission, November 17, 1997).

28. Operating profit for 1996 is a pro-forma amount for a predecessor company to Aurora Foods, Inc.

29. Aurora Foods, Inc., Form 10-K annual report to the Securities and Exchange Commission, December 1999, p. 2.

30. *The Value Line Investment Survey, Ratings and Reports* (New York: Value Line Publishing, Inc., April 14, 2000), p. 1011.

31. *The Wall Street Journal*, November 6, 1994, p. A1.

32. General Electric Co., Form 10-K annual report to the Securities and Exchange Commission, December 1997, p. F-25.

33. Ibid., p. F-29.

34. *The Wall Street Journal*, November 6, 1994, p. A1.

35. Data provided by *The Value Line Investment Survey, Ratings and Reports* (New York: Value Line Publishing, Inc., May 26, 2000), p. 2125.

36. SunTrust Banks, Inc., annual report, December 1998, p. 69.

37. *The Wall Street Journal*, November 4, 1996, p. C1.

38. Sears Roebuck & Co., Form 10-K annual report to the Securities and Exchange Commission, December 1994, p. 34.

39. Accounting and Auditing Enforcement Release No. 1140, *Order Instituting Public Administrative Proceedings Pursuant to Section 21C of the Securities Exchange Act of 1934, Making Findings, and Imposing Cease-and-Desist Order* (Washington, DC: Securities and Exchange Commission, June 30, 1999).

40. Fine Host Corp., Form 10-K/A amended annual report to the Securities and Exchange Commission, December 25, 1996, p. F25.

41. Refer to Accounting and Auditing Enforcement Release No. 1272, *In the Matter of Cendant Corporation, Respondent* (Washington, DC: Securities and Exchange Commission, June 14, 2000).

42. Refer to SFAS No. 2, *Accounting for Research and Development Costs* (Norwalk, CT: FASB, October 1974) and SFAS No. 86, *Accounting for the Costs of Computer Software to be Sold, Leased, or Otherwise Marketed* (Norwalk, CT: FASB, August 1985).

43. SFAS No 142, *Goodwill and Other Intangible Assets* (Norwalk, CT: FASB, June 2001).

44. Cisco Systems, Inc., annual report, July 1999, p. 41.

45. MCI WorldCom, Inc., Form 8-K report to the Securities and Exchange Commission, September 14, 1998, p. 4.

46. *The Wall Street Journal*, May 1, 1998, p. B6.

47. Ibid., October 1, 1996, p. B9.

48. Micro Warehouse, Inc., Form 10-K annual report to the Securities and Exchange Commission, December 1996, Exhibit 11.

49. *The Wall Street Journal*, October 26, 1999, p. A12.

50. H. Schilit, as quoted in *The Wall Street Journal,* November 24, 1999, p. C1.

51. *The Wall Street Journal*, November 22, 1999, p. A4.

52. Fine Host Corp., Form 10-K annual report to the Securities and Exchange Commission, December 1996, p. F7.

53. Fine Host Corp., Form 8-K report to the Securities and Exchange Commission, February 6, 1998, p. 2.

54. Ibid., Exhibit 99-1.

55. Scienter is a term used to describe an intent to deceive, manipulate, or defraud [(*Ernst & Ernst v. Hochfelder*, 425 U.S. 185, 193n. 12 (1976)]. More is said about scienter and fraud in financial reporting in Chapter 4.

56. Refer to Accounting and Auditing Enforcement Release No. 1179, *Securities and Exchange Commission v. Francis A. Tarkenton, Donald P. Addington, Rick W. Gossett, Lee R. Fontaine, William E. Hammersla, III, Eladio Alvarez and Edward Welch, Civil Action File No. 1:99-CV-2497* (Washington DC: Securities and Exchange Commission, September 28, 1999).

57. *The Wall Street Journal,* December 14, 1992, p. B4.

58. Accounting and Auditing Enforcement Release No. 543, *Order Instituting Public Proceeding and Opinion and Order Pursuant to Section 21C of the Securities Exchange Act of 1934 In the Matter of Comptronix Corporation* (Washington, DC: Securities and Exchange Commission, March 29, 1994).

59. In acknowledging its accounting irregularities, the company noted, "False entries have been made in the company's books and records which would affect the accuracy of some of the information contained in these documents." Leslie Fay Companies, Inc., announcement accompanying annual report, February 1, 1993.

60. Accounting and Auditing Enforcement Release No. 689, *Order Instituting Public Proceedings Pursuant to Section 8A of the Securities Act of 1933 and Section 21C of the Securities Exchange Act of 1934 and Findings and Cease-and-Desist Order of the Commission in the Matter of Kurzweil Applied Intelligence, Inc.* (Washington, DC: Securities and Exchange Commission, July 25, 1995).

61. Accounting and Auditing Enforcement Release No. 283, *Securities and Exchange Commission v. Minkow, et al.* (Washington, DC: Securities and Exchange Commission, November 8, 1990).

62. M. Stevens, *The Big Six: The Selling Out of America's Top Accounting Firms* (New York: Simon & Schuster, 1991), pp. 28 29.

63. *The Wall Street Journal,* January 6, 2000, p. A1.

64. Accounting and Auditing Enforcement Release No. 757, *Order Instituting Proceedings Pursuant to Rule 102(e) of the Commission's Rules of Practice, Making Findings and Imposing Sanctions in the Matter of Ronal A. Romito, CPA* (Washington, DC: Securities and Exchange Commission, February 1, 1996).

65. California Micro Devices Corp. 10-K annual report to the Securities and Exchange Commission, March 1996, p. 13.

66. *The Wall Street Journal,* August 13, 1998, p. A1.

67. Cendant Corp., Form 10-K/A annual report to the Securities and Exchange Commission, December 1997, p. 4.

68. Ibid.

69. Accounting and Auditing Enforcement Release No. 1272, *In the Matter of Cendant Corporation, Respondent* (Washington, DC: Securities and Exchange Commission, June 14, 2000).

70. A change resulting from a new accounting standard will be accounted for in accordance with the provisions of that standard. Such accounting treatment might be handled prospectively, impacting current and future periods. Alternatively, it might be handled as a cumulative-effect adjustment, with an adjustment for all prior-year earnings effects handled as a cumulative current-year charge or credit to earnings. In limited circumstances, a new accounting standard may specify that the change should be handled by restating prior-year financial statements.

71. Kimberly Clark Corp., Form 10-K annual report to the Securities and Exchange Commission, December 1999, Exhibit 13.

72. There are a limited number of exceptions to this treatment. However, the details are beyond the scope of this chapter.

73. Costco Wholesale Corp., Form 10-K annual report to the Securities and Exchange Commission, August 1999, pp. 29–30.

74. Fine Host Corp., Form 8-K report to the Securities and Exchange Commission, February 6, 1998, p. 2.

75. Statement of Auditing Standards No. 53, *The Auditor's Responsibility to Detect and Report Errors and Irregularities* (New York: American Institute of Certified Public Accountants, 1988).

76. Statement of Auditing Standards No. 82, *Consideration of Fraud in a Financial Statement Audit* (New York: American Institute of Certified Public Accountants, 1997).

CHAPTER THREE

Earnings Management: A Closer Look

While the problem of earnings management is not new, it has swelled in a market that is unforgiving of companies that miss their estimates.[1]

Flexibility in accounting allows it to keep pace with business innovations. Abuses such as earnings management occur when people exploit this pliancy. Trickery is employed to obscure actual financial volatility.[2]

The need to meet Wall Street expectations has become a consuming preoccupation of CEOs and boards across the nation.[3]

We need another two cents to make our earnings-per-share number. I've found a penny; it's up to someone else to find the other.[4]

You have to give this quarter to the CFO. It looks like he welded shut the cookie jar of discretionary spending.[5]

Despite significant attention on earnings management from regulators and the financial press, academic research has shown limited evidence of earnings management.[6]

So let us accept that earnings management, per se, is not a bad thing. In fact, it is expected and demanded, both inside and outside businesses, by all stakeholders in the capital markets.[7]

Reported earnings have a powerful influence on the full range of a firm's business activities and the decisions made by its management. The preoccupation of companies with meeting Wall Street expectations reflects management concerns with potential negative consequences on the value of a company's shares if it fails to meet those expectations.

In response to this prospect, management may view it as its responsibility to do, within limits, everything possible to ensure that the consensus forecast of Wall Street analysts is met or exceeded, or to manage earnings, as the activity is often described.

Consider the earnings performance of Cisco Systems in relation to consensus earnings expectations. The $0.18 per-share pro-forma earnings of Cisco Systems for its fiscal 2001 first quarter beat the $0.17 consensus analyst estimate. This marked the 13th straight quarter in which Cisco beat the consensus forecast by one penny. There is a small possibility that this outcome is due to chance, but it is very small. The chairman of the SEC sees earnings management that is designed to produce earnings that meet or exceed Wall Street's consensus earnings as problematic.

Of course, meeting Wall Street's earnings expectations is only one of many earnings targets that might affect management's behavior and lead to earnings management. Others include an earnings target needed to support the success of an initial public offering (IPO), a minimum earnings level needed to earn incentive compensation, or a threshold for complying with a financial covenant in a debt or credit agreement. This chapter examines these and other motivating conditions for earnings management and considers available evidence as to whether earnings management is, in fact, being practiced, whether it is effective, and whether it is always bad or might at times be good.

Before proceeding, it should be noted that the terms *earnings management* and *financial numbers game* frequently are used interchangeably. However, as seen in Chapters 1 and 2, the financial numbers game is viewed here in a broader sense, as encompassing more than just managed earnings. Earnings management generally is viewed to be an interperiod concept, where earnings are moved from one period to the next. For example, earnings in a future year might be reduced or increased in an effort to raise or lower earnings in the current year. The financial numbers game includes steps taken to manage earnings, and thus it encompasses these interperiod activities. However, the financial numbers game also includes intraperiod activities, where earnings or cash flows are moved around within a single period's financial statements. For example, in Chapter 2 it was noted that in 1999 IBM netted the gain on sale of its Global Network against selling, general, and administrative expenses. Because it affected only 1999, this was an intraperiod action that gave the impression that the company was being effective in reducing its recurring selling, general, and administrative expenses.

The financial press and the SEC are very focused on the term *earnings management*. For this reason, we deemed it necessary to take a closer look at the topic.

WHAT IS EARNINGS MANAGEMENT?

For an expression that is so common, little effort has been made to provide careful definitions of earnings management. A selection from among the limited available definitions and descriptions is provided in Exhibit 3.1.

The common theme of the definitions in the exhibit is that of altering results. Actions are taken to create earnings that would not result in the absence of these steps. The reference to an "altered impression" in the first definition does not necessarily imply that

---

Exhibit 3.1 Defining Earnings Management

Earnings management is the active manipulation of accounting results for the purpose of creating an altered impression of business performance.[a]

Given that managers can choose accounting policies from a set (e.g., GAAP), it is natural to expect that they will choose policies so as to maximize their own utility and/or the market value of the firm. This is called earnings management.[b]

During 1999 we focused on financial reporting problems attributable to abusive earnings management by pubic companies. Abusive earnings management involves the use of various forms of gimmickry to distort a company's true financial performance in order to achieve a desired result.[c]

---

[a]C. Mulford and E. Comiskey, *Financial Warnings* (New York: John Wiley & Sons, 1996), p. 360.

[b]W. Scott, *Financial Accounting Theory* (Englewood Cliffs, NJ: Prentice-Hall, 1997), p. 295.

[c]Securities and Exchange Commission, *Annual Report* (Washington, DC: Securities and Exchange Commission, 1999), p. 84.

---

earnings management produces a less meaningful measure of earnings. For example, it is possible that a managed earnings number is a better indicator of expected future earnings. Moreover, the volatility of a managed earnings series may provide a more realistic index of financial risk than an unmanaged series. In this regard, it has been suggested that "These considerations lead to the interesting, and perhaps surprising, conclusion that a little bit of earnings management is a good thing."[8]

The emphasis on choice of accounting *polices* in the second definition is probably intended to be broader than the term *policies* might suggest. The range of potential earnings management techniques extends well beyond the selection of accounting policies. Consider, for example, the choice of the accounting policy of straight-line depreciation. The full impact of this method on earnings also is affected by necessary estimates of both useful life and salvage or residual value. These also add to the flexibility of GAAP.

In Chapter 2, earnings management was described as a special form of the financial numbers game, where the flexibility of GAAP is employed to guide earnings toward a predetermined target. In this view, earnings management is held to remain within the flexibility afforded by GAAP. However, a reference to abusive earnings management is made in the third definition in the exhibit. This definition, as provided by the Securities and Exchange Commission, would imply that some earnings management falls within the flexibility found in GAAP, while in other situations it crosses the line to become *abusive*. That is, earnings that have been abusively managed are held to materially misrepresent true financial performance. If detected, these companies become potential targets for action by the SEC.

Earnings management, whether within or outside the flexibility afforded by GAAP, is purposeful and done in response to certain motivating conditions and incentives.

INCENTIVES AND CONDITIONS FOR EARNINGS MANAGEMENT

The desire to meet or exceed consensus earnings estimates is a powerful earnings-management incentive. A dramatic decline in market capitalization is often the consequence of not meeting a consensus earnings estimate. This shrinkage in value is usually greater in the case of firms in industries with very high valuations. Examples of markers of lofty valuations would include high ratios of price to earnings, price to EBITDA (earnings before interest, taxes, depreciation, and amortization), price to sales, or price to book value per share.

In Chapter 1 we provided a summary of the potential rewards that may be earned by those who play the financial numbers game. Here we look more carefully at the conditions that motivate earnings management and the resulting incentives that may reward the activity.

Earnings Management: Conditions and Associated Incentives

It is important to distinguish between the conditions that motivate earnings management from the underlying incentives to manage earnings. For example, the condition that underlies forecast-based earnings management is usually that earnings, prior to any earnings management, are below their consensus estimate. The incentive behind managing earnings is to avoid, among other things, shrinkage in market capitalization.[9] The conditions that are conducive to earnings management are distinguished from circumstances that are conducive to fraudulent financial reporting. Here, conducive conditions include weak internal controls, inexperienced management, complex transactions, and a weak board of directors.[10]

There is a reasonable amount of research, in addition to anecdotal evidence, indicating that the conditions identified in Exhibit 3.2 are associated with earnings management activity. A sampling of this work is summarized later in this chapter. Notice that only in the case of items 8 and 9 is the earnings management technique identified. The combination of the technique employed, as well as the related condition and incentive, will bear on whether earnings management achieves its objective.

For example, assume in case 1 of the exhibit that the earnings target, the consensus earnings forecast, is met by accelerating the shipment of goods at the end of the quarter. Unless this action is widely recognized as raising sales to a level that is not sustainable, the consensus forecast probably will be seen as having been met. Alternatively, assume that the target is met by selling an investment at a gain. While this may cause earnings to be equal to or greater than the consensus forecast, analysts may remove the gain from reported earnings on the basis that it is (1) nonrecurring and (2) had not been incorporated in their earnings forecast.[11] That is, even though earnings have been managed, the technique employed may not be effective. The consensus forecast still would be seen as having been missed, and share price, other things being equal, would decline.[12]

Finally, assume that a material understatement of an expense accrual makes it possible to achieve the consensus earnings forecast. This may be effective simply because the market is unaware that the earnings target was achieved by this undisclosed activity. Moreover, such an action could be held to constitute an intentional and material mis-

---

Exhibit 3.2   Earnings Management: Conditions and Incentives

Condition	Incentive
Earnings are somewhat short of the consensus earnings forecast in the market.	To avoid a potentially sharp drop in share price
A firm is preparing for an initial public offering of its shares.	To present the best possible earnings picture so as to maximize the price at which the issue is sold
Earnings are just above the minimum level required to earn incentive compensation, or close to exceeding the maximum beyond which no additional incentive compensation is earned.	To cause earnings to remain between the minimum and maximum earnings level so as to maximize incentive compensation
A firm, either because of size or industry membership, or both, is a potential target for adverse political activity.	To minimize the political costs of size and/or industry membership by avoiding what might be considered excessive profit levels
A firm is close to violation of an earnings-related financial covenant in a credit or debt agreement.	To avoid the potential adverse effects of a covenant violation, for example, an interest rate increase, a demand for security or immediate repayment
Earnings are either somewhat above or below a long-term trend believed by management to be sustainable.	To avoid an improper market response to earnings being temporarily off trend
Earnings volatility is induced by a series of nonrecurring items.	To reduce earnings volatility so that a valuation penalty, associated with a perceived higher level of risk, is not assessed
A change in the top management of the firm has taken place.	To take large write-offs immediately upon the arrival of new management, relieving future results of the charges and permitting blame to be assigned to outgoing management
Large losses associated with restructuring and related charges have been accrued in the past.	To reverse any overstated portion of the accruals in order to achieve earnings goals in later periods

statement of earnings. This would be outside the bounds of GAAP and close to or within the territory of fraudulent financial reporting.

The SEC has identified a number of cases of earnings management, whether effective or not, that it believes were aimed at meeting earnings projections or compensation benchmarks. In a speech, SEC commissioner Isaac C. Hunt, Jr., reported that:

> Last year [1999], the Division brought 18 actions alleging that the purposes of these frauds was to engage in earnings management for the purpose of meeting projections and compensation benchmarks. In one particularly egregious case, the CEO of Unison Healthcare handed the company controller a piece of paper and said, "Here's the numbers we need to get to" and "I don't care how we get there."[14]

A sampling of cases in which the SEC believes that earnings were managed toward projected amounts is provided in Exhibit 3.3. Notice that most of the entries in that exhibit relate to the first item of Exhibit 3.2, managing earnings to an internal or external projection. Moreover, three cases (Bankers Trust, Informix, and Peritus) include the management of revenue to target amounts. One entry relates to item 3 of Exhibit 3.2, the management of earnings for purposes of affecting the amount of performance bonuses (Thor Industries).

Some of the steps taken by firms to meet targets extend well beyond simply stretching the flexibility inherent in GAAP. The Bankers Trust case involved the improper conversion of unclaimed funds. False entries were made in the case of both Thor Industries/General Coach and Unison Healthcare.

It is important, for both the producers and users of financial statements, to know whether earnings management techniques fall within or outside the boundaries of GAAP. In addition, as noted above, application of an earnings management technique may produce the target earnings and yet not be effective. Hence, assessing the likely effectiveness of an earnings management technique is essential.

EARNINGS MANAGEMENT TECHNIQUES

The most common class of earnings management techniques involves simply using the flexibility that exists in GAAP, or as former SEC chairman Arthur Levitt has said, the pliancy in GAAP.[15] Mr. Levitt's two statements quoted at the opening of this chapter could be taken to imply that all earnings management is improper. Note the reference in the first quote to "the problem of earnings management."[16] The second quoted statement has a similar tone: "Abuses such as earnings management occur when people exploit this pliancy," which refers to the flexibility inherent in the application of GAAP.[17] However, the third definition of earnings management in Exhibit 3.1 makes reference to the problems created for the SEC by "abusive" earnings management. This suggests that, within limits, the SEC would not consider earnings management to be problematic. Cases that go beyond these limits are presumably those that become the targets of SEC actions, with the most egregious being the subject of administrative action and possible civil or criminal proceedings.

Exhibit 3.3   SEC-Identified Cases of Managing Earnings to Projections

Company	SEC Earnings Management Statement
Bankers Trust AAER[a] No. 1143, July 19, 1999	". . . participated in a scheme to improperly convert unclaimed funds in the bank's custody to Bankers Trust reserve and income accounts in order to meet the bank's revenue and expense targets."
CUC/Cendant AAER No. 1275, June 14, 2000	". . . her supervisors told her that CUC's chief financial officer had generated the adjustments to inflate CUC's quarterly results so that the results would meet the earnings expectations of Wall Street analysts."
IBD Communications Group, Inc. AAER No. 1296, August 28, 2000	"The Commission's complaint alleged that Subikoff, Cheramy and Wann fraudulently inflated IBD's first quarter earnings from \$9 million to \$15 million in order to meet analysts' projections."
Informix Corporation AAER No. 1215, January 11, 2000	The fraudulent conduct described herein was driven by some former managers' perceived need to meet or exceed the Company's internal revenue and earnings goals, which were based, in part, on financial analysts' expectations.
KnowledgeWare AAER No. 1179, Sept. 28, 1999	". . . engaged in a fraudulent scheme to inflate KnowledgeWare's financial results to meet sales and earnings projections."
Peritus Software Services, Inc. AAER No. 1215, April 13, 2000	The inclusion of the revenue (improperly recognized) enabled Peritus to report revenue in line with analysts' expectations.
Thor Industries/General Coach AAER No. 1172, Sept. 28, 1999	"According to the complaint, to conceal his theft, give the appearance that the subsidiary was operating at a profit when it was not, and to earn performance bonuses, Buchanan made false entries to the subsidiary books and records over a several year period."
Unison Healthcare Corp. AAER No. 1170, Sept. 28, 1999	"According to the complaint, the false adjustment enabled Unison to report earnings in line with analysts' estimates."

[a]AAER refers to the Securities and Exchange Commission's Accounting and Auditing Enforcement Release for the indicated date.

Earnings Management within the Boundaries of GAAP

Beyond the listing of five topical areas by former SEC chairman Levitt, there are no authoritative listings of actions that could be considered earnings management.[18] Rather, those suggested usually are identified simply by considering areas of flexibility within GAAP and anecdotes based on experience. A sampling of possible earnings management techniques or accounting activities that might be used for earnings-management purposes is provided in Exhibit 3.4. No presumption is made at this point that the employment of any of these techniques or activities would be outside the bounds of the flexibility inherent in GAAP.

Some of the listed items in Exhibit 3.4 are largely discretionary in nature. This would be true of items 1 to 3, which deal with depreciation-related changes. However, activity in this area may simply be a response to changing expectations regarding underlying productivity patterns, durability, and market conditions for used assets. It is exceptionally difficult to establish that any observed behavior in this area represents conscious earnings management.

This is a recurrent theme in the area of earnings management. Whereas a particular action might be seen as consistent with an earnings-management motivation or incentive, it is difficult to prove an underlying intent. Proof of earnings management sometimes is established in cases of abusive earnings management. Here the fruits of investigations by the SEC, plus testimony and admissions by involved company personnel, can establish that earnings management was the goal of the observed activity.

Other items listed in Exhibit 3.4 are routine accounting activities that are an essential part of the implementation of GAAP. This is true of all of the items from 4 to 20. While the activity is required in the implementation of the requirements of GAAP, each of these areas has a characteristic in common: the need to exercise varying degrees of estimation and judgment. It is this feature, among others, that former SEC chairman Levitt no doubt had in mind when he declared that:

> Flexibility in accounting allows it to keep pace with business innovations. Abuses such as earnings management occur when people exploit this pliancy. Trickery is employed to obscure actual financial volatility.[19]

For example, consider item 4 dealing with determining the allowance for uncollectible accounts or loans receivable. There is some evidence that banks may use the adjustment for loan losses to manage earnings. An earnings shortfall might be avoided simply by booking a somewhat lower loss adjustment. The degree of uncertainty in making such an accrual is great, and it would be difficult to demonstrate that the adjustment was understated.

Item 11, restructuring accruals, has received considerable attention as a possible earnings management tool. Here the pattern is to overstate the restructuring accrual and then reverse a portion of it into earnings if needed to reach an earnings target. As with the loss accrual, the degree of uncertainty and the need for the exercise of considerable judgment makes it very difficult to, ex ante, demonstrate that the charge is overstated.

Much of the potential for earnings management with the items listed in the exhibit is the result of accelerating the recognition of revenue and deferring the recognition of expenses. Chapters 6 through 8 include the details underlying many of these matters. A discussion of the technical details underlying each of the entries goes beyond the objectives of this chapter.

The items in Exhibit 3.4 are presented neutrally in terms of whether they exceed the boundaries of the flexibility in GAAP. Beyond the boundaries of conventional GAAP, according to Mr. Levitt, is a "gray area where the accounting is being perverted, where managers are cutting corners, and where earnings reports reflect the desires of management rather than the underlying financial performance of the company."[20] Presumably, a black area lies beyond the gray. Movement from gray to black raises the likelihood of action being taken by the SEC and/or others. Examples of those who have gone the proverbial "bridge too far" include such names as Donnkenny, Informix, W.R. Grace, Livent, Phar-Mor, and Sunbeam.[21]

Exhibit 3.4 Potential Earnings Management Techniques or Activities

1. Changing depreciation methods, (e.g., accelerated to straight-line)
2. Changing the useful lives used for depreciation purposes
3. Changing estimates of salvage value used for depreciation purposes
4. Determining the allowance required for uncollectible accounts or loans receivable
5. Determining the allowance required for warranty obligations
6. Deciding on the valuation allowance required for deferred tax assets
7. Determining the presence of impaired assets and any necessary loss accrual
8. Estimating the stage of completion of percentage-of-completion contracts
9. Estimating the likelihood of realization of contract claims
10. Estimating write-downs required for certain investments
11. Estimating the amount of a restructuring accrual
12. Judging the need for and the amount of inventory write-downs
13. Estimating environmental obligation accruals
14. Making or changing pension actuarial assumptions
15. Determining the portion of the price of a purchase transaction to be assigned to acquired in-process research and development
16. Determining or changing the amortization periods for intangibles
17. Deciding the extent to which various costs such as landfill development, direct-response advertising, and software development should be capitalized
18. Deciding on the proper hedge-classification of a financial derivative
19. Determining whether an investment permits the exercise of significant influence over the investee company
20. Deciding whether a decline in the market value of an investment is other than temporary

Next we present some examples of earnings management carried well beyond the limits of the flexibility inherent in the application of GAAP and into the realm of alleged fraudulent financial reporting.

Earnings Management: Into the Darkness

If carried too far, efforts to manage earnings result in misstatements or omissions of material amounts or proper disclosures. The actions are intended to deceive the users of the financial statements.[22] The terms *accounting irregularities* and *fraudulent financial reporting* often are used to describe such activities. As discussed in Chapter 1, the two terms tend to be used interchangeably. However, a determination that fraud is involved normally requires a showing that someone used the misstated statements to their detriment. In the following discussion, we simply use the expression *abusive earnings management* to label the described activities. Activities might be seen to be abusive without an ultimate determination that they represented fraudulent financial reporting.

Abusive Earnings Management

Numerous examples of abusive earnings management are provided in the Accounting and Auditing Enforcement Releases (AAERs) of the SEC. A sampling from AAERs is presented in Exhibit 3.5. Some other examples were presented in Exhibit 3.3 from SEC disclosures of firms employing abusive earnings management procedures.

Most of the items in Exhibit 3.5 involve the misuse of normal accounting activities. These include the recognition of sales, the accrual of expenses, the capitalization of costs, and the write-off of assets. However, the SEC saw implementation of these accounting activities to have moved beyond the exercise of the legitimate flexibility in the application in GAAP.

Revenue Recognition   The premature recognition of revenue, or in some cases the recognition of wholly fictitious revenue, is one of the more common forms of abusive earnings management. In a recent study, fully one-half of firms engaged in fraudulent financial reporting employed improper revenue recognition.[23]

Some of the items in Exhibit 3.5 represent very dramatic moves from aggressive to abusive earnings management. Examples of abusive earnings management include holding the books open and continuing to record shipments that clearly belong in subsequent periods and recording sales without the shipment of goods (Advanced Medical Products). Of the two, recording nonexistent sales, referred to as fictitious revenue recognition, is more abusive than holding the books open, a form of premature revenue recognition. While both misrepresent sales and profits, actual sales do exist in the case where the books are held open to record currently sales that belong in a later period.

Expense Recognition   The understatement of expenses, which has the corollary effect of also overstating assets or understating liabilities, is another form of abusive earnings management. Cendant provides an example of expense understatement and associated reserve or liability understatement. Moreover, when it needed to reach its earnings

Exhibit 3.5   Examples of Abusive Earnings Management

Company	Nature of Abusive Earnings Management
Advanced Medical Products, Inc. AAER[a] No. 812, Sept. 5, 1996[a]	• Improperly recognized revenue upon shipments to field representatives—goods still under company's control • Improperly held open its accounting periods and continued to book sales • Recognized sales without shipping the goods actually ordered • Recognized full sale amount on partial shipments
Cendant Corporation AAER No. 1272, June 14, 2000	• Both understated reserves and reversed reserves into earnings • Overstated acquisition-related reserves and then reversed portions into earnings • Failed to record membership charge-backs and cancellations • Improperly charged asset write-offs against acquisition reserves
Chambers Development AAER No. 767, March 5, 1996	• Improper cost capitalization, especially interest capitalization
First Merchants Acceptance Corp. AAER No. 1166, Sept. 28, 1999	• Understated its allowance for credit losses by misrepresenting the payment status of accounts
Hybrid/Ikon, Inc. AAER No. 1281, June 29, 2000	• Improperly recognized as a sale a transaction that provided an absolute right of return through a side letter
Informix Corp. AAER No. 1215, Jan. 11, 2000	• Recognized revenue on transactions with reseller customers who were not creditworthy • Recognized revenue on disputed claims against customers • Recognized revenue on transactions granting rights to refunds and other concessions
Intile Designs, Inc. AAER No. 1259, May 23, 2000	• Underreported value of ending inventory so as to decrease property taxes
Pepsi-Cola P.R. AAER No. 1171, Sept. 28, 1999	• Understated allowances for sales discounts
System Software Associates, Inc. AAER No. 1285, July 14, 2000	• Recognized revenue on sales with significant uncertainties about customer acceptance of the product and collectibility of the contract price and significant vendor obligations remained

[a]AAER refers to the Securities and Exchange Commission's Accounting and Auditing Enforcement Release for the indicated date.

forecasts, Cendant even reversed these *understated* reserves into earnings. Cendant worked both sides of this street by also overstating acquisition-related reserves. Again, as needed, it also reversed these overstated amounts into earnings. The SEC uses some very harsh language in describing the Cendant activities:

> The scheme was driven by senior management's determination that CUC would always meet the earnings expectations of Wall Street analysts and fueled by disregard for any obligation that the earnings reported needed to be real.[24]

Notice that the above SEC declaration identifies managing earnings toward Wall Street's expectations as the underlying motivation for this behavior. This does not rule out the influence of some of the other incentives listed in Exhibit 3.2 as well.

EVIDENCE OF EARNINGS MANAGEMENT

Investors, analysts, auditors, and regulators should be interested in determining whether earnings management is being practiced. Closely tied to this determination is the issue of why earnings are being managed. A wide range of potential earnings-management incentives was presented in Exhibit 3.2. Actions that on the surface appear to be very similar may have quite different motivations and implications. For example, a firm might marginally overstate a restructuring reserve in order to offset a realized investment gain so that the resulting net income remains closer to what management believes to be its sustainable level or trend. This could be seen as a way for management to convey inside information to the market about its profit prospects.[25] Alternatively, a firm might under-accrue an operating expense in order to mask deterioration in financial performance.

Management's conveying of inside information to investors and others could be viewed as a beneficial use of earnings management. However, underaccruing an expense to obscure deterioration in performance could not be viewed as being in the interests of anyone other than current management and perhaps short-term investors.[26] It is this latter application of earnings management that has captured the attention of the SEC and earned the pejorative term *abusive* earnings management.

A rising stream of SEC enforcement actions provides some concrete evidence of the existence of earnings management. Some of this evidence has already been presented in Exhibits 3.3 and 3.5, where attention was focused on illustrations of SEC-identified cases of managing earnings and sales to projections, either those of the firm or the market, and abusive earnings management.[27] Beyond this, there is some academic work that suggests the presence of earnings management.

Earnings Management Evidence: SEC Actions

Earnings management that has resulted in SEC Accounting and Auditing Enforcement Release actions is considered by the SEC to be abusive earnings management. Here the actions taken by company management attempt to create an illusion of performance that is materially at odds with reality. The AAERs normally make reference to sections of the applicable securities acts that have been violated. The actions are often identified as constituting fraudulent financial reporting.

By contrast, the objective of the academic studies is simply to determine whether management's behavior, as it manifests itself in financial statement data and relationships, is consistent with earnings management. For example, some studies have examined the hypothesis that management will take steps to influence earnings in order to maximize earnings-based incentive compensation.[28] Little or no effort is taken to identify specific earnings management techniques. Moreover, distinguishing between earnings management that is in a white, gray, or black region—that is, within GAAP, at the fringes of GAAP, and beyond GAAP—is usually not part of the research plan.

The examples of abusive earnings management included in Exhibits 3.3 and 3.5 are expanded on in Exhibit 3.6 to provide a somewhat richer set of abusive earnings-management activities. This set includes earnings-management activities along with actions taken to impede (cover up) their discovery.

The recognition of premature or fictitious revenue represents the most common form of abusive earnings management in cases cited by the SEC in its AAERs. Companies gravitate toward areas with the potential for a material dollar effect on earnings and also where a wide gray area provides room to maneuver.[29] Revenue recognition is rich on both of these dimensions. The SEC enforcement actions against cases of premature or fictitious revenue recognition are well represented in the exhibit. The premature or fictitious recognition of revenue is discussed and illustrated at length in Chapter 6.

While not specifically identified in the examples in Exhibit 3.6, most cases of abusive earnings management also involve lying, typically to outside accountants or bankers, misrepresentation, and the failure to disclose material facts that are essential to ensure that the financial statements are not misleading.

Exhibit 3.6 Additional Abusive Earnings Management and Cover-up Activities

Company	Abusive Earnings Management and Cover-ups
ABS Industries, Inc. AAER[a] No. 1240, Mar. 23, 2000	• Recorded bill-and-hold sales in the absence of customer requests • The product recorded as sold was neither billed nor shipped • There was no fixed commitment to purchase the goods • In some cases goods were not even complete • Customer copies of the bill-and-hold invoices discarded so that the customer would not be billed

(continues)

Exhibit 3.6 *(Continued)*

Company	Abusive Earnings Management and Cover-ups
Aviation Distributors, Inc. AAER No. 1340, Nov. 8, 2000	• Recognized revenue on goods that had not been shipped • Created false invoices, purchase orders, and shipping documents to cover up activities.
Centennial Technologies, Inc. AAER No. 1310, Sept. 26, 2000[b]	• Improperly recognized sales revenue from invalid or nonexistent sales • Included fake items in inventory • Created fake sales documentation on shipments of fruit baskets to its customers and others
Craig Consumer Electronics, Inc. AAER No. 1317, Sept. 27, 2000	• Disguised inventory overstatements by creating false bills of lading that were scanned into a computer and then consignee was changed from the supplier to Craig
Guilford Mills, Inc. AAER No. 1287, July 24, 2000	• Made false entries to the general ledger of Hofmann Laces (a Guilford subsidiary) (a typical false entry would decrease trade accounts payable and cost of sales in the same amount, thus increasing earnings)
Health Management, Inc. AAER No. 1308, Sept. 25, 2000	• Overstated inventories to meet earnings expectations • Lied to auditors about the existence of in-transit inventory • Falsified an accounts receivable aging
Sirena Apparel Group, Inc. Litigation Release No. 16730 Sept. 27, 2000	• Held open the March 1999 fiscal quarter until the sales target for the period was met • Changed the computer clock so that a (false) date within the quarter would be printed on the company's invoices • Created false shipping documents to correspond with false invoice dates
Solucorp Industries Ltd. AAER No. 1337, Oct. 31, 2000	• Backdated a license agreement in order to cover up improper revenue recognition

[a]AAER refers to the Securities and Exchange Commission's Accounting and Auditing Enforcement Release for the indicated date.

[b]The goal was to create a shipping document that could then be altered and used to support what would appear to be a legitimate shipment of goods. Centennial is not in the fruit business.

As can be seen in Exhibit 3.6, a wide range of cover-up techniques is used. Examples noted in this small set of SEC cases include the following:

- Discarding invoice copies
- Creating false documents: invoices, purchase orders, shipping documents, and other records
- Including fake items in inventory[30]
- Recording false journal entries
- Backdating agreements
- Changing computer clocks
- Scanning in and altering legitimate documents

Reading a substantial number of AAERs is a sobering experience. They reveal that abusive earnings management is clearly with us and that some managers will go to almost any length to alter the apparent financial performance of the firm. Moreover, they demonstrate substantial determination and creativity on the part of the (typically) senior management of the companies involved. The combination of collusion and creativity, as well as the apparent willingness to risk imprisonment, presents a formidable challenge when it comes to detecting these activities. The combination of the conditions and incentives for earnings management, outlined in Exhibit 3.2, exerts an influence that some company officers find irresistible.

The prevalence of abusive earnings management cannot be judged simply from the number of cases pursued by the SEC. With only a couple of hundred cases a year, and over 10,000 SEC registrants, one might argue that abusive earnings management is not a significant threat. However, the initiatives taken in this and related areas by the leadership of the SEC imply that they see abusive earnings management as a significant problem. Moreover, our discussions with members of the business community, along with the survey results presented in Chapter 5, leave us with the impression that the cases pursued by the SEC may simply be the tip of an iceberg.

Again, the activity of the SEC clearly provides concrete evidence of earnings management. Some of the academic research in this area, which adopts quite different methodologies, also provides additional evidence.

Earnings Management Evidence: Academic Research

Academic research provides some evidence of earnings management. The SEC evidence is based on an accumulation of enforcement cases, and it includes the testimony, specific documentation, and, in some cases, admissions by offending company management. The academic studies are based mainly on the statistical analysis of large samples and publicly available financial information. Moreover, the studies rely on statistical models whose capacity to detect earnings management, if present, may not be very strong. However, the results of some studies, which mainly provide basic descriptive data, are consistent with the presence of earnings management.[31] There is a large and growing body of academic work in this area, and the intent here is to only provide a limited sampling of this research.

Evidence from Descriptive Studies

Descriptive studies focus on the possible incentives to achieve specific earnings outcomes.[32] They include, among others, the desire to avoid losses and decreases in earnings as well as to meet or exceed analyst consensus forecasts. The results of these studies are summarized in Exhibit 3.7.

Considering the findings to be consistent with the presence of earnings management is based on the assumption that there should be more symmetry in the distributions of most of these measures. That is, small losses and small profits should be of similar incidence, as should small increases and small decreases in profits. Moreover, the cases where actual results just exceed consensus forecasts should be comparable to small shortfalls of actual results.

The conditions summarized in Exhibit 3.7 are consistent with companies managing earnings to create these outcomes. The weakness of the supporting studies is the relative absence of controls in the design of the research. That is, one cannot rule out the possibility that excluded variables drive these results, not earnings management. This legitimate criticism aside, we believe that findings are strongly supportive of the conclusion that companies engage in earnings management in response to a variety of different earnings-related incentives.

Studies Using Statistical Models

Early work using statistical models tested the hypothesis that earnings management was used to maximize the bonuses or incentive compensation of managers. Some of the areas considered in later work investigated whether earnings management was used to maximize the proceeds from both initial and seasoned stock offerings, to prevent the violation of financial covenants, and to meet consensus analyst forecasts of earnings.

Bonus Maximization   Healy studied the possibility that earnings management was practiced in companies that had bonus or incentive compensation plans based on reported

---

Exhibit 3.7   Evidence of Earnings Management from Descriptive Studies

- Small reported losses are rare.
- Small reported profits are common.
- Small declines in profits are rare.
- Small increases in profits are common.
- Large numbers of consensus forecasts are either just met or exceeded by a small amount.
- Small numbers of just-missed consensus forecasts (i.e., a shortfall of actual earnings) are rare.

earnings.[33] The assumption was that managers would attempt to manage earnings so that their incentive compensation would be maximized. Bonuses for the plans included in the study were determined by reported net income.

Without exploring the various technical aspects of this study, earnings management was approximated by the change in accruals across a reporting period. The accruals were seen to be approximated by the difference between the reported earnings and cash flow. If accruals changed across a period so that they represented a larger net asset balance, then this growth was considered the amount by which earnings were managed up. Alternatively, if the balance declined across the period, then earnings were viewed as having been managed down. The total change in accruals was considered to be discretionary and designed to manage earnings.[34]

The key features of the Healy study are expectations about the behavior of total accruals, that is, income increasing or income decreasing. If earnings were above a cap—the maximum amount of income on which incentive compensation could be earned—income-decreasing accruals are predicted. Because the maximum bonus has already been earned, additional earnings provide no further compensation benefit. Similarly, if earnings were below a floor or bogey—the minimum earnings necessary to earn incentive compensation—then it is expected that earnings would be managed down still further. Taking charges in the current period increases the likelihood of earnings in subsequent periods being high enough to earn incentive compensation. Income-increasing accruals are predicted to be dominant in the range between the bogey and the cap. Here earnings increases will increase incentive compensation.

Healy's findings were consistent with the above predictions. Accruals were mainly income decreasing when earnings were below the bogey and above the cap. Forty-six percent of accruals were positive when earnings were in the range between the bogey and the cap.[35] However, only 9% and 10% of accruals were positive when earnings were either below the bogey or above the cap, respectively. These results are consistent with more income-increasing earnings management being practiced in the interval where income increases boost incentive compensation.

There has been considerable subsequent work on whether earnings are managed to maximize incentive compensation. Healy's early work has been criticized for assuming that all of the changes in accruals were discretionary, that is, due to efforts to manage earnings. However, a more recent study by Guidry, Leone, and Rock concludes that: "The evidence is consistent with business-unit managers manipulating earnings to maximize their short-term bonus plans."[36] Work by Gaver, Gaver, and Austin also provides some support for Healy's findings. However, they see the earnings management behavior as possibly explained by the objective of income smoothing as opposed to bonus maximization.[37] After a review of a large body of this research, Scott concluded that "despite methodological challenges, there is significant evidence that managers use accruals to manage earnings so as to maximize their bonuses, particularly when earnings are high."[38]

Maximizing the Proceeds from either Seasoned or Initial Stock Offerings   Recent work by Shivakumar finds that in the case of seasoned offerings, income and accruals, which are income increasing, are abnormally high. This is seen to be consistent with earnings management aimed at maximizing the proceeds from the stock offering.[39] Shivakumar also concludes that this earnings management does not mislead investors, and states that earnings management, "rather than being intended to mislead investors may actually be the rational response of issuers to anticipated market behavior at offering announcements."[40] That is, the market apparently expects firms to manage earnings up before offerings. Or, as Shivakumar observes: ". . . investors appear to rationally infer this earnings management at equity offerings and, as a result, reduce their price response to unexpected earnings released after offering announcements."[41]

There is also some evidence of earnings management aimed at maximizing the price received on initial public offerings (IPO). A study by Friedlan found that firms made accruals that increased net income in the period before the IPO.[42]

Preventing the Violation of Financial Covenants　The violation of a financial covenant in a credit agreement may well impose costs on firms and also restrict their managerial flexibility. Studies of earnings management and financial covenants have focused on samples of firms that had covenant violations. The findings of these studies are generally consistent with efforts by firms to manage earnings up just before or during the period of the covenant violations.[43]

Meeting Consensus Analyst Forecasts　Recent work supports the position (already documented by AAERs of the SEC) that firms manage earnings in order to meet or exceed consensus analyst forecasts of earnings. Work by Payne and Robb tested the proposition that "managers will move earnings towards analysts' forecasts when pre-managed earnings are below expectations."[44] Their findings supported this expectation. Moreover, work by Kasznik, which focused on management as opposed to analyst forecasts, reported ". . . evidence consistent with the prediction that managers use positive discretionary accruals to manage reported earnings upward when earnings would otherwise fall below management's earnings forecasts."[45]

These findings are generally consistent with expectations about the circumstances in which earnings management would be practiced. As with any single statistical study of this nature, the conclusions always must be considered somewhat tentative. Moreover, statistical studies are capable of identifying only an association and not a cause-and-effect relationship.

The fact that some firms appear to engage in earnings management does not necessarily mean that earnings management is effective.

EFFECTIVENESS OF EARNINGS MANAGEMENT

The effectiveness of earnings management is determined by whether it results in the associated incentive being realized.[46] These incentives, as outlined in Exhibit 3.2, range from the avoidance of declines in share values to maximizing incentive compensation and avoiding violations of financial covenants in debt or credit agreements.

The effectiveness of earnings management depends on the combination of the earnings-management techniques used, the motivating conditions, and the incentives. It is only possible to conjecture about the effectiveness of some of the nine combinations of conditions and incentives listed in Exhibit 3.2. However, some key considerations for selected cases are discussed below.

To Avoid Share-Price Declines from Missed Earnings Forecasts

Exhibit 3.3 presented a number of SEC enforcement actions that involved abusive earnings management used to meet earnings projections. In retrospect, because of their discovery and prosecution, these earnings-management actions ultimately were not effective. However, at the time the managed earnings numbers were reported, share price declines may well have been avoided.

Key to Effectiveness

The key to the effectiveness of projections-oriented earnings management is that both analysts and the market accept the managed results as indicative of the firm's real financial performance. However, an earnings target typically will not be seen as having been met if the earnings shortfall is covered by, for example, nonrecurring or nonoperating increases in earnings.

It is standard practice for news items on company earnings releases to include commentary on whether the consensus earnings forecast was achieved. If present, nonrecurring items are removed from actual results to produce a *pro-forma* or *operating* result. It is this earnings result that is then compared to the consensus forecast. Implicit in this practice is that Wall Street analysts do not include nonrecurring items in their forecasted amounts. In addition, it is usually held that earnings without the inclusion of nonrecurring items are a better measure of periodic financial performance. The relevant portions of several such items follow:

> Excluding investment income and other one-time items, the company posted a loss of $8.2 million, or four cents a share. Analysts expected Intuit to report a loss of nine cents a share.[47]
>
> The figures, however, do include unspecified equity gains. Absent those gains, H-P would have reported earnings of 97 cents per share. Analysts surveyed by First Call/Thompson Financial had expected earnings of 85 cents per share.[48]
>
> Excluding one-time items, Comcast said it recorded a loss of $208 million, or 22 cents a share. That was wider than the 15 cents a share expected by First Call/Thomson Financial.[49]

Role of Pro Forma Earnings and Associated Adjustments

Removing nonrecurring items from reported results can involve a substantial degree of judgment. As a result, pro forma or operating earnings may lack comparability. The concept of nonrecurring, which guides the determination of pro forma and operating earnings, is not well defined in GAAP. Recent debates in this area have involved the inclusion or exclusion of gains on the sale of investments, especially by technology firms with substantial holdings in newer technology firms.[50] Contention also has focused on the role played by extraordinary gains in determining whether Fannie Mae met the market's consensus earnings forecast. Without this gain, which amounted to three cents per share, Fannie Mae would have fallen short of the consensus forecast by three cents. A survey of forecast-contributing analysts found that nine felt that the extraordinary item should be included in earnings used to judge whether the forecast was met and two believed that it should not be included.[51] The majority analyst position was strongly influenced by the fact that Fannie Mae had produced extraordinary gains and losses (from debt retirements) in a majority of quarters for at least a decade.

It should be clear that booking a nonrecurring benefit for the purpose of meeting a consensus earnings forecast may not be effective. This is especially true if the amount is material and well disclosed in the financial statements or associated notes. It follows that firms under extreme pressure to make their numbers may employ earnings-management techniques that are unlikely to be detected. For example, the use of a number of individually immaterial items of income may not be picked up on an analyst's radar.

A variety of items that were removed from net income for purposes of judging whether the consensus forecast was met are provided in Exhibit 3.8. Most of the listed items are plausible adjustments based on their nonrecurring character. The rationale for some is less obvious. The adjustment for goodwill amortization by CNET Networks is common in the determination of EBITDA. Its presence here is probably more industry specific and reflects the view that goodwill does not have a limited life, and, therefore, its amortization should not be included in judging financial performance. Notice that goodwill amortization was also an adjustment for Juniper Networks and Palm, Inc.

The treatment of payroll taxes incurred by companies upon the exercise of stock options by their employees as a pro forma earnings adjustment is common in the technology sector.[52] Disclosures of these payroll taxes by BEA Systems, Inc., provides the logic of adding them back to net income in arriving at pro-forma earnings:

> The company is subject to employer payroll taxes when employees exercise stock options. These payroll taxes are assessed on the stock option gain, which is the difference between the common stock price on the date of exercise and the exercise price. The tax rate varies depending upon the employees' taxing jurisdiction. Because we are unable to predict how many stock options will be exercised, at what price and in which country, we are unable to predict what, if any, expense will be recorded in a future period.[53]

BEA Systems makes the case that these options-related payroll taxes are similar to nonrecurring items. They share their lack of predictability or their irregular character. As such, they are not part of the earnings prediction process and are therefore added back to actual net income. They do, of course, represent an operating cash outflow.

Closing an Earnings Expectation Gap with Nonrecurring Items

Efforts to meet the consensus earnings estimate of Wall Street will in many cases prove to be ineffective. That is, credit often will not be given for closing the gap between earnings and the consensus forecast if the revenue and gain increases or loss and expense decreases are judged to be nonrecurring or nonoperating. Many of the items in Exhibit 3.8 that would move earnings toward a target would be reversed in the process of computing pro forma or operating earnings. While in no sense a recommendation that more clandestine tactics be employed, it seems clear that the booking of nonrecurring items

Exhibit 3.8   Items Excluded in Judging Actual Earnings versus Consensus Forecasts

Company	Exclusions
Advanced Micro Devices, Inc. (third quarter, 2000)	• Gain on sale of telecommunications business
Amazon.com, Inc. (fourth quarter, 2000)	• Losses on equity investments • Stock-based compensation expense • Amortization of intangibles • Write-downs of impaired assets
Chevron Corp. (third quarter, 2000)	• Environmental remediation charge • Asset write-downs • Tax adjustment charges • Gains on sales of marketable securities
CNET Networks, Inc. (third quarter, 2000)	• Goodwill amortization • Net gains on investments • Income taxes
Handspring, Inc. (first quarter, 2001)	• Amortization of deferred stock compensation
JDS Uniphase Corp. (third quarter, 2000)	• Merger-related charges • Payroll taxes on stock-option exercises • Some investment income
Juniper Networks, Inc. (second quarter, 2000)	• Amortization of goodwill • Deferred compensation
Navistar International Corp. (second quarter, 2000)	• Research and development tax credit
Palm, Inc. (first quarter, 2001)	• Amortization of goodwill and other intangibles • Purchased in-process technology • Separation costs
3Com Corp. (first quarter, 2001)	• Realignment costs • Income from discontinued operations • Gains on investments • Merger-related costs
Saks, Inc. (second quarter, 2000)	• Merger integration costs
Texas Instruments, Inc. (third quarter, 2000)	• Micro Technology investment gain • Purchased in-process R&D • Pooling-of-interests transaction costs
Toys 'R' Us, Inc. (second quarter, 2000)	• Losses from Toysrus.com
TRW, Inc. (third quarter, 2000)	• Consolidation of air bag operations • Automotive restructuring charges • Unrealized noncash losses on currency hedges
Venator Group, Inc. (second quarter, 2000)	• Cost of store closings • Divestitures

Sources: Company news and earnings releases and associated news reports

typically will be ineffective in closing an earnings shortfall and by extension in avoiding a reduction in share value.

What Remains to Effectively Close the Earnings Gap?

If booking nonrecurring revenues or gains will not be effective in closing the earnings gap, what, if anything, will? In some cases, it appears that companies have boosted end-of-period sales by offering special incentives. This might work, but it is also possible that results will be discounted somewhat by analysts on the grounds that the sales increment may not be sustainable. Cutting back on discretionary spending also could be considered. Again, analysts may infer that this happened by noting a decline in the selling, general, and administrative expense area. Recall that this tactic was cited in one of the opening chapter quotes: "You have to give this quarter to the CFO. It looks like he welded shut the cookie jar of discretionary spending."[54]

In addition to the above actions, it might be possible to close part of the gap simply by making sure that expense accruals are closer to the lower range of acceptable limits. The opposite posture would be taken with any revenue accruals.

In all of these efforts to close the gap between actual earnings and consensus expectations, care must be taken that the result not be seen to represent an intentional and material misrepresentation of earnings. However, closing a one- or two-cent gap may require the exercise of only limited amounts of flexibility, such that the amount would not be held to be material under conventional standards. It may well be seen by some as the responsible thing to do, especially if missing the consensus by a penny or two could trim off millions or billions of dollars of market capitalization.

Finally, if nothing else appears to be available, it might be possible to expand the scope of losses or expenses that are added back in arriving at pro forma earnings, which are used to assess whether the forecast is met.

To Maximize Earnings-Based Incentive Compensation

It may be possible to use a wide range of earnings-management techniques in an effort to maximize incentive compensation. There is some evidence that various accruals are used to move earnings into ranges that benefit the compensation of covered executives.[55] However, a key issue is the manner in which earnings are defined for purposes of computing incentive compensation.

There will be maximum flexibility in taking earnings-management steps to maximize incentive co___ when the base for determining the additional compensation is ___ ne. However, it may be that the earnings base for the determi-___ sation will make some of the same adjustments used in devel-___ gs used in judging whether a consensus forecast is met.

___ this area may involve efforts to either raise or lower earn-___ would attempt to increase earnings beyond the minimum ___ nal compensation, but not above the maximum amount on ___ on may be earned. If earnings, prior to any earnings-___ e maximum income amount upon which incentive compensation is based, then earnings might be managed down to this maximum. These earnings might then be recognized in a subsequent period, where they might then increase the amount of incentive compensation received.

To Minimize Debt-Covenant Violations

There are powerful incentives to avoid the violation of debt covenants. Covenant violations may result in immediate calls for debt repayment, increases in interest rates, require the borrower to put up collateral, and other negative actions. However, earnings management may be effective in avoiding violations of financial covenants that are affected by the level of earnings.

It is common to have a variety of financial covenants that are affected by the amount of net income reported. Covenants based on earnings before interest, taxes, depreciation, and amortization (EBITDA) are a common example. In addition, maximum ratios of debt to shareholders' equity, minimum amounts of shareholders' equity, and minimum fixed-charge coverage ratios are all affected by the level of reported earnings.

As with meeting projections and maximizing incentive compensation, increasing earnings through earnings management techniques may not alter the amount of earnings or shareholders' equity used in measuring compliance. For example, it is common for debt or credit agreements to require that the covenant measures be computed based on GAAP consistently applied. This means that an increase in earnings from an accounting change would not count toward covenant compliance.

The authors consulted with a bank on an issue of an accounting change and whether a borrower was in compliance with a covenant that required the maintenance of a minimum amount of shareholders' equity. In anticipation of a covenant violation by the borrower, the bank was planning to raise the interest rate on the financing and also to require security from the borrower. The accounting change added $2 million to shareholders' equity, an amount sufficient to avoid a violation, if it were counted in measuring covenant compliance. It turned out that in invoking GAAP in the bank's credit agreement with the borrower, the bank did not specify that GAAP was to be *consistently* applied. As a result, the shareholders' equity increase counted and the borrower did not have a covenant violation. Alternatively, if the covenants were measured on the basis of GAAP consistently applied, then the increase in equity would not be included in judging covenant compliance. That is, the borrower would have violated the covenant.

Earnings management designed to ward off earnings-related financial covenants will be effective only if the method employed will be counted as part of earnings for purposes of determining covenant compliance. In the very competitive market for business loans, borrowers should be in a relatively strong position. They may be able to use this position to bargain for as few restrictions on the earnings increases that may be counted toward covenant compliance.

To Minimize Certain Political Costs

As noted in Chapter 1, there may be circumstances when it is not in a company's interests to appear to be exceptionally profitable. This has been especially true for petroleum companies over the years. If rising profits are associated with rising prices at the pump, there will be political pressure to either control prices or to apply excess-profits taxes to the earnings of the oil companies. In more recent years, oil was released from U.S. strategic reserves in an effort to reduce prices.

Negotiations with unions over wages are certainly not helped if there is the impression that the affected firms are exceptionally profitable. A perceived ability to pay more can cause a union to be more resolute in advancing its demands than would be the case if earnings were more modest.[56] Earnings management might be employed in this circumstance actually to manage earnings down. However, the effectiveness of this earnings management will hinge on the recognition or acceptance of the reduced profit level as being legitimate by the unions and other key players.

Other Conditions and Incentives for Earnings Management

Evaluating the likely effectiveness of the other condition/incentive combinations in Exhibit 3.2 raises some of the same issues as those already discussed. The effectiveness of the first entry in that exhibit, where earnings are short of the consensus forecast, is determined by the market's response to earnings management, the objective of which is to meet consensus earnings expectations. However, the effectiveness of earnings management in the case of the third item, incentive compensation, and the fifth item, debt covenants, will turn on contract issues. Will the earnings-management effects be treated as altering earnings as defined by the contracts?

Maximizing Initial Public Offering Proceeds

The effectiveness of earnings management for the remaining issues in Exhibit 3.2 depends principally on the market's response to the altered results. In the IPO case, an expectation already exists that IPO firms will dress up their statements to the extent possible. It is like the senior prom; everybody wants to look his or her best. Therefore, the market may simply apply a valuation discount to account for the earnings management that is expected to take place.

Smoothing and Managing Earnings toward a Long-term Trend

Regarding the sixth item from Exhibit 3.2, management usually will have expectations concerning the long-term trend in earnings. Temporary conditions may cause results to deviate significantly from that trend. To avoid a misinterpretation by the market, steps may be taken to manage earnings toward the trend. In a sense, earnings management is used to convey what may be inside information about the firm's long-term trend in earnings. Commenting on this circumstance, Scott noted that "earnings management can be a vehicle for the communication of management's inside information to investors."[57]

In response to the seventh condition noted in the exhibit, reducing the volatility of reported earnings, also known as income smoothing, shares much in common with managing earnings to a long-term trend. In the case of income smoothing, management attempts to convey a sense of greater earnings stability and, therefore, less risk. Implicit in this practice is the assumption that, in the absence of income smoothing, the market might overestimate the firm's risk and undervalue its shares.

In each of the above cases, there is the prospect that the market will frustrate the intentions of management. This will be true if the market identifies the earnings-management actions being taken and removes their effects from reported earnings. In this case the earnings management will not be effective.

Change in Control and Write-offs

The eighth motivation/condition combination in Exhibit 3.2, a change in top management, is often viewed as an opportune time to take large write-offs. The need to take these write-offs can conveniently be blamed on the outgoing management. In addition, these charges relieve future earnings of their burden and help the new management to fulfill a pledge to improve future profitability. Potential behavior of this type was recently discussed in connection with management changes at DaimlerChrysler AG:

> There has been growing speculation that Mr. Zetsche [new CEO] will make fourth-quarter results look as bad as possible in order to get the worst of Chrysler's problems behind him. That would enable Mr. Zetsche to blame Chrysler's problems on his predecessor.[58]

As behavior of this type becomes more routine, its effectiveness in helping to shift blame for the write-offs to the replaced management declines. Moreover, the valuation implications of the increase in future earnings resulting from overly aggressive write-offs is somewhat problematic, suggesting that a positive market reaction to higher future earnings may not be forthcoming.

Restructuring Accruals and Reversals

Former SEC chairman Levitt took particular aim at the ninth item in Exhibit 3.2, an overstatement of restructuring and related charges. As a result, the likelihood that it will be practiced as frequently and continue to go unnoticed by analysts is reduced. Regarding restructuring charges Mr. Levitt said, in part:

> Why are companies tempted to overstate these charges? When earnings take a major hit, the theory goes that Wall Street will look beyond a one-time loss and focus only on future earnings. And, if these charges are conservatively estimated with a little extra cushioning, that so-called conservative estimate is miraculously reborn as income when estimates change and future earnings fall short.[59]

For restructuring and related charges to be effective, future reversals of the charges must be brought into earnings without notice. Thus, the charges must be ignored when they are originally recorded and not detected when subsequently returned to earnings. It is increasingly unlikely that both acts will go unidentified. There has been strong regulatory pressure to provide fulsome disclosures of restructuring charges, both when they are initially accrued and as they are subsequently discharged.[60]

IS EARNINGS MANAGEMENT GOOD OR BAD?

Assessing the merits of earnings management hinges on the nature of the steps taken to manage earnings and the objective of the earnings management. As we have seen, steps taken to manage earnings can range from the employment of conventional GAAP flexibility, to flexibility that strains its GAAP connection, to behavior that goes well beyond GAAP boundaries and into the dark realm of fraudulent financial reporting. The earnings-management actions are usually the result of one or more of the conditions and incentives summarized in Exhibit 3.2.

Views on the character of earnings management range from good, to of no consequence, to bad. The no-consequence view typically comes from the academic community and is based on the assumption that there is full disclosure of the earnings management. Moreover, normally investors are considered to be the potentially affected group, as can be seen in this quotation:

> While practitioners and regulators seem to believe that earnings management is both pervasive and problematic, academic research has not demonstrated that earnings management has a large effect on average on reported earnings, or that whatever earnings management does exist should be of concern to investors.[61]

The authors of this quotation no doubt assume that, with full disclosure, the market will efficiently process the effects of earnings management on financial performance and securities will be priced properly. However, it is unlikely that this position could be maintained in cases of abusive earnings management such as are summarized in Exhibits 3.3, 3.5, and 3.6. That is, efforts to materially misrepresent the financial performance of a firm must be considered to be harmful. This is the dominant theme of those survey results in Chapter 5 that deal with whether earnings management is good or bad.

A CEO recently characterized "bad" earnings management in this way: "Bad earnings management, that is, *improper earnings management*, is intervening to hide real operating performance by creating artificial accounting entries or stretching estimates beyond a point of reasonableness."[62] This same CEO also characterized good earnings management as "reasonable and proper practices that are part of operating a well-managed business and delivering value to shareholders."[63] This CEO suggested that the sale of an asset to offset a revenue shortfall is within the scope of good earnings management. The setting was one in which the delayed closing of a contract would cause earnings to fall short of expectations. The gain on the asset sale would simply replace the gain expected to be booked when the contract was closed in the following quarter. As the CEO explained:

> If something has been sitting around that is less valuable to the company than before, and an interested buyer can be found, then why not take advantage of making the asset sale and maintaining the stability of the bottom line? Properly disclosed, of course, the resulting trend is not misleading.[64]

Whether earnings management is seen to be good, bad, or indifferent is a complex matter. Motivation, perspective, conditions, and methods will all bear on characterizations of specific cases of earnings management.

Meeting the Consensus Forecast

It is clear that a good deal of earnings-management activity is aimed at helping firms to meet or exceed the forecasts of management or the consensus earnings forecasts of analysts.[65] If the effects of earnings-management actions are accepted for purposes of meeting the forecast, then shareholders and company management will benefit by avoiding a decline in market value. Managing earnings effectively for this purpose generally will require the use of either real actions, such as accelerating shipments or cutting discretionary spending, or the exercise of flexibility that is within the boundaries of GAAP. Booking a well-disclosed nonrecurring gain is unlikely to be accepted as closing a gap between the earnings forecast and actual results.

It is important that reasonable disclosure of the steps taken to manage earnings be provided in order to ensure that the benefit reaped by shareholders and management is not at the expense of others. In the case of abusive earnings management, where investors have no knowledge of the activity, benefits reaped by current shareholders and management would be at the expense of others. For example, a purchaser of shares, whose decision was influenced by questionable tactics, may suffer subsequently if the abusive earnings management becomes known.

Maximizing Proceeds from Initial or Seasoned Share Issues

A firm may believe that it is in its interests to manage earnings prior to initial (IPO) or seasoned equity offerings (SEO) in order to maximize the proceeds from its share issue. The common sentiment is that firms do try to look their financial best prior to these offerings. As long as the earnings management falls within the boundaries of GAAP, and there is full and fair disclosure, it seems unlikely that investors in these shares would be harmed. Given an expectation of pre-IPO or SEO earnings management, one would expect that the pricing of the IPO to discount for the somewhat inflated pre-IPO results.

However, available research suggests that, at least in the case of SEOs, investors may not see through the earnings management associated with these offerings. Rather, the performance of these issues suggests a possible overpricing upon issuance of the shares followed by underperformance of the shares in subsequent periods.[66] The implication is that short-term investors in the offerings might benefit but that longer-term investors may be harmed.

Maximizing Incentive Compensation

There is some evidence that earnings are managed so as to maximize incentive compensation. If the design of the incentive-compensation agreement incorporates the possibility of earnings management, then any actions to manage earnings would appear to be harmless. The recipients of incentive compensation simply will earn the additional compensation expected in the design of the plan.

However, there may be harmful effects if those covered by the incentive compensation plan use earnings-management techniques that were not contemplated in the plan's design. The amount of incentive compensation earned will be excessive. Here management will benefit at the expense of shareholders. Further, if the earnings management activities are abusive, then there may be a material misstatement of financial performance. Others who rely on the firm's financial statements, such as lenders, regulators, employees, and prospective investors, also may be harmed.

Avoiding Financial Covenant Violations

Earnings management may make it possible to avoid negative consequences associated with violation of a financial covenant in a credit agreement. The borrower would benefit by avoiding the violation. Moreover, the lender should not be harmed as long as the earnings-management techniques employed are within the range of those contemplated and permitted by the debt or credit agreement.

Avoiding a covenant violation by using techniques that are neither permitted by the credit agreement nor disclosed to the lender will benefit the borrower at the lender's expense. The lender will not have an opportunity either to waive the violation or to take steps to protect its position as intended by the credit agreement and associated covenants.

Reducing Earnings Volatility

A traditional view is that volatility in reported earnings is a sign of heightened risk, resulting in a higher risk premium and valuation discount. This view gave rise to the practice of income smoothing, a subset of earnings management, long before there were any discussions of managing earnings to a consensus earnings forecast. Today the pivotal role played by consensus forecasts appears to have displaced the emphasis on income smoothing.

However, a role for income smoothing may remain to the extent that management attempts to guide analysts' forecasts. An earnings stream that is smooth and growing is still valued in the marketplace. If, through income smoothing, management is successful in guiding analysts' forecasts to match its own earnings expectations, then this form of earnings management would be considered to be effective. The end result will be fewer earnings forecast surprises and, potentially, a higher share price.

SUMMARY

This chapter has outlined the key features and practices of earnings management, the conditions under which earnings management is likely to be pursued, and the associated incentives. Evidence of earnings management and issues of its effectiveness also have been considered. Moreover, the issue of whether earnings management should be considered to be good or bad, and under what circumstances, has been explored.

Key points made in the chapter include the following:

- Earnings management attempts to create an altered impression of business performance. These efforts may employ techniques that fall within, at the edge of, or beyond the boundaries of the flexibility that is inherent in generally accepted accounting principles.

- A range of conditions and incentives underlie earnings management. Currently one of the most common condition/incentive combinations is (1) earnings that, premanagement, will fail to meet the consensus expectations of Wall Street, and (2) the desire to avoid the shrinkage in market value that may follow the failure to meet these expectations. Other common incentives include maximizing incentive compensation and avoiding the violation of earnings-related financial covenants in credit agreements.

- The Securities and Exchange Commission launched a major campaign against abusive earnings management in 1998. Company officers face the prospect of civil, and possibly criminal, prosecution if their efforts to manage earnings are seen to involve fraudulent financial reporting.

- Key targets of the SEC's campaign include (1) big-bath charges, (2) creative acquisition accounting, (3) cookie jar reserves, (4) materiality judgments, and (5) revenue-recognition practices.

- Clear evidence of *abusive* earnings management is available in the Accounting and Auditing Enforcement Releases of the SEC. If the number of AAERs is related to the number of SEC registrants, one might conclude that abusive earnings management is not common. Another commonly held view is that the cases identified and pursued by the SEC represent only the tip of the iceberg of abusive earnings management.

- Evidence of earnings management from academic research is somewhat supportive. The research designs of this work often rely on statistical models applied to large samples of firms. Their power to isolate behavior consistent with earnings management is rather problematic. Also, this work provides little or no insight into the details of earnings management, unlike the SEC evidence. However, this work continues to be strengthened and stronger results should be forthcoming. The more simple research designs, which focus mainly on descriptive statistics, provide stronger evidence of earnings management. Supportive findings include the rarity of small losses and small declines in profits and the large numbers of consensus forecasts that are either just met or exceeded by a small amount.

- Earnings management often must have a stealth quality to be fully effective. For example, recording and disclosing a nonrecurring gain on the sale of an investment normally will not be counted toward meeting the consensus earnings expectations of Wall Street. However, earnings management that can undetectably increase earnings may make it possible for a firm to issue shares at higher prices.[67]

- Various techniques used to conceal abusive earnings management are revealed in the SEC's AAERs. They include discarding document copies, creating false documents—in some cases by scanning and altering legitimate documents, backdating agreements, lying to auditors, and booking wholly false entries.

- Broad statements about whether earnings management is either good or bad are difficult to make. Much depends on the steps taken and the motivation for the earnings management. Good earnings management might include real actions taken or accounting flexibility that is exercised within the boundaries of GAAP, if full disclosure is provided about current and prospective financial performance. Bad earnings management would include earnings management practices described in this chapter as abusive. Here the goal is to misrepresent and mislead statement users about a firm's financial performance.

GLOSSARY

Abusive Earnings Management   A characterization used by the Securities and Exchange Commission to designate earnings management that results in an intentional and material misrepresentation of results.

Accounting and Auditing Enforcement Release (AAER)   Administrative proceedings or litigation releases that entail an accounting or auditing-related violation of the securities laws.

Accounting Irregularities   Intentional misstatements or omissions of amounts or disclosures in financial statements done to deceive financial statement users. The term is used interchangeably with *fraudulent financial reporting*.

Administrative Proceeding   An official SEC document reporting a settlement or a hearing scheduled before an administrative judge of an alleged violation of one or more sections or rules of the securities laws.

Aggressive Accounting   A forceful and intentional choice and application of accounting principles done in an effort to achieve desired results, typically higher current earnings, whether the practices followed are in accordance with generally accepted accounting principles or not. Aggressive accounting does not become allegedly fraudulent, even when generally accepted accounting principles have been breached, until an administrative, civil, or criminal proceeding has alleged that fraud has been committed. In particular, an intentional, material misstatement must have taken place in an effort to deceive financial statement readers.

Audit Committee   A subcommittee of a company's board of directors assigned the responsibility of ensuring that corporate financial reporting is fair and honest and that an audit is conducted in a probing and diligent manner.

Big Bath Charges   A wholesale write-down of assets and accrual of liabilities in an effort to make the balance sheet particularly conservative so that there will be fewer expenses to serve as a drag on earnings in future years.

Bill and Hold Practices   Product sales along with an explicit agreement that delivery will occur at a later, often yet-to-be-determined, date.

Bogey   The level of earnings in an incentive compensation or bonus plan below which no incentive compensation or bonus is earned. Also termed a *floor*.

Cap The level of earnings in an incentive compensation or bonus plan above which no additional incentive compensation or bonus is earned. Also termed a *ceiling*.

Consensus Earnings Estimates   The average of earnings-per-share estimates by analysts. These estimates are collected from analysts and distributed by a number of firms.

Cookie Jar Reserves   An overly aggressive accrual of operating expenses done in an effort to reduce future-year operating expenses by reversing portions of the accrued liability into earnings.

Creative Accounting Practices   Any and all steps used to play the financial numbers game, including the aggressive choice and application of accounting principles, both within and beyond the boundaries of generally accepted accounting principles, and fraudulent financial reporting. Also included are steps taken toward earnings management and income smoothing.

Creative Acquisition Accounting   The allocation to expense of a greater portion of the price paid for another company in an acquisition in order to reduce acquisition-year earnings and boost future-year earnings by relieving them of the burden of these charges. Acquisition-year expense charges include purchased in-process research and development and overly aggressive accruals of future operating expenses.

Earnings Management   The active manipulation of earnings toward a predetermined target. This target may be one set by management, a forecast made by analysts, or an amount that is consistent with a smoother, more sustainable earnings stream. Often earnings management entails taking steps to reduce and "store" profits during good years for use during slower years. This more limited form of earnings management is known as income smoothing.

EBITDA   Earnings before interest, taxes, depreciation, and amortization.

Fictitious Revenue   Revenue recognized from a nonexistent sale or other transaction.

Financial Covenants   Provisions in credit or debt agreements that call for the maintenance of certain amounts or relationships. A positive covenant might require the maintenance of a minimum ratio of current assets to current liabilities or of a minimum amount of shareholders' equity. A negative covenant could restrict the amounts of dividend payments or capital expenditures. These covenants are designed to provide the lender with some degree of control over the activities of the debtor and, by so doing, to increase the likelihood of being repaid.

Financial Numbers Game   The use of creative accounting practices to alter a financial statement reader's impression of a firm's business performance.

Fraudulent Financial Reporting   Intentional misstatements or omissions of amounts or disclosures in financial statements that are done to deceive financial statement users. The term is used interchangeably with *accounting irregularities*. A technical difference exists in that with fraud it must be shown that a reader of financial statements containing intentional and material misstatements used those financial statements to his or her detriment. The term *fraudulent financial reporting* is used here only after it has been demonstrated in an administrative, civil, or criminal proceeding, such as that of the Securities and Exchange Commission, or a court, that a fraud has been committed.

GAAP   Generally accepted accounting principles.

Income Smoothing   A form of earnings management designed to remove peaks and valleys from a normal earnings series. The practice includes taking steps to reduce and "store" profits during good years for use during slower years.

Market Capitalization   The market value of shares outstanding as well as the book value of current and noncurrent long-term debt.

Materiality   A characterization of the magnitude of a financial statement item's effect on a company's overall financial condition and performance. An item is material when its size is likely to influence decisions of investors or creditors.

Nonrecurring Items   Revenues or gains and expenses or losses that are not expected to recur on a regular basis. This term is often used interchangeably with *special items*.

Operating Earnings   A term frequently used to describe earnings after the removal of the effects of nonrecurring or nonoperating items.

Operational Earnings Management   Management actions taken in the effort to create stable financial performance by acceptable, voluntary business decisions. An example: a special discount promotion to increase flagging sales near the end of a quarter when targets are not being met.[68]

Premanaged Earnings   Earnings before the effects of any earnings-management activities.

Pro-Forma Earnings   Reported net income with selected nonrecurring items of revenue or gain and expense or loss deducted from or added back, respectively, to reported net income. Occasionally selected nonoperating or noncash items are also treated as adjustment items.

Restructuring Charges   Costs associated with restructuring activities, including the consolidation and/or relocation of operations or the disposition or abandonment of operations or productive assets. Such charges may be incurred in connection with a business combination, a change in an enterprise's strategic plan, or a managerial response to declines in demand, increasing costs, or other environmental factors.

Scienter   A mental state embracing intent to deceive, manipulate, or defraud [(*Ernst & Ernst v. Hochfelder*, 425 U.S. 185, 193 n. 12 (1976)].

Special Items   Significant credits or charges resulting from transactions or events that, in the view of management, are not representative of normal business activities of the period and that affect comparability of earnings.[69] This term is often used interchangeably with *nonrecurring items*.

Sustainable Earnings   A measure of reported earnings from which the effects of all nonrecurring items of revenue or gain and expense or loss have been removed. Sustainable earnings are seen to be a better foundation upon which to base earnings projections.

Treadway Commission Also known as the National Commission on Fraudulent Financial Reporting. A special committee formed in 1985 to investigate the underlying causes of fraudulent financial reporting. The commission was named after its chairman, former SEC commissioner James Treadway. The commission's report, published in 1987, stressed the need for strong and independent audit committees for public companies.

Underlying Results   Earnings after removing the effects of nonrecurring or nonoperating items.

NOTES

1. Arthur Levitt, "The Numbers Game," speech at the New York University Center for Law and Business, September 28, 1998, p. 3. Available at: www.sec.gov/news/speeches/spch220.txt.
2. Ibid.
3. L. Quinn, "Accounting Sleuths," *Strategic Finance*, October 2000, p. 56.
4. This statement was part of a casual conversation struck up by one of the authors while on an airplane. The other party was the anonymous CEO of a midsize public company. He "found" his penny by reversing a portion of an accrued liability. He decided that it was too large!
5. *The Wall Street Journal*, July 19, 2000, p. A1. The quoted statement is attributed to Don Young, an analyst with Paine-Webber.
6. P. Dechow and D. Skinner, "Earnings Management: Reconciling the Views of Accounting Academics, Practitioners, and Regulators," *Accounting Horizons*, June 2000, p. 235.
7. W. Parfet, "Accounting Subjectivity and Earnings Management: A Preparer Perspective," *Accounting Horizons*, December 2000, p. 486.
8. W. Scott, *Financial Accounting Theory* (Upper Saddle River, NJ: Prentice-Hall, 1997), p. 296.
9. It is also possible that earnings would be managed down if actual earnings were coming in well above the consensus estimates. A concern would be that the current high level of earnings would lead to expectations for future results that could not be satisfied.

10. For more on conducive conditions, see C. Mulford and E. Comiskey, *Financial Warnings* (New York: John Wiley & Sons, 1996), p. 394–398. Another very useful source is M. Beasley, J. Carcello, and D. Hermanson, *Fraudulent Financial Reporting: 1987–1997: An Analysis of U.S. Public Companies* (New York: American Institute of Certified Public Accountants, 1999).

11. Agilent Technologies, Inc. presents an exception to the practice of removing nonrecurring gains in judging whether earnings have met the target or not. Agilent had provided guidance to analysts regarding the amount and timing of gains on the sale of certain leased assets. "Unlike a restructuring charge, which was added back to net income in judging whether Agilent had met its target, however, that gain on asset sales was included in the consensus estimate." *The Wall Street Journal*, November 21, 2000, p. B6. Since the gain had been included in the earnings estimates of the analysts, it was not removed from actual earnings is judging whether the consensus earnings estimate was met.

12. Falling short of a consensus forecast still may result in an increase in share price if other positive news is reported along with the disappointing earnings. For example, an Internet retailer may have added more new customers than anticipated.

13. A possible example of this condition and associated incentive is found in the change in DaimlerChrysler AG's management. "There has been growing speculation that Mr. Zetsche [new CEO] will make fourth-quarter results look as bad as possible in order to get the worst of Chrysler's problems behind him. That would enable Mr. Zetsche to blame Chrysler's problems on his predecessor." *The Wall Street Journal*, November 21, 2000, p. A3.

14. Isaac C. Hunt, Jr., "Current SEC Financial Fraud Developments" (Washington, DC: Securities and Exchange Commission, March 3, 2000), p. 5. This appeared in a speech given by Mr. Isaac and is available at: www.sec.gov/news/speeches/spch351.htm.

15. Ibid. Levitt, "The Numbers Game."

16. Ibid.

17. Ibid.

18. These included the areas of: (1) big-bath charges, (2) creative acquisition accounting, (3) cookie-jar reserves, (4) materiality, and (5) revenue recognition. Ibid., pp. 3–5.

19. Ibid., p. 3.

20. Ibid., p. 2.

21. The "bridge too far" reference is a prophetic statement made by a senior officer involved in the planning for Market Garden, a large World War II allied airborne operation into the Netherlands. As the plan was laid out, a series of four key bridges was identified that had to be secured for the success of the operation. When the fourth bridge was identified, this officer remarked that he thought that it was "a bridge too far." Three bridges were secured, but the fourth was not. Market Garden failed at great cost in men and materiel.

22. For examples of carrying earnings management too far, see a summary of 30 SEC enforcement actions aimed at financial reporting fraud: "Details of the 30 Enforcement Actions" (Washington, DC: Securities and Exchange Commission, September 28, 1999). This document is available on the SEC web site at: www.sec.gov/news/extra/finfrds.htm.

23. Beasley, Carcello, and Hermanson, *Fraudulent Financial Reporting*, p. 24.

24. Accounting and Auditing Enforcement Release No. 1272, *In the Matter of Cendant Corporation, Respondent* (Washington, DC: Securities and Exchange Commission, June 14, 2000). Cendant was a combination of two companies: HFS and CUC. The abusive earnings management was conducted by the former CUC entity.

25. For a discussion of this and related points, see Scott, *Financial Accounting Theory*, chapter 11.

26. Earnings management that is designed to obscure deterioration in performance will eventually be discovered. When it is, existing shareholders will suffer. Those shareholders selling their shares before the discovery of the earnings management may benefit from the practice.

27. For a recent distillation of SEC actions against fraudulent financial reporting see Beasley, Carcello, and Hermanson, *Fraudulent Financial Reporting*.

28. The lower bound of this earnings-management region is a level of company earnings below which no incentive compensation is earned. The upper bound, if present, is a maximum earnings level above which no additional incentive compensation is earned. The earnings management goal is to keep company earnings within this region and, ideally, at the upper limit if compensation is to be maximized.

29. This flexibility has been reduced somewhat by the issuance by the SEC of Staff Accounting Bulletin (SAB) 101, *Revenue Recognition in Financial Statements* (Washington, DC: Securities and Exchange Commission, December 3, 1999). This SAB is discussed at length in Chapter 6.

30. Centennial Technologies, included in Exhibit 3.6, produced 27,000 PC cards that looked like typical product. However, they consisted only of an outer casing and no inner circuitry.

31. A paper that has been exceptionally helpful to the authors in this section is by P. Dechow and D. Skinner, "Earnings Management," pp. 235–250. The information summarized in Exhibit 3.7 owes much to their work.

32. Examples of key studies include: L. Brown, "Managerial Behavior and the Bias in Analysts' Earnings Forecasts," Working Paper, Georgia State University, 1998; D. Burgstahler, "Incentives to Manage Earnings to Avoid Earnings Decreases and Losses: Evidence from Quarterly Earnings," Working Paper, University of Washington, 1997; D. Burgstahler and I. Dichev, "Earnings Management to Avoid Earnings Decreases and Losses," *Journal of Accounting and Economics*, December 1997, pp. 99–126; D. Burgstahler and M. Eames, "Management of Earnings and Analyst Forecasts," Working Paper, University of Washington, 1998; F. Degeorge, J. Patel, and R. Zeckhauser, "Earnings Management to Exceed Thresholds," *Journal of Business*, January 1999, pp. 1–33; C. Hayn, "The Information Content of Losses," *Journal of Accounting and Economics*, September 1995, pp. 125–153; and S. Richardson, S. Teoh, and P. Wysocki, "Tracking Analysts' Forecasts over the Annual Earnings Horizon: Are Analysts' Forecasts Optimistic or Pessimistic?" Working Paper, University of Michigan, 1999.

33. P. Healy, "The Effect of Bonus Schemes on Accounting Decisions," *Journal of Accounting and Economics*, April 1985, pp. 85–107.

34. In a subsequent paper, Dechow et al. criticized the assumed absence of any nondiscretionary component to the change in accruals. The authors identified that portion of the change in accruals that could be considered to be nondiscretionary. Refer to P. Dechow, J. Sabino, and R. Sloan, "Implications of Nondiscretionary Accruals for Earnings Management and Market-Based Research, Working Paper, University of Michigan, 1998.

35. Healy, "The Effect of Bonus Schemes on Accounting Decisions," p. 96.

36. F. Guidry, A. Leone, and S. Rock, "Earnings-Based Bonus Plans and Earnings Management by Business-Unit Managers," *Journal of Accounting and Economics*, January 1999, pp. 113–142.

37. J. Gaver, K. Gaver, and J. Austin, "Additional Evidence on Bonus Plans and Income Management," *Journal of Accounting and Economics*, February 1995, pp. 3–28.

38. Scott, *Financial Accounting Theory*, p. 302.

39. L. Shivakumar, "Do Firms Mislead Investors by Overstating Earnings before Seasoned Offerings?," *Journal of Accounting and Economics*, June 2000, pp. 339–371.

40. Ibid., p. 369.

41. Ibid.

42. J. Friedlan, "Accounting Choices of Issuers of Initial Public Offerings," *Contemporary Accounting Research*, Summer 1994, pp. 1–31. Other studies on earnings management and seasoned offerings include: S. Rangan, "Earnings Management and the Performance of Seasoned Equity Offerings," *Journal of Financial Economics*, October 1998, pp. 101–122 and S. Teoh, I. Welch, and T. Wong, "Earnings Management and the Underperformance of Seasoned Equity Offerings," *Journal of Financial Economics*, October 1998, pp. 63–99.

43. A. Sweeney, "Debt-Covenant Violations and Managers' Accounting Responses," *Journal of Accounting and Economics*, May 1994, pp. 281–308, and M. DeFond and J. Jiambalvo, "Debt Covenant Violation and Manipulation of Accruals," *Journal of Accounting and Economics*, January 1994, pp. 145–176.

44. J. Payne and S. Robb, "Analysts Forecasts and Earnings Management," *Journal of Accounting, Auditing and Finance*, Fall 2000, p. 389.

45. R. Kasznik, "On the Association between Voluntary Disclosure and Earnings Management," *Journal of Accounting Research*, Spring 1999, p. 79.

46. An example: Assume that a firm is close to violation of a debt-to-worth covenant in a credit agreement. A change in accounting policy that increases earnings, and with it shareholders' equity, could be seen as earnings management designed to avoid a covenant violation. The underlying incentive is to avoid the negative consequences of a covenant violation, for example, an increase in interest, a demand for collateral, or a reduction in debt maturity. For this earnings management to be effective, the earnings increase from the change in accounting must be permitted to increase shareholders' equity for purposes of measuring covenant compliance. This may or may not be the case depending on the specific conditions in the credit agreement.

47. *The Wall Street Journal*, August 23, 2000, p. B7.

48. Ibid., August 17, 2000, p. A3.

49. Ibid., November 7, 2000, p. B11.

50. Ibid., October 12, 2000, pp. C1–C2.

51. Ibid., July 14, 2000, p. A2.

52. Ibid., August 7, 2000, pp. C1–C2.

53. BEA Systems, Inc., annual report, January 2000, p. 39.

54. *The Wall Street Journal*, July 19, 2000, p. A1.

55. Healy, "The Effect of Bonus Schemes on Accounting Decisions."

56. An airline's union contract for its pilots includes a condition that could alter their job security in the event of a substantial economic downturn. One downturn measure is a one-third projected reduction in 12 months' pretax earnings, excluding extraordinary debits and credits. If there is ever an effort to invoke this feature, what are or are not extraordinary debits and credits will no doubt have to be litigated. Based on "Contract 2000 Highlights," the tentative United Airlines Pilots agreement, p. 1.

57. Scott, *Financial Accounting Theory*, p. 296.

58. *The Wall Street Journal*, November 21, 2000, p. A3.

59. Levitt, "The Numbers Game," p. 4.

60. The SEC has provided guidance in the area of restructuring charges in Staff Accounting Bulletin: No. 100—*Restructuring and Impairment Charges*, November 24, 1999. This SAB is available on the SEC web site: www.sec.gov/interps/account/sab100.htm. Guidance is also provided in Emerging Issues Task Force items of the Financial Accounting Standards Board: EITF Issue No. 94-3, *Liability Recognition for Certain Employee Termination Benefits and Other Costs to Exit an Activity (including Certain Costs Incurred in a Restructuring)* and EITF 95-3, *Recognition of Liabilities in Connection with a Purchase Business Combination.*

61. Dechow and Skinner, "Earnings Management," pp. 235–236.

62. Parfet, "Accounting Subjectivity and Earnings Management," p. 485. Mr. Parfet is the chairman and CEO of MPI Research, Inc., and a member of the Financial Accounting Foundation.

63. Ibid.

64. Ibid.

65. For research that documents this form of earnings management, see: Payne and Robb, "Analysts Forecasts and Earnings Management," pp. 371–389, and Kasznik, "On the Association between Voluntary Disclosure and Earnings Management," pp. 57–81.

66. Rangan, "Earnings Management and the Performance of Seasoned Equity Offerings," and Teoh, Welch, and Wong, "Earnings Management and the Underperformance of Seasoned Equity Offerings."

67. Dechow and Skinner, "Earnings Management," p. 245.

68. The essential content of this entry is from Parfet, "Accounting Subjectivity and Earnings Management," p. 485.

69. Shell Oil Company, *Third Quarter Earnings Release*, November 2, 2000.

CHAPTER FOUR

The SEC Responds

*Therefore, I am calling for immediate and coordinated action:
technical rule changes . . . to improve the transparency of financial
statements; enhanced oversight of the financial reporting process . . .
and nothing less than a fundamental cultural change on the part of
corporate management as well as the whole financial community. . . .[1]*

THE CHAIRMAN'S SPEECH

With the above announcement in a speech on September 28, 1998, to the New York University Center for Law and Business, Arthur Levitt, then chairman of the Securities and Exchange Commission, announced an all-out war on the kinds of accounting and reporting procedures collectively referred to here as creative accounting practices. During recent years, the SEC has witnessed an increase in what the agency termed "accounting hocus pocus."[2] In the chairman's view, the increased use of accounting gimmickry to sway reported financial results was due to a predilection on the part of the financial markets to punish companies that missed their consensus earnings forecasts. He noted an example of one U.S. company that missed its so-called numbers by one cent and saw its market value decline by more than 6 percent in a single day. In the chairman's view, corporate managements were under extreme pressure to make their numbers and were bowing to that pressure, putting the integrity of our financial reporting system at risk.

The chairman noted that accounting principles were not meant to be a straitjacket. Flexibility is necessary to permit financial reporting to handle differences in business structures and keep pace with business innovations. However, according to the chairman, companies are using that flexibility to create illusions in their financial reports, illusions that are anything but true and fair reporting.

In its regulatory role, the SEC is clearly of preeminent importance to the financial reporting process in the United States. The agency has front-line responsibility to help limit the use of creative accounting practices in financial reports filed with it. Given this responsibility and the new diligence being shown by the SEC to address many of the creative accounting practices being reported on here, a review of the problems the SEC sees with financial reporting and the new directions it is taking was deemed necessary.

Five Creative Accounting Practices

According to the SEC's chairman, companies are using or, rather, abusing five accounting practices to control their reported financial results and position. The first three of these accounting practices, big bath charges, creative acquisition accounting, and cookie jar reserves, were considered together with other forms of earnings management in Chapters 2 and 3. The fourth item, materiality, is used by companies to stretch the flexibility found in generally accepted accounting principles as they account for individually immaterial items in a manner that is outside the boundaries of GAAP. Treatment of the topic is provided in Chapter 9. The fifth item, revenue recognition, is studied in Chapter 6, the chapter on recognizing premature or fictitious revenue. Exhibit 4.1 lists the five creative accounting practices with the location of where each topic is afforded primary treatment.

Big Bath Charges

Companies are using large restructuring charges to clean up their balance sheets—thus the term *big bath*. The temptation is for companies to overstate these charges because investors will look beyond the one-time loss and focus only on future earnings. If some extra cushioning can be built into the charge that is taken, making it overly conservative, then the amount of that extra cushioning is "miraculously reborn as income when estimates change or future earnings fall short."[3]

The chairman's position is not opposed to restructuring charges generally. Such strategic actions are part of managing a changing business. Rather, his position is that

---

Exhibit 4.1   Five Creative Accounting Practices Identified by SEC Chairman

Creative Accounting Practice	Location of Primary Treatment
1. Big bath charges	Chapter 2
	Chapter 3
2. Creative acquisition accounting	Chapter 2
	Chapter 3
3. Cookie jar reserves	Chapter 2
	Chapter 3
4. Materiality and errors	Chapter 9
5. Revenue recognition	Chapter 6

Source: Arthur Levitt, "The Numbers Game," speech given to the New York University Center for Law and Business.

---

such charges should be recorded without including a "flushing [of] all associated costs—and maybe a little extra—through the financial statements."[4]

Creative Acquisition Accounting

The second gimmick used by reporting companies to create financial statement illusions is creative acquisition accounting. As the number of acquisitions, consolidations, and spin-offs have increased in recent years, so has the use of "merger magic."[5] In particular, that magic is the creative use of purchased in-process research and development. Companies are classifying an ever-growing portion of the price paid in an acquisition to purchased in-process R&D, writing it off as a one-time charge and removing any future earnings drag. While not stated, the chairman's implication is that more of the acquisition price paid should be allocated to goodwill or other intangibles and, where relevant, amortized over future years' earnings.

Another creative accounting practice used by companies completing acquisitions is to create large liabilities for future operating expenses. These liabilities purportedly represent future costs associated with the recently completed business combination. What they may include, however, is a portion of normal future operating expenses. By charging those to the acquisition, future earnings are boosted.

Cookie Jar Reserves

The third item uses unrealistic assumptions to estimate liabilities. The practice entails reducing earnings during good years by stashing amounts in cookie jars, then reaching into the jars when needed during bad times. The chairman specifically mentioned sales returns, loan losses, and warranty costs.

He gave a specific example of an unusual accounting treatment, recalling a company that took a large one-time charge to "reimburse franchisees for equipment."[6] That equipment, which appeared to include more than what might be considered equipment, had yet to be purchased. Moreover, the announcement of the equipment charge was done at a time when the company announced that future earnings were expected to grow at 15% per year.

Materiality

The fourth item used by companies to adjust earnings to desired levels is the abuse of the concept of materiality. The chairman noted that materiality helps to build flexibility into financial reporting. Some items may be so insignificant that they are not worth measuring and reporting with exact precision. The concept of materiality can be misused by intentionally recording transactions incorrectly within a defined percentage ceiling. However, because the effect on the bottom line is, supposedly, too small to matter, adjustment of the error is unnecessary. Of course, even immaterial items can add a penny or two to reported earnings per share, keeping them in line with analyst forecasts.

Revenue Recognition

More concerned here about improperly boosting earnings, the chairman identified the fifth method of manipulating income as incorrectly recognizing revenue. Revenue recognition was likened to a bottle of fine wine. Just like a bottle of fine wine, where the cork should not be popped before it is ready, revenue should not be recognized until the proper time. He noted that it is improper to recognize revenue before a sale is complete, before the product is delivered to a customer, or at a time when the customer still has options to "terminate, void or delay the sale."[7]

Beyond the SEC's Five Practices

This focus by the SEC on five specific creative accounting practices notwithstanding, we have observed numerous examples of creative accounting practices employed in other areas. For this reason, we discuss creative accounting practices dealing with aggressive capitalization of expenditures and extended amortization periods in Chapter 7 and generally all other misstatements of assets and liabilities in Chapter 8. Because we also felt that financial statement readers can be misled by financial statement classifications, we added topics dealing with the formatting of the income statement in Chapters 9 and 10 and the statement of cash flows in Chapter 11.

THE ACTION PLAN

The SEC chairman noted that U.S. capital market supremacy is based on the reliability and transparency of financial statements. Thus, the problems with financial reporting noted in his speech are a problem for the financial community in this country and not just for the companies involved. Accordingly, he called for immediate and coordinated community action, a cooperative public-private sector effort.

Specifically, the SEC chairman's action plan is a multipoint program designed for both regulators and the regulated to not only maintain but increase public confidence in financial reporting. His nine-point action plan is divided into four categories:

1. Improving the accounting framework
2. Enhancing outside auditing
3. Strengthening the audit committee process
4. Pursuing cultural change

These categories and the nine action-plan program steps are summarized in Exhibit 4.2 and detailed below.

Improving the Accounting Framework

In this first category of the action plan, he outlined six program steps designed to make financial statements themselves more transparent and reliable. The first is a proposal to require well-detailed disclosures about the impact of changes in accounting assumptions. This disclosure requirement is proposed as a supplement to the financial statements showing, for account balance changes, the beginning and ending balances and cross-period activity, including adjustments. The direct objective here is to better enable finan-

Exhibit 4.2   SEC Chairman's Nine-Point Action Plan to Return Reliability and Transparency to Financial Reporting in the United States

Category	Action Plan Program Step
Improving the Accounting Framework	1. Better disclosure of impact of changes in accounting assumptions
	2. Clarified accounting rules for purchased in-process research and development, large acquisition write-offs, and restructuring charges
	3. Guidance on qualitative factors for determining materiality in accounting measurements
	4. Interpretive guidance for revenue recognition
	5. Prompt resolution of FASB's definition of liabilities
	6. Targeted reviews of public companies announcing restructuring liability reserves, major write-offs, or other earnings-management practices
Enhancing Outside Auditing	7. Call to auditors to review the way audits are performed and determine if changes are needed
Strengthening the Audit Committee Process	8. Blue-ribbon panel to develop recommendations to strengthen audit committees
Pursuing Cultural Change	9. Corporate management and Wall Street to examine reporting environment, to reward open and transparent reporting and punish creative accounting practices

Source: Derived from Arthur Levitt, "The Numbers Game," speech given to the New York University Center for Law and Business.

cial statement users to understand the nature and effects of restructuring liabilities and other loss accruals.

The second point is a challenge to the accounting profession to clarify the accounting rules for purchased in-process research and development, large acquisition write-offs, and restructuring charges. In the chairman's view, there is too much gray area and flexibility surrounding the accounting for these items.

In his third point, the chairman addresses his concerns about the misuse of materiality, which can be used as an excuse to deliberately misstate performance. He noted the example of a company that used a materiality ceiling of 6% of earnings to justify an error. According to the chairman, that is not the manner in which materiality thresholds are to be used. He directed the SEC staff to study the problem and publish guidance that emphasizes the need to consider qualitative, not just quantitative, factors of earnings. In this way, materiality guidelines will consider all relevant factors that should impact an investor's decision.

In the fourth action point, the SEC staff is directed to consider interpretive accounting guidance for revenue recognition. The objective here is a clearer insight into what are and what are not proper revenue recognition practices. Acknowledging new, tighter guidance for software revenue recognition, outlined in Chapter 6, the chairman directed the SEC staff to determine whether the software revenue recognition standards can be applied to other service companies.

The fifth point is directed at private sector accounting standard setters, in particular, the Financial Accounting Standards Board (FASB). The chairman encouraged the board to pursue a prompt resolution of ongoing projects to clarify the definition of liabilities. In particular, the FASB has an ongoing deliberation of issues raised in a 1990 discussion memorandum that focuses on the characteristics of liabilities and equity, *Distinguishing between Liability and Equity Instruments and Accounting for Instruments with Characteristics of Both*.[8]

The SEC plans to reinforce the regulatory initiatives contained in these accounting-change action steps. In the sixth point of his nine-point program, the chairman indicated that the SEC will formally target reviews of public companies that announce restructuring liability reserves, major write-offs, or other practices that appear to manage earnings.

Enhancing Outside Auditing

The seventh point is directed at the auditing profession. In the chairman's view, auditors are the watchdogs in the financial reporting process. They put the equivalent of a "good housekeeping seal of approval on the information investors receive."[9] In this view, the integrity of the information contained in financial reports must take priority over any desire for cost efficiencies or competitive advantage in the audit process. In addition, a high-quality audit requires well-trained auditors who are well supervised. The chairman wondered aloud whether, given the high number of audit failures being observed in recent years, the professionals actually doing the audits were sufficiently trained and supervised. In his words, "We cannot permit thorough audits to be sacrificed for re-engineered approaches that are efficient, but less effective."[10] To address this potential problem, he ordered all constituencies involved in the audit process to review the ways audits are performed and determine if changes are needed.

Strengthening the Audit Committee Process

Audit committees are subcommittees of corporate boards of directors assigned the responsibility of ensuring that corporate financial reporting is fair and honest and that the audit is conducted in a probing and diligent manner. A good audit committee is a tough-minded group of independent members of the board of directors that have appropriate financial accounting and reporting knowledge. The SEC chairman noted that many audit committee members are not sufficiently independent from management, do not have the requisite financial accounting and reporting knowledge, and do not meet often enough to make a difference in a company's reporting environment. He contrasted the character and composition of two different audit committees. One committee had little expertise in the basic principles of financial reporting and met only twice per year for 15 minutes before a regular board meeting. Every member of the second committee had a financial background, had no personal ties to the chairman or the company, and met monthly to ask tough questions of management and the outside auditors. In the latter case, according to the chairman, investor interest was better served.

In point 8 of the SEC's action plan, the chairman announced the formation of a blue-ribbon panel sponsored by the New York Stock Exchange and the National Association of Securities Dealers. The purpose of this panel, the Blue Ribbon Committee on Improving the Effectiveness of Corporate Audit Committees, is to develop a series of recommendations intended to empower audit committees to better function as the ultimate guardian of investor interests and corporate accountability.

Pursuing Cultural Change

In the ninth and final point of the action plan, the chairman challenged corporate management and Wall Street to look carefully at the current reporting environment. He reminded managements that the integrity of their financial numbers is directly related to the long-term interests of their corporations. Temptations abound to employ creative accounting practices. However, the rewards are ultimately self-destructive. As to Wall Street, he encouraged market participants to punish firms that rely on deception in financial reporting rather than those that use openness and transparency.

SUBSEQUENT DEVELOPMENTS

Arthur Levitt's address was a watershed event. It rang a starting bell and announced that the SEC was going after creative accounting practices from several directions in a concerted way. The financial markets of the United States are the envy of the world, and Levitt was convinced that reporting problems were putting their preeminence at risk. He would not let that happen.

In the time following the SEC chairman's speech, we have seen numerous developments on many fronts that can be attributed directly to the SEC's new found diligence.

Accounting Framework

Developments in the SEC's accounting framework area are summarized in Exhibit 4.3 and detailed below.

Consistent with their accounting directives, the SEC issued three new Staff Accounting Bulletins (SABs). SAB 99 *Materiality*, was issued in August 1999.[11] The bulletin reiterates the SEC's view that materiality cannot be judged based on quantitative measures alone, but must consider qualitative factors as well. The bulletin also notes that in determining materiality, offsetting misstatements cannot be netted but must be considered separately. Finally, the bulletin states that intentional misstatements of immaterial items are not permitted.

In November 1999, the SEC issued SAB 100 *Restructuring and Impairment Charges*.[12] In this bulletin, the SEC expresses its views on the accounting for and dis-

---

Exhibit 4.3   Summary of Developments in the Accounting Framework since the SEC Chairman's Speech

---

SEC issued SAB 99: *Materiality.*

SEC issued SAB 100: *Restructuring and Impairment Charges.*

SEC issued SAB 101: *Revenue Recognition.*

FASB issued SFAS No. 141: *Business Combinations.*

FASB issued SFAS 142: *Goodwill and Other Intangible Assets.*

FASB deferred reconsideration of purchased in-process research and development to comprehensive project on R&D.

FASB planned exposure draft and final statement on the definition of liabilities.

SEC filed numerous accounting fraud civil suits.

SEC announced heightened pursuit of criminal prosecutions for accounting fraud.

Sources: Securities and Exchange Commission Internet Web Site, June 2000, and Financial Accounting Standards Board, *Status Report,* April 17, 2000.

---

closure of expenses commonly reported in connection with exit activities and business combinations. The bulletin includes exit costs—the costs to exit a business activity, including employee termination benefits and other costs such as lease termination fees and asset disposal costs—within the broader term *restructuring charges.* Restructuring charges are the costs associated with restructuring activities, including the consolidation and/or relocation of operations or the disposition or abandonment of operations or productive assets. Generally, the bulletin prohibits the accrual of exit costs prior to the date that a company's management is committed to an exit plan. Moreover, there must be a detailed budget of the various costs associated with an exit plan strategy. The bulletin concludes with detailed disclosure requirements for exit costs, including adjustments to any previously accrued exit-plan liability.

Also following closely after the chairman's speech was SAB 101, *Revenue Recognition.*[13] SAB 101 notes that accounting rules for revenue recognition are not comprehensive but rather a collection of industry and transaction-specific guidelines. The bulletin, however, does not change any of the existing rules on revenue recognition. It clarifies the basic criteria for revenue recognition found in those existing rules and explains how the SEC applies them to other transactions that the existing rules do not specifically address. Generally, the bulletin takes the newly updated and carefully considered revenue recognition requirements for software revenue and applies them to other product and service sales. Using those requirements, the bulletin maintains that before revenue can be recognized, four criteria must be met:

1. There is persuasive evidence of an arrangement
2. Delivery has occurred or services have been rendered

3. The seller's price to the buyer is fixed or determinable

4. Collectibility is reasonably assured

Also contained in the accounting framework portion of Arthur Levitt's speech were appeals to the FASB to clarify the accounting rules for purchased in-process research and development, large acquisition write-offs, and restructuring charges, and to resolve its ongoing projects that will clarify the definition of liabilities.

The FASB has made much progress on accounting for business combinations. It has published two statements, SFAS No. 141, *Business Combinations* and SFA No. 142, *Goodwill and Other Intangible Assets.*[14] In them, the board emphasizes the need to recognize all of the net assets acquired, including intangible assets, and measure them at their fair values, with any excess of the purchase price over the fair value of net assets acquired being recognized as goodwill. Goodwill will no longer be amortized but will be reviewed periodically for evidence of value impairment.

A careful application of these provisions likely would reduce the portion of an acquisition cost allocated to purchased in-process R&D. Moreover, granting companies the ability to report income without goodwill amortization may lessen their motives to minimize amounts allocated to goodwill.

The FASB did consider specifically addressing the accounting for purchased in-process R&D as part of the project on business combinations. However, it postponed consideration of that issue until a future date when it could consider accounting for R&D costs more comprehensively.

Currently, the FASB is not deliberating the topic of restructuring charges. However, the SEC's recently issued SAB 100, *Restructuring and Impairment Charges,* gives detailed accounting direction for that topic.

The FASB has near-term plans to issue an exposure draft on the definition of liabilities. However, as of the time of this writing, the proposed date of a final statement is not known.

To help ensure that its new accounting directives and existing accounting rules were being followed carefully, minimizing the extent to which creative accounting practices were being employed, the SEC chairman indicated that the commission will formally target reviews of public companies that announce restructuring liability reserves, major write-offs, or other practices that appear to manage earnings. There is ample evidence to indicate that the SEC is adhering to this plan.

The primary responsibility for carrying out the SEC's plan to review more carefully the filings of selected companies falls on the SEC's Division for Corporation Finance. Soon after the chairman's speech, the division announced the creation of an earnings management task force whose task is to identify potential cases of earnings-management activities. Then, in early 1999, the division notified 150 publicly traded companies that special charges reported by them in 1998 might be reviewed for potential accounting violations. The division also notified selected bank holding companies that their loan-loss provisions for 1998 might be reviewed.

Adding heat to the fire, around the same time that the Division for Corporation Finance announced its plans, the SEC's Division of Enforcement announced that as part of a stepped-up campaign to curb accounting fraud, it expected to bring several civil cases against public companies. According to Richard Walker, director of the Division of Enforcement, the fraud-fighting underscores "how serious we are about accurate financial statements."[15]

Identified early in the Enforcement Division's war on alleged accounting fraud were W.R. Grace & Co. and Livent, Inc. W.R. Grace was allegedly using excess reserves to lower operating expenses and bring the company's earnings into line with previously set targets.[16] Management at Livent, Inc., was accused by the SEC of manipulating income over an eight-year period by fraudulently overstating fixed assets and theatrical performance preproduction costs.[17]

Within months, the division had filed additional enforcement actions against 68 people alleging misrepresented financial statements at 15 different companies. Exhibit 4.4 identifies the 15 companies snared in the fraud sweep and summarizes the nature of the cases against them.

As seen in the exhibit, the SEC's fraud sweep included suits against a wide number of firms. Companies caught in the probe included finance firms, such as First Merchants Acceptance Corp. and Mercury Finance Co.; manufacturers, such as Thor Industries, Inc., and Computone Corp.; service companies, such as Itex Corp. and Unison Healthcare Corp.; and technology firms, such as KnowledgeWare, Inc., and WIZ Technology, Inc. The allegedly fraudulent acts by these firms included everything from improper revenue recognition to inflated assets, from the deliberate issuance of false and misleading press releases to concealed embezzlements. Given the wide-ranging nature of the SEC's campaign and the high number of firms and individuals accused of wrongdoing, it is clear that the Division of Enforcement was serious about accurate financial statements.

However, even after this wide-ranging series of civil actions, the SEC was concerned that some managements still might not be convinced that it was serious about cleaning up financial reporting in the United States. Accordingly, within months of the announcement of the civil actions against the 15 firms, the SEC announced that it would work more closely with criminal prosecutors to attack corporate accounting fraud. In a speech to the American Institute of Certified Public Accountants, Richard Walker said that the commission continues to see "an unacceptably high number of busted audits."[18] Thus, he announced that the commission would work more closely with U.S. attorneys' offices to pursue criminal charges against executives involved in fraudulent financial reporting. According to Mr. Walker, "Cook the books, and you will go directly to jail without passing Go."[19]

Mr. Walker cited an example of a case the Enforcement Division was pursuing against two executives of Unison Healthcare, Inc., now known as RainTree Healthcare Corp. According to testimony in the case, Unison's CEO allegedly handed the controller a note that contained "the numbers we need to get to" and said, "I don't care how we get there."[20]

Civil charges typically result in cease and desist orders or other sanctions and a monetary fine. Beyond such penalties, however, there is also the threat of criminal charges, with the possibility of incarceration. Such an announcement would certainly be an attention getter.

Exhibit 4.4   Summary of SEC Enforcement Actions Filed against Defendants at 15 Different Companies Announced in September 1998

Company	Nature of Charge
C.E.C. Industries Corp.	• Material overstatement of assets and revenue
Computone Corp.	• Fraudulent transaction reporting to overstate income
Dominican Cigar Corp.	• Falsely claimed to own assets
FastComm Communications Corp.	• Fraudulently recognized revenue from transactions that were subject to material contingencies
First Merchants Acceptance Corp.	• Did not write off delinquent and uncollectible accounts • Took artificial steps to make accounts appear current
Itex Corp.	• False and misleading disclosures about business performance • Failed to disclose numerous suspect and sham barter deals
KnowledgeWare, Inc.	• Inflated earnings primarily through premature revenue recognition practices
Materials Sciences Corp.	• Improperly overstated inventories and understated accounts payable • Maintained improper and inadequate internal controls
Mercury Finance Co.	• Did not write off delinquent and uncollectible accounts • Falsified records to offset declining revenue
Model Imperial, Inc.	• Recorded unsubstantiated gain from barter transaction, improper sales revenue, and sham sales • Overstated gross profit on retail sales and paid commercial bribes
Pepsi-Cola Puerto Rico Bottling Co.	• Reported fictitious profits while the company actually operated at a loss
Photran Corp.	• Reported premature and fictitious revenue • Improperly recognized revenue from consignment sales
Thor Industries, Inc.	• Embezzlement with false entries to conceal the theft
Unison Healthcare Corp.	• Artificial increase in revenue and earnings with phantom journal entries
WIZ Technology, Inc.	• Deliberate issuance of false and misleading press releases

[1]The charges are alleged acts that violate the Securities Acts.

Source: Securities and Exchange Commission Internet Web Site, September, 1999.

Outside Audits

The SEC's newfound diligence on cleaning up corporate financial reporting went beyond even the civil and criminal cases brought against company managements. The SEC is aware that auditors may play a role in permitting accounting problems at the companies they audit. Thus, as part of his division's crackdown, Mr. Walker announced that it would begin bringing enforcement cases against "weak-kneed auditors."[21] In particular, the division is concerned about cases involving auditors who also are providing consulting services for fear the auditors were not being as diligent in their pursuit of reporting problems.

In response to these concerns of the SEC, the Public Oversight Board formed a special committee, the Panel on Audit Effectiveness. The Public Oversight Board is an independent private-sector body that oversees the audit practices of certified public accountants who work with SEC-regulated companies. The Panel on Audit Effectiveness was created to perform a comprehensive review and evaluation of the way independent audits of financial statements of publicly traded companies are performed. The panel's work included a review of a sample of audits of public companies and a survey of interested parties as to audit effectiveness.

In June 2000 the panel released its preliminary findings. Overall, it found that the accounting profession and the quality of its audits are fundamentally sound. It noted that the model underpinning financial statement audits is appropriate, "although, in need of updating, enhancing and implementing more consistently."[22] According to the panel, the audit profession has not kept pace with a rapidly changing environment and needs to address directly the issue of fraudulent financial reporting. Some of the panel's recommendations are provided in Exhibit 4.5.

As seen in this exhibit, most of the panel's recommendations are for the audit profession to be more diligent in doing what its members already do. However, the recommendation for auditors to perform fraud-seeking audit procedures, so-called forensic-type procedures, on every audit is a new and big step.

Arthur Levitt was pleased with the panel's recommendations. In a press statement released at the time of the panel's report, he noted, "Implementation of the specific recommendations made by the panel to improve the audit process through more comprehensive and vigorous audit methodologies and standards will engender greater confidence among investors that they are receiving high-quality audits."[23]

Audit Committees

In February 1999 the Blue Ribbon Committee on Improving the Effectiveness of Corporate Audit Committees issued a series of recommendations.[24] These recommendations were representative of those included in a 1987 report of the National Commission on Fraudulent Financial Reporting, also known as the Treadway Commission, named after its chairman, former SEC commissioner James Treadway.[25] The Treadway Commission had been formed in 1985 to investigate the underlying causes of fraudulent financial reporting. That committee had determined that financial frauds arose because of undue pressure that builds on management, including pressure for short-term results to meet

---

Exhibit 4.5   Summary of Major Recommendations of Public Oversight Board Panel on Audit Effectiveness, June 2000

Fraud-seeking–type audit procedures should be performed on every audit to enhance the prospects of detecting financial statement fraud.

Audit firms should review and, if needed, enhance their audit methodologies, guidance, and training materials.

Audit standards that guide audit practice should be written in a more specific and definitive manner.

Audit firms should put more emphasis on high-quality audits in training, performance evaluations, compensation, and promotion decisions.

A stronger peer-review process is needed for review of audit practices followed by firms auditing SEC-regulated companies.

Audit committees should preapprove nonaudit services performed by audit firms above certain preestablished amounts.

A stronger disciplinary process is needed over firms auditing SEC-regulated companies.

Source: Public Oversight Board Panel on Audit Effectiveness, Press Release, *Panel on Audit Effectiveness Releases Exposure Draft,* June 6, 2000.

---

bonus-plan requirements and/or the expectations of investors. To help create a reporting environment that could withstand such pressure, a body was needed that was effectively immune to it. An independent audit committee fit the role well. The Treadway Commission's primary contribution was the recommendation for a stronger and more independent audit committee that was active in the financial reporting process.

The report of the Blue Ribbon Committee on Improving the Effectiveness of Corporate Audit Committees included several recommendations regarding the nature and function of audit committees. These recommendations are summarized in Exhibit 4.6.

Among its recommendations, the Blue Ribbon Committee recommended that an audit committee should be comprised of at least three members who are financially literate and independent of the company and its management. At least one member should have accounting or related financial management expertise. Audit committees should be guided by a formal written charter that includes, among other things, a proviso that the outside auditor is ultimately accountable to the board of directors and the audit committee. Other recommendations include the stipulation that a company's outside auditor should discuss with the audit committee the auditor's judgments about the quality, not just the acceptability, of the accounting principles applied by a company. There was also a call for a letter from the audit committee to the shareholders in a company's annual SEC filing noting that management and the audit committee have discussed matters of financial reporting, including the quality of the accounting principles applied. On December 15, 1999, the SEC adopted virtually all of the Blue Ribbon Committee's recommendations.

Exhibit 4.6 Summary of Major Recommendations of Blue-Ribbon Committee on Improving the Effectiveness of Corporate Audit Committees

---

Audit committee should have a minimum of three members who are independent and financially literate

At least one member of audit committee should have accounting or related financial management expertise.

Formal written charter should guide audit committee.

Audit committee should discuss issues of financial statement quality with outside auditor.

Audit committee should provide letter to shareholders noting that matters of financial statement quality have been discussed with auditors and management.

Source: M. Young, ed., *Accounting Irregularities and Financial Fraud: A Corporate Governance Guide* (New York: Harcourt, Inc., 2000).

Cultural Changes

The SEC has less direct control over instituting cultural changes in corporate managements and Wall Street than it does over the contents of financial reports filed with it, the quality of audits, and the independence of audit committees. Certainly the new diligence the commission is showing in the pursuit of civil and criminal penalties for questionable accounting practices should, over time, lead to a more transparent financial reporting culture.

However, the chairman's call to Wall Street to punish firms that rely on deception in financial reporting was arguably unnecessary. Numerous stories abound of breathtaking declines in share prices accompanying disclosures of questionable accounting practices. For example, shares of Boston Scientific Corp. declined more than 20% across three days in November 1998 when it disclosed that it had improperly booked millions of dollars in sales. Similarly, shares of Tyco International, Ltd., declined 24% over a three-week period in October 1999 after news of questionable accounting for acquisitions surfaced. Even worse, on a single day in April 1999, the share price of McKesson HBOC, Inc., declined 48% when news surfaced of accounting problems, primarily related to revenue recognition, at the recently acquired HBO & Co.

In fact, so prepared are investors to sell shares on even a hint of accounting impropriety that even a rumor of a probe by the SEC into a company's accounting practices can send its shares lower. Lucent Technologies, Inc., learned this difficult lesson when its share price declined 5.5% on a single day in January 2000 when unconfirmed rumors circulated that the SEC might investigate the company.[26]

Will It Make a Difference?

When Mr. Levitt made his speech to the New York University Center for Law and Business, he was fed up with the financial reporting environment that he perceived had developed in the United States. His proposals were designed to bring about significant and lasting change. There is anecdotal evidence available to indicate that change is occurring.

For example, in acquisitions of technology firms, the portion of the purchase price allocated to purchased in-process research and development declined to 45% of the purchase price in late 1998 from 72% of the purchase price between 1985 and mid-1996.[27] Moreover, companies are revising downward the portion of acquisition prices allocated to in-process R&D in prior-year acquisitions and restating previously filed financial statements. Additional data indicate that the amount of other special charges, including other merger-related charges, asset write-downs, and restructuring charges, also have declined in recent years. Referring to numbers observed in mid-1999, Jack Ciesielski, head of a watchdog group on accounting practices and advisor to analysts and the FASB, noted, "As the impact of the SEC's campaign sunk in, corporate charges really took a nose dive in the second quarter."[28]

We are also seeing changes in the way firms in certain industries are recording revenue. For example, data collected by Bear Stearns revealed that "At least 32 companies have changed the way they book revenue as a result of the Securities and Exchange Commission's heightened scrutiny of revenue accounting."[29] Companies are generally slowing the timing of their revenue recognition. For example, discount club retailers are moving to recognize revenue over the period of a membership rather than up front. Other companies, in particular certain Internet companies, are actually reducing the absolute amount of the revenue being recognized. In cases where they serve simply as agents to facilitate sales, many are now recognizing revenue for only an agency fee computed as a portion of the sales price rather than for the entire sales price itself.

While it is still early, there is reason to believe that the financial reporting environment in the United States is changing. The above examples of declines in various special charges and changes in revenue recognition practices indicate that change is occurring.

Interestingly, there are some who believe that the SEC has gone too far. For example, a spokesman for the Financial Executives Institute (FEI) said, "Many members believe Mr. Levitt is painting all corporations with the same brush, unfairly so."[30] As another member of the FEI noted, "The SEC shouldn't punish the whole financial community for the sins of a few."[31] Another agrees, stating "They're throwing their weight around."[32] While generally supportive of the SEC's reform campaign, an executive at Merrill Lynch noted that the SEC seemed to be second-guessing even legitimate accounting methods. The executive sounded an alarm, stating that if the SEC does "a lot of scrutiny of the minutiae of individual judgments that go into the financial-reporting process, then that would be a problem."[33] These warnings notwithstanding, however, we think that the new diligence of the SEC is needed and ultimately will lead to a better reporting environment.

Does that mean that creative accounting practices will be eliminated? Will companies no longer play the financial numbers game? Even with improvements in financial reporting, we still expect to see cases of creative accounting practices being discovered, leading to write-downs, restatements, and share-price declines. The game may be played by fewer participants, but it will not go away. The SEC's mandates have not eliminated and cannot eliminate the game's potential rewards. Accordingly, there will remain pressure on individuals to manipulate their reported financial results and position. Under that pressure, there will be those who bend and break.

An additional word of caution is needed. Those who play the game will likely become more careful. They will seek new and more creative accounting practices to manipulate their financial statements. Accordingly, the reader of financial statements must be doubly prepared to examine them carefully to ferret out information that may prove to be misleading.

ENFORCING THE SECURITIES LAWS

Given the SEC's heightened concern about the accuracy of financial statements filed with it, we deemed it appropriate to look more closely at how the SEC's Division of Enforcement enforces the securities laws that govern financial reporting. In this section, we look closer at the securities laws themselves, including key sections and rules of the laws that deal with accounting issues and we examine the workings of the Division of Enforcement, including the penalties available to it in the event of noncompliance.

Securities Acts

Collectively, the Securities Act of 1933 (1933 Act) and the Securities Exchange Act of 1934 (1934 Act) provide for registration of issuers of securities, for standardized disclosure of financial and other information, and for oversight and compliance enforcement. The acts were prompted by a strong perceived need at the time for federal regulation of U.S. securities markets following years of broad-based stock market speculation and price manipulation fostered in part by a general lack of corporate disclosure.

The 1933 Act was designed to protect the investing public from fraudulent practices in the purchase and sale of newly issued securities. Generally, the act made it illegal for any security to be issued that had not been registered with the SEC. Moreover, in a registration statement, an issuer must provide a description of its business and holdings, a description of the security being offered and associated risks, information about company management, and a complete set of audited financial statements. The registration statement must be signed by the issuer's principal officers and by a majority of its board of directors.

The 1934 Act established the SEC and extended the corporate disclosure requirements. Generally, while the 1933 Act contained disclosure requirements for newly issued securities, under the 1934 Act the disclosure requirements became ongoing. That is, as long as the securities of an issuer subject to the requirements of the 1933 Act were outstanding, the subject company would be required to file periodic reports with the SEC to update the information contained in its original filing. The purpose of these recurring disclosure requirements was to ensure that the public gets accurate and timely information about the company.

Regular, periodic filings are required of all companies with more than 500 shareholders and $10 million in total assets, whether a company's securities are listed and traded on a national exchange or not. Under section 13, *Periodical and Other Reports*, of the 1934 Act, three basic reports must be filed with the SEC: Form 10-K, an annual report, Form 10-Q, a quarterly report, and Form 8-K, a report filed to disclose major events affecting the company such as a major acquisition, a change in control, or bankruptcy.[34] Financial statements must be included with Forms 10-K and 10-Q, and in Form 10-K the financial statements must be audited. As with the registration statement, Form 10-K must be signed by the company's principal officers and a majority of its board of directors. Thus, both the 1933 and the 1934 acts include representations by key individuals who are at risk if, later, the company's financial statements prove to be false.

Enforcement Actions

The SEC's Division of Enforcement is responsible for investigating potential violations of the Securities Acts. Violations involving financial reporting that are deemed to be a misrepresentation or omission of important information would fall under the division's jurisdiction. Cases for investigation are identified from many sources, including its own surveillance activities, other divisions of the SEC, self-regulatory organizations, the financial press, and investor complaints.

If, after an investigation, the staff of the division believes that a case can be made against a company or its management, authorization is sought to begin an administrative or judicial proceeding. Once the division gets authority to proceed, it typically will seek to reach a settlement with the targeted parties. If settlement talks are not fruitful, a hearing will be scheduled. Depending on the seriousness of the alleged wrongdoing and its technical nature, that hearing will be either an administrative proceeding in front of an administrative law judge or a civil hearing before a federal court judge.

Whether resulting in a negotiated settlement or scheduled for an administrative hearing, cases deemed appropriate for an administrative proceeding will be reported by the SEC in official documents known as administrative proceedings. Cases considered to be more appropriate for a judicial proceeding, whether settled or scheduled for a federal court hearing, will be reported by the SEC in official documents known as litigation releases. Both types of documents are regularly published by the SEC and appear chronologically on the SEC's web site.[35]

Administrative proceedings and litigation releases published by the SEC will include all violations of the Securities Acts, whether they are accounting related or not. When issues involving financial reporting and disclosure are involved, the SEC also will label the related administrative proceeding or litigation release as an Accounting and Auditing Enforcement Release (AAER). Thus, accounting-related actions taken by the commission will be reported as administrative proceedings or as litigation releases, and both will also be labeled as AAERs.

Financial Reporting and Disclosure Provisions

Enforcement actions against companies and individuals involving financial reporting and disclosure issues typically focus on several sections and rules of the 1933 and 1934 acts. Given its ongoing disclosure requirements, key sections and rules of the 1934 Act are particularly prominent, especially three subsections from Section 13—Section 13(a), Section 13(b)(2)(A), and Section 13(b)(2)(B).

Section 13(a) is referred to as the "periodic reporting" provision of the 1934 Act. Failure to file timely annual and quarterly reports with the commission could indicate a violation of this section. Section 13(a) states in part:

> Every issuer of a security . . . shall file with the Commission, in accordance with such rules and regulations as the Commission may prescribe as necessary or appropriate for the proper protection of investors . . .
>
> 1. Such information and documents . . . as the Commission shall require to keep reasonably current the information and documents required to be included in or filed with an application or registration statement . . .
> 2. Such annual reports . . . certified if required by the rules and regulations of the Commission by independent public accountants, and such quarterly reports . . . as the Commission may prescribe.[36]

Section 13(b)(2)(A) is referred to as the "books and records" provision of the 1934 Act. The section requires that issuers maintain accurate and reasonably detailed financial records. Evidence that financial statements contain errors and are not "accurate," as interpreted by the commission, could indicate a violation of this section of the Securities Act. Section 13(b)(2)(A) states in part:

> Every issuer which has a class of securities registered . . . and every issuer which is required to file reports . . . shall—
>
> A. make and keep books, records, and accounts, which, in reasonable detail, accurately and fairly reflect the transactions and dispositions of the assets of the issuer.[37]

Section 13(b)(2)(B) is referred to as the "internal control" provision of the 1934 Act. The section is designed to assure that a company filing with the commission maintains a system of internal controls that is sufficient to provide financial information that portrays the transactions and events affecting it, consistent with management's authorization and in accordance with generally accepted accounting principles. Evidence that financial statements are not in accordance with GAAP, or of transactions that have been accounted for outside of corporate prescriptions, even if by a rogue member of management, could indicate a violation of this section of the Securities Act. Section 13(b)(2)(B) states in part:

> Every issuer which has a class of securities registered . . . and every issuer which is required to file reports . . . shall—
>
> B. devise and maintain a system of internal accounting controls sufficient to provide reasonable assurances that—
>   i. transactions are executed in accordance with management's general or specific authorization;
>   ii. transactions are recorded as necessary (I) to permit preparation of financial statements in conformity with generally accepted accounting principles or any other criteria applicable to such statements, and (II) to maintain accountability for assets;

    iii. access to assets is permitted only in accordance with management's general or specific authorization; and

    iv. the recorded accountability for assets is compared with the existing assets at reasonable intervals and appropriate action is taken with respect to any differences.[38]

Selected rules of the 1934 Act that are especially relevant for enforcement of accounting and reporting issues are Rule 12b-20, *Additional Information*, Rule 13b2-1, *Falsification of Accounting Records*, Rule 13a-1, *Requirements of Annual Reports*, and Rule 13a-13, *Quarterly Reports on Form 10-Q and Form 10-QSB*. The purpose of these rules is to clarify and sharpen the accounting and reporting requirements of the Securities Act.

Rule 12b-20, *Additional Information*, generally holds that financial statements must include all information needed to prevent them from being misleading. The rule states:

> In addition to the information expressly required to be included in a statement or report, there shall be added such further material information, if any, as may be necessary to make the required statements, in the light of the circumstances under which they are made, not misleading.[39]

Rule 13b2-1, *Falsification of Accounting Records*, maintains that no person shall directly or indirectly falsify accounting records. The rule states in part:

> No person shall, directly or indirectly, falsify or cause to be falsified, any book, record or account subject to . . . the Securities Exchange Act.[40]

Rules 13a-1, *Requirements of Annual Reports*, and 13a-13, *Quarterly Reports on Form 10-Q and Form 10-QSB,* clarify the need for annual and quarterly reporting. Rule 13a-1 states in part:

> Every issuer having securities registered . . . shall file an annual report on the appropriate form authorized or prescribed therefore for each fiscal year after the last full fiscal year for which financial statements were filed in its registration statement. Annual reports shall be filed within the period specified in the appropriate form.[41]

Rule 13a-13 states in part:

> . . . every issuer that has securities registered . . . and is required to file annual reports . . . shall file a quarterly report on Form 10-Q and Form 10-QSB within the period specified . . . for each of the first three quarters of each fiscal year of the issuer. . . .[42]

Generally Accepted Accounting Principles and the Securities and Exchange Commission

Section 13(b)(2)(B) states in part that internal controls in place should permit preparation of financial statements "in conformity with generally accepted accounting principles."[43] The SEC has generally permitted the private sector, and since 1973, the

Financial Accounting Standards Board, to develop accounting principles for use in the United States. Accounting principles developed by the FASB have the full support of the SEC. As such, the SEC does not play a major role in the development of accounting principles.

The commission does, however, make its mark on generally accepted accounting principles. For example, the SEC will prod the FASB into taking quicker action on accounting issues where it sees a need. The reference earlier to the SEC chairman's call for clarification on the definition of liabilities is a case in point. The SEC was also instrumental in pushing the FASB to develop accounting and disclosure requirements for financial derivatives, eventually leading to SFAS No. 133, *Accounting for Derivatives Instruments and Hedging Activities*.[44]

In other instances, the SEC may refuse to accept an accounting standard established by the FASB, leading the FASB to reconsider and revise its position. For example, in 1962 the Accounting Principles Board (APB), a predecessor to the FASB, released a standard calling for deferral of the investment tax credit, with recognition in income over the life of the related asset—the so-called deferral method.[45] The SEC balked at this approach, preferring instead to see the investment tax credit recognized in income currently—the so-called flow-through method. The APB went along with the SEC and amended its standard, permitting both the deferral and flow-through methods.[46] In another example, in 1977 the FASB released a standard for oil- and gas-producing companies calling for only very limited capitalization of exploration expenditures—the so-called successful-efforts method.[47] Here again, the SEC did not consider the practice acceptable. Eventually the FASB amended its standard, permitting both the successful-efforts method and a more liberal "full-cost" method.[48]

The SEC also will communicate problems to the FASB, respond to accounting standards proposed by the FASB, known as exposure drafts, and provide the FASB with counsel upon request. Finally, the SEC will, on occasion, issue its own standards for accounting and disclosure practices for companies falling under its jurisdiction. Good examples of such rules generated by the SEC are the Staff Accounting Bulletins on materiality, restructuring charges, and revenue recognition, recently released by the SEC in response to the chairman's action plan.

Antifraud Provisions

Financial reports are considered to be fraudulent when they violate the antifraud provisions of the Securities Acts. The antifraud provisions are contained in one section of the 1933 Act and one section and one rule of the 1934 Act. Section 17(a) of the Securities Act of 1933 states:

a. **Use of interstate commerce for purpose of fraud or deceit**. It shall be unlawful for any person in the offer or sale of any securities by the use of any means or instruments of transportation or communication in interstate commerce or by the use of the mails, directly or indirectly—
   1. to employ any device, scheme, or artifice to defraud, or
   2. to obtain money or property by means of any untrue statement of a material fact or any omission to state a material fact necessary in order to make the statements

made, in the light of the circumstances under which they were made, not misleading, or

3. to engage in any transaction, practice, or course of business which operates or would operate as a fraud or deceit upon the purchaser.[49]

The antifraud section of the 1934 Act is Section 10(b), which states,

It shall be unlawful for any person, directly or indirectly, by the use of any means or instrumentality of interstate commerce or of the mails, or of any facility of any national securities exchange—

b. To use or employ, in connection with the purchase or sale of any security registered on a national securities exchange or any security not so registered, any manipulative or deceptive device or contrivance in contravention of such rules and regulations as the commission may prescribe as necessary or appropriate in the public interest or for the protection of investors.[50]

Rule 10b-5 of the 1934 Act is also considered to be a component of the antifraud provisions of the Securities Acts. The rule states:

It shall be unlawful for any person, directly or indirectly, by the use of any means or instrumentality of interstate commerce, or of the mails or of any facility of any national securities exchange,

a. To employ any device, scheme, or artifice to defraud,
b. To make any untrue statement of a material fact or to omit to state a material fact necessary in order to make the statements made, in the light of the circumstances under which they were made, not misleading, or
c. To engage in any act, practice, or course of business which operates or would operate as a fraud or deceit upon any person, in connection with the purchase or sale of any security.[51]

The antifraud provisions are broad and, taken at face value, could be construed to include almost all forms of misstatement made by a company's management, whether within or outside its financial statements. However, through case law, it has been demonstrated that to violate the antifraud provisions of the Securities Acts, a defendant must act with scienter—an intent to defraud. Consider, for example, an interpretation of the antifraud provisions found in an administrative proceeding involving Waste Management, Inc.

The SEC alleged that Waste Management violated the antifraud provisions of the 1934 Act by publicly supporting projected results for the company's second quarter in June 1999 at a time when the company was aware of significant adverse trends affecting its business that rendered its forecast unreasonable. The commission's interpretation of the antifraud provisions is provided below. It states clearly the role of scienter in violating the antifraud provisions:

Section 10(b) of the Exchange Act and Rule 10b-5 thereunder prohibit any person, in connection with the purchase or sale of a security, from making an untrue statement of material fact or from omitting to state a material fact necessary in order to make statements made, in light of the circumstances under which they were made, not misleading. To violate Section 10(b) and Rule 10b-5, a defendant must act with scienter, . . . *defined as a mental state embracing intent to deceive, manipulate, or defraud.* . . . Recklessness also has been found to satisfy the scienter requirement. . . . The mental states of a corporation's officers may be imputed to the corporation for purposes of establishing its scienter. . . . A fact is material if there is a substantial likelihood that a reasonable investor would consider the information to be important.[52]

The SEC felt that Waste Management's actions violated the antifraud provisions. Waste Management did not admit or deny these allegations. The company did make an offer of settlement to cease and desist its alleged actions, which the commission accepted.

Application Examples

To demonstrate how the SEC applies the aforementioned sections and rules of the 1934 Act, specific details of three enforcement actions are provided. The companies involved are America Online, Inc., FastComm Communications Corp., and System Software Associates, Inc.

America Online, Inc.   In an AAER dated May 2000, the commission accepted an offer of settlement from America Online, Inc. (AOL), to "cease and desist from causing any violations, and any future violations of Sections 13(a) and 13(b)(2)(A) of the Exchange Act and Rules 13a-1 and 13a-13 thereunder."[53] AOL made the settlement offer without admitting or denying the SEC's allegations. During its 1995 and 1996 fiscal years, AOL had been capitalizing certain direct advertising costs that the commission felt should have been expensed as incurred. After a lengthy discussion of the facts of the case, the SEC noted that AOL's capitalization policy made the company's financial statements inaccurate and not in compliance with generally accepted accounting principles. Moreover, because the company's policy resulted in the recording as an asset advertising costs that should not be reported as such, books, records, and accounts that accurately reflect the transactions and dispositions of its assets were not being maintained. Collectively, according to the SEC, these actions violated Sections 13(a) and 13(b)(2)(A) and Rules 13a-1 and 13a-13 of the 1934 Act.

FastComm Communications Corp.   In an AAER dated September 1999, the SEC charged that FastComm Communications Corp. "engaged in two transactions that led to the fraudulent recognition of revenue in certain of the Company's financial statements during 1993 and 1994."[54] According to the SEC, these transactions were entered into with the knowledge and participation of its former vice president of contracts and administration, Charles DesLaurier. In the first transaction, "FastComm recognized $185,000 in revenue on a sale of telecommunications products that were not completely assembled and not fully functional as originally shipped, and that a certain number were packaged and shipped after the close of the fiscal quarter."[55] In the second transaction, the SEC noted:

FastComm improperly recognized revenue of $579,000 during the quarter ended February 5, 1994, on two sales to a South American customer. This represented approximately one-third of its sales revenue for that period. When finished product was not available for ship-ment to satisfy these orders, unfinished product was shipped to a freight-forwarder's ware-house to be held until recalled by FastComm. Moreover, this shipment to the warehouse was not completed by midnight of the last day of the quarter, and thus some or all of the unfinished product was packaged and shipped after the close of the fiscal quarter.[56]

The SEC maintained that the manner in which these transactions were accounted for was in violation of Section 13(a), the periodic reporting provision, Section 13(b)(2)(A), the books and records provision, and Section 13(b)(2)(B), the internal control provision, of the 1934 Act.

The SEC also alleged that FastComm and DesLaurier were in violation of Section 10(b), an antifraud provision of the 1934 Act. According to the SEC, the company's actions were done with scienter, and accordingly, the Commission brought the allegation of fraud.

FastComm and DesLaurier consented, without admitting or denying the Commis-sion's allegations, to the entry of final judgments against them. The Company was enjoined from future violations of Section 10(b), Section 13(a), Section 13(b)(2)(A), and Section 13(b)(2)(B) of the 1934 Act. Given that the Company was recently emerging from a reorganization proceeding, it was not required to pay a civil penalty. DesLaurier was permanently enjoined from future violations of Section 10(b) of the 1934 Act and from aiding and abetting violations of Section 13(a) and Rules 12b-20, 13a-1, and 13a-13, also of the 1934 Act. He was also ordered to pay a civil penalty of $20,000.

System Software Associates, Inc.   In an AAER filed in July 2000, the SEC charged Sys-tem Software Associates, Inc., its former CEO and chairman of the board, Roger Covey, and its former CFO Joseph Skadra with "fraudulent accounting practices that resulted in massive investor losses."[57]

The complaint alleged that Covey and Skadra caused System Software to misstate its financial results during its fiscal years 1994 through 1996 by improperly reporting rev-enue on sales of a development-stage UNIX-language software product. Customers who purchased the product allegedly experienced severe and continuing difficulties with its performance and often rejected it. According to the SEC, revenue was not earned and should not have been recognized because "there existed significant uncertainties about customer acceptance of the product and collectibility of the contract price and significant vendor obligations remained. . . ."[58] The commission also alleged that System Software recognized revenue from sales of its UNIX product that were subject to side letters or other material contingencies that effectively negated the sales.

System Software, Covey, and Skadra were charged with violating or aiding and abet-ting violations of Section 17(a) of the Securities Act of 1933 and Sections 10(b), 13(a), 13(b)(2)(A), and 13(b)(2)(B) and Rules 10b-5, 12b-20, 13a-1, and 13a-13 of the 1934 Act. At the time of this writing, these and other charges had not been resolved.

The charges against America Online, FastComm Communications, and System Soft-ware demonstrate well how the commission uses the Securities Acts, and especially the identified sections and rules, to pursue and clean up perceived accounting abuses. Issues of accounting that hinge on judgment that, in the opinion of the SEC, move beyond the boundaries of GAAP are handled without allegations of fraud. However, when there is perceived fraud, the SEC does not hesitate to incorporate alleged violations of the antifraud provisions of the Securities Acts into its complaints.

Penalties

The SEC has a wide range of penalties available to it for punishment of violations of the Securities Acts. The simplest penalty is a cease-and-desist order or a permanent injunction where the defendant is enjoined from future violations on penalty of contempt of court. For more egregious acts, wrongdoers can be prohibited from ever again serving as an officer or director of a registered company. Professionals, such as lawyers and accountants, who are found to violate the securities laws can be censured, suspended, or barred from practicing before the SEC. Such suspensions can be for a set time interval or permanent. Civil monetary penalties are also available. In addition, a defendant can be forced to disgorge any bonuses or incentive compensation amounts received that were calculated on the basis of what the commission deems to be inaccurate financial results. Finally, given the severity of the violation and the extent to which the commission perceives the existence of fraudulent intent, the case can be referred to the U.S. Department of Justice for criminal prosecution.

The America Online case noted above did not involve alleged fraudulent acts. It was resolved with a cease-and-desist order.[59] In contrast, the FastComm case, which did involve alleged fraudulent acts, resulted in injunctions against future violations of securities laws and a civil monetary penalty of $20,000.[60]

In the KnowledgeWare case discussed in Chapter 2, Francis Tarkenton, the company's former CEO and chairman of the board, was enjoined from future violations of the securities laws. In addition, he agreed to pay a civil monetary penalty of $100,000 and disgorged $54,187 plus interest in incentive compensation that was received on the basis of the company's materially overstated earnings.[61]

In another case, Kevin Kearney, a certified public accountant and former manager of financial reporting at CUC International, Inc., a predecessor company of Cendant Corp., was denied the privilege of appearing or practicing before the commission as an accountant. After five years, Mr. Kearney may request that the commission consider his reinstatement.[62]

Other Consequences

The monetary fines assessed on defendants for alleged acts of fraudulent financial reporting seem low, almost inconsequential. The low amounts may suggest to some that it is worth trying to get away with reporting transgressions. It is important to keep in mind, however, that the SEC's monetary fines are not necessarily the end of the matter. As noted, there is always the threat of criminal prosecution, which provides a dark cloud that can hang over defendants for some time. In addition, other costs may accrue to players of the financial numbers game, beyond the potential civil and criminal penalties, that dwarf, in financial terms, the direct costs that the SEC may assess. The significant reduction in shareholder value that accompanies the often-breathtaking declines in share prices following announcements of accounting problems and SEC investigations is one such consequence. Others include the costs associated with class action litigation and the reduced liquidity associated with a delisting of a company's shares by an organized share-trading exchange.[63]

Criminal Prosecution   In Chapter 2 we presented the example of Aurora Foods, Inc. In early 2000 the company restated its results for the last two quarters of 1998 and three quarters of 1999, wiping out $81,562,000 of pretax earnings for those two years. The company had recognized revenue prematurely and had improperly capitalized promotional expenses paid to retailers.

Less than a year after the announced restatement, a federal grand jury indicted four of the company's former executives on charges they engaged in "a criminal conspiracy to cook the company's books."[64] According to prosecutors, the former executives had annual bonuses that were tied directly to Aurora's earnings. They took steps to boost those earnings by "improperly classifying [promotional expenses] as assets and in others by directing underlings to understate the expenses in the company's records."[65] The criminal charges faced by the former executives include conspiracy, securities fraud, making false statements in the company's public financial filings, keeping false books and records, and lying to the company's independent auditor.

Numerous examples of successful criminal prosecutions of corporate executives found guilty of financial fraud are provided in Exhibit 4.7. As can be seen in the exhibit, in recent years criminal prosecutors have been successful in prosecuting financial frauds.

Exhibit 4.7   Selected Criminal Prosecutions of Financial Fraud

Executive	Company	Sentence
Eddie Antar	Crazie Eddie, Inc.	6 years 10 months
Earl Brian	Financial News Network, Inc.	5 years
Cosmo Corigliano	CUC International, Inc.	Pending
Chan Desaigoudar	California Micro Devices Corp.	36 months
Donald Ferrarini	Underwriters Financial Group, Inc.	12 years 1 month, under appeal
Patrick Finn	Phar-Mor, Inc.	2 years 9 months
Steven Hoffenberg	Towers Financial Corp.	20 years
Maria Messina	Livent, Inc.	Pending
James Murphy	Centennial Technologies, Inc.	1 year 3 months community confinement
Paul Polishan	Leslie Fay Companies, Inc.	Pending
Richard Rubin	Donnkenny, Inc.	Pending
Paul Safronchik	Home Theater Products International, Inc.	37 months
Q. T. Wiles	Miniscribe Corp.	30 months

Sources: Data compiled from *CFO*, September 2000, and *Fortune*, August 2, 1999.

Class Action Litigation   Almost immediately after the announcement of a financial reporting problem significant enough to require restatement of prior-period results, class action lawyers likely will have identified investors who have lost money on their investments in the subject company. Using information that the SEC is investigating reporting problems and that prior-year results are in error, suits may be filed in the names of losing investors who are seeking to be named as representatives of an entire class of similar investors. These suits will target many potential defendants, including the company, its officers, the audit committee and other members of the board of directors, underwriters, selling shareholders, and the outside auditors. The complaints will seek redress for investment losses incurred as the result of allegedly false filings made with the SEC.

For example, in a class action lawsuit filed against certain representatives of Safety-Kleen Corp. by the firm of Grant & Eisenhofer, P.A. on behalf of the company's bondholders, two institutional investors claimed more than $30 million in damages. The action was brought against Safety-Kleen's officers, directors, controlling shareholders, accountants, and underwriters. The suit alleged, among other things, that the company's financial statements for the years ended August 31 1997, 1998, and 1999 were "false and misleading, and had to be withdrawn by Safety Kleen and its auditors, PricewaterhouseCoopers LLP."[66] These financial statements, according to the lawsuit, had been used in connection with the sale of the bonds and also had been used after their sale, "artificially inflating the price of the bonds in the aftermarket."[67]

Ultimately, a consolidated complaint that is representative of the class will arise from the many individual complaints that have been filed. Depending on the facts and circumstances of the case, the consolidated complaint likely will include claims that key sections of the securities laws, including Section 10(b) and Rule 10b-5 of the 1934 Act and others, have been violated. While the use of a jury trial to hear both sides of the case is a possibility, it is more likely that the end result of such a lawsuit will be a cash settlement. Such settlements can reach many millions of dollars and exceed by a significant margin any liability insurance the company may have in place for just such a possibility.

In 1999, for example, Cendant Corp. agreed to a $2.83 billion settlement, the largest ever in a shareholder class action, in conjunction with its 1998 accounting scandal. As noted at the time, the settlement "will allow shareholders to recoup some of the losses they suffered when Cendant's share price plunged by more than 50% after an accounting fraud was disclosed last year."[68] Also settling a lawsuit over the accounting problems at Cendant was the company's auditors, Ernst & Young LLP, which agreed to a cash settlement of $335 million.

Delisting of a Company's Shares   In addition to the SEC, companies must also be concerned about the regulatory power of the stock exchanges and associations on which their shares are traded. National securities exchanges, securities associations, and clearing agencies are self-regulatory organizations that are registered with the SEC. In the United States, there are several such bodies, including the New York Stock Exchange, the American Stock Exchange, and the National Association of Securities Dealers, Inc. The stock of most public companies is bought and sold over one or more of these exchanges. In order to have an orderly and liquid market for their stock, affording prompt trades in a fair and honest environment, it is important that companies' shares are listed on a regulated exchange.

To get listed and stay listed, companies must meet certain financial and other qualitative requirements and demonstrate good corporate governance. Companies that are found to have accounting problems may be unable to meet continued listing requirements and find themselves the subject of delisting proceedings.

Financial listing requirements typically focus on such quantifiable measures as net tangible assets, market capitalization, profitability, and a company's share price. For example, among the financial requirements for initial listing on Nasdaq (National Association of Securities Dealers Automated Quotation System), an issuer must have net tangible assets of $4 million, a market capitalization of $50 million, *or* net income of $750,000 in the most recently completed fiscal year or in two of the last three most recently completed fiscal years. In addition, an issuer must have a minimum share price of $4. For continued listing, these financial requirements become net tangible assets of $2 million, a market capitalization of $35 million, *or* net income of $500,000 in the most recently completed fiscal year or in two of the last three most recently completed fiscal years. The minimum share price requirement is dropped to $1. For listing on Nasdaq's more prestigious National Market System, the financial listing requirements are more stringent.

Qualitative listing requirements, including such corporate governance standards as the need to provide shareholders with timely annual and interim reports, the need for independent directors, an audit committee, and an annual meeting of shareholders, give the exchanges more room for applying judgment in deciding whether to delist a company's securities. For example, Nasdaq's Marketplace Rules note that Nasdaq constantly reviews an issuer's corporate governance activities and that it may take appropriate action, including the placing of restrictions on or additional requirements for listing, or the denial of a security's listing, if it determines that "there have been violations or evasions of such corporate governance standards."[69] Depending on the facts, news that accounting problems have led the SEC to investigate a company's management for alleged violations of the antifraud provisions of the securities laws could give an exchange such as Nasdaq the ammunition its needs to consider delisting that company's securities.

When a company's shares are delisted, it can choose to list on a lesser-known exchange that has less stringent listing requirements. For example, a company that is delisted from Nasdaq may choose to have its securities listed on the much-less-regulated Bulletin Board. The problem is that such lesser-known exchanges have much less visibility and, likely, lower trading volumes. As a result, there is less liquidity for a company's shares and, probably, a lower price.

Companies at Risk for Fraud

In their most extreme form, creative accounting practices become fraudulent. As seen in this chapter, the costs to the shareholder or debt holder of a company whose financial statements are alleged to be fraudulent can be significant. In an effort to better prepare readers to either avoid such situations or at least reduce exposure to them, the attributes

---

Exhibit 4.8 Attributes of Companies at Risk for Fraudulent Financial Reporting

---

Small companies, in particular, with assets and revenue less than $100 million

Weak internal control environment with unchecked CEO or CFO

No audit committee or one that meets less than twice per year

Board of directors dominated by insiders or individuals with significant equity ownership and little experience serving as directors of other companies

Family relationships exist among directors and/or officers

Source: M., Beasley, J. Carcello, and D. Hermanson, *Fraudulent Financial Reporting: 1987–1997: An Analysis of U.S. Public Companies* (New York: Committee of Sponsoring Organizations of the Treadway Commission, 1999).

---

of companies that are more at risk for fraudulent financial reporting are summarized in Exhibit 4.8.

The attributes summarized here were drawn from a research report published by Beasley, Carcello, and Hermanson. The authors studied the details of 200 cases of alleged financial statement fraud using Accounting and Auditing Enforcement Releases filed by the Division of Enforcement of the SEC over the period 1987 to 1997. Some of the more noteworthy findings are summarized in the exhibit.

The findings are consistent with some of the thoughts expressed by Mr. Levitt in his speech "The Numbers Game" and reported earlier in this chapter.[70] In particular, the exhibit indicates that a strong, independent board of directors and audit committee form an important cornerstone to any public company's corporate governance structure. The remaining chapters of this book are devoted to helping the reader identify companies that are involved not only in potentially fraudulent financial reporting but instances of creative accounting practices, whether they result in allegations of fraud or not.

SUMMARY

The SEC has not been idle as numerous examples of creative accounting practices, sometimes entailing alleged fraudulent activity, have surfaced in recent years. Concerned about the integrity of the financial reporting system in the United States, the SEC has mounted a direct attack on what it views to be the causes of questionable reporting. This chapter provides details of the problems the SEC sees with the current reporting environment, identifies what the commission is doing about these problems, and discusses the tools available to the commission to ensure compliance with its reporting regulations.

Key points made in the chapter include the following:

- In his speech, "The Numbers Game," Arthur Levitt, chairman of the SEC, announced an all-out war on what was termed accounting hocus pocus.[71]
- The chairman identified five creative accounting practices as being particularly objectionable:
  1. Big bath charges
  2. Creative acquisition accounting
  3. Cookie jar reserves
  4. The misuse of materiality
  5. Revenue recognition
- The chairman announced a multipoint action plan designed to increase public confidence in financial reporting, divided into four categories:
  1. Improving the accounting framework
  2. Enhancing outside auditing
  3. Strengthening the audit committee process
  4. Pursuing cultural change
- To demonstrate that the commission was serious about instituting a tighter, more stringent reporting environment, numerous enforcement actions were filed against a large collection of defendants alleging reporting fraud.
- Early developments indicate that newly found diligence at the SEC is having an effect. For example, companies are reducing the portion of acquisition prices allocated to purchased in-process research and development, and revenue recognition practices are becoming more conservative.
- Some market participants believe that the SEC has gone too far and has involved itself too greatly in accounting minutiae. However, this view seems to be in the minority, and there is no evidence that the SEC plans to back down.
- Efforts of the SEC notwithstanding, creative accounting practices are not expected to disappear. They may change form and become more carefully hidden, but the financial pressures that help to bring them about remain.
- The SEC's Division of Enforcement is used to enforce the securities laws. Depending on many factors, including the nature and severity of the reporting problem, the division may use an administrative action or a civil suit to prosecute alleged violations of selected sections and rules of the Securities Act of 1933 and the Securities Exchange Act of 1934
- The SEC does not establish generally accepted accounting principles but rather relies on the private sector, primarily the Financial Accounting Standards Board, for that purpose. However, the commission does have a voice in the process of establishing accounting standards and uses it.
- Alleged fraudulent financial reporting entails violations of the antifraud provisions of the securities laws, in particular, Section 17(a) of the 1933 Act and Section 10(b) and Rule 10b-5 of the 1934 Act.
- The Division of Enforcement has many penalties available to it, including cease-and-desist orders, suspensions for individuals from serving as officers of public compa-

nies, suspensions for accountants and lawyers from practicing in front of the SEC, and monetary fines. In more egregious cases of alleged fraud, civil cases are referred for criminal prosecution.

- Beyond the direct penalties that may be administered, other very significant consequences may result from accounting misdeeds, including share-price declines, class action litigation, and a delisting of a company's shares.

- Financial reporting fraud is more likely at smaller companies with a weak internal control environment and a board of directors that does not have independent members, that has family relationships among its members and/or the company's officers, and that does not have an audit committee.

GLOSSARY

Accounting and Auditing Enforcement Release (AAER) An administrative proceeding or litigation release that entails an accounting or auditing-related violation of the securities laws.

Administrative Proceeding Official SEC record of a settlement or a hearing scheduled before an administrative judge of an alleged violation of one or more sections or rules of the securities laws.

Antifraud Provisions Specific sections and rules of the 1933 Act and 1934 Act that are designed to reduce fraud and deceit in financial filings made with the SEC. The antifraud provisions are Section 17(a) of the 1933 Act and Section 10(b) and Rule 10b-5 of the 1934 Act.

Audit Committee A subcommittee of a company's board of directors assigned the responsibility of ensuring that corporate financial reporting is fair and honest and that an audit is conducted in a probing and diligent manner.

Big Bath A large, nonrecurring charge or expense used to clean up a company's balance sheet, making it more conservative, some would say excessively so, in an effort to reduce costs in future years and boost future earnings.

Blue Ribbon Committee on Improving the Effectiveness of Corporate Audit Committees A committee formed in response to SEC chairman Arthur Levitt's initiative to improve the financial reporting environment in the United States. In a report dated February 1999, the committee made recommendations for new rules for regulation of financial reporting in the United States that either duplicated or carried forward the recommendations of the Treadway Commission.

Bulletin Board An electronic affiliation of market makers that offers traders real-time electronic quotes but for which trades must be executed by phone call to a market maker. Few regulations cover securities traded on the Bulletin Board beyond the need to file regular financial reports with the SEC.

Cookie Jar Reserves An overly aggressive accrual of operating expenses and the creation of liability accounts done in an effort to reduce future-year operating expenses.

Creative Acquisition Accounting The allocation to expense of a greater portion of the price paid for another company in an acquisition in an effort to reduce acquisition-year earnings and boost future-year earnings. Acquisition-year expense charges include purchased in-process research and development and an overly aggressive accrual of future operating expenses.

Division for Corporation Finance A department of the SEC that reviews corporate filings with the SEC and assists companies with interpretations of SEC rules and recommends new rules for adoption by the SEC.

Litigation Release   Official SEC record of a settlement or a hearing scheduled before a civil court judge of an alleged violation of one or more sections or rules of the securities laws. Typically, a litigation release entails a more serious violation of the securities laws than an administrative proceeding.

Materiality   A financial statement item's effect on a company's overall financial condition and operations. An item is material when its size is likely to influence a decision of an investor or creditor.

National Association of Securities Dealers Automated Quotation System (Nasdaq)   An electronic securities market comprised of competing market makers whose trading is supported by a communications network that provides links to readily available information on quotes, trade reports, and order executions.

National Commission on Fraudulent Financial Reporting   See *Treadway Commission.*

National Market System   The largest listing section of Nasdaq where listing requirements are more stringent and where the shares of larger, more prestigious companies trade.

Panel on Audit Effectiveness   A special committee of the Public Oversight Board that was created to perform a comprehensive review and evaluation of the way independent audits of financial statements of publicly traded companies are performed. The panel found generally that the quality of audits is fundamentally sound. The panel did recommend the expansion of audit steps designed to detect fraud.

Public Oversight Board   An independent private-sector body that oversees the audit practices of certified public accountants who work with SEC-regulated companies.

Restructuring Charges   Costs associated with restructuring activities, including the consolidation and/or relocation of operations or the disposition or abandonment of operations or productive assets. Such charges may be incurred in connection with a business combination, a change in an enterprise's strategic plan, or a managerial response to declines in demand, increasing costs, or other environmental factors.

Staff Accounting Bulletin (SAB)   Interpretations and practices followed by the staff of the Office of the Chief Accountant and the Division of Corporation Finance in administering the disclosure requirements of the federal securities laws.

Securities Act of 1933 (1933 Act)   Law passed by Congress to protect the investing public from fraudulent practices in the purchase and sale of newly issued securities.

Securities Exchange Act of 1934 (1934 Act)   Law passed by Congress that established the SEC and extended corporate disclosure requirements to make them ongoing for publicly traded securities.

Treadway Commission   Also known as the National Commission on Fraudulent Financial Reporting, a special committee formed in 1985 to investigate the underlying causes of fraudulent financial reporting. The commission was named after its chairman, former SEC commissioner James Treadway. The commission's report, published in 1987, stressed the need for strong and independent audit committees for public companies.

NOTES

1. A. Levitt, "The Numbers Game," remarks to New York University Center for Law and Business, September 28, 1998, p. 5. The speech is available at: www.sec.gov/news/speeches/spch220.txt.

2. Ibid., p. 3.

3. Ibid., p. 3.

4. Ibid., p. 3.

5. Ibid., p. 3.

6. Ibid., p. 4.

7. Ibid., p. 5.

8. Financial Accounting Standards Board Discussion Memorandum, *Distinguishing between Liability and Equity Instruments and Accounting for Instruments with Characteristics of Both* (Norwalk, CT: Financial Accounting Standards Board, 1990).

9. Levitt, "The Numbers Game," p. 6.

10. Ibid., p. 6.

11. Securities and Exchange Commission, Staff Accounting Bulletin 99, *Materiality* (Washington, DC: Securities and Exchange Commission, August 13, 1999).

12. Securities and Exchange Commission, Staff Accounting Bulletin 100, *Restructuring and Impairment Charges* (Washington, DC: Securities and Exchange Commission, November 24, 1999).

13. Securities and Exchange Commission, Staff Accounting Bulletin 101, *Revenue Recognition* (Washington, DC: Securities and Exchange Commission, December 3, 1999).

14. Statement of Financial Accounting Standards No. 141, *Business Combinations* and SFAS No. 142, *Goodwill and Other Intangible Assets* (Norwalk, CT: Financial Accounting Standards Board, June 2001).

15. *The Wall Street Journal*, December 24, 1998, p. A3.

16. Accounting and Auditing Enforcement Release No. 1140, *In the Matter of W.R. Grace & Co., Inc., Respondent* (Washington, DC: Securities and Exchange Commission, June 30, 1999).

17. Accounting and Auditing Enforcement Release No. 1095, *In the Matter of Livent, Inc., Respondent* (Washington, DC: Securities and Exchange Commission, January 13, 1999).

18. *The Wall Street Journal*, December 8, 1999, p. A6.

19. Ibid.

20. Ibid. Refer also to Accounting and Auditing Enforcement Release No. 1162, *In the Matter of Raintree Healthcare Corporation, formerly known as Unison Healthcare Corporation, and Lisa M. Beuche, Respondents, Securities and Exchange* (Washington, DC: Securities and Exchange Commission, September 28, 1999).

21. *The Wall Street Journal*, December 8, 1999, p. A6.

22. Panel on Audit Effectiveness, Press Release, *Panel on Audit Effectiveness Releases Exposure Draft*, June 6, 2000.

23. Securities and Exchange Commission, Press Release, *Chairman Levitt Issues Statement on the Report and Recommendations of the Panel on Audit Effectiveness*, June 6, 2000.

24. Report of Blue Ribbon Committee on Improving the Effectiveness of Corporate Audit Committees (Washington, DC: Blue Ribbon Committee on Improving the Effectiveness of Corporate Audit Committees, 1999).

25. Report of the National Commission on Fraudulent Financial Reporting (Washington, DC: National Commission on Fraudulent Financial Reporting, 1987).

26. *The Wall Street Journal*, January 17, 2000, p. B8.

27. Research data collected by Z. Deng and B. Lev, as reported in *The Wall Street Journal*, March 22, 1999, p. C3.

28. *The Wall Street Journal*, September 13, 1999, p. A4.

29. Ibid., March 15, 2000, p. B10.

30. Ibid., November 17, 1998, p. A2.

31. Ibid., February 1, 1999, p. A2.

32. Ibid.

33. Ibid.

34. Securities Exchange Act of 1934, §13 (1934).

35. The URL is http:/www.sec.gov/. There is a link for the Enforcement Division.

36. Securities Exchange Act of 1934, §13(a) (1934).

37. Ibid., §13(b)(2)(A) (1934).

38. Ibid., §13(b)(2)(B) (1934).

39. Ibid., Rule 12b-20 (1934).

40. Ibid., Rule 13b2-1 (1934).

41. Ibid., Rule 13a-1 (1934).

42. Ibid., Rule 13a-13 (1934).

43. Ibid., §13(b)(2)(B)ii (1934).

44. SFAS No. 133, *Accounting for Derivatives Instruments and Hedging Activities* (Norwalk, CT: FASB, June 1998).

45. Accounting Principles Board Opinion No. 2, *Accounting for the "Investment Credit"* (New York: Accounting Principles Board, 1962).

46. APB Opinion No. 4 (Amending No. 2), *Accounting for the "Investment Credit"* (New York: Accounting Principles Board, March 1964).

47. SFAS No. 19, *Financial Accounting and Reporting by Oil and Gas Producing Companies* (Norwalk, CT: FASB, December 1977).

48. SFAS No. 25, *Financial Accounting and Reporting by Oil and Gas Producing Companies* (Norwalk, CT: FASB, February 1979).

49. Securities Act of 1933, §17(a) (1933).

50. Securities Exchange Act of 1934, §10(b) (1934).

51. Ibid., Rule 10b-5 (1934).

52. Accounting and Auditing Enforcement Release No. 1277, *In the Matter of Waste Management, Inc., Respondent* (Washington, DC: Securities and Exchange Commission, June 21, 2000), § IV, emphasis added.

53. Accounting and Auditing Enforcement Release No. 1257, *In the Matter of America Online, Inc., Respondent* (Washington, DC: Securities and Exchange Commission, June 21, 2000), § III. It should be noted that in offering to settle the accounting matter, AOL did not admit or deny the SEC's findings.

54. Accounting and Auditing Enforcement Release No. 1187, *Securities and Exchange Commission v. Fastcomm Communications Corporation, Civil Action No. 99-1448-A* (Washington, DC: Securities and Exchange Commission, September 28, 1999), para. 1.

55. Ibid., p. 2.

56. Ibid., p. 3.

57. Accounting and Auditing Enforcement Release No. 1285, *Securities and Exchange Commission v. System Software Associates, Inc., Roger Covey and Joseph Skadra, Civ. No. 00C4240* (Washington, DC: Securities and Exchange Commission, July 14, 2000), para 1.

58. Ibid., para. 2.

59. Accounting and Auditing Enforcement Release No. 1257.

60. Accounting and Auditing Enforcement Release No. 1187.

61. Accounting and Auditing Enforcement Release No. 1179, *Securities and Exchange Commission v. Francis Tarkenton, Donald P. Addington, Rick W. Gossett, Lee R. Fontaine, William E. Hammersla, III, Eladio Alvarez and Edward Welch, Civil Action File No. 1:99-CV-2497* (Washington, DC: Securities and Exchange Commission, September 28, 1999).

62. Accounting and Auditing Enforcement Release No. 1284, *In the Matter of Kevin T. Kearney, CPA, Respondent* (Washington, DC: Securities and Exchange Commission, July 13, 2000).

63. For a more in-depth look at the topics of class action litigation and stock delisting, the reader is referred to M. Young, *Accounting Irregularities and Financial Fraud: A Corporate Governance Guide* (New York: Harcourt Professional Publishing, Inc., 2000).

64. *The Wall Street Journal,* January 24, 2001, p. B11.

65. Ibid.

66. Press Release, Grant & Eisenhofer, P.A., July 19, 2000.

67. Ibid.

68. *The Wall Street Journal*, December 8, 1999, p. A4.

69. *The Nasdaq Stock Market, Marketplace Rules* (New York: The Nasdaq Stock Market, 1997), p. 9.

70. Levitt, "The Numbers Game."

71. Ibid.

CHAPTER FIVE

Financial Professionals Speak Out

It [earnings management] gives the appearance of greater stability than is the reality. As a consequence, when the day of reckoning comes, which it inevitably does, the fall is much farther than it needs to be.[1]

Absolutely, earnings management can harm investors. At its worst, it can keep negative items hidden beyond when it would be reasonable to expect such items to have been communicated externally. Investors would have made investment decisions based on less than complete data.[2]

I believe that most investors are not sophisticated enough to detect earnings management and it may create a misperception of how good earnings really are.[3]

You cannot detect earnings management—even abnormal balance sheet changes can be explainable. If management is managing earnings and the auditors sign off, you will never know.[4]

It helps companies who manipulate earnings for the purpose of maintaining stability in their stock price by smoothing earnings over time, rather than sending volatile earnings reports to the market.[5]

Meeting or beating analysts' estimates is important these days. As long as this is done within GAAP rules, earnings-management tools are very helpful to investors.[6]

There is little systematic information available on the views of financial professionals about the financial numbers game, how the game is played and might be detected, and whether and under what circumstances it might be considered to be either good or bad. Also, we know little about their views regarding the compliance with GAAP of the var-

---

Exhibit 5.1 Survey Introduction Letter

Dear:

The subject of "creative accounting" (also referred to as "earnings management") was dramatically brought to the fore by Arthur Levitt, former Chairman of the Securities and Exchange Commission, in a September 1998 speech at New York University. Mr. Levitt's talk was titled *The Numbers Game,* and in it he provided current examples of "creative accounting" and also challenged "the broad spectrum of capital market participants, from corporate management to Wall Street analysts to investors, to stand together and re-energize the touchstone of our financial reporting system: transparency and comparability." Since this speech, the SEC has launched a number of initiatives aimed at reducing creative accounting.

Mr. Levitt pointed to the desire of management to meet Wall Street earnings expectations as a major contributor to a rise in "creative accounting." While acknowledging the legitimacy of flexibility in the application of generally accepted accounting principles (GAAP), Mr. Levitt identified a "gray area where the accounting is being perverted; where managers are cutting corners; and, where earnings reports reflect the desires of management rather than the underlying financial performance of the company."

Mr. Levitt noted that, "Flexibility in accounting allows it to keep pace with business innovations, and that abuses such as *earnings management* (emphasis added) occur when people exploit this pliancy. Trickery is employed to obscure actual financial volatility." Elsewhere, in the 1999 Annual Report of the SEC, *abusive earnings management* is held to "involve the use of various forms of gimmickry to distort a company's true financial performance in order to achieve a desired result."

We are writing a book to be titled *The Financial Numbers Game.* As with a previous book, *Financial Warnings*, we hope to bring to bear the wisdom and experience of important producers and users of financial statements. To this end, we are asking CFOs, analysts, lenders, CPAs, accounting academics, and advanced MBA students to share their experience and views with us.

We would be extremely grateful to you if you could take 15 or 20 minutes to respond to the attached questionnaire. Most of the questions are objective in nature and can be answered quickly. Please place the completed questionnaire in the envelope provided. We hope that, among other things, you will see this as an opportunity for you to register your views on these important matters. If you would like a copy of the results of this survey, please send your address to us by email. This will preserve confidentiality.

Very truly yours,	Very truly yours,
Eugene E. Comiskey	Charles W. Mulford
Callaway Professor of Accounting	Invesco Professor of Accounting

Source: Financial Numbers Game Survey

ious techniques employed in the financial numbers game. The goal of this chapter is to contribute to this void by reporting the results of a survey of financial professionals.

SURVEY OF FINANCIAL PROFESSIONALS

The views of various financial professionals add greatly to the richness of our consideration of the financial numbers game and earnings management. Any single individual has only a limited set of experiences. However, access to the collective experiences of financial professionals from a variety of different occupations can greatly enhance the quality and content of our investigation.

To provide some context for the survey, we included a letter from the authors to each of the surveyed financial professionals along with the survey instrument. A copy of the letter is provided in Exhibit 5.1. The letter was individually addressed and printed on the letterhead of the DuPree College of Management at the Georgia Institute of Technology.

The campaign launched by the Securities and Exchange Commission, under the leadership of former SEC chairman Arthur Levitt, is the focal point of the letter. The thrust of Mr. Levitt's views is that the numbers game has gone too far and that some companies are abusing the legitimate flexibility in the application of GAAP to produce financial results that distort performance. Given the investor-protection role of the SEC, Mr. Levitt's remarks carry the clear implication that investors stand to be harmed by the abusive earnings management practiced by companies. The survey collects the views of financial professionals on a variety of issues raised by Mr. Levitt:

- Is the SEC's campaign necessary?
- What constitutes legitimate flexibility in the application of GAAP?
- When does earnings management become abusive?
- How can earnings management be detected?
- Can investors benefit from earnings management?
- Are investors harmed by earnings management?

Survey Instrument

The survey instrument is comprised of three sections. The first section includes descriptions of 20 techniques that could be used to manage earnings. Many of these techniques have actually been the targets of enforcement actions by the Securities and Exchange Commission. Survey respondents were asked to classify each of the techniques in terms of their relationship to generally accepted accounting principles (GAAP). The four classifications are as follows:

1. Action is within the flexibility afforded by GAAP.
2. Action is at the outer limits of the flexibility afforded by GAAP.
3. Action is beyond the limits of GAAP flexibility but is not fraudulent financial reporting.
4. Action constitutes fraudulent financial reporting.

The 20 earnings management techniques that the respondents were asked to classify are provided in Exhibit 5.2.

A review of the listing in the exhibit will reveal that some of the techniques represent real actions and not simply the acceleration or delay in the recognition of revenue or expenses. For example, items 5 to 8 and 10 to 11 involve management actions that were motivated by the desire to achieve certain earnings outcomes. It would be reasonable to expect respondents to select classification number "1" from the above listing. That is, these real actions are not in conflict with GAAP, even though they may be prompted by the desire to manage earnings.

Other techniques in Exhibit 5.2 clearly stretch the limits of the flexibility inherent in GAAP, while some appear to go well beyond GAAP. Some of these extreme cases—such as items 1, 9, 12, 13, 15, 16, 17, and 18—could be candidates for SEC investigation and a possible determination that they represent fraudulent financial reporting.

The second section of the survey calls for respondents to indicate their degree of agreement or disagreement with a series of 10 statements dealing with earnings management. The statements deal with the goals of earnings management, whether it can help or hurt investors, and whether or not earnings management has become more common over the past decade. Respondents were asked to indicate the degree of their agreement or disagreement with the statements using the following choices:

1. Definitely yes
2. Yes
3. No
4. Definitely no
5. No opinion

The 10 statements that respondents were asked to classify are listed in Exhibit 5.3.

The last section of the survey asked respondents to provide written responses to each of these questions:

- Based upon your experience, what are some of the more common earnings management practices that you have observed?
- When examining financial statements, what techniques or procedures have you found to be helpful in detecting earnings management? That is, how do you detect the presence of earnings management?
- If you believe that earnings management has the potential to harm investors or others, please briefly indicate how.
- If you believe that earnings management has the potential to be helpful to investors or others, please briefly indicate how.

Survey Respondents

The survey respondents included chief financial officers, analysts, lenders, CPAs, and accounting academics. About three-quarters of the accounting academics are also CPAs

Exhibit 5.2 Survey Items on the Classification of Earnings Management Techniques

1. Goods are shipped to a customer and a sale is recognized. The purchaser is provided an oral right-of-return agreement and no provision for expected returns is recorded by the seller.
2. An airline uses an optimistic estimate of useful life in depreciating its flight equipment.
3. An auto company records an addition to its warranty liability that it knows to be too small.
4. A firm overaccrues a restructuring provision in order to be able to reverse a portion of the accrual into future earnings if needed in order to meet company earnings targets.
5. Advertising expenditures are accelerated in the fourth quarter of the current year so as not to exceed the earnings target for the current year and to increase first-quarter earnings in the next year.
6. Production is expanded beyond current requirements in order to capitalize more overhead into inventory and by so doing increase incentive compensation for company officers.
7. Credit standards are relaxed at year-end in order to boost sales and with it earnings for the year just ending.
8. A schedule of price increases, to take effect early in the next year, is announced during the fourth quarter in order to boost sales and earnings in the year just ending.
9. Books are held open for several days after the close of the year to record additional sales in the year just ended.
10. Shipments close to year-end are delayed in order to provide an increase in sales for the first quarter of the next year.
11. Investments are sold to recognize a gain in order to offset a special charge arising from an asset write-down.
12. Goods are shipped to a customer who has not yet placed an order but probably will during the next quarter.
13. Sales are recognized on goods shipped to reseller customers who are not creditworthy.
14. Revenue is recognized on disputed claims against customers, prior to a definitive settlement.
15. Sales are recognized upon the shipment of goods to a company's field representatives.
16. Total order revenue is recognized even though only partial shipments were made.
17. Revenue is recognized upon the consignment of goods but prior to their subsequent sale by the consignee.
18. The value of an ending inventory is understated in order to decrease property taxes.
19. Sales revenue is recognized when there are significant uncertainties about customer acceptance of the product and of ability to pay.
20. Sales revenue is recognized when an absolute right of return is provided by means of a "side" letter, which is outside of standard firm policies.

Source: Financial Numbers Game Survey

Exhibit 5.3   Survey Items on the Motivations and Objectives of Earnings Management

---

1. It is common for companies to manage earnings or to play the financial numbers game, that is, to exploit the flexibility found in the application of GAAP.
2. The SEC's campaign against earnings management is necessary.
3. A common goal of earnings management is to reduce earnings volatility.
4. A common goal of earnings management is to support or increase stock prices.
5. A common goal of earnings management is to increase earnings-based incentive compensation.
6. A common goal of earnings management is to meet consensus earnings forecasts of analysts.
7. Investors are sometimes harmed by earnings management practices.
8. Earnings management can be helpful to investors.
9. The practice of earnings management has become more common over the past decade.
10. The new SEC Fair Disclosure Regulation (known on the street as Reg. FD), which attempts to ensure that all investors have equal access to material financial information, will result in an increase in earnings management activity aimed at meeting the consensus forecasts of analysts.

Source: Financial Numbers Game Survey

---

with varying amounts of practice experience. We also surveyed some advanced master's of business administration (MBA) students. The graduate students mainly specialized in accounting or finance and most had several years of business experience prior to returning to graduate studies.

A total of 191 finance professionals completed the survey. The questionnaires were distributed during the winter and spring of 2001. The respondents by occupational groups included:

	Number	*Percent*
Accounting academics	59	31
Chief financial officers	30	16
Security analysts	24	12
Lenders	21	11
Certified public accountants	21	11
Advanced MBA students	36	19
Total	191	100

A variety of means were used to identify and solicit these professionals to complete the survey questionnaire. In some cases the authors used their personal contacts with financial professionals to obtain survey responses. This was especially true with the accounting academics. The 59 responses from academics were obtained by sending 120 questionnaires to senior accounting academics. Each was well known to one or both of the authors. This, along with their interest in the project and inclination to cooperate with other academics, explains their very high response rate: 59/120 equals 49%. The 30 responses from CFOs were obtained from 460 questionnaires sent to large public companies. Here the response rate was far lower but rather typical for surveys that do not rely on any personal connection or other relationship with the population surveyed: 30/460 equals 6%. In addition, some CFOs indicated that their companies had policies that prohibited completing questionnaires.

A combination of mailings, at much lower levels than in the case of the CFOs, and direct contacts were used to obtain the responses from the analysts, lenders, and CPAs. The graduate students were enrolled in a graduate elective course in accounting and financial analysis taught by one of the authors.

SURVEY RESULTS

The survey results are presented and discussed in the order in which the three sections appeared in the survey questionnaire:

1. Classification of earnings-management techniques in terms of their compliance with GAAP
2. Classification of statements about earnings management, such as frequency, objectives, and helpful versus harmful
3. Written comments on earnings management observed, detection of earnings management, and whether earnings management is helpful or harmful

Classification of Earnings Management Techniques

These instructions for the classification of the earnings-management techniques were provided:

> Classify each of the management actions listed below by circling one classification from among the four options provided. In making the classifications, assume that the effect of the action is material to the financial performance or financial position of the firm. Moreover, the firm understands each of these actions; they are not simply mistakes. A reasonable definition of fraudulent financial reporting is: an intentional, material misstatement that is taken in an effort to deceive financial statement readers. If you would like to make any comments about any of the statements, please simply write them on the copy by the relevant numbered item.

The results are reported as averages by earnings-management technique and group and as weighted averages by earnings-management technique for the 6 categories of respondents. This means that an average response of 1.5 for a particular technique indicates that it is viewed as more in line with GAAP than another technique with an average of 3.5. The averages by respondent category (academics, CFOs, etc.) are presented to determine the extent to which views concerning GAAP compliance vary across the groups. Observed differences between group averages cannot be given too much weight in view of the relatively small sample sizes in some of the groups.[7] A summary of the results on the classification of 20 earnings management actions is provided in Exhibit 5.4.

Commentary on the Respondent Classifications

A summary of the responses received together with commentary by survey number is provided below.

1. Goods are shipped to a customer and a sale is recognized. The purchaser is provided an oral right-of-return agreement and no provision for expected returns is recorded by the seller.

The mean classification of 2.62 places this action beyond the limits of GAAP flexibility. Twenty-six of the 59 academics classified this action as a 4, as did 14 of the 30 CFOs. On the other hand, only 7 of the 24 analysts assigned this action a 4. If having some returns is a reasonable expectation, then earnings would clearly be overstated by failing to record a provision for returns. Some respondents qualified their choice based on the likelihood of returns. The key in classifying this case is the combination of materiality and acting with scienter (the intent to deceive, manipulate, or defraud). The average respondent saw the action here as beyond GAAP flexibility but not as extending to fraudulent financial reporting. However, the academics and CFOs leaned more to the extreme of fraudulent financial reporting classification.[8]

2. An airline uses an optimistic estimate of useful life in depreciating its flight equipment.

A mean classification here of 1.65 indicates that respondents saw this action as within the flexibility afforded by GAAP. A number of respondents qualified their support for the within-GAAP classification by assuming that optimistic was also realistic.

3. An auto company records an addition to its warranty liability that it knows to be too small.

Exhibit 5.4 reveals that all respondent groups saw this action as beyond GAAP. However, 46 respondents classified this action from 1 to 3, with most being 3. These respondents may have found it difficult to determine, from the information given, that there was the intent to deceive, a requirement for classification as fraudulent financial reporting.

4. A firm overaccrues a restructuring provision in order to be able to reverse a portion of the accrual into future earnings if needed in order to meet company earnings targets.

As with number 3, the respondents generally saw this action as beyond GAAP. A total of 45 respondents classified this action as a 3. As all of these actions were to be consid-

Exhibit 5.4 Twenty Earnings Management Actions: Their Compliance with GAAP

| Action | Weighted Means | Mean Rankings by Respondent Group | | | | | |
		ACPA	CFO	FA	Lender	CPA	MBA
1.	2.62	2.98	3.00	2.83	2.33	2.30	1.83
2.	1.65	1.46	1.70	1.67	1.62	1.70	1.47
3.	3.48	3.63	3.73	3.54	3.57	3.90	3.28
4.	3.41	3.65	3.83	2.96	2.96	3.90	3.11
5.	1.50	1.36	1.50	1.54	1.29	1.78	1.72
6.	1.97	1.49	1.73	2.13	2.38	2.56	2.44
7.	1.59	1.36	1.60	1.79	1.57	1.50	1.86
8.	1.13	1.03	1.07	1.29	1.19	1.20	1.19
9.	3.66	3.79	3.93	3.42	3.81	3.20	3.44
10.	1.73	1.72	1.67	1.75	1.38	2.33	1.83
11.	1.27	1.08	1.00	1.42	1.10	1.00	1.86
12.	3.67	3.74	3.93	3.25	3.48	3.50	3.75
13.	2.58	2.71	2.47	2.29	2.20	3.20	2.69
14.	2.87	2.89	2.67	2.91	2.90	3.10	2.89
15.	3.52	3.76	3.57	3.46	3.33	3.80	3.17
16.	3.57	3.63	3.90	3.21	3.00	4.00	3.63
17.	3.61	3.79	3.93	3.21	3.52	3.90	3.28
18.	3.82	3.82	3.87	3.58	4.00	3.90	3.83
19.	3.12	3.18	3.33	2.96	2.95	3.10	3.08
20	3.20	3.51	3.57	2.88	2.38	3.30	3.06
Averages	2.70	2.73	2.80	2.60	2.55	2.86	2.67

Source: Financial Numbers Game Survey

ACPA = academics, most of whom are also CPAs

CFO = chief financial officer or comparable senior financial position, e.g., controller, etc.

FA = Financial analyst, CFAs in most cases

Lender = Commercial bank lender

CPA = CPA in public practice

MBA = Advanced MBA students, most with some work experience, and enrolled in advanced elective courses in accounting and finance

Note: The weighted means are the sum of the weighted means (weighted by the number of respondents in each group relative to total respondents) for each of the 20 statements.

ered as having a material effect on financial performance, classification as beyond GAAP, a 3, should be seen as a minimum. As noted in question 3, classification as fraudulent financial reporting, a 4, also requires the additional criterion of the intent to deceive. Later sections will consider views on whether earnings management can be viewed as helpful to investors and others. Whereas overaccruing a restructuring provision may be seen as beyond GAAP, the motivation could be to preserve share value by meeting earnings expectations or reducing earnings volatility, which may not be seen as an intent to deceive. This could explain the significant number of classifications as 3 in this case.

5. Advertising expenditures are accelerated in the fourth quarter of the current year so as not to exceed the earnings target for the current year and to increase first quarter earnings in the next year.

Items 5 to 8 are all operational or real actions, that is, they involve business practices and not simply, for example, the acceleration of revenue or the deferral of expenses. As such, they should not be seen as being in conflict with GAAP. The weighted averages of 1.50, 1.97, 1.59, and 1.13, respectively, of actions 5 through 8 indicate that each group considered the actions to be consistent with GAAP. Accelerating advertising expenditures could be seen as a way to reduce the volatility of earnings.

6. Production is expanded beyond current requirements in order to capitalize more overhead into inventory and by so doing increase incentive compensation for company officers.

This real action, with an average ranking of 1.97, is viewed as being closer to pushing the limits of GAAP flexibility. This is somewhat odd since it does not raise a GAAP issue. This average ranking may reflect some concern about the possible ethical issue that this action presents. Is this action by company officers to raise their incentive compensation also in the interests of the shareholders?[9] An inventory buildup absorbs cash flow and could raise the possibility of the need for a future inventory write-down. As one academic respondent observed: "An action may not violate GAAP (or be related to GAAP) but still results in misleading or even fraudulent reporting. Items 5 to 8 fall into this area." A CFO who classified this as 1 suggested that "most companies have codes of business conduct with policies that might not allow this." A CPA who provided no classification stated that this was not a reporting matter but rather an issue of "plan design and ethics."

7. Credit standards are relaxed at year-end in order to boost sales and with it earnings for the year just ending.

The average ranking of 1.59 also indicates no conflict between this real action and GAAP. However, a number of respondents annotated their response indicating that their classification of this action as a 1 assumed that an appropriate increase in the bad debt allowance was recorded. In addition, this is a case where a bad business decision may have been made to achieve a desired earnings objective.

8. A schedule of price increases, to take effect early in the next year, is announced in the fourth quarter in order to boost sales and earnings in the year just ending.

This is another real action that may not seem to be either related to or inconsistent with GAAP. A CFO who classified this as 2 noted that "In many cases this is difficult to prevent even if *not* desired."

9. Books are held open for several days after the close of the year to record additional sales for the year just ended.

The average ranking of 3.66 places this action into the domain of fraudulent financial reporting. This activity has been a common target in SEC enforcement actions. These are sales that belong in the next year. Of course, this will make it more difficult to achieve profit expectations in the coming year—borrowing from Peter to pay Paul.

10. Shipments close to year-end are delayed in order to provide an increase in sales for the first quarter of the next year.

This is another real action, and its average ranking of 1.73 is consistent with the rankings of the other real actions. However, the delay in shipments could be seen as understating the performance of the current and potentially overstating the performance of the following year. While it may not be the intent, this could be misleading, even though it is not in conflict with GAAP.

11. Investments are sold to recognize a gain in order to offset a special charge arising from an asset write-down.

Another real action with an average ranking of 1.27. The motivation here may well be to reduce the volatility of earnings, one of the more common helpful features of earnings management, according to survey respondents, discussed in subsequent sections. Several respondents qualified their within-GAAP classification with the assumption that both the charge and gain were disclosed, that is, not netted.

12. Goods are shipped to a customer who has not yet placed an order but probably will during the next quarter.

This action is unambiguously a violation of GAAP. The average ranking of 3.67 indicates that the respondent groups also viewed this as potentially fraudulent financial reporting.

13. Sales are recognized on goods shipped to reseller customers who are not creditworthy.

Somewhat surprisingly, this action appears to be seen as less objectionable than booking sales in the absence of an order. In order to recognize revenue, GAAP requires that the sale amount be collectible. The average ranking is 2.58 for this action versus 3.67 for action 12. However, about 20 respondents indicated that their response assumed the recording of an appropriate allowance for bad debts. In most cases a classification of 1 or 2 was recorded but would have been a 3 or 4 in the absence of an allowance. This action clearly raises questions about the wisdom of this business decision. Moreover, it is questionable that an appropriate allowance for bad debts could be determined in the case of customers who are not creditworthy. The addition of a statement that an allowance was not recorded would have moved the average ranking closer to the fraudulent reporting classification.

14. Revenue is recognized on disputed claims against customers prior to a definitive settlement.

Disputed customer claims are most common in the case of contractors and contract reporting. Here the relevant GAAP permits the recognition of revenue on disputed claims if the likelihood of receiving the amounts is probable and estimable.[10] The average ranking of 2.87 places this action close to being beyond the flexibility afforded by

GAAP. However, recognition is consistent with GAAP assuming that the judgments about the likelihood of collection and associated amounts are reliable.

15. Sales are recognized upon the shipment of goods to a company's field representatives.

A sale to a field representative does not normally represent the shifting of the risk of ownership. The average ranking of 3.52 indicates that respondents saw this action as well beyond the flexibility inherent in GAAP. A total of 136 respondents classified this action as fraudulent financial reporting.

16. Total order revenue is recognized even though only partial shipments were made.

Where applicable, shipment is normally the gold standard for revenue recognition. With an average ranking of 3.57, respondents saw this action as beyond the flexibility provided by GAAP.

17. Revenue is recognized upon the consignment of goods but prior to their subsequent sale by the consignee.

This is clearly at odds with GAAP; a consignment is not a sale, and revenue should not be recognized until the goods are sold by the consignee. The average rank of 3.61 indicates that this deviation from GAAP is, on average, understood by the respondents.

18. The value of an ending inventory was understated in order to decrease property taxes.

This action was in fact a basis for a SEC enforcement action. In addition to the inventory understatement, profits and tax obligations also were understated by this action. The financial statements were misleading and the act was deliberate. The average ranking of 3.82 was the most severe ranking for all of the 20 earnings-management actions.

19. Sales revenue was recognized when there were significant uncertainties about customer acceptance of the product and of the customer's ability to pay.

With an average ranking of 3.12, respondents felt that this action went beyond GAAP, but they were not generally prepared to consider it to be fraudulent financial reporting. There may well have been concerns about the levels of uncertainty concerning customer acceptance and the ability to pay.

20. Sales revenue was recognized when an absolute right of return was provided by means of a "side" letter, which is outside of standard firm policies.

The average ranking of 3.20 indicates that respondents considered this action to be beyond the flexibility inherent in GAAP. Several respondents classified this action as within GAAP based on the assumption that an adequate reserve for returns could be established.

Implications of Respondent Classifications

The key classifications that should be correctly classified most frequently are those that involve actions that go beyond the flexibility inherent in GAAP and especially those actions that could potentially represent fraudulent financial reporting. Significant harm can be done to all stakeholders if firms are determined to have engaged in fraudulent financial reporting. On average, the actions that could be considered potentially fraudulent were classified as such. That is, actions 2, 9, 12, and 15 through 18 had average classification ranks of about 3.5 or higher. On balance, financial professionals recognize potentially fraudulent actions if they are presented to them. Whether such actions actually would be detected on a timely basis is a separate matter.

However, within each of the groups there are some respondents who did not classify potentially fraudulent actions as such. If the classification of a potentially fraudulent action, a 4, were instead classified as either within or at the edge of GAAP flexibility—that is, a 1 or a 2—then there were a total of 127 misclassifications. This represents an overall rate of misclassification of 9% (127 misclassifications divided by a total of 1337 classifications for the 7 potentially fraudulent actions).

Making the classifications clearly involves the exercise of judgment, and some respondents felt that the character of some of the actions was not totally clear and that more information was needed. However, on an overall basis, the results do appear to be reasonable for each of the actions presented for classification. Further judgments about the significance of differences across groups of respondents are limited by the size of the samples for some of the groups.

Views on Earnings Management Motivations and Objectives

Survey respondents also were asked to express varying degrees of agreement or disagreement with a number of statements about earnings management in this section. The possible responses are:

1. Definitely yes
2. Yes
3. No
4. Definitely no
5. No opinion

Analysis of Numerical Responses

The results of this section, displayed in Exhibit 5.5, are reported in terms of the average of choices 1 to 4. A score of 1.5 indicates more agreement with the statement than one of 3.5. As in the analysis of results in the previous section, averages for each respondent group, as well as weighted averages for the combined groups, are reported.

The responses to the first two items are quite consistent across the five groups of financial professionals surveyed.[11] While the averages range from 1.31 to 2.00, they indicate strong support for (1) earnings management being common and (2) the SEC's campaign against earnings management being necessary. These results should provide a degree of support for those who believe that abusive earnings management is an important issue, especially for the SEC. The SEC's concern with earnings management appears to be shared by a range of different financial professionals.

The responses to items 3 through 6 also indicate agreement with what often are claimed to be the underlying motivations for earnings management: (3) reducing earnings volatility, (4) supporting or increasing stock prices, (5) increasing earnings-based compensation, and (6) meeting consensus earnings forecasts.

Exhibit 5.5 Earnings Management: Motivations and Objectives

	Weighted Average	ACPA	FA	Lender	CPA	MBA
1. Earnings management is common	1.46	1.55	1.33	1.31	1.70	1.50
2. The SEC's campaign against abusive earnings management is necessary	1.88	1.89	2.00	1.92	1.80	1.94
3. Common goal of earnings management is to reduce earnings volatility	1.72	1.68	1.65	1.92	1.50	1.97
4. Common goal of earnings management is to support or increase stock prices	1.67	1.72	1.55	1.69	2.00	1.72
5. Common goal of earnings management is to increase earnings-based compensation	1.89	2.00	1.84	1.85	1.67	1.97
6. Common goal of earnings management is to meet consensus earnings forecasts	1.62	1.68	1.55	1.62	1.40	1.78
7. Investors are sometimes harmed by earnings-management practices	1.63	1.68	1.67	1.77	1.40	1.69
8. Earnings management can be helpful to investors	2.28	2.37	2.32	2.00	2.57	2.33
9. Earnings management has become more common over the past decade	1.80	2.00	1.53	1.77	1.70	1.85
10. Reg. FD will increase earnings management to meet consensus earnings forecasts	2.63	2.95	2.53	2.42	2.44	2.55

Source: Financial Numbers Game Survey

ACPA = academics, most of whom are also CPAs

CFO = chief financial officer or comparable senior financial position, e.g., controller, etc.

FA = Financial analyst, CFAs in most cases

Lender = Commercial bank lender

CPA = CPA in public practice

MBA = Advanced MBA students, most with some work experience, and enrolled in advanced elective courses in accounting and finance

On items 7 and 8, respondents were in stronger agreement with the statement that earnings management could hurt investors (weighted average of 1.63) as opposed to help (weighted average of 2.28) investors.

The respondents agreed (item 9) that earnings management has become more common over the past decade. Finally, the results on item 10, whether the SEC regulation on full disclosure would increase earnings management to meet consensus earnings forecasts, do not appear to support this prospect. Here the expectation has been that somewhat less guidance might be provided, as a result of Reg. FD, to analysts by management. This would in turn require more earnings management to meet analysts' expectations.

Other Respondent Commentary

In addition to the numerical choices made by survey respondents, space also was provided on the questionnaire to add written comments. A selection of these comments is provided in Exhibit 5.6. Additional and more expansive commentary on some of these items is provided in the following section.

Views on Earnings Management

This section of the survey asked for written responses on (1) earnings-management techniques that respondents had observed, (2) how they believed that earnings management could be detected, and also whether earnings management had the potential to (3) harm or (4) help investors and others.

Earnings Management Techniques Observed in Practice

The survey respondents provided a total of 227 examples of earnings-management techniques that they had observed. Interestingly, some CFO respondents felt the need to emphasize that they had not observed these earnings-management techniques in their companies. After reviewing all of the responses, the techniques were grouped into six categories, with a seventh category used for other diverse items. The categories and the number of techniques reported are presented in Exhibit 5.7.

The results in the exhibit reveal that the timing of expense recognition was the most commonly observed earnings-management technique. The combination of the expense-recognition classifications of (a) timing of operating expenses and (b) big-bath charges and cookie jar reserves represent 110, or 48.5%, of the total of 227 earnings-management techniques reported by the survey respondents. Making a distinction between these two categories sometimes involved close calls. The key was distinguishing between large nonrecurring charges, which were used to create reserves that later could be reversed into earnings, and the more routine fine-tuning of expense recognition.

Earnings management that is based on the timing of revenue recognition is the next most frequent earnings-management technique. This representation by revenue recognition is comparable to that in a recently reported 10-year study of fraudulent financial reporting. While the categories in the fraudulent reporting study were somewhat differ-

---

Exhibit 5.6   Comments by Survey Respondents to Earnings Management Statements

---

Earnings management is common
- Smart analysts and investors have a fair idea that this happens.—ACPA
- Yes, where motivation exists, which is commonplace. Not as much as in the past, but economic turn down represents serious motivation.—ACPA
- Yes, GAAP affords the flexibility to do so.—CFO

The SEC's campaign against abusive earnings management is necessary
- Yes, but they have gone overboard to a point where leading practitioners are afraid to exercise professional judgment.—ACPA
- Yes, but at best they will mitigate the practice slightly.—ACPA
- Yes, if the CPAs will not, somebody should.—ACPA
- Yes, but I would support a less blunt instrument than the approach I perceive is being used by the SEC.—ACPA
- No. An ambivalent answer since much earnings management is transparent.—ACPA
- Yes, using the flexibility afforded by GAAP is prudent business. Going beyond (abusive) is not.—CFO
- Yes, industry needs to police itself and evolve appropriate consequences for improper behavior by management.–FA
- No, it is important that companies play by the same rules and it is inconceivable to believe that earnings shouldn't fluctuate in ranges year to year. Straight-line trends should be uncommon.—CPA

Common goal of earnings is to reduce earnings volatility
- To the extent that meeting or exceeding expectations reduces volatility.—ACPA

Common goal of earnings management is to support or increase stock prices
- Yes, it does not mean that it is necessarily successful.—ACPA
- Yes, decreased EPS variance is often associated with higher valuations.—FA

Common goal of earnings management is to increase earnings-based compensation
- Yes, but this may be an overemphasized goal.—ACPA
- Yes, the impression is that options are the primary compensation nowadays. Hence, the effect of earnings on compensation may be indirectly through stock price.—ACPA
- Yes, management is not the owner. They are economically motivated hired hands who have significant control over their own compensation. The behavior is predictable.—FA

Common goal of earnings management is to meet consensus earnings forecasts
- Yes, this is an unfortunate pressure on companies that did not exist to some extent before.—ACPA
- Yes, but only when companies go outside the flexibility afforded by GAAP.—CFO
- Yes, but most companies manage consensus estimates by calling analysts whose estimates appear out of line.—FA

Exhibit 5.6 *(Continued)*

Investors are sometimes harmed by earnings-management practices

- Yes, management decisions that are focused on short-term needs will invariably compromise the long-term performance.—FA
- Yes, probably hurts potential investors or those who are currently investing based on *inflated* earnings.—CPA

Earnings management can be helpful to investors

- Yes, to the degree that it permits better firm valuation estimates by providing information on permanent and transitory components of income.—ACPA
- No, mild earnings management aimed at reducing earnings volatility could be useful, but otherwise no.—ACPA
- Yes, sustained earnings growth consistent with earnings expectations is better for investors than volatile swings quarter to quarter.—CFO
- Yes, but only in the short term.—CPA

Earnings management has become more common over the past decade

- Yes, more pressure on management to meet earnings to have improving stock performance.—ACPA
- Yes, more emphasis on meeting analyst forecasts.—ACPA
- Yes, due to requirements to meet quarterly earnings estimates and the incredible volatility of the markets.—CPA

The SEC's regulation on fair disclosure will increase earnings management to meet consensus earnings forecasts

- Yes, prior to Reg. FD, management would steer analysts toward their numbers. Now analysts will create their own number and management will need to steer their number toward whatever analysts created.—FA

Source: Financial Numbers Game Survey

ACPA = Academics, most of whom are also CPAs

CFO = Chief financial officer or comparable senior financial position, e.g., controller

FA = Financial analyst, CFAs in most cases

Lender = Commercial bank lender

CPA = CPA in public practice

MBA = Advanced MBA students, most with some work experience, and enrolled in advanced elective courses in accounting and finance

ent from those used in Exhibit 5.7, that study showed expense recognition to be somewhat more common than revenue recognition.[12] Of course, the survey reported in this chapter is not confined to earnings management that could be considered to be fraudulent financial reporting.

The substantial representation of "real" actions used to manage earnings was somewhat surprising. That is, management decisions involving the actual conduct of business often are used to manage earnings. For example, an asset might be sold to produce a gain to offset an operating loss. Real actions are distinguished from most other earnings-management techniques that simply involve the timing of the recognition of revenues or expenses.

The area of inventory accounting was next to last in terms of specifically identified earnings-management techniques. Last-in, first-out (LIFO) dipping and inventory misstatements were some of the techniques more frequently identified by survey respondents.[13] The rather low representation of inventory accounting in earnings management may simply reflect the growth in the economy of firms for whom inventories are not a significant factor.

Changes in accounting policies and practices, although often mentioned as likely earnings-management techniques, represented only 3.5% of total earnings-management techniques that were reported. Their visibility or transparency may make them less effective as earnings-management techniques, assuming that they are fully and fairly disclosed—something that may not always be the case. A representative sampling of the items included in the survey categories from Exhibit 5.7 is provided in Exhibit 5.8.

Detection of Earnings Management

We asked the survey respondents also to indicate how earnings-management practices could be detected. The survey respondents provided a total of 190 possible detection

---

Exhibit 5.7   Reported Earnings Management Techniques Observed in Practice

Category	Number	Percentage
Timing of operating expenses	71	31.3
Big bath charges and cookie jar reserves	39	17.2
Revenue recognition	42	18.5
Real actions	31	13.6
Inventory accounting	19	8.4
Changes in accounting policies and practices	8	3.5
Other techniques	17	7.5
Totals	227	100.0

Source: Financial Numbers Game Survey

Exhibit 5.8   Earnings Management Techniques from the Survey

Timing of Operating Expenses
- Underestimation of allowances—ACPA
- Accrual of losses and expenses to meet EPS forecasts—ACPA
- Under provisioning for bad debts, returns, etc.—ACPA
- Warranty reserve adjustments—CFO
- Manipulation of reserves and accruals—CFO
- Aggressive capitalization of costs—CFO
- Justifying the absence of write-downs until the "time is right"—CFO
- Optimistic depreciation and amortization terms—FA
- Accelerating expenses in a good year and revenue in a bad year—CPA
- Managing discretionary accruals, such as workers' compensation and general liability, for the self-insured—CPA
- Overaccruals in high earnings periods so as not to set expectations too high—Lender
- Reserves boosted to even the flow of earnings in future periods—Lender

Big Bath Charges and Cookie Jar Reserves
- Cookie jar reserves are far and away the most common practice I observed in public accounting—ACPA
- Overreserving for current contingencies to build reversible earnings to hedge future periods—ACPA
- Conservative valuation reserves—warranty, inventory obsolescence, etc.—with subsequent reversal to operations—CFO
- Overaccrual of restructuring reserves and subsequent crediting to smooth earnings—CFO
- Outside the bounds of GAAP, establishment of general reserves covering no particular exposure—CFO
- The practice of "saving a little for the future" has been common—usually by having excessive reserves—CFO
- Special charges offsetting gains—FA
- Large write-offs—FA
- Overuse of restructuring charges—CPA
- Excess bad debt reserves in good years—CPA
- Overuse of special charges that are taken back into income at a later date—Lender
- Overaccruals are done all the time—Lender

Revenue Recognition
- Premature booking of revenue—ACPA
- Keeping year end "open" through the first few days of the following year—ACPA
- Bill-and-hold sales—ACPA
- Recording out-of-period revenue—CFO
- Recognition of income on service contracts prior to services being performed—CFO
- Recognition of sales prior to actual shipment to third party; i.e., loads still on dock for export sales—CFO
- Front-ending sales or revenue that should be spread out over a much longer period—FA

(continues)

Exhibit 5.8 *(Continued)*

- I do a lot of construction contractor work—percentage-of-completion is a huge abuse—CPA
- Sales recognized in the wrong period—CPA
- Holding books open after month or quarter end—MBA

Real Actions

- Postponing R&D and advertising—ACPA
- Channel stuffing—ACPA
- Motivating customers to order product ahead of their needs at quarter ends—CFO
- Timing of plant maintenance activities—CFO
- Reducing advertising spending to improve earnings—CFO
- Buying or selling derivatives to hedge earnings volatility—FA
- Selling receivables—FA
- Granting more lenient credit terms—FA
- Selling assets at gains—CPA
- Repurchasing common stock to increase earnings per share—Lender
- Delaying or accelerating shipments to smooth earnings—Lender

Inventory Accounting

- Adjusting inventory allowances—ACPA
- Adjusting production to increase overhead charged to inventory—ACPA
- LIFO dipping—ACPA
- Inventory valuation—FA
- Obsolete inventory—Lender

Changes in Accounting Policies and Practices

- Changes in depreciable lives—ACPA
- Changes in estimates—CFO
- Changes in revenue recognition policies—FA
- Changes in accounting practices, e.g., capitalization, revenue recognition, LIFO to FIFO—MBA

Miscellaneous

- Business combinations accounting—ACPA
- Fictitious entries—CFO
- Misclassification of items below operating earnings line—FA
- Using gains on sales to close down outmoded facilities is the most often used—FA

Source: Financial Numbers Game Survey
ACPA: Academic, also typically a CPA
CFO: Chief financial officer or comparable position
FA: Financial analyst, typically a CFA
CPA: Certified public accountant in public practice
Lender: Bank lender
MBA: Advanced MBA student

techniques. Several respondents provided statements about the futility of efforts to detect earnings management instead of suggesting detection techniques. This is not a view shared by the authors of this book, but we provide their statements in the spirit of full disclosure:

- Most detection techniques are ineffective. Earnings management is too easily masked. Earnings management often is uncovered when it masks a substantive change in a company's operations—ACPA
- With an unqualified opinion, detection of earnings management is extremely difficult. The summary of accounting policies does provide some information. Most of the issues that the SEC has addressed have been, in my opinion, due to *audit failure*— ACPA
- You cannot detect earnings management—even abnormal balance-sheet changes can be explainable. If management is managing earnings and the auditors sign off, you will never know—CFO

The large sample of potential detection techniques provided by the survey respondents indicates that many do not share negative opinions about the ability to detect earnings management. However, the thrust of the above statements does have some merit. That is, the detection of earnings management can be very difficult. Most of the cases of abusive earnings management, which became the subjects of accounting and auditing enforcement releases of the SEC, had gone on for years without detection. In addition, most involved the active participation and collusion of top management of the companies and included active efforts to subvert the efforts of the outside auditors.

Discussions and illustrations of how earnings management might be detected are provided throughout this book. While the task of detection remains formidable, we believe that the discussion and illustration of earnings management detection, supplemented by the detection techniques provided by the survey respondents, can increase the likelihood that material cases of earnings management will be detected.

However, it is important to note that none of the detection techniques provided by the survey respondents, or presented elsewhere in the book, provides conclusive evidence of earnings management. That is, they all should be thought of as yellow and not red flags, warnings and not condemnations. They indicate that the conditions and circumstances revealed by the detection technique sometimes are associated with earnings management. Further investigation, including discussions with a firm's management or outside auditors, normally are needed before a conclusion that earnings management is taking place could be made.

Exhibit 5.9 provides a classified breakdown of the 190 detection techniques provided by survey respondents. The detection techniques did not fit as neatly into a limited number of categories as was true of earnings-management techniques. A rather large number of detection techniques end up simply being classified "other." As with any such classification, there are some close calls made in some of the classifications, and in a number of cases an item might fit into more than a single category. However, each technique was classified only into a single category.

Exhibit 5.9   Techniques for the Detection of Earnings Management

Category	Number	Percentage
Trend analysis (analytical review)	50	26.3
High-likelihood conditions or circumstances	27	14.2
Footnote review	16	8.4
Days statistics	15	7.9
Relationship of actual to estimates	11	5.8
Incentives and conducive conditions	7	3.7
Cash-flow and accrual relationships	8	4.2
Other techniques	56	29.5
Totals	190	100.0

Source: Financial Numbers Game Survey

Representative examples of the items included in each of the categories in Exhibit 5.9 are provided in Exhibit 5.10.

Trend analysis tops the list in terms of the separately identified detection techniques. Scanning numbers, conditions, and relationships across a series of periods is one of the most important tools of financial analysis. It has a long tradition of use, usually under the title of analytical review, by auditors. Some might have expected more specialized or esoteric methods. However, the value of this fundamental analytical technique is very clear, given its dominance of the listing in Exhibit 5.9.

High-likelihood conditions represent circumstances that often are associated with the presence of earnings management. A plea to conduct a careful review and analysis of footnotes is one of the most common exhortations in financial analysis. However, this exhortation can be fruitless if users of statements lack the technical skills to process foot-note information adequately, a circumstance that is far too common. This is especially true with the expansion in the past decade of footnotes in terms of numbers, length, and technical complexity.

Days statistics are also a powerful analytical tool, and their application is explained and illustrated in other chapters of this book. A close proximity of actual and estimated earnings can provide a strong incentive to manage earnings so that earnings expectations are met. The presence of other incentives and conducive conditions should alert the analyst to be on the lookout for earnings-management activity. Similarly, a divergence of cash flow and accrual relationships may be a sign of earnings management activity.

Some of the techniques contributed by lenders and CPAs may not be available to other users. Cut-off and subsequent events testing are standard auditing procedures that require access that usually would be available only to auditors or insiders such as CFOs. Notice that the recommendation to review aging schedules (for accounts receivable) where a financing arrangement is in place may provide lenders with the necessary access.

Exhibit 5.10   Examples of Earnings-Management Detection Techniques

Trend Analysis (Analytical Review)

Conduct comparative ratio analysis—ACPA

Conduct ratio and trend analysis—ACPA

Look for flipping between conservatism one period and aggressive reporting in another—ACPA

Review special charges in conjunction with note disclosures; look at over time—ACPA

Make a quarter-by-quarter comparison of financial statements with the past year—CFO

Check for increases or decreases in reserves offsetting other trends, e.g., sales increases offset by increased reserves—CFO

Review the sources of significant changes in margins—CFO

Review past trends in revenue and expenses—FA

Compare revenue growth versus EPS growth—FA

Review the reasons for changes in effective tax rates—FA

Review credit policy changes or large fluctuations in write-offs—CPA

Look for large changes in revenue and expenses in the fourth quarter—Lender

Review cases of high shipping volume at the first of the next month—MBA

High-Likelihood Conditions

Be suspicious of disclosures that barely meet the minimum, or don't even get that far—ACPA

Examine unusual and nonrecurring transactions—ACPA

Review changes in accounting methods without clear justification—ACPA

Review quarter-end manual entries—CFO

Look closely at fourth-quarter adjustments—CFO

Critically review explanations that are offered each year for charges and reversals of charges in subsequent years—CFO

Review changes in accounting policies and/or estimates, e.g., useful life, pension plan return, etc.—FA

Force management to provide greater detail on reserve calculations—CPA

Look at major areas of judgment, e.g., accruals and reserves—CPA

Review aging of receivables, inventory, and payables—Lender

Footnote Analysis

Read accounting policies footnote and compare to previous year—ACPA

Read inventory footnotes carefully for evidence of LIFO dipping—ACPA

Review pension and Other Post-Employment Benefits (OPEB) footnotes for changes in assumptions—ACPA

Review footnote disclosures for unusual gains in periods of weak operating results—CFO

Read notes closely to find accounting or valuation changes, e.g., pension assumptions—Lender

(continues)

Exhibit 5.10 *(Continued)*

Days Statistics

Accounts receivable increase faster than sales—ACPA

Look for excessive aging of accounts receivable—CFO

Review inventory-to-sales ratio changes—CFO

Days on hand information is a good early indicator of issues—FA

Relationships of Actual Results to Estimates

Review trends of meeting or beating analysts' consensus forecasts—ACPA

Review the proximity of reported earnings and EPS amounts to analysts' estimates—CFO

I have found that companies that continually meet expectations "to the penny" are usually managing earnings—CFO

An examination of the EPS trend is a good start. If a company shows consistent EPS growth for several years, it is probably managing earnings—FA

Review earnings versus consensus estimates—CPA

Incentives

I look for opportunities to manage and reasons to manage, i.e., incentives—ACPA

Understand the financial reporting and other pressures on management and assess risk of misstatement in the light of this analysis—ACPA

Review disclosures to determine the level of estimates inherent in the financial statements—CFO

Consider the current climate in which management is operating. Is there a need to manage earnings?—Lender

Consider the existence of compensation-based incentives to manage earnings—Lender

Cash Flow and Accrual Relationships

I examine the relationship of net income to cash flow from operating activities over time for a firm. If net income is systematically greater than zero, while cash flow from operating activities is less than zero, management may be manipulating—ACPA

Income before tax is significantly in excess of cash flow—you can manage earnings much easier than cash flow—CFO

Other Techniques

A management that is not forthcoming to questions—ACPA

Analyze and test significant accruals and deferrals—ACPA

Review credit terms—CFO

Try to match shipments and sales to market data on consumer takeaway—CFO

Examine offsetting gains and losses—CFO

The consistent announcement of restructuring charges when it doesn't appear that estimates will be met and the subsequent nonuse of charges will be returned to income—CFO

Look for nonrecurring items—FA

Exhibit 5.10   *(Continued)*

Cutoff testing—CPA
Subsequent events testing—CPA
Comparisons to the industry—Lender
Reviewing aging schedules—Lender
Thorough questioning of management and their CPAs about accounting practices—Lender
I ask the CFO how revenue and expenses are recorded—Lender
Benchmarking accounting policy with the industry—MBA

ACPA: Academic, also typically a CPA

CFO: Chief financial officer or comparable position

FA: Financial analyst, typically a CFA

CPA: Certified public accountant in public practice

Lender: Bank lender

MBA: Advanced MBA student

Earnings Management: Harmful or Helpful?

The larger question of whether earning management is harmful or helpful has received less attention than whether firms engage in earnings management, both how and to what extent. The survey results presented here expand on the earlier, mainly numerical, analysis of whether earnings management is harmful or helpful that was provided in Exhibits 5.5 and 5.6. Written commentary on earnings management as harmful or helpful is classified and discussed in the balance of this section. The survey respondents provided 121 written statements concerning how earnings management could harm investors and others. Alternatively, only 66 statements were provided on how earnings management could be helpful to investors and others.

Earnings Management as Harmful   Statements indicating how investors could be harmed are categorized as follows:

	Number	*Percentage*
Distorts financial performance	54	45
Inflates or deflates stock prices	33	27
Hurts firm performance	8	7
Other reasons	26	21
Total	121	100

A sampling of the statements from each of the above categories is provided in Exhibit 5.11.

Exhibit 5.11   Statements about How Earnings Management Harms Investors

---

Distorts Financial Performance

It masks the *true* economic performance of the firm and understates volatility (risk) of the business—ACPA

It gives the appearance of greater stability than is the reality. As a consequence, when the day of reckoning comes, which it inevitably does, the fall is much further than it needs to be, yielding larger investor losses than should have been—ACPA

When earnings management masks fraud, it has the potential to harm investors—ACPA

Smoothed earnings give investors a false sense of the amount and timing of future cash flows—ACPA

Can harm investors if earnings management activities cover up negative trends—CFO

Answer with a question: How can an investor make informed investment decisions when they are misled by the management of the company in which they are investing?—CFO

Can lead one to invest in a company where earnings are not as dependable as reported—CFO

Can overstate sales and trends. Earnings management is terrible for investors—CFO

Earnings management, to the extent that it distorts the true picture of the company's operations, is harmful to investors. Prudent financial management to minimize the cost of capital, however, is an important duty of company senior management—FA

It is most damaging when overly optimistic assumptions are made in recording sales and earnings that at a later date must be retracted with sizable losses recognized at long last—FA

A banker might make a bad loan—CPA

Volatility, the unpredictability of a business can be masked. Abilities of management to manage through the good and bad times can be oversold—CPA

No real means for investors to assess the information—Lender

It covers up operating problems—Lender

If the management tactics are fraudulent, eventually a restatement will occur. In this case, investors who are unaware of management practices could be hurt—MBA

Affects Stock Prices

Stock price is artificially inflated and followed by an unexpected fall—ACPA

To the extent that it is not transparent, earnings management could support artificially high stock prices—ACPA

Reduces confidence in reported numbers, resulting in higher discount for uncertainty and lower stock prices—ACPA

Usually results in overstated stock valuation—CFO

Earnings management harms investors because the company will eventually get caught and the stock will be punished—CFO

Artificial maintenance of an inflated stock price can certainly harm investors. However, the punitive nature of today's markets for those companies who miss market expectations and do not manage earnings is also damaging—CFO

If companies run out of options to manage earnings, the stock prices may fall—FA

Exhibit 5.11 *(Continued)*

Earnings management could either inflate or keep stock price low depending on whether earnings are managed up or down. Inflating stock price will come back to bite the company and investors—Lender

Hurts Firm Performance

When earnings management involves taking more risks, e.g., relaxing credit standards, it increases the probability that the company will suffer losses—ACPA

Widespread earnings management can increase the cost of capital to all firms that access U.S. capital markets—ACPA

Provides excessive compensation and security for top level executives—ACPA

Earnings management taken to excess, where poor business decisions are taken as a result, will weaken the business in the long run—CFO

Encourages management to pursue strategies that may not maximize firm value in the long run—FA

Takes management's attention away from their true task, i.e., managing the firm—FA

Inappropriate increases in bonuses—Lender

Managing earnings takes significant effort away from managing true profit and loss—CPA

Management may be expending inappropriate resources to manage earnings or making short-term decisions that are detrimental to long-term performance—CPA

Other Reasons

Occasionally earnings management leads to manipulation that leads to fraud and devastates the firm, ruining lives of all involved in the firm—ACPA

Some earnings management cannot be detected—ACPA

Evidence of earnings management over time reduces the credibility of corporate management—ACPA

Distorts the predictability of future cash flows—CFO

Potentially unable to detect operational difficulties—CFO

Accounting should be results neutral, just reporting what has happened and not affecting the actual results—CFO

It will lead management to use more questionable accounting practices in order to smooth earnings to meet security analysts' expectations—FA

Intentional deception is viewed very unfavorably in the marketplace—Lender

ACPA: Academic, also typically a CPA

CPA: Certified public accountant in public practice

CFO: Chief financial officer or comparable position

Lender: Commercial bank

FA: Financial analyst, typically a CFA

MBA: Advanced MBA student

Earnings Management as Helpful   The 66 statements suggesting that earnings management could be helpful are categorized as follows:

	Number	*Percentage*
Reduces earnings volatility	16	24
Provides a share-price benefit	15	23
Signals management's private information	9	14
Helps to meet forecasts	6	9
Rationalizes expectations	4	6
Other reasons	16	24
Total	66	100

A sampling of the statements from each of these categories is provided in Exhibit 5.12.

The reduction in earnings volatility is the most frequently mentioned benefit of earnings management. The recurrent theme is that a smoother earnings stream is likely to benefit share value and also may reflect favorably on management of the firm. Earnings management as a means of signaling management's private information is cited only by the academics. Positive information possessed by management can be signaled to investors by managing earnings up. Alternatively, negative information can be signaled to investors by managing earnings down.

With all the attention given to consensus analyst earnings estimates, the identification of meeting such expectations as a potential benefit of earnings management is not surprising. The rationalization of expectations could be seen as another avenue for guiding expectations toward reality. In fact, this action is comparable to management using earnings management to signal its superior information about the level of future earnings.

Exhibit 5.12   Statements that Earnings Management May Be Helpful to Investors

Reduces Earnings Volatility

The ability to reduce earnings volatility is an indicator of financial strength—ACPA

It can reduce earnings volatility and thereby increase returns because the market perceives the earnings to be more predictable, i.e., less risky—ACPA

I think that intent is the key. Some accruals management might be helpful to preserve core-underlying trends—ACPA

Smoothing rather than volatility is often useful—CFO

Even if management of a company is running the business well for the long term, uncontrolled earnings volatility can lead to unfounded concerns of management ability and result in a lower price-to-earnings ratio. Smoothing earnings legitimately, e.g., pacing expenditures, improves investor confidence—CFO

Exhibit 5.12 *(Continued)*

Reducing some volatility from the EPS stream can be okay if it is within a fair band around the normal earnings trend line—FA

Minor adjustments to smooth EPS can produce investor confidence to buy and hold for the long term and avoid the Street's constant noise to trade—FA

Could sometimes be used to offset a loss from an extraordinary item, e.g., selling investments at a gain to offset losses—CPA

In the absence of fraud, a smooth stream of earnings will help the investor over time— Lender

Provides a Share-Price Benefit

Mild earnings management that simply reduces price volatility over time can be helpful in stabilizing investment return and investor activities—ACPA

Smoothes out certain nonrecurring items that might otherwise lead to increased stock price volatility—ACPA

Conservative accounting practices within GAAP are prudent business actions to provide a shock absorber to unforeseen negative events. Sustained earnings growth consistent with expectations creates value for all stakeholders—CFO

Earnings management helps eliminate extreme volatility in the stock price when a company does not meet the analysts' consensus estimate—CFO[14]

May result in higher stock prices over the short term—FA

With the hypersensitivity of the stock market, some earnings management has been required to temper the effects of the peaks and valleys or routine variations in business. Without the ability to report consistency or stability, a stock could fluctuate radically— CPA

It helps companies who manipulate earnings for the purpose of maintaining stability in their stock price by smoothing earnings over time, rather than sending volatile earnings reports to the market and having stock price fluctuate wildly—Lender

Signals Management's Private Information

It could be used to signal managers' superior information concerning future returns— ACPA

Management can use accruals to communicate superior information about future outcomes—ACPA

Can be used as a signaling tool about otherwise unobservable information—ACPA

Legitimate earnings management can convey information about management plans and expectations—ACPA

Helps to Meet Forecasts

Since stock prices may be affected by whether or not earnings forecasts have been met, earnings management can help those investors in the short term—ACPA

Meeting or beating analysts' estimates is important these days. As long as this is done within GAAP rules, earnings management tools are very helpful to investors—Lender

(continues)

Exhibit 5.12 *(Continued)*

Rationalizes Expectations

Within reason, earnings management can help to rationalize expectations in periods where there may be unusual charges or credits in current earnings—CFO

Perhaps okay if an extraordinarily good quarter occurs and some genuine sales or earnings are deferred to a later date to avoid extra-optimistic assumptions on the part of investors—FA

Other Reasons

May act as a counterbalance to the rules of GAAP that create rough edges—ACPA

If the quality of earnings is defined as the ability to forecast future cash flows and managing earnings can increase quality (because of GAAP deficiencies), then earnings management can be helpful—ACPA

Some definitions of earnings management may include useful activities, such as risk management through the use of derivative instruments—ACPA

For cyclical firms, earnings management helps investors to more properly view earnings power and determine firm value—FA

ACPA: Academic, also typically a CPA

CPA: Certified public accountant

CFO: Chief financial officer or comparable position

Lender: Commercial bank lender

FA: Financial analyst, typically a CFA

MBA: Advanced MBA student

SUMMARY

Earnings management has attracted much attention in recent years, but there is still relatively little systematic information available about the nature of earnings management and how and why it is practiced. The survey results presented in this chapter are designed to help fill this void. Key points made in the chapter, based on the survey, include the following:

- Financial professionals are generally in agreement on when earnings management crosses the line between the exercise of the legitimate flexibility inherent in GAAP and abusive or fraudulent financial reporting. However, a nontrivial subset of professionals appears to understate the potential seriousness of certain earnings-management actions.

- Financial professionals agree that earnings management is common, that it has increased over the past decade, and that the SEC campaign against abusive earnings management is necessary.

- The major objectives of earnings management are to reduce earnings volatility, support or increase stock prices, increase earnings-based compensation, and meet consensus earnings forecasts of analysts.

- The major categories of earnings-management actions, in order of frequency, are the timing of expense recognition, big bath and cookie jar reserves, the timing of revenue recognition, and real actions. While not in conflict with GAAP, real actions still could be used to produce misleading results.
- Trend analysis (analytical review), analysis of high-likelihood conditions and circumstances, footnote review, days statistics, and the proximity of actual to estimated results are the most frequently mentioned earnings-management detection techniques.
- Earnings management is viewed as more likely to be harmful than helpful.
- Harmful earnings-management effects are seen to include the distortion of financial performance, inflation of share prices, and potential damage to firm performance.
- Possible helpful effects from earnings management include a reduction in earnings volatility and share-price volatility, the potential for management to signal its private information, and helping to meet forecasts and rationalize expectations.

GLOSSARY

Absolute Right of Return Goods may be returned to the seller by the purchaser without restrictions.

Abusive Earnings Management A characterization used by the Securities and Exchange Commission to designate earnings management that results in an intentional and material misrepresentation of results.

Analytical Review The process of attempting to infer the presence of potential problems through the analysis of ratios and other relationships, often over time.

Bill and Hold A sales agreement where goods that have been sold are not shipped to a customer but as an accommodation simply are segregated outside of other inventory of the selling company or shipped to a warehouse for storage awaiting customer instructions.

Channel Stuffing Shipments of product to distributors who are encouraged to overbuy under the short-term offer of deep discounts.

Consignment A shipment of goods to a party who agrees to try to sell them to third parties. A sale is not considered to have taken place until the goods are sold to a third party.

Consignor A party shipping goods to a consignee. The consignee then makes an effort to sell the goods for the account of the consignor.

Consignee A party to whom goods are shipped under a consignment agreement from a consignor. Until ultimate sale, the goods remain the property of the consignor.

Days Statistics Measures the number days' worth of sales in accounts receivable (accounts receivable days) or days' worth of sales at cost in inventory (inventory days). Sharp increases in these measures might indicate that the receivables are not collectible and that the inventory is not salable.

Field Representatives Company employees who negotiate sales transactions on behalf of their employers.

LIFO Dipping Reducing LIFO inventory quantities and, as a result, including older and lower costs in the computation of cost of sales, resulting in an increase in earnings.

Real Actions (Earnings) Management Involves operational steps and not simply acceleration or delay in the recognition of revenue or expenses. The delay or acceleration of shipment would be an example.

NOTES

1. Accounting academic respondent.
2. Chief financial officer respondent.
3. Analyst respondent.
4. Chief financial officer respondent.
5. Lender respondent.
6. Lender respondent.
7. In view of the limited sample sizes and nonrandom character of most of the samples, no effort is made to test for statistical differences between the means of the various groups.
8. One chief financial officer provided the following comment on this case: "Not a realistic example. If history showed a pattern of returns, where policy was no right of return, they would have to provide a reserve or auditors would be all over them."
9. This action might be seen to be in the shareholders' interests if the goal were to increase incentive compensation by increasing the value of stock options. However, the intent was to frame the action as tied to increasing earnings-based incentive compensation.
10. Statement of Position No. 81-1, *Accounting for Performance of Construction-Type and Certain Production-Type Contracts* (New York: American Institute of Certified Public Accountants, July 15, 1981), para. 65–67. Earlier GAAP, SFAS No. 5, *Accounting for Contingencies* (Norwalk, CT: Financial Accounting Standards Board, March 1975), para. 17, held that contingent gains are not normally reflected in the accounts.
11. The CFO survey did not include this element. We expected it to be difficult to get CFOs to respond to the survey. Therefore, to reduce its length somewhat, we decided to exclude this element from the CFO version of the survey. Our low, but not unexpected, response rate from the CFOs would probably have been even lower if the questionnaire had been longer.
12. M. Beasley, J. Carcello, and D. Hermanson, *Fraudulent Financial Reporting: 1987–1997, An Analysis of U.S. Public Companies*, Research Commissioned by the Committee of Sponsoring Organizations of the Treadway Committee (NJ: American Institute of Certified Public Accountants, 1999), p. 24.
13. LIFO dipping refers to increases in earnings that result from a reduction in inventory that causes older and lower inventory costs to be included in the calculation of cost of sales. A lower cost of sales increases earnings. The expressions *LIFO dipping* and *LIFO liquidations* tend to be used interchangeably.
14. This statement continues: "The penalty can cause significant losses for investors when the stock price crashes and street expectations are not met. While I do not advocate earnings management, it would seem that a company reversing an accrual (with some justification) or booking an accrual or contingency at somewhat less than the company policy to meet expectations wouldn't be harmful to investors. This would presume this type of behavior wasn't a regular occurrence and it wasn't material to the financials."

CHAPTER SIX

Recognizing Premature or Fictitious Revenue

Lucent Technologies, Inc., continuing to pay the price for years of pushing for faster growth than it could sustain, significantly restated revenue from the last quarter and said it expects a "substantial" loss . . . We mortgaged future sales and revenue in a way we're paying for now . . .[1]

The people said the biggest problem was the old Sunbeam's practice of overstating sales by recognizing revenue in improper periods, including through its "bill and hold" practice of billing customers for products, but holding the goods for later delivery.[2]

The scheme began with the Supervisors arranging for a shipment of $1.2 million in software to one of Insignia's resellers and concealing side letters that granted extremely liberal return rights.[3]

Undetected by auditors, according to . . . testimony in a criminal trial of Cal Micro's former chairman and former treasurer, were a dozen or more accounting tricks. . . . They include one particularly bold one: booking bogus sales to fake companies for products that didn't exist.[4]

Reported revenue and its rate of growth are key components in the understanding of corporate financial performance. The account is displayed prominently on the income statement as the top line. It provides a preliminary indication of success and directly affects the amount of earnings reported and, correspondingly, assessments of earning power. For many companies, especially start-up operations that have not yet become profitable, valuation often is calculated as a multiple of revenue. We will not soon forget the stratospheric valuations enjoyed, although briefly, by Internet companies as market participants raced to value their meager but growing revenue streams with ever increasing multiples.

In this setting it is not surprising that premature or fictitious revenue recognition is often at the top of the list of tools used in playing the financial numbers game.

IS IT PREMATURE OR FICTITIOUS REVENUE?

Premature revenue recognition and fictitious revenue recognition differ in the degree to which aggressive accounting actions are taken. In the case of premature revenue, revenue is recognized for a legitimate sale in a period prior to that called for by generally accepted accounting principles. In contrast, fictitious revenue recognition entails the recording of revenue for a nonexistent sale. It is often difficult, however, to assign a label to such revenue recognition practices because of the large gray area that exists between what is considered to be premature and what is considered to be fictitious revenue recognition.

Goods Ordered But Not Shipped

Revenue recognized for goods that have been ordered but that have not been shipped at the time of recognition would be considered by most to be premature. Twinlab Corp., for example, restated results for 1997 and 1998 because "some sales orders were booked but not 'completely shipped' in the same quarter."[5] The company made an apparently valid sale to a presumably creditworthy customer. Revenue was recognized prematurely, however, because the full order had not been shipped to the customer. Twinlab had not yet earned the revenue.

In a similar example of premature revenue recognition, Peritus Software Services, Inc., received a purchase order for its year 2000 software product in August 1997. The company recorded revenue under this order in the quarter ended September 1997 even though the software was not shipped until November 1997.[6]

In some instances of premature revenue recognition, companies will ship product after the end of a reporting period to fill orders received prior to the end of that period. In order to include the late shipments in sales for the period just ending, the books will be left open well into the new period. Pinnacle Micro, Inc., used this practice and became rather brazen about its premature revenue recognition practices.

For approximately one year following its initial public offering in July 1993, the company consistently reported increasing sales and earnings. Like any young and growing company, Pinnacle established ambitious sales targets. At times, however, those targets became difficult to meet. If shipments for a quarter were not up to target, the shipping department was instructed to continue shipping until the sales goal was met. In order to recognize revenue from such shipments made after the end of a quarter, employees were instructed to predate packing lists, shipping records, and invoices to conceal the fact that orders had not been shipped until later. To facilitate such predating, the calendar on a computer that generated an automatic shipping log was reset to an earlier date. On several occasions there was insufficient product available to fill orders needed to meet sales goals. Accordingly, even manufacturing had to continue after the end of a reporting period to generate product for use in shipments dated prior to that period's end. This practice continued, getting progressively worse, until a newly hired controller, who refused to get involved, contacted the company's audit committee and independent auditors and advised them of the postperiod shipments.[7] In the end, financial results were restated to remove the prematurely recognized revenue. The restatement effects were significant. Net income for 1993 was reduced from $2.6 million to $1.6 million and net income for the fourth quarter of that year was restated to a loss of $804,000 from a profit of $652,000.

Goods Shipped But Not Ordered

A more aggressive action than recording sales for goods not yet shipped would entail product shipment and revenue recognition in advance of an expected order. Given the lack of an actual order, such an act would, in our view, entail fictitious revenue recognition. If the expected order is received later, some might argue that the transaction involved, at worst, premature revenue recognition.

For example, among several aggressive revenue recognition actions, Digital Lightwave, Inc., recorded revenue on the shipment of product to a customer that, at the time, had not placed an order. The units shipped were, in fact, demonstration units for which there was never a firm commitment for purchase. The shipped units were later returned to the company and the revenue was reversed.[8] Revenue should not have been recognized in the first place. Similarly, Ernst & Young LLP resigned as the independent auditor for Premier Laser Systems, Inc., because of a disagreement over the company's accounting practices. In particular, a customer claimed that "it didn't order certain laser products that Premier Laser apparently booked as sales."[9]

Late in 1998, Telxon Corp., a manufacturer of bar-code scanning equipment, was interested in being acquired by its longtime competitor and once hostile suitor, Symbol Technologies, Inc. Curiously, Telxon was now pushing for a quick deal and stipulated that Symbol would not be allowed to look at the company's books before completing the purchase. Telxon's results looked healthy enough. In the third quarter ended September 1998, net income before nonrecurring items was up 47% on a 13% increase in revenue. However, Symbol balked at such an arrangement and insisted on being allowed to complete a full due-diligence review of Telxon's finances. Interested in a deal, Telxon relented.

What Symbol found was not pretty. In particular, a single sale for $14 million worth of equipment was recorded toward the end of the September quarter. That equipment was sold to a distributor with no purchase agreement from an end buyer. To make matters worse, the financing for the purchase was backed by Telxon. This single sale was very important to Telxon's results because, without it, the company's revenue would be flat and it would have reported a loss for the quarter.

Symbol's interpretation of the $14 million transaction was that it was not a bona-fide sale but rather a secured financing arrangement. In effect, inventory had been shipped to Telxon's distributor, awaiting sale. In this view, while product had been shipped, there was effectively no valid order and, thus, no sale. Telxon had recognized revenue prematurely. Soon after the Symbol review, Telxon restated its results to remove the premature recognition effects of the $14 million deal along with other questionable transactions.[10]

Selected examples of premature revenue recognition are provided in Exhibit 6.1.

More Egregious Acts

In going beyond simply recognizing revenue for product shipments prior to an expected order, some companies will record sales for shipments for which orders are not expected, or, even worse, they will record sales for nonexistent shipments. Revenue recognized in such situations would be considered fictitious.

For example, during 1997 and 1998, sales managers at Boston Scientific Corp. were particularly eager to meet or exceed sales goals. To facilitate increased, although fictitious sales of the company's medical devices, commercial warehouses were leased and unsold goods were shipped there. To mask the fact that these "noncustomers" never paid for the goods, credits were later issued and the same goods were later "resold" to different customers. In other cases, product was shipped to distributors who had not placed orders. Sometimes these distributors were not even in the medical device business. Credits were then issued when these distributors returned the shipments, although by then revenue had been recognized in an earlier period.[11] Such alleged acts clearly would constitute fictitious revenue recognition.

Exhibit 6.1 Examples of Premature Revenue Recognition

Company	Premature Revenue
Acclaim Entertainment, Inc. AAER No. 1309, September 26, 2000	• Recognized revenue on a foreign distribution agreement in advance of required product delivery
Bausch & Lomb, Inc. AAER No. 987, November 17, 1997	• Used aggressive promotion campaign to encourage orders and shipments that could not be economically justified
Peritus Software Services, Inc. AAER No. 1247, April 13, 2000	• Revenue recognized for valid order that was not shipped until a later period
Pinnacle Micro Corp. AAER No. 975, October 3, 1997	• Books left open and revenue recognized for shipments made in a later period
Telxon Corp. *The Wall Street Journal*, December 23, 1998, p. C1	• Shipment to reseller that was not financially viable
Twinlab Corp. *The Wall Street Journal*, February 25, 1999, p. B9	• Revenue recognized for valid orders that were not completely shipped

Source: SEC's Accounting and Auditing Enforcement Release (AAER) or article from *The Wall Street Journal* for the indicated date.

California Micro Devices Corp. provides a particularly egregious example of fictitious revenue recognition. As noted in the opening quotes to this chapter, the chip maker's acts of revenue recognition included "booking bogus sales to fake companies for products that didn't exist." In fact, evidence obtained in a criminal trial of the company's former chairman and former treasurer indicated that one-third of its $45 million of revenue in fiscal 1994 was spurious. Facing ever more aggressive revenue goals, managers at the company began relaxing their definition of what constitutes a sale. Revenue was soon being recognized for product shipped to customers before it was ordered, and those sales were not reversed when the product was returned. In other cases, distributors were paid special handling fees to accept product that had unlimited rights of return. Revenue was recognized when product was shipped to those distributors. As the fiction developed, the company began recording sales for fake shipments. In fact, as the alleged fraud grew and more of the company's staff became involved in it, a running joke developed in which staff would say to each other, "like in a Bugs Bunny cartoon, 'What's wevenue?' "[12]

One final example of fictitious revenue recognition is that of Mercury Finance Co. In early 1997 the fast-growing auto loan company announced that it had uncovered phony bookkeeping entries, including fictitious revenue, that led it to overstate earnings in 1995 and 1996. In fact, in 1996 earnings were overstated by more than 100%.[13] In this case, much of the fictitious revenue was recognized by the stroke of a pen—through journal entries recorded without even the semblance of a sale. The erroneous entries accompanied other operational problems at the company from which it never recovered, ultimately leading to a bankruptcy filing.

Cover-up Activities

Commonly found among cases of fictitious revenue recognition are steps taken by management to cover up its acts. Such cover-up activities might take the form of backdating invoices, changing shipping dates, or creating totally false records. The actions taken often are limited only by the imagination of those concocting the scheme and may be more offensive than the original acts of fictitious revenue recognition themselves.

For its fiscal year ended September 1993, Automated Telephone Management Systems, Inc. (ATM) reported revenue of $4.9 million. Included in that revenue total was a $1.3 million sale of telecommunications equipment to a single customer, National Health Services, Inc. (National Health). National Health, however, did not actually purchase the goods in question. In fact, the company did not take delivery or pay for them. Instead, National Health's president signed documents that simply made it appear as if the $1.3 million sale had taken place. In particular, he signed a sales contract, a document indicating completion of installation of the equipment in question, and an audit confirmation letter, all of which were provided to ATM's independent auditors as support for the sale. For signing these bogus documents, he was provided $17,000 in gifts and payments. Eventually the scheme was uncovered and National Health's president found himself in the middle of an SEC enforcement action along with management of ATM.[14]

In 1991 a distributor for Cambridge Biotech Corp. took delivery of $975,000 worth of product at the direction of Cambridge's CEO. The distributor had no obligation to pay for the goods delivered. Later that year, Cambridge's CFO devised a scheme to retrieve the product and simultaneously make it appear as if the distributor had paid the $975,000 price. To effect the plan, Cambridge ordered other product from a third company for an amount approximately equal to the value of the original shipment. The order was a sham order, however, and was in actuality an order to take delivery of the same product that had been shipped to the distributor in the first place. The goods were shipped back to Cambridge from the distributor. Then, by paying for the goods, Cambridge provided the distributor with the money needed to "pay" for the original shipment. It was a convoluted plan and one that netted to zero; however, Cambridge was able to report revenue, profit, and cash flow.

In another transaction, Cambridge shipped product valued at $817,000 to a distributor whom the company had negotiated to acquire. Here again the distributor had no obligation to pay for the product that had been shipped. Cambridge recognized revenue for the transaction amount and showed a receivable. Later, in completing the purchase of the distributor, the $817,000 was netted from the acquisition price.

A third transaction was even more involved, entailing even greater cover-up actions. Here Cambridge management convinced a trading company to order $600,000 worth of product. Cambridge recognized revenue for $600,000 even though the trading company had no real obligation to pay for the order. Then Cambridge agreed to purchase goods worth $48,640 from another company, one that was related to the trading company. The agreed purchase price was set at $737,349. Cambridge then paid the related company the $737,349 and took delivery of the $48,640 in goods purchased. The related company paid $600,000 to the trading company, which used the money to pay for the original order. The related company kept $88,709 to pay for the goods ordered, shipping costs, duties, and taxes, and as a "commission" on the transaction.[15]

These three transactions are only representative of the great lengths taken by management of Cambridge Biotech to cover up its recognition of fictitious revenue. There were others. Fortunately, the transactions were uncovered and the company's cover-up activities were foiled.

Selected examples of cover-up activities seen in the area of revenue recognition are summarized in Exhibit 6.2.

A Precise Demarcation Is Not Practical

We have looked at many examples of both premature and fictitious revenue recognition. In some instances identifying when revenue has been recognized prematurely is very straightforward. Most would agree that revenue is recognized prematurely when it is recorded for a shipment made immediately after a period's cutoff date to fill a valid order from a creditworthy customer. The revenue is not fictitious because the sale exists. It was recorded early. Most also would agree that revenue recorded for nonexistent sales to nonexistent customers is fictitious. Here a sale simply does not exist. Between these two extremes, however, within that gray area noted earlier, it is difficult to get consensus on what constitutes premature and what constitutes fictitious revenue recognition. Fortunately, such a precise demarcation is not necessary.

Exhibit 6.2   Revenue Recognition Cover-up Activities

Company	Cover-up
Advanced Medical Products, Inc. AAER No. 812, September 5, 1996	• Did not mail invoices and monthly statements to "customers" that had not placed orders
Automated Telephone Management Systems, Inc. AAER No. 852, October 31, 1996	• Prepared fictitious sales contract, completion of installation document, and audit confirmation letter
Cambridge Biotech Corp. AAER No. 843, October 17, 1996	• Provided money to customer to pay for an order, netted receivable out as part of an acquisition of a customer, paid commission to a third party to provide funds to customer to pay amount due
Cendant Corp. AAER No. 1272, June 14, 2000	• Charges to cancellation reserve kept off the books
Cylink, Inc. AAER No. 1313, September 27, 2000	• Shipments made to third-party warehouse
Informix Corp. AAER No. 1215, January 11, 2000	• Backdated license agreements to earlier periods
Laser Photonics, Inc. AAER No. 971, September 30, 1997	• Did not record credit memos for returns
Photran Corp. AAER No. 1211, December 3, 1999	• Backdated order and shipping documents • Shipments made to third-party warehouse
Premier Laser Systems, Inc. AAER No. 1314, September 27, 2000	• Prepared fictitious customer order form • Shipments made to third-party warehouse

Source: SEC's Accounting and Auditing Enforcement Release (AAER) for the indicated date.

For purposes of analysis, a precise labeling of premature or fictitious revenue is less important than acknowledging that revenue has been recognized improperly. In both cases, revenue has been reported on the income statement that does not belong. Expectations about earning power will have been unduly influenced in a positive way. Certainly the more egregious the acts of improper revenue recognition become, the greater will be the penalty that ultimately is exacted. But all forms of improper revenue recognition typically will have some form of penalty, including a negative market reaction. Accordingly, the point of view taken here is that all forms of improper revenue recognition, whether premature or fictitious, should be avoided whenever possible.

WHEN SHOULD REVENUE BE RECOGNIZED?

Managers, accountants, and regulators have struggled for decades with the question of when revenue should be recognized. As our economy evolves and new forms of products, services, and transactions arise, the appropriate timing of revenue recognition becomes more difficult to define. In its most elemental form, revenue should be recognized when it is earned and realized or realizable. Revenue is earned when a company has substantially accomplished what it must do to be entitled to the benefit represented by the revenue being recognized. Revenue is realized when goods and services are exchanged for cash or claims to cash. Revenue is realizable when assets received in exchange for goods and services are readily convertible into known amounts of cash or claims to cash.

While this definition of revenue might appear to be appropriate for most transactions, often it is deficient. In particular, problems often arise in determining when revenue is earned. Consider the software industry, which has struggled with problems of revenue recognition for years. The industry has evolved from what was effectively the sale of a product—the software—to something that is more of an ongoing subscription. Services provided by the software firm, which extend well beyond the date of sale, include not only installation and training but also such customer services as ongoing telephone support and unspecified product upgrades and enhancements. With such services being provided over extended periods, determining when the revenue is earned becomes a problem.

Initially, there was no specific guidance as to when revenue should be recognized in the software industry. Accordingly, the industry struggled to determine when its revenue was earned, and companies formulated revenue recognition practices that were quite divergent. For example, it was not long ago that software companies were employing such revenue recognition policies as the following:

From the annual report of BMC Software, Inc.:

> Revenue from the licensing of software is recognized upon the receipt and acceptance of a signed contract or order.[16]

From the annual report of American Software, Inc.:

> Upon entering into a licensing agreement for the standard proprietary software, the company recognized eighty percent (80%) of the licensing fee upon delivery of the software documentation (system and user manuals), ten percent (10%) upon delivery of the software (computer tapes with source code), and ten percent (10%) upon installation.[17]

From the annual report of Autodesk, Inc.:

> Revenue from sales to distributors and dealers is recognized when the products are shipped.[18]

From the annual report of Computer Associates International, Inc.:

> Product license fee revenue is recognized after both acceptance by the client and delivery of the product.[19]

Note how each company defined quite differently when the revenue from an initial software licensing agreement was to be recognized. BMC Software was most aggressive and considered the revenue earned when an order was received. American Software waited until shipment but, curiously, recognized most of the revenue associated with a transaction when the system and user manuals were shipped. At that time, the software itself had not been shipped. Autodesk waited until the software was shipped, while Computer Associates was most conservative, recognizing revenue when the product was delivered and accepted by the client. With such diverse revenue recognition practices, it was difficult to compare financial performance across companies in the same industry.

As they became aware of the problem in the industry, accounting regulators began to chip away at the inherent flexibility in software revenue recognition. Accounting policies for revenue recognition gradually were tightened until an important document, Statement of Position 97-2, *Software Revenue Recognition* (SOP 97-2), was issued by the Accounting Standards Executive Committee of the American Institute of CPAs.[20] Generally, for software that does not entail significant production, modification, or customization, SOP 97-2 indicates that the following four criteria must be met before software revenue can be recognized:

1. Persuasive evidence of an arrangement exists.
2. Delivery has occurred.
3. The vendor's fee is fixed or determinable.
4. Collectibility is probable.

More specifically, SOP 97-2 requires that before software revenue can be recognized, there must be a valid order from a third-party customer, the software has been shipped, the price is not dependent on a future varying number of users or units distributed, and the total sale price is collectible. Note how the past practices of BMC Software and American Software would not be in accordance with this statement. In fact, as a direct result of changes in accounting policies for revenue recognition in the software industry, both companies changed their revenue recognition practices, linking recognition to software shipment.

SOP 97-2 also provides direction for software arrangements involving multiple elements, such as upgrades and enhancements, ongoing telephone support, and other services, such as installation, training, and consulting. Such services go well beyond the actual shipment of a software product and require special attention. When such additional elements are part of a software sale, the total software license fee must be divided among the various elements, including the software itself, based on their relative fair market values. Revenue then is recognized over time as performance takes place for each element of the total package. As a result, revenue recognition is delayed beyond the software delivery date for what can amount to a significant part of the total sale.

Consider the revenue recognition policy for Microsoft Corp., as provided in the company's annual report:

Revenue from products licensed to original equipment manufacturers is recorded when OEMs ship licensed products while revenue from certain license programs is recorded when the software has been delivered and the customer is invoiced. Revenue from packaged product sales to and through distributors and resellers is recorded when related products are shipped. Maintenance and subscription revenue is recognized ratably over the contract period. Revenue attributable to undelivered elements, including technical support and Internet browser technologies, is based on the average sales price of those elements and is recognized ratably on a straight-line basis over the product's life cycle. When the revenue recognition criteria required for distributor and reseller arrangements are not met, revenue is recognized as payments are received. Costs related to insignificant obligations, which include telephone support for certain products, are accrued. Provisions are recorded for returns, concessions and bad debts.[21]

The policy is very descriptive and appears to abide well with the requirements of SOP 97-2. Note that revenue is not recognized until product is shipped, either by the company itself or by its OEMs (original equipment manufacturers). Revenue associated with maintenance and subscription activities and other elements, such as technical support and browser technologies, is deferred and recognized over time, as earned. The company describes this policy further as follows:

> A portion of Microsoft's revenue is earned ratably over the product life cycle or, in the case of subscriptions, over the period of the license agreement. End users receive certain elements of the Company's products over a period of time. These elements include items such as browser technologies and technical support. Consequently, Microsoft's earned revenue reflects the recognition of the fair value of these elements over the product's life cycle.[22]

Microsoft's policy has led to the deferral of a significant amount of revenue. Using amounts provided in the company's annual report, deferred revenue at June 30, 2000, was $4.87 billion, up from $4.2 billion in 1999.

In some instances, a software sale requires significant production, modification, or customization to suit a particular customer's needs. In such cases, SOP 97-2 calls for use of contract accounting. In particular, the percentage-of-completion method should be used when the software vendor can make reasonably dependable estimates of the extent of progress toward completion, of contract revenue and contract costs. Here software revenue is recognized as progress is made toward completion of the total software installation. When conditions for use of the percentage-of-completion method are not met, the completed-contract method is appropriate. Here software revenue is not recognized until the software installation is complete.

Advent Software, Inc., notes use of the following policy for software sales requiring an extended production period:

> Revenues for interface and other development and custom programming are recognized using the percentage of completion method of accounting based on the costs incurred to date compared with the estimated cost of completion.[23]

More is said about contract accounting in a subsequent section of this chapter.

The SEC Clarifies Criteria for Revenue Recognition

The Securities and Exchange Commission has long been aware that companies often use aggressive revenue recognition practices to play the financial numbers game. Recall from Chapter 4 that revenue recognition was one of the five creative accounting practices specifically identified by the SEC as requiring action. To address the problems it sees with revenue recognition, the commission issued Staff Accounting Bulletin No. 101, *Revenue Recognition in Financial Statements* (SAB 101). SAB 101 noted that in many industries, such as the software industry, and for many non–industry-specific revenue recognition situations, such as with leases or when a sale entails a right of return, specific revenue recognition guidance exists. The SEC did not want its SAB 101 to infringe on those preexisting standards. However, the commission noted that in many other ongoing situations no specific guidance was provided to help accountants and managers determine when revenue is earned and realized or realizable. This Staff Accounting Bulletin was written to provide such guidance.

SAB 101 borrows its revenue recognition criteria from SOP 97-2, the software revenue statement. In fact, the criteria for revenue recognition in SAB 101—persuasive evidence of an arrangement, delivery has occurred or services have been rendered, the seller's price to the buyer is fixed or determinable, and collectibility is reasonably assured—are identical to those contained in SOP 97-2. In the paragraphs that follow, each of these criteria is given careful consideration. Examples are provided to show how they are applied and how companies that seek to record premature or fictitious revenue might abuse them.

Persuasive Evidence of an Arrangement

Practice varies across companies and industries as to what constitutes a valid arrangement or purchase order. In some instances a verbal order may be the norm, followed by a written confirmation. In others, a sale may require a written and signed sales agreement. SAB 101 specifically notes that if customary business practice is to use a signed sales agreement, then revenue should not be recognized without it. For example, a written sales agreement may be prepared and signed by an authorized representative of the selling company. While verbally agreeing to the terms of the contract, the purchasing company's representative may not have signed the agreement until approved by the company's legal department. Even though the purchasing company's representative provides verbal assurances of the company's interest in the product or service, according to SAB 101 persuasive evidence of an arrangement does not exist. Revenue should not be recognized.

Examples of revenue recognition in the absence of an arrangement often entail the total lack of an order. For example, Structural Dynamics Research Corp. sold its software products in the Far East through company representatives who acted as company sales agents. These sales agents would place orders with Structural Dynamics for product in the absence of orders from end users. The orders were therefore not final but were instead contingent on sales to legitimate end users. The orders themselves even contained conditional language; in fact, some were labeled as conditional purchase orders. Nonetheless, Structural Dynamics recognized revenue related to the orders. The product that was sold under them often was shipped to a freight forwarder and held there until an end user purchased the product and sought delivery. Payment was piecemeal, tied to purchases by end users. Often end users never materialized, and the related receivables were written off.[24]

Cylink Corp. also provides an example of revenue recognized for a shipment made in the absence of a firm order. The company recognized revenue for a shipment to a third-party warehouse on an order placed by a small international distributor. The sale was contingent on the distributor's ability to obtain a letter of credit. When that letter of credit was not granted, company management decided to store the shipped product in the warehouse awaiting a future sale. Given the sale's contingent nature, revenue should not have been recognized.[25]

In one of the opening quotes to this chapter, Lucent Technologies, Inc., indicated, "We mortgaged future sales and revenue in a way we're paying for now."[26] In effect, the company was admitting to premature revenue recognition—revenue was recognized currently that should have been recognized at a later date. The company restated results for its fiscal fourth quarter, reducing revenue by $679 million. The bulk of that adjustment, in fact, $452 million worth, was for equipment that it took back from distributors when they did not sell it. Apparently the company made verbal commitments to the distributors that it would take the equipment back if it was not sold. After the large and difficult adjustment, the company changed its revenue recognition practices to postpone revenue recognition until after end user customers had purchased the product. However, the company continues to suffer from its earlier accounting misdeeds; the Enforcement Division of the Securities and Exchange Commission decided to conduct a "formal investigation into possible fraudulent accounting practices" at the firm.[27]

Informix Corp. provides a clear example of revenue recognition in the absence of a formal arrangement. To meet end-of-quarter revenue and earnings goals, company sales personnel often rushed to conclude as many transactions as possible. The company's written policy was that revenue on any license agreement is not recognized for a reporting period unless the agreement is signed and dated prior to that period's end. However, in numerous instances, sales personnel were unable to obtain signed license agreements from customers prior to a period's end. Nonetheless, there was an accepted practice at the company of signing license agreements after a period's end and then backdating them to appear as if they had been executed prior to that time.[28]

Sensormatic Electronics, Inc. mastered the art of premature revenue recognition with several creative accounting practices. In each case, the company had a valid order; that is, there was persuasive evidence of an arrangement. However, the scheduled delivery date was for a later reporting period. For example, goods were shipped and revenue was recognized for orders received near the end of a reporting period but for which delivery was requested for a few days into a new period. To avoid an early delivery, the carrier was asked to delay delivery until the requested delivery date. For shipments with even longer delivery horizons, goods were shipped to company warehouses and stored until the requested delivery date. Revenue was recognized at the time of shipment to the company warehouse. On other occasions, customers issued purchase orders with FOB (free-on-board) destination terms. In such instances, title passes and revenue should be recognized when the goods reach their destination. However, the company accounted for such transactions as FOB shipping point transactions, recognizing revenue at the time the goods were shipped. While this act and others performed by the company might accelerate revenue recognition by as little as a few days, those few days typically would be enough to boost end-of-period revenue by a sufficient amount to meet revenue and earnings growth targets.

Kurzweil Applied Intelligence, Inc., also used warehouses to store shipped goods that had not been ordered. Across a two-year period straddling the company's initial public offering in August 1993, the company recorded millions of dollars in phony sales. While the goods were supposedly sold to customers, they were instead shipped and stored at a local warehouse controlled by the company. To hide the scheme, company managers allegedly forged customer signatures, altered other crucial documents, and occasionally, when needed, shifted unsold good between warehouses.[29]

Channel Stuffing

Channel stuffing is closely related to revenue recognition for shipments made in the absence of outstanding orders. However, in the case of channel stuffing, orders are in fact received. Channel stuffing refers to shipments of product to distributors who are encouraged to overbuy under the short-term offer of deep discounts. While at the time of shipment, an order is in hand, revenue is recognized somewhat prematurely by the seller because its customers are purchasing goods that will not be needed or resold until a later period. The seller is effectively borrowing sales from a later period. In such cases, sales are not sustainable.

Some would refer to the practice of channel stuffing as trade loading, a term traditionally used in the tobacco industry. This quote describes the practice well: "Trade loading is a crazy, uneconomic, insidious practice through which manufacturers—trying to show sales, profits, and market share they don't actually have—induce their wholesale customers, known as the trade, to buy more product than they can promptly resell."[30]

For example, in a particularly aggressive marketing and promotion campaign, Bausch & Lomb, Inc., offered deep discounts on contact lenses to distributors for product purchased during the third quarter of 1993. The promotion enabled the company to exceed its third-quarter sales forecast. In the process, however, the company sold distributors enough inventory to meet or exceed their fourth-quarter needs. Then in December of that same year, the company used other promotional tactics and extended payment terms to convince distributors to buy even more product. In some instances distributors bought enough product in two weeks to service their needs for up to two years.[31] While Bausch & Lomb technically had orders for the product shipped, one could clearly question whether revenue recognition was economically justified.

Side Letters

Sometimes a sales transaction may include what appears to be a legitimate order from a creditworthy customer, or, in the terms of the SEC, there exists persuasive evidence of an arrangement. However, outside of normal corporate reporting channels is a separate agreement between some member or members of a company's management and the customer. This separate agreement, or side letter as they have become known, effectively neutralizes the purchase transaction between the company and its customer. Note that there is nothing inherently wrong with a side letter that is generally known by company management and is used to clarify or modify terms of a sales agreement without somehow undermining the agreement as a whole. The problem with side agreements arises when they are maintained outside of normal reporting channels and are used to negate some or all terms of the disclosed agreement.

Stipulations of an improper side letter might include: liberal rights of return; rights to cancel orders at any time; contingencies, such as the need to raise funds on the part of the customer, that if not met make the sale null and void; being excused from payment if goods purchased are not resold; or, even worse, a total absolution of payment. As a result, there is no arrangement per se between the two companies. A sale has not taken place and revenue should not be recognized.

Insignia Solutions, PLC, a software company, sold product to resellers and offered limited rights of return. The company provided for estimated future returns that were deducted from gross revenue in deriving net revenue. The estimate of returns was calculated by measuring inventory on hand at resellers that exceeded a 45-day supply. In a significant sale to a single reseller, the sales manager, at the direction of the sales vice president, signed a side letter offering a more liberal right of return than normally provided. Then, after the shipment, a subordinate was instructed to report only 10% of the inventory held by the reseller. By underreporting inventory, amounts on hand at the reseller were made to appear to be much less than the 45-day supply that would require an additional provision for returns. As a result, the company was able to report higher net revenue than would have been reported in the absence of the side letter and the misstatement of inventory.[32]

Sales personnel and management at Informix Corp. used a variety of both written and oral side agreements to encourage orders by resellers that effectively rendered their sales agreements unenforceable. Terms varied and included such provisions as:

- Committing the company to use its own sales force to find customers for resellers
- Offering to assign future end user orders to resellers
- Extending payment terms beyond 12 months
- Committing the company to purchase computer hardware or services from resellers under terms that effectively refunded all, or a substantial portion, of the license fees paid by them
- Diverting the company's own future service revenue to resellers as a means of refunding their license fees
- Paying fictitious consulting or other fees to resellers to be repaid to the company as license fees[33]

Given the liberal use of limits on their sales agreements, it is evident that in the presence of these side letters, a true sales arrangement was not in effect. Revenue should not have been recognized.

In a review of SEC enforcement actions against companies with alleged premature or fictitious revenue recognition practices, many companies were noted with side letters to their sales agreements. Common among the provisions of these side letters were liberal rights of return and extended payment terms, often to a point where no payment was expected unless the product shipped was resold. A summary of popular provisions contained in side letters is provided in Exhibit 6.3.

Exhibit 6.3   Sales-Agreement Side Letters

Company	Side-Letter Provisions
Cylink Corp. AAER No. 1313, September 27, 2000	• Provided right to exchange software products for hardware
Engineering Animation, Inc. AAER No. 1332, October 5, 2000	• Absolved reseller of payment unless software resold
Hybrid Networks, Inc. AAER No. 1281, June 28, 2000	• Provided absolute right of return
Informix, Corp. AAER No. 1133, May 17, 1999	• Committed company to use its own sales force to find customers for reseller • Offered to assign future end-user orders to resellers • Extended payment terms beyond 12 months • Committed company to make future purchases from resellers under terms that effectively refunded license fees paid by them • Diverted company's own future service revenue to resellers as a means of refunding their license fees • Agreed to pay fictitious consulting or other fees to resellers to be repaid to the company as license fees
Insignia Solutions, PLC AAER No. 1215, January 11, 2000	• Provided more liberal rights of return
Kendall Square Research Corp. AAER No. 776, April 29, 1996	• Absolved customers of payment obligation if anticipated funding not received
KnowledgeWare, Inc. AAER No. 1179, September 28, 1999	• Provided unconditional right of return • Absolved reseller of payment unless software resold
McKesson HBOC AAER No. 1329, October 11, 2000	• Offered rights for continuing negotiation • Offered right to cancel agreement
Platinum Software Corp. AAER No. 780, May 9, 1996	• Offered right to cancel agreement
Scientific Software-Intercomp, Inc. AAER No. 1057, July 30, 1998	• Excused payment • Treated sales agreement as ineffective until goods resold

Source: SEC's Accounting and Auditing Enforcement Release (AAER) for the indicated date.

Interestingly, as seen in the exhibit, most of the companies with side agreements were in the software industry. It is unclear why the practice was so prevalent with software firms. Possibly the relative youth of the industry, the specialized nature of many software sales, and the very low cost of production for software products all played a role. Given the prevalence of software firms having difficulties with revenue recognition, it is not surprising that the software industry became the focus for revenue recognition enforcement actions by the SEC.

Rights of Return

Several of the companies providing side letters to their customers permitted liberal rights of return. There is nothing inherently wrong with recognizing revenue in the presence of a return privilege. Even with returns, persuasive evidence of a sales arrangement can exist. In fact, most sales provide for some form of return. However, several conditions must be met before revenue with a return privilege can be recognized. In order to recognize revenue in the presence of a right of return, the sales price must be fixed or determinable and payment cannot be contingent on resale. In addition, the buyer must be economically separate from the seller, the obligation to pay must not be affected by the theft or destruction of the product sold, and, importantly, the seller must be able to estimate future returns.[34]

General Motors Corp. provides return privileges and recognizes revenue at the time of sale. A provision for returns is recorded at that time. The company describes its revenue recognition policy as follows:

> Sales are generally recorded when products are shipped or when services are rendered to independent dealers or other third parties. Provisions for normal dealer sales incentives, returns and allowances, and GM Card rebates are made at the time of vehicle sales.[35]

The return privileges offered by companies that used side letters with rights of return were too liberal, effectively negating the sales. Also, it is likely that they were not reducing the amounts of revenue recognized for estimated future returns.

Even without side letters, however, companies can get into trouble recognizing revenue when return privileges are offered. Typically, the problem arises because insufficient provisions for returns are recorded. For example, Laser Photonics, Inc., did not provide sufficient amounts for estimated returns of its laser products. Then when products were returned, the company simply did not record credit memos for the returns.[36]

CUC International, Inc., a predecessor company to Cendant Corp., was effectively a club that sold shopping memberships. Much like estimated returns, with each membership sale the company would set aside a percentage to cover estimated cancellations. These estimated cancellations were properly excluded from revenue and were reported as part of the company's membership cancellation reserve, a liability account. When cancellations were received, they were charged against the cancellation reserve and had no effect on income.

At one point in the late 1980s, however, the company experienced an unexpected spike in cancellations that was outsized relative to the cancellation reserve. Rather than take a single charge to the reserve that would render it inadequate for future cancellations and require an accompanying charge to earnings, the company decided to hold the cancellations off-books for a month in order to smooth out its impact on the reserve. This decision served as a precedent, and the off-books lag increased in future periods as the company looked for opportunities to boost earnings.[37]

As devised, the company's policy was correct, and presumably an accurate amount was originally reported in its cancellation reserve. It was only after steps were taken to thwart this otherwise well-intentioned accounting practice that the company began to misstate its operating results.

Related-Party Revenue

Underlying the SEC's requirement for persuasive evidence of an arrangement before revenue can be recognized is the assumption that any sale agreement reached is the result of an arm's length transaction negotiated with a separate entity that can pursue its own interests. A related party is an entity whose management or operating policies can be controlled or significantly influenced. The related-party entity simply cannot pursue its own interests without considering those of the other party. Related parties include investees in whom a significant voting-share interest is held (typically 20% or more), trusts created for the benefit of employees, principal owners, management, and immediate family members of owners or management.

With related-party revenue, the issue is whether a sale would have taken place in the absence of the affiliation between the two parties. Has one party unduly pressured the other into the sales transaction? No stipulations in revenue recognition policy preclude the recognition of revenue in such related-party situations. What generally accepted accounting principles do call for is full disclosure. That is, in related-party transactions, a reporting company must disclose the nature of the relationship, a description of the transactions, their dollar amounts, their effects on the financial statements, and amounts due to and from the related parties.[38] Companies that have recognized revenue in related-party transactions without providing full disclosure of the relationship have drawn the attention of the enforcement division of the SEC.

CEC Industries Corp. was a Nevada corporation that had only limited sources of recurring revenue. Yet, in its fiscal year ended March 1996, sales revenue increased to $2,387,608 from $68,223 in 1995 and $600 in 1994. However, as was later determined, a substantial portion of the revenue reported in 1996 was the result of an asset exchange transaction with a related party. In the transaction, CEC transferred a parcel of vacant land to the related party in exchange for a promissory note collateralized by the company's preferred stock that was owned by the related party. CEC received no down payment for the purchase of land and had no reasonable basis to believe that the related party would pay for it. In the absence of a significant nonrefundable cash commitment on the part of the buyer, revenue should not have been recognized on this sale.[39] Compounding the problem, however, was the fact that, based on our reading of the company's 10-K annual report filing with the SEC for the year ended March 31, 1996, the related-party transaction was not disclosed. To a reader of the company's annual report, the sale looked like an arm's length transaction.

Lernout & Hauspie Speech Products NV (L&H) had a particularly promising software product for speech recognition. Moreover, the company's finances, as reported, reflected success. Revenue grew to $212 million in 1998 from $99 million in 1997 and surged again to $344 million in 1999. Profits, which had been elusive in years past, appeared for the first time in 1999 when the company reported net income of $42 million.[40] However, behind the rosy revenue figures were some troubling recognition practices involving related-party relationships.

For example, significant amounts of the company's revenue were for sales to some 30 start-up companies located in Singapore and Belgium. L&H helped found these start-ups. The company did maintain, however, that they were owned by independent investors who sought to use its software for new applications. As was later determined in an audit-committee report, most of these start-ups were not buying software licenses per se. Rather, they were paying L&H for products that had not yet been developed and were effectively paying to develop future products. The start-ups were thus funding L&H's research and development activities.

L&H also had a cozy relationship with a venture capital fund, Flanders Language Valley Fund, NV, which the founders of L&H helped to start. In instances documented in Lernout's audit committee report, L&H signed a contract for the sale of software to a customer shortly before the Flanders Fund invested in that same customer. Certainly L&H should have disclosed the related-party nature of this revenue.[41] To a discerning eye, the revenue did not have the same recurring prospects as revenue recognized from a self-financed, unrelated party. Future sales would likely lag if the Flanders Fund did not continue to provide financing.

Delivery Has Occurred or Services Have Been Rendered

This criterion of revenue recognition says effectively that revenue must be earned before it is recognized. Certainly the manner in which revenue is earned varies greatly depending on the nature of the product being sold or the service provided.

Sales Revenue

In the vast majority of cases in which products are sold, revenue is recognized at the time of shipment. Consider the revenue recognition policy employed by Hewlett-Packard Co.:

> Revenue from product sales is generally recognized at the time the product is shipped, with provisions established for price protection programs and for estimated product returns.[42]

The company recognizes revenue for product sales at the time of shipment, reducing the amount recognized for estimates of product returns. The provisions for price protection referred to in the note incorporate the effect on earnings of price concessions offered to resellers to account for price reductions occurring while inventory is held by them.

A policy of recognizing revenue for product sales at the time of shipment seems simple enough. However, it is interesting to see the extent to which variations on that theme, including some deceitful acts, are observed in practice.

Advanced Medical Products, Inc., often recorded revenue for what were referred to as "soft sales," or sales for which customers had expressed an interest but had not committed to a signed purchase order. Often, to facilitate revenue recognition, this equipment was shipped to field representatives or even to the company's corporate offices awaiting a firm order. However, on at least one occasion the company recorded a sales accrual for such a soft sale that was not even shipped. On other occasions the company recognized revenue for backordered equipment. These were legitimate orders for equipment that, due to a shortage of finished product, could not be filled. On still other occasions, the company was able to partially fill its orders with shipments, although revenue was recognized as if complete shipments had taken place.[43]

Laser Photonics, Inc., was in the process of developing a more powerful version of its standard medical laser. The company built prototypes of this laser, but they typically malfunctioned with use and were never put into commercial production. Yet, in 1992, the company accrued two sales of these new lasers. A commercial shipper picked up one of them at the company's facilities. Soon thereafter, however, the shipping instructions were canceled and the laser was returned. The company placed it in warranty repair status. The second laser was shipped to an airport warehouse and was also returned to the company. While a credit memo was promised to the purchaser, a credit was never issued.[44]

FastComm Communications Corp. manufactured analog and digital products to access computer networks. With a valid order in hand, the company recognized revenue on the shipment of product to a customer even though the product shipped did not have the full complement of memory chips ordered by the customer. While the company received payment for this order, revenue was not earned and should not have been recognized.[45]

Styles on Video, Inc., developed a system that permitted retail eyeglass customers to see how they would look when wearing varying eyeglass styles. To operate the system, the retailer would need to use proprietary software that the company sold on specialized access disks. Three days before the company's 1993 fiscal year end, it recognized revenue for a $500,000 sale of that software. The problem was that the software was not shipped and development was not complete.[46] Clearly, revenue was not earned in this case.

Bill-and-Hold Transactions   In some sales, a valid order is received and the goods are complete and ready for shipment. However, for various reasons—for example, a lack of available space or sufficient inventory in distribution channels—the customer may not be ready to take delivery. A bill-and-hold transaction is effected when an invoice is issued, but the goods in question are simply segregated outside of other inventory of the selling company or shipped to a warehouse for storage, awaiting customer instructions.

The SEC stipulates several criteria that must be met before revenue can be recognized in advance of shipment. These criteria, which are summarized in Exhibit 6.4, also would guide revenue recognition for bill-and-hold transactions.

Thus, assuming that the exhibit criteria are satisfied, revenue can be recognized in bill-and-hold transactions. Problems do arise, however, when companies take shortcuts with some of the criteria specified by the SEC. Consider the case of Sunbeam Corp. The consumer products company employed extensive use of bill-and-hold practices as a sales promotion campaign. During 1997 the company sold barbecue grills to retailers at

---

Exhibit 6.4 Criteria for Recognizing Revenue in Advance of Shipment

1. The risks of ownership have passed to the buyer.
2. The customer must have made a fixed commitment to purchase the goods, preferably in written documentation.
3. The buyer, not the seller, must request that the transaction be on a bill-and-hold basis. The buyer must have a substantial business purpose for ordering the goods on a bill and hold basis.
4. There must be a fixed schedule for delivery of the goods. The date for delivery must be reasonable and must be consistent with the buyer's business purpose.
5. The seller must not have retained any specific performance obligations such that the earning process is not complete.
6. The ordered goods must have been segregated from the seller's inventory and not be subject to being used to fill other orders.
7. The goods must be complete and ready for shipment.

Source: Staff Accounting Bulletin No. 101, *Revenue Recognition in Financial Statements* (Washington, D.C.: Securities and Exchange Commission, December 3, 1999).

---

bargain prices before the normal buying season for such products. The company had an agreement with its customers that it would deliver the goods as its customers requested them. These transactions failed most of the criteria used by the SEC to regulate revenue recognition in bill-and-hold situations. In effect, Sunbeam was using the deals to recognize revenue prematurely, borrowing sales from the first and second quarters of 1998.[47]

As another example of the improper use of bill-and-hold transactions, consider Digital Lightwave, Inc. On the last day of the quarter in June 1997, the company recognized revenue of $1.5 million for 40 units of a 60-unit order. The sale comprised 28% of the company's revenue for the quarter. Bill-and-hold accounting treatment was used as the goods were not shipped at the time of recognition. The bill-and-hold treatment accorded the sale was based on the terms and conditions contained in a letter from the company's customer. However, that letter was dated July 3, 1997, a date that was after revenue from the sale had already been recognized.

There were many things wrong with this transaction, not the least of which was the fact that the goods were not shipped and the customer's letter supposedly arranging bill-and-hold treatment was received after the quarter had ended. However, even if the letter had been received before the quarter's end, its terms did not support bill-and-hold treatment. For example, the letter did not specify that the risk of ownership had passed to the customer. In addition, it was the company and not the customer that had decided to structure the transaction as bill and hold. Further, the goods were not complete at the time of sale and could not have been shipped even if the customer wanted them. In fact, there was no scheduled delivery date and payment had not been arranged. Revenue under the terms of a bill-and-hold transaction should not have been recognized.[48]

Customer Acceptance   In some sales, uncertainty may exist about customer acceptance of the product sold. For example, the customer may have the right to test the delivered product or to require the seller to perform additional services subsequent to delivery, or identify other work that must be done before accepting the product. To be effective, these conditions must be part and parcel of any sales agreement. Generally, revenue should not be recognized until all conditions of acceptance are satisfied or the rejection period has lapsed.

Adac Laboratories, Inc., sold nuclear-medicine devices used to diagnose cancer and heart disease. Upon receipt of a valid order, the company traditionally recognized revenue at the time of shipment. However, its customers were not obligated to pay for the equipment purchased until it was installed and working properly. Frequently this was several months later. In a change of accounting for revenue that led to a restatement of its results for 1996 and 1997, the company moved to recognize revenue more slowly, appropriately factoring in the installation process.[49]

As another example, the mode of operations for Advanced Medical Products, Inc., was to ship product, pursuant to customer orders, to field representatives who were responsible for equipment installation and training. The company recognized revenue at the time of shipment from its warehouse to its field representative. However, at that point, revenue was not earned. The equipment was not installed and training had not taken place. Even worse, the customer had not taken possession of the products ordered.[50]

Service Revenue

Often a revenue transaction entails the provision of a service as opposed to the sale of a product. Here revenue recognition is dependent on completion of the promised services. For example, as stated in the Raytheon Co. annual report:

> Service revenue is recognized ratably over contractual periods or as services are performed.[51]

While, as with Raytheon, recognizing service revenue may appear to be straightforward, measuring the provision of service can become quite complicated. Consider the case of MicroStrategy, Inc. The company was accused by the SEC of prematurely recording revenue from software sales by "booking sales before determining the full extent of services it would have to provide in connection with those sales."[52] That is, in addition to its software product, which the company had in fact shipped, it also provided other services related to a software sale. The company divided its contracts for software and services into separate elements, recording revenue up front on some of them while deferring revenue on others. After being investigated by the SEC, the company changed its policy and began to defer revenue on all such contracts, recognizing it over the contract term. In the view of the SEC, the company earned its revenue on these contracts over time. The effect on the company's financial position was significant, shaving approximately $50 million from revenue for 1999. The company's share price dropped 62% with the announcement of the accounting change and, as of this writing, had not recovered. Interestingly, the share-price decline occurred in spite of the fact that the company expected no material change in its operating cash flow or the amount of revenue it ultimately expected to recognize. Clearly, the actual amount of revenue recognized in any one period is important to market participants.

Up-front Service Fees   Some firms collect up-front fees for services to be provided over extended periods. As the related services are provided over time, revenue should be deferred and recognized as services are provided. In recent years there have been many examples where revenue related to up-front service fees has not been recognized over time. However, pursuant to the SEC's new statement on revenue recognition, SAB 101, these firms are changing their methods of accounting for such up-front service fees. Membership shopping clubs are a case in point. Consider the recent change in accounting for membership fees announced by BJ's Wholesale Club, Inc.:

> During the fiscal year ended January 30, 1999, the Company adopted changes in methods of accounting for membership fee revenues and preopening expenses. The Company had previously recognized membership fee revenues as income when received. Under its new accounting method, the Company now recognizes membership fee revenues as income over the life of the membership, which is typically twelve months.[53]

The significant impact that deferral can have on the amount of revenue recognized in any one period is made clear in disclosures provided by Costco Wholesale Corp.:

> Membership fee revenue represents annual membership fees paid by substantially all of the Company's members. In accordance with historical and industry practice, annual membership fees are recognized as income when received. Effective with the first quarter of fiscal 1999, the Company will change its method of accounting for membership fee income from a "cash basis", which historically has been consistent with generally accepted accounting principles and industry practice, to a "deferred basis."
>
> If the deferred method (assuming ratable recognition over the one year life of the membership) had been used in fiscal 1998, net income would have been $444,451,000 or $1.96 per share (diluted). The Company has decided to make this change in anticipation of the issuance of a new Securities and Exchange Commission (SEC) Staff Accounting Bulletin regarding the recognition of membership fee income.
>
> The change to the deferred method of accounting for membership fees will result in a one-time, non-cash, pre-tax charge of approximately $197,000,000 ($118,000,000 after-tax, or $.50 per share) to reflect the cumulative effect of the accounting change as of the beginning of fiscal 1999 and assuming that membership fee income is recognized ratably over the one year life of the membership.[54]

Using disclosures provided by the company, net income in 1998 of $459,842,000 under its former policy of immediate recognition of up-front membership fees would be reduced to $444,451,000 under the new deferral policy. Also noteworthy was the cumulative effect of the change on earnings of prior years. That amount, $118,000,000 after tax, also would serve to reduce shareholders' equity.

While not a membership shopping club, Maxim Group, Inc., also collected up-front fees for service. As part of an announcement of a restatement of its results for the year ended January 31, 1999, the flooring retailer indicated that it was changing its method of recognizing revenue for funds received from suppliers who paid for shelf space at the company's stores. Historically, the company had recognized such fees up-front, at the time of receipt. With the change, however, the company would defer such revenue, recognizing it over the time period covered by the shelf-space agreement. This latter policy is consistent with the SEC's preferred accounting for such fees.

Finance-Related Income   Closely related to service revenue is finance-related income. Like other industries, this industry is not immune to revenue recognition problems.

Green Tree Financial Corp., like other subprime lenders, enjoyed a remarkable financial ride during the mid-1990's. Subprime lenders funded loans to borrowers of lower credit standing to facilitate purchases of such durable goods as used cars and mobile homes. Green Tree was primarily a mobile-home lender. The company would finance the purchase of mobile homes by individuals from dealers. After making a large number of such loans, the company would package and sell them to investors as loan-backed securities. The company would continue to service the underlying loans, collecting interest and principal from the borrowers and remitting a portion of that interest and the underlying principal to its investors. At the time of sale, the company would use gain-on-sale accounting. It would record as profit the excess of (1) the sales price and the present value of the estimated interest income that it expected to receive on the loans above the amounts funded on the loans over (2) the present value of the interest they had agreed to pay the buyers of the loan-backed securities. When properly executed, there is nothing inherently wrong with this process. However, Green Tree, like other subprime lenders, was somewhat aggressive in the assumptions used in calculating the present value of the amount of interest to be received. These assumptions included such subjective estimates as the rate of default by the underlying borrowers, the rate at which the loans were repaid, and the interest rate used in calculating present value. By aggressively understating the default rate, repayment rate, and interest rate used to discount the resulting payment stream, the company was able to report a higher gain on the sale of the packaged loans. As a result, that gain on sale was overstated.[55] More conservative assumptions would have led to a lower up-front gain amount. If collection experience subsequently showed these assumptions to be overly conservative, then additional income could have been recognized at that later point.

Xerox Corp. also has had financial reporting problems related to premature revenue recognition. The company often uses sales-type lease accounting to account for shipments of its copiers and other office equipment placed on long-term leases. In a sales-type lease, a manufacturer, such as Xerox, records up-front gross profit for the excess of the present value of the lease payments to be received across a lease term over the cost to manufacture the leased equipment. Interest income also is recognized on the lease receivable as it is earned over the lease term. Assumptions about the interest rate that is used to calculate the present value of the lease payments to be received impacts directly the amount of gross profit that can be recognized when a lease is signed and the amount of interest income recognized over the lease term. Higher interest rates result in lower present value amounts and lower up-front profit measures with correspondingly higher interest income measures over the lease term. However, as the assumed interest rate is lowered, the present value of the lease payment stream is increased, raising the amount of up-front gross profit recognized and lowering the amount of interest income recorded over the lease term.

Many of Xerox's leasing customers were located in Latin America, where the rate of inflation was high. High rates of inflation called for the use of higher interest rates in calculating present value. In an aggressive fashion, however, Xerox used interest rate-assumptions that were too low for the circumstances, permitting the company to recognize higher amounts of up-front profit.[56] A portion of this profit was recognized prematurely and should have been recorded as interest income over the lease terms.

Revenue Recognition by Certain E-Commerce Firms   Until the bubble burst in spring of 2000, e-commerce firms, or "dot-coms" as they were commonly called, reaped rich valuations that were calculated as multiples of revenue. While these companies reported recurring losses, investors reasoned that as long as revenue continued to grow rapidly, profits would materialize eventually.

Revenue still plays a principal role in the valuation of these companies. Given its significance, it is especially important for revenue to be properly reported. For the majority of e-commerce firms, revenue recognition is straightforward. Revenue for product sales is recognized on shipment. Advertising revenue and revenue for other services are recognized when the services are provided. Consider the revenue recognition policy employed by the online auction firm EBay, Inc.:

> Online transaction revenues are derived primarily from placement fees charged for the listing of items on the EBay service and success fees calculated as a percentage of the final sales transaction value. Revenues related to placement fees are recognized at the time the item is listed, while those related to success fees are recognized at the time that the transaction is successfully concluded. A transaction is considered successfully concluded when at least one buyer has bid above the seller's specified minimum price or reserve price, whichever is higher, at the end of the transaction term.[57]

The company did note that as a result of SAB 101, it would recognize placement fee revenue over an auction transaction's term.

For some firms in this sector, however, there are questions surrounding revenue recognition practices. The concerns center on whether some companies with only a tangential role in the sale of a product may be grossing up revenue. When an e-commerce firm arranges an online transaction between a buyer and seller, the key question that arises is whether that firm should be permitted to report an amount paid by a buyer as revenue and an amount paid to a seller as cost of sales. Instead, it is thought that only a sales agent's commission should be reported for arranging the transaction.

The Emerging Issues Task Force of the FASB addressed the topic and decided that in order to be able to recognize revenue and cost of sales rather than just an agent's commission, a firm must be fully involved in a purchase and sale transaction. As such, the firm actually would purchase a product from a manufacturer or supplier at a negotiated price, take title to the product, establish a sales price and shipping charge, arrange for shipment, assume credit risk for collection and collect payment, ensure that products reach their customers, and process returns. If an e-commerce firm is not fulfilling these actions, then it is acting more as a sales agent, arranging a transaction between a buyer and seller, for which only a commission should be recorded.[58]

Two companies that have been singled out in this debate are Ventro Corp. and Price-line.com, Inc.[59] Ventro handles web sales of specialty medical products and medical research goods. The company maintains that it fulfills all of the requirements for recognizing revenue and cost of goods sold in the transactions it arranges. However, the company does admit that it takes title to products sold for only a very short time, usually the time it takes to complete shipment. Also, suppliers typically determine prices in negotiations with customers and tend to absorb the costs of returns. Finally, credit risk is next to nil because of the high credit quality of the companies involved. Priceline.com arranges online sales of discounted airline tickets. The company maintains that it does buy the tickets it sells and bears the cost of refunds. The risk of ownership and resale is not too high, however, because the company only takes into inventory tickets that it knows will be resold.

Both companies, Ventro Corp. and Priceline.com, may be correct in their self-assessments of revenue recognition practices. Undoubtedly it will take time for the industry to mature and for revenue recognition practices to become clearer and more generally accepted. More is said about this topic in Chapter 9.

Contract Accounting

When an extended period is required for completion of a product or service, contract accounting is commonly called for. While often contract accounting is considered relevant only for construction contractors, it is needed in many industries, including railroads, shipbuilding, road construction, various types of equipment manufacturers, engineering, and software.[60]

With contract accounting, revenue is recognized in one of two ways: (1) the percentage-of-completion method, which recognizes revenue as progress is made toward completion, and (2) the completed-contract method, which recognizes revenue when a contract is complete. The percentage-of-completion method is the more popular of the two and should be used when reasonably dependable estimates of progress toward completion, contract revenue, and contract costs can be made.[61] The completed-contract method is the default method and is reserved for those limited instances when dependable estimates of progress toward completion, contract revenue, and contract costs cannot be made. According to available data, in the United States the completed-contract method is used in approximately 3% of all contracts.[62]

Note that with the percentage-of-completion method, revenue is recognized even before a product or service is formally delivered. The contractor recognizes revenue as progress is made toward completion. Estimates of progress must be made and typically are based on costs incurred as a percentage of total estimated contract costs. As the contractor makes progress toward completion, costs incurred plus profit recognized, which have not been billed, are recorded as a current asset, commonly referred to as cost plus estimated earnings in excess of billings or, more simply, unbilled accounts receivable. As billing takes place, unbilled accounts receivable are reduced and accounts receivable are recorded.

The percentage-of-completion method can be abused by anyone interested in misleading financial statement readers. Aggressive estimates of progress toward completion can be made by increasing the costs incurred on a contract or through overly optimistic estimates of the costs to complete one (i.e., underestimating total contract costs). Either way, the completion percentage will appear to be higher, permitting the accelerated recognition of contract revenue.

For example, 3Net Systems, Inc., developed computer laboratory software that required considerable development for each customer installation. On several occasions the company applied the percentage-of-completion method to recognize software revenue. However, the company misrepresented its progress toward completion and overstated the amount of revenue recognized.[63]

In an example of fictitious revenue recognition under the percentage-of-completion method, consider the vintage and infamous case of Stirling Homex Corp. The company recognized ever-increasing amounts of revenue as it made progress toward completion of contracts for the modular housing units it manufactured.[64] The problem was that it did not have valid contracts for these units and simply was completing them and shipping them to remote sites for storage.

The Seller's Price to the Buyer Is Fixed or Determinable

Certainly in the vast majority of revenue transactions, there exists an agreed-on price for a provided product or service. Before revenue can be recognized, that fee must be a set amount that is not subject to refund or adjustment.

Consider the revenue generated by membership shopping clubs mentioned earlier. While a membership fee is paid up front, many of these clubs allow customers to cancel their memberships at any time during a membership term for a full refund of the fee paid. A strict interpretation of SAB 101 would say that because of the extended refund period, the membership fee is not determinable until the end of the membership period when the refund option expires. Revenue in such a transaction should be deferred until the end of the membership period. The SEC did, however, soften its stance on this position. If the amount of a membership fee, exclusive of expected refunds, was fixed and reliable, estimates of refunds could be made for a large pool of homogeneous members on a timely basis using company-specific historical data, then membership fee revenue could be recognized over a membership term.[65]

In some transactions, a customer may be given a payment term that extends over a substantial portion of the period during which the customer is expected to use or market the related products. The concern here is that the underlying product's continuing value may be reduced due to the subsequent introduction of enhanced products by the vendor or its competitors. As a result, the vendor may be under pressure to offer the customer price concessions, refunds, or new products. In such situations, especially when the payment term extends beyond one year, revenue should not be recognized by the seller until collection is made.

In other transactions, a customer may be permitted to exchange a purchased product for another product over some extended period. As with extended payment terms, in the presence of such an exchange option, the original sales price cannot be considered fixed or determinable.

In the earlier section on revenue recognition in the presence of side letters, we saw many examples of side letters to sales agreements that negated the fixed price provisions of SAB 101. Examples noted in Exhibit 6.3 include Cylink Corp., which provided the right to exchange software products for hardware, Engineering Animation, Inc., which absolved its resellers of any payment responsibility unless the software was resold, Informix Corp., which extended payment terms beyond 12 months, and Kendall Square Research Corp., which absolved customers of their payment obligations if anticipated funding was not received.

Collectibility Is Reasonably Assured

Closely related to a fixed or determinable sales price is the issue of whether the sales price is collectible or not. Collectibility hinges first and foremost on the transacting of business with a creditworthy customer. For example, Alias Research, Inc., recorded $1.5 million in revenue, its fourth largest sale ever, from the sale of software to a reseller that did not have the ability to pay. In other transactions, Alias agreed not to collect payment and to attempt to obtain financing for customers, which was unlikely.[66]

Profit Recovery Group International, Inc., provides services designed to recover over-payments made to vendors for its clients. These overpayments might be due to such factors as missed price concessions or errors. When the company detects a mistaken payment, it notifies its client and records revenue for an amount equal to 30% to 50% of the amount to be recovered. The client then seeks a refund from its vendor, a process that can take up to a year to complete. Profit Recovery gets paid only after its client successfully collects the refund. There is, of course, an issue of collectibility here. For example, the vendor may have a legitimate defense, negating the refund. Moreover, given the extended period that exists between revenue recognition and collection, general uncertainties call collection into question.[67]

Boston Chicken, Inc., used a franchise system to grow its revenue stream quickly. However, the company itself financed the costs of initial franchise fees and store construction for its franchisees. The poor financial performance of its franchised stores called into question the collectibility of those loans and whether initial franchise revenue should have been recognized.[68]

Beyond the issue of whether a customer is creditworthy or not, collectibility can be questioned when customers are given payment terms that extend beyond one year or when collection is tied to some other event, such as the resale of the product or receipt of anticipated funding. Examples of these acts seen earlier include many of the companies reported in Exhibit 6.3, such as Engineering Animation, Inc., Informix Corp., and Kendall Square Research Corp.

DETECTING PREMATURE OR FICTITIOUS REVENUE

A careful analysis can be helpful in detecting revenue that has been recognized in a premature or fictitious manner. Steps that are particularly useful in this regard are outlined below. These steps also may prove helpful in detecting revenue that has been recognized properly but whose sustainability nonetheless can be questioned.

Understand the Policy for Revenue Recognition

It is very easy to avoid a careful read of the footnotes that accompany an annual report. The small print and accompanying accounting terminology make the reading dense and slow-going. The notes, however, are a treasure trove of information about the company and the manner in which it accounts for the business it transacts. In particular, the first footnote, the accounting policy note, is a must-read. Among the accounting policies employed will be a company's disclosed method of revenue recognition.

In reading the revenue recognition note, it is important to understand when during the term of a sale or service transaction revenue is recognized. For example, is revenue recognized before delivery or performance? If so, it is important to determine whether the revenue is, in fact, earned or not. Is it recognized at the time of delivery or performance? An affirmative response would help assuage questions about whether the revenue is earned. However, if some significant effort remains open, such as installation, training, or other post-sale support, then it is reasonable to expect that some portion of the revenue should be deferred. Is there a right of return or price protection? Has the company provided for potential returns? For price protection, which grants customers automatic refunds or credits for declines in market prices, have sufficient allowances been made? It is important to note that the more that estimates are used in the recognition of revenue—for example, in determining the amount of revenue to defer for installation, training, or other post-sale support, or in measuring the amounts of potential returns, or in calculating allowances for price protection—the more open that revenue becomes to creative accounting practices. Beyond these questions, it is important to note whether there has been a change in the manner in which revenue is recognized. If so, is it now being recognized earlier than before or later? Why is that?

Answering these questions will provide a better understanding of a company's revenue recognition policy. With a better understanding, questionable revenue recognition practices can be detected more readily.

Earlier we looked at Profit Recovery Group International, Inc., which provides services designed to recover for its clients overpayments made to vendors. For example, Kmart Corp. mistakenly may not have received a purchase discount to which it was entitled. Through its specialized group of auditors, Profit Recovery would determine and inform Kmart that it has overpaid a particular vendor. Kmart would then bill that vendor for the amount of overpayment. Until its policy was changed in 1999, Profit Recovery recorded revenue for the transaction, typically at 30% to 50% of the amount to be recovered, at the time it notified Kmart of the overpayment. Revenue was recognized at this early point even though Profit Recovery did not bill Kmart for its services and also did not expect payment until its client collected the overcharge, which could take as long as one year.

Before changing its policy, Profit Recovery provided the following revenue recognition note:

> . . . the Company recognizes revenues at the time overpayment claims are presented to and approved by its clients, as adjusted for estimated uncollectible claims. . . . the Company believes that it has completed substantially all contractual obligations to its client at the time an identified and documented claim which satisfies all client-imposed guidelines is pre-

sented to, and approved by, appropriate client personnel. The Company further believes that at the time a claim is submitted and accepted by its client, such claim represents a valid overpayment due to the client from its vendor.[69]

A careful review and understanding of such a note, possibly supplemented with a clarification from company management, would alert the reader to the substantial time period and related uncertainty for collection that remained at the time the company recognized revenue. It was this very uncertainty that led the Center for Financial Research and Analysis, among others, to question the policy.[70] These questions likely encouraged the company to change its policy, a change that led to an after-tax charge of $29.2 million in 1999.

Watch Accounts Receivable

Often, revenue that is recognized in a premature or fictitious manner is not collected.[71] Accordingly, a balance sheet account, other than cash, will increase as this revenue is recognized. Typically that balance sheet account is accounts receivable.[72] It is important to keep this relationship in mind because unusual increases in accounts receivable commonly accompany questionable revenue, whether due to uncertainties about the earnings process or about collectibility.

Recall that Sunbeam Corp. used aggressive accounting tactics, including a questionable bill-and-hold scheme, to boost revenue in 1997. In a bill-and-hold arrangement, while recognized, revenue collection is delayed. Accordingly, one should see an accompanying increase in accounts receivable. Annual sales and accounts receivable data, together with annual rates of change and days accounts receivable (A/R days), are provided in Exhibit 6.5.

As seen in the exhibit, the noteworthy growth in sales of 18.7% in 1997 over 1996 was accompanied by a 38.5% increase in accounts receivable. As a result, A/R days increased to 92.3 days in 1997 from 79.2 days in 1996. Even if the company were not recognizing revenue prematurely, at a minimum, questions regarding the collectibility of its accounts receivable should be raised.

Quarterly data are useful for more timely evaluations of revenue recognition practices. In 1994 an investigation into the accounting practices at California Micro Devices Corp. found that significant amounts of fictitious revenue had been recognized. In fact, as much as one-third of the company's revenue for 1994 was fictitious. To determine the extent to which these erroneous amounts could be detected, quarterly sales and accounts receivable data, together with quarterly rates of change and A/R days, are provided in Exhibit 6.6. The data provided are through the quarter ending March 1994, the latest quarter for which data were available prior to a restatement of the company's results.

Note the significant buildup in accounts receivable as the company became more aggressive in its revenue recognition policies. In most of the quarters for which data are presented in the exhibit, accounts receivable grew more quickly than sales. The end result was an unsustainable increase in A/R days. This was true particularly in fiscal 1994 when accounts receivable showed a dramatic bulge.

As seen in Exhibit 6.6, it is difficult to overstate the importance of checking the level of A/R days. An increase in accounts receivable that is faster than an increase in revenue

---

Exhibit 6.5   Sunbeam Corp., Selected Account Balances and Statistics, Years Ending December 31, 1995, 1996, and 1997 (thousands of dollars, except days and percentage amounts)

	1995	1996	1997
Revenue	$1,016,883	$984,236	$1,168,182
Percent increase (decrease) from prior year	—	(3.2%)	18.7%
Accounts receivable	$216,195	$213,438	$295,550
Percent increase (decrease) from prior year	—	(1.3%)	38.5%
A/R days[a]	77.6	79.2	92.3

[a]A/R days calculated by dividing accounts receivable by revenue per day, where revenue per day is revenue divided by 365.

Source: Data obtained from Disclosure, Inc., *Compact D/SEC: Corporate Information on Public Companies Filing with the SEC* (Bethesda, MD: Disclosure, Inc., December 2000). Amounts reported are as originally filed and do not reflect the effects of any restatements.

Exhibit 6.6   California Micro Devices Corp., Selected Quarterly Account Balances and Statistics, Years Ending June 30, 1993 and 1994 (thousands of dollars, except days and percentage amounts)

	Fiscal Year 1993				Fiscal Year 1994		
	Sept.	Dec.	Mar.	June	Sept.	Dec.	Mar.
Revenue	$7,564	$8,173	$8,237	$9,033	$9,315	$10,212	$11,341
Percent increase from prior quarter	—	8.1%	.8%	9.7%	3.1%	9.6%	11.1%
Accounts receivable	$8,449	$9,916	$10,531	$12,341	$12,647	$16,997	$19,386
Percent increase from prior quarter	—	17.4%	6.2%	17.2%	2.5%	34.4%	14.1%
A/R days[a]	101.9	110.7	116.7	124.7	123.9	151.9	156.0

[a]Quarterly A/R days calculated by dividing accounts receivable by quarterly revenue per day, where quarterly revenue per day is quarterly revenue divided by 91.25.

Source: Data obtained from Disclosure, Inc., *Compact D/SEC: Corporate Information on Public Companies Filing with the SEC* (Bethesda, MD: Disclosure, Inc., December 2000). Amounts reported are as originally filed and do not reflect the effects of any restatements.

is not a problem if it is for only a limited period and does not result in a collection period for accounts receivable that is significantly at odds with the credit terms being offered. In the exhibit, accounts receivable increased faster than revenue for several quarters. By the end of the March quarter 1994, A/R days had increased to 156.0 days, indicating that the company was taking approximately five months to collect its outstanding invoices. It would be hard for most companies to justify such an extended collection period.

A significant buildup in accounts receivable also would have highlighted the aggressive revenue recognition practices at Cylink Corp. As a result of these aggressive practices, the company was forced by the SEC to restate results for the year ending December 1997 and quarters ending March 1998 and June 1998.[73] Annual and quarterly sales and accounts receivable data, together with quarterly rates of change and A/R days for the company, are provided in Exhibit 6.7.

As can be seen in the exhibit, Cylink Corp. struggled to maintain sales levels in the quarters ending March 31, 1998, and June 30, 1998, that were on par with results posted for 1997. Nonetheless, accounts receivable grew faster than sales, resulting in an increase in A/R days to very high levels.

Exhibit 6.7   Cylink Corp., Selected Account Balances and Statistics, Year Ending December 31, 1997, Quarters Ending March 31, 1998, and June 30, 1998 (thousands of dollars, except days and percentage amounts)

	Year Ending December 31,		Quarter Ending March 31,		Quarter Ending June 30,	
	1996	**1997**	**1997**	**1998**	**1997**	**1998**
Revenue	$25,793	$49,333	$16,182	$15,829	$18,269	$18,035
Percent increase (decrease) from prior year	—	91.3%	—	(2.2%)	—	(1.3%)
Accounts receivable	$12,682	26,245	$14,017	$21,840	$17,242	$28,430
Percent increase (decrease) from prior year	—	107.0%	—	55.8%	—	64.9%
Days A/R[a]	179.5	194.2	79.0	125.9	86.1	143.8

[a]Annual A/R days calculated by dividing accounts receivable by annual revenue per day, where annual revenue per day is annual revenue divided by 365. Quarterly A/R days calculated by dividing accounts receivable by quarterly revenue per day, where quarterly revenue per day is quarterly revenue divided by 91.25.

Source: Data obtained from 10-Q quarterly reports with the Securities and Exchange Commission and Disclosure, Inc., *Compact D/SEC: Corporate Information on Public Companies Filing with the SEC* (Bethesda, MD: Disclosure, Inc., December 2000). Amounts reported are as originally filed and do not reflect the effects of any restatements.

Steps Taken to Thwart Detection

Depending on their willingness to deceive financial statement readers, managers who take steps to recognize revenue prematurely or fictitiously also may attempt to cover up their acts. Aware that analysts will look for sustained relationships between sales and accounts receivable as part of their search for questionable revenue, unscrupulous managers may record artificial adjustments to accounts receivable to keep them in line.

Such steps were taken at Comptronix, Inc., during a financial reporting fraud that ran from 1987 to 1991. Company management transferred amounts from accounts receivable to property, plant, and equipment using an elaborate deposit mechanism arranged with a local bank. The scheme made it appear as if accounts receivable were being collected and that the cash was being used to buy new equipment.

Interestingly, even though accounts receivable was kept somewhat in line, other accounts grew by fictitious amounts. In this case the property, plant, and equipment line item, relative to sales, grew to a distorted amount. Over the time period covered by the reporting fraud at the company, property, plant, and equipment grew 24% faster than sales. Sales divided by property, plant, and equipment declined accordingly. When the fraud was discovered in 1991, the company reported property, plant, and equipment relative to sales that was 2.2 times the normal amount implied by industry norms.[74]

It is important to remember that when revenue is recognized in a premature or fictitious manner, one or more accounts on the balance sheet must increase by a corresponding amount. If accounts receivable is not used, then some other account must be selected. Typically, the related balance sheet accounts used are not cash or investments, because these accounts are more amenable to a precise verification. Another unlikely candidate is inventory, because analysts will readily pick up problems as the reporting company's investment in inventory grows to an outsize amount relative to its sales. The more likely accounts to be used are the property, plant, and equipment accounts and other assets, which can include anything from prepaid expenses to land held for sale. These accounts tend not to be examined as carefully and as routinely as inventory and accounts receivable.

Companies also might offset an improper increase in revenue with a decrease in any number of liability accounts. Such an approach would be rare, however, because as revenue is increased, a liability would need to be reduced, eventually to zero, necessitating the use of some other account.

Thus, in detecting premature or fictitious revenue, it is important to remember that any balance sheet account—in particular accounts receivable and possibly property, plant, and equipment, and other assets—is a potential storage location for misreported amounts. Care should be taken in evaluating relationships among these accounts, in particular their relationship to revenue and their rate of change relative to the rate of change in revenue. Calculated relationships (e.g., revenue divided by property, plant, and equipment) with revenue should be compared with industry norms and amounts for competitors. Explanations should be obtained for significant differences. In Chapters 7 and 8 we look at the valuation of other assets and liabilities and consider how they might be misstated, whether or not due to premature or fictitious revenue.

Consider Physical Capacity

Another factor to consider in evaluating whether revenue is premature or fictitious is whether the reporting company has the physical capacity to generate the amount of revenue being reported. Admittedly, a check on measures of revenue to physical capacity will be sensitive only to the more egregious cases of fictitious revenue recognition.

Consider the example of Flight Transportation, Inc., an air charter carrier. In 1980 and 1981 the company recorded flights that were not made and overstated tourist charter revenue by 62% and 54%, respectively. The president of another air charter company that Flight Transportation sought to acquire questioned how Flight Transportation had the physical capacity to generate the amount of air charter revenue that it was reporting. He decided not to sell his company. As was later learned, Flight Transportation reported that it had flown 120 flights in 1980, 12 during the first three quarters and 109 during the fourth quarter, a next-to-impossible feat given the size of the company's fleet. [75]

In this example, calculating revenue per plane would have been helpful in surfacing serious questions. With other companies in varying industries, different measures of physical capacity will be appropriate. For retailers, revenue per square foot of retail space would make sense. For real estate management companies, revenue per square foot of leased space would be appropriate. For other companies, it might be revenue per employee or revenue per property, plant, and equipment, or even total assets. The proper measure to use would depend on the company and the circumstances. Note that a routine calculation of revenue in relationship to the amount of property, plant, and equipment would have helped to surface the problems at Comptronix, Inc., referred to earlier.

CHECKLIST TO DETECT PREMATURE OR FICTITIOUS REVENUE

A checklist of items to consider in detecting premature or fictitious revenue is provided in Exhibit 6.8. While the questions are simple, many requiring only a yes or no answer, they are designed to require thought, necessitating that the reader consider all aspects of the financial statements and footnotes. In answering them, examples presented in the chapter should be considered so that the reader is more attuned to the implications of the answers provided for the possibility of premature or fictitious revenue.

Exhibit 6.8   Checklist to Detect Premature or Fictitious Revenue

A. What is the company's revenue recognition policy?
   1. Before delivery or performance?
      a. Is it really earned?
   2. At delivery or performance?
      a. Is there a right of return or price protection?
         i.   Has the company provided adequately for returns or price adjustments?

(continues)

Exhibit 6.8 *(Continued)*

---

    b. Does the company offer side letters offering a right of return or price protection not contained in the actual sale contract?

      i. Do side letters effectively negate the sale?

  3. After delivery or performance and full customer acceptance?

B. Was there a change in the revenue recognition policy?

  1. Did the change result in earlier revenue recognition?

C. Are there any unusual changes in revenue reported in recent quarters?

  1. What is revenue for each of the last four to six quarters?

  2. Does any one quarter show unusual activity not explained by seasonal factors?

  3. How do quarterly changes in revenue compare with the industry or selected competitors?

    a. For companies with a strong seasonal effect, changes in quarterly revenue should be calculated using amounts taken from the same quarter of the previous year.

    b. If quarterly data are not available, or if quarterly data give misleading signals, annual data can be used. Three or more years of data should provide a sufficient number of data points to get a meaningful indicator of potential problems.

D. Review disclosures of related-party transactions.

  1. Is there evidence of significant related-party revenue?

    a. Is this revenue sustainable?

E. Does the company have the physical capacity to generate the revenue reported?

  1. What is revenue per appropriate measure of physical capacity for each of the last four to six quarters?

  2. How do the measures compare with the industry or with selected competitors?

    a. Possible measures of revenue per physical capacity:

      i. Revenue per employee

      ii. Revenue per dollar of property, plant, and equipment

      iii. Revenue per dollar of total assets

      iv. Revenue per square foot of retail or rental space

F. Are there signs of overstated accounts receivable or other accounts that might be used to offset premature or fictitious revenue?

  1. Compare the percentage rate of change in accounts receivable, property, plant, and equipment, and other assets with the percentage rate of change in revenue for each of the last four to six quarters.

    a. What are the implications of differences in the rates of change in these accounts and revenue?

  2. Consider whether unexplained changes in other asset or liability accounts might be explained by premature or fictitious revenue.

  3. Compute A/R days for each of the last four to six quarters.

    a. What are the implications of changes noted in A/R days over the last four to six quarters?

Exhibit 6.8 *(Continued)*

---

     b. How does the absolute level of A/R days and changes therein compare with the industry and selected competitors?

G. Does the company use the percentage-of-completion method for long-term contracts?

    1. Is management experienced in applying the method?

    2. Has the company reported losses in prior years from cost overruns?

    3. Depending on data availability, compare the percentage rate of change in unbilled accounts receivable with the percentage rate of change in contract revenue for each of the last four to six quarters.

        a. If unbilled accounts receivable is increasing faster than contract revenue, it implies that amounts recognized as revenue are not being billed.

           i. Is there a particular reason why amounts recognized as revenue are not being billed?

          ii. Note that for some contractors, quarterly data may give misleading signals. Certain key contract benchmarks may not have been met during the quarter, limiting amounts billed over that short of a time frame. In these cases, annual data should be used.

SUMMARY

Given its importance to earning power and corporate valuation, it is not surprising that revenue recognition plays a significant role in the financial numbers game. Accordingly, the SEC often focuses its enforcement actions on premature and fictitious revenue recognition. Using many of these enforcement actions supplemented with examples from other sources, this chapter looks at the broad topic of revenue recognition, including when it should be recognized and the steps companies might take to recognize it in a premature or fictitious manner. Key points raised in the chapter include the following:

- Premature revenue entails revenue recognition for a legitimate sale or service transaction in a period prior to that called for by generally accepted accounting principles. Fictitious revenue is revenue recognized for a nonexistent sale or service transaction. At these extremes, premature revenue can be readily differentiated from fictitious revenue. Within these extremes, a large gray area exists where a clear demarcation between the two is not practical. It is important to note, however, that whether revenue is recognized in a premature or fictitious manner, assessments of earning power will be overstated.

- Fictitious revenue recognition often involves some number of cover-up activities on the part of management designed to support the reporting of nonexistent results. Examples include the preparation of totally fictitious documents, backdating of valid agreements, keeping accounts off the books, and shipping goods to company-controlled warehouses.

- The SEC has clarified and tightened the requirements for revenue recognition. To recognize revenue there must be persuasive evidence of an arrangement, delivery has occurred or services have been rendered, the seller's price to the buyer is fixed or determinable, and collectibility is reasonably assured.
- While technically fulfilling the criteria for revenue recognition, channel stuffing, where deep discounts are offered to encourage orders that are uneconomic from the buyer's perspective, results in the recognition of revenue that is not sustainable.
- Side letters sometimes are used to surreptitiously negate the terms of a sale. Revenue should not be recognized in such cases.
- Under specific criteria, revenue that is subject to a right of return can be recognized. It is important for the estimated amount of any return to be deducted from the revenue amount reported.
- Related-party revenue, when a sale or service transaction is conducted with an entity over which the selling company has influence, must be clearly disclosed. Disclosure permits the reader to form an opinion as to the sustainability of the revenue recognized.
- Very specific criteria must be met before revenue can be recognized in advance of shipment. These criteria guide the recognition of revenue in bill-and-hold transactions. Among the criteria is the stipulation that bill-and-hold transactions must be arranged at the request of the buyer.
- Service fees cannot be recognized until the related services are provided.
- Contract accounting is employed when an extended period is required for completion of a product or service. Under contract accounting, there are two methods of reporting revenue. Under the percentage-of-completion method, revenue is recognized as progress is made toward completion. Under the completed-contract method, revenue is recognized at completion.
- In detecting premature or fictitious revenue the following points are important:
  1. The revenue recognition footnote contains important information on the timing of revenue recognition
  2. A close relationship exists between revenue and accounts receivable
  3. Other balance sheet accounts, including property, plant, and equipment and other assets, might be used to offset premature or fictitious revenue
  4. A company may not have the physical capacity to generate the revenue being reported.

GLOSSARY

Accounts Receivable Days (A/R Days)   The number of days it would take to collect the ending balance in accounts receivable at the year's average rate of revenue per day. Calculated as accounts receivable divided by revenue per day (revenue divided by 365).

Bill and Hold   A sales agreement where goods that have been sold are not shipped to a customer but, as an accommodation, simply are segregated outside of other inventory of the selling company or shipped to a warehouse for storage, awaiting customer instructions.

Channel Stuffing   Shipments of product to distributors who are encouraged to overbuy under the short-term offer of deep discounts.

Completed-Contract Method   A contract accounting method that recognizes contract revenue only when the contract is completed. All contract costs are accumulated and reported as expense when the contract revenue is recognized.

Contract Accounting   Method of accounting for sales or service agreements where completion requires an extended period.

Cost Plus Estimated Earnings in Excess of Billings   Revenue recognized to date under the percentage-of-completion method in excess of amounts billed. Also known as unbilled accounts receivable.

Earned Revenue   When a company has substantially accomplished what it must do to be entitled to the benefit represented by a revenue transaction.

Emerging Issues Task Force   A separate committee within the Financial Accounting Standards Board composed of 13 members representing CPA firms and preparers of financial statements whose purpose is to reach a consensus on how to account for new and unusual financial transactions that have the potential for creating differing financial reporting practices.

Fictitious Revenue   Revenue recognized on a nonexistent sale or service transaction.

Free-on-Board (FOB) Destination   A shipping arrangement agreed to between buyer and seller where title to the goods sold passes when the goods in question reach their destination. When goods are shipped FOB destination, revenue is properly recognized when the goods reach their destination.

Free-on-Board (FOB) Shipping Point   A shipping arrangement agreed to between buyer and seller where title to the goods sold passes when the goods in question are delivered to a common carrier. When goods are shipped FOB shipping point, revenue is properly recognized when the goods are delivered to the common carrier.

Gain-on-Sale Accounting   Up-front gain recognized from the securitization and sale of a pool of loans. Profit is recorded for the excess of the sales price and the present value of the estimated interest income that is expected to be received on the loans above the amounts funded on the loans and the present value of the interest agreed to be paid to the buyers of the loan-backed securities.

Percentage-of-Completion Method   A contract accounting method that recognizes contract revenue and contract expenses as progress toward completion is made.

Premature Revenue   Revenue recognized for a confirmed sale or service transaction in a period prior to that called for by generally accepted accounting principles.

Price Protection   A sales agreement provision where price concessions are offered to resellers to account for price reductions occurring while inventory is held by them awaiting resale.

Realizable Revenue   A revenue transaction where assets received in exchange for goods and services are readily convertible into known amounts of cash or claims to cash.

Realized Revenue   A revenue transaction where goods and services are exchanged for cash or claims to cash.

Related Party   An entity whose management or operating policies can be controlled or significantly influenced by another party.

Revenue Recognition   The act of recording revenue in the financial statements. Revenue should be recognized when it is earned and realized or realizable.

Right of Return   A sales agreement provision that permits a buyer to return products purchased for an agreed-upon period of time.

Sales Revenue   Revenue recognized from the sales of products as opposed to the provision of services.

Sales-type Lease   Lease accounting used by a manufacturer who is also a lessor. Up-front gross profit is recorded for the excess of the present value of the lease payments to be received across a lease term over the cost to manufacture the leased equipment. Interest income also is recognized on the lease receivable as it is earned over the lease term.

Service Revenue   Revenue recognized from the provision of services as opposed to the sale of products.

Side Letter   A separate agreement that is used to clarify or modify the terms of a sales agreement. Side letters become a problem for revenue recognition when they undermine a sales agreement by effectively negating some or all of an agreement's underlying terms and are maintained outside of normal reporting channels.

Trade Loading   A term used for channel stuffing in the domestic tobacco industry.

Unbilled Accounts Receivable   Revenue recognized under the percentage-of-completion method in excess of amounts billed. Also known as cost plus estimated earnings in excess of billings.

NOTES

1. *The Wall Street Journal*, December 22, 2000, p. B2.
2. Ibid., October 20, 1998, p. A3.
3. Accounting and Auditing Enforcement Release No. 1133, *In the Matter of Insignia Solutions PLC, Respondent* (Washington, DC: Securities and Exchange Commission, May 17, 1999), para. 6.
4. *The Wall Street Journal*, January 6, 2000, p. A1.
5. Ibid., February 25, 1999, p. B9.
6. Accounting and Auditing Enforcement Release No. 1247, *In the Matter of Peritus Software Services, Inc., Respondent* (Washington, DC: Securities and Exchange Commission, April 13, 2000).
7. Accounting and Auditing Enforcement Release No. 975, *In the Matter of Pinnacle Micro, Inc., Scott A. Blum, and Lilia Craig, Respondents* (Washington, DC: Securities and Exchange Commission, October 3, 1997).
8. Accounting and Auditing Enforcement Release No. 1243, *In the Matter of Beth A. Morris and Steven H. Grant, Respondents* (Washington, DC: Securities and Exchange Commission, March 29, 2000).
9. *The Wall Street Journal*, May 27, 1998, p. A10.
10. Ibid., December 23, 1998, p. C1.
11. Ibid., August 22, 2000, p. B11.
12. Ibid., January 6, 2000, A1.
13. Ibid., January 30, 1997, p. A3 and Accounting and Auditing Enforcement Release No. 1166, *Securities and Exchange Commission v. Lawrence Borowiak* (Washington, DC: Securities and Exchange Commission, September 28, 1999).
14. Accounting and Auditing Enforcement Release No. 852, *Order Instituting Public Proceeding Pursuant to Section 21C of the Securities Exchange Act of 1934, Making Findings and*

Cease-and-Desist Order in the Matter of Troy Lee Wood (Washington, DC: Securities and Exchange Commission, October 31, 1996).

15. Accounting and Auditing Enforcement Release No. 843, *In the Matter of Cambridge Biotech Corporation, Respondent* (Washington, DC: Securities and Exchange Commission, October 17, 1996).

16. BMC Software, Inc., annual report, March 1991, p. 42.

17. American Software, Inc., annual report, April 1991, p. 39.

18. Autodesk, Inc., annual report, January 1992, p. 28.

19. Computer Associates International, Inc., annual report, March 1992, p. 20.

20. Statement of Position 97-2: *Software Revenue Recognition* (New York: Accounting Standards Executive Committee, October 1997).

21. Microsoft Corp., annual report, June 2000. Information obtained from Disclosure, Inc., *Compact D/SEC: Corporate Information on Public Companies Filing with the SEC* (Bethesda, MD: Disclosure, Inc. December 2000).

22. Ibid.

23. Advent Software, Inc., annual report, December 1999. Information obtained from Disclosure, Inc., *Compact D/SEC*.

24. Accounting and Auditing Enforcement Release No. 903, *In the Matter of Lynn K. Blattman, Respondent* (Washington, DC: Securities and Exchange Commission, April 10, 1997).

25. Accounting and Auditing Enforcement Release No. 1313, *In the Matter of Cylink Corp., Respondent* (Washington, DC: Securities and Exchange Commission, September 27, 2000).

26. *The Wall Street Journal,* December 22, 2000, p. B2.

27. Ibid., February 9, 2001, p. A3.

28. Accounting and Auditing Enforcement Release No. 1215, *In the Matter of Informix Corp., Respondent* (Washington, DC: Securities and Exchange Commission, January 11, 2000).

29. *Business Week,* September 16, 1996, p. 90.

30. *Fortune,* December 4, 1989, p. 89.

31. Accounting and Auditing Release No. 987, *In the Matter of Bausch & Lomb Incorporated, Harold O. Johnson, Ermin Ianacone, and Kurt Matsumoto, Respondents* (Washington, DC: Securities and Exchange Commission, November 17, 1997).

32. Accounting and Auditing Enforcement Release No. 1133.

33. Accounting and Auditing Enforcement Release No. 1215, *In the Matter of Informix Corp., Respondent* (Washington, DC: Securities and Exchange Commission, January 11, 2000).

34. Statement of Financial Accounting Standards No. 48, *Revenue Recognition When Right of Return Exists* (Norwalk, CT: Financial Accounting Standards Board, June 1981).

35. General Motors Corp., annual report, December 1999. Information obtained from Disclosure, Inc. *Compact D/SEC.*

36. Accounting and Auditing Enforcement Release No. 971, *In the Matter of Laser Photonics, Inc., Respondent* (Washington, DC: Securities and Exchange Commission, September 30, 1997).

37. Accounting and Auditing Enforcement Release No. 1272, *In the Matter of Cendant Corp., Respondent* (Washington, DC: Securities and Exchange Commission, June 14, 2000).

38. Statement of Financial Accounting Standards No. 57, *Related-Party Disclosures* (Norwalk, CT: Financial Accounting Standards Board, March 1982).

39. Accounting and Auditing Enforcement Release No. 1220, *In the Matter of William L. Clancy, CPA, Respondent* (Washington, DC: Securities and Exchange Commission, February 7, 2000).

40. Lernout & Hauspie Speech Products NV, annual report, December 1999. Information obtained from Disclosure, Inc. *Compact D/SEC.*

41. *The Wall Street Journal,* December 19, 2000, C1.

42. Hewlett-Packard Co., annual report, October 1999. Information obtained from Disclosure, Inc. *Compact D/SEC.*

43. Accounting and Auditing Enforcement Release No. 812, *In the Matter of Advanced Medical Products, Inc., Clarence P. Groff and James H. Brown, Respondents* (Washington, DC: Securities and Exchange Commission, September 5, 1996).

44. Accounting and Auditing Enforcement Release No. 971, *In the Matter of Laser Photonics, Inc., Respondent* (Washington, DC: Securities and Exchange Commission, September 30, 1997).

45. Accounting and Auditing Enforcement Release No. 1184, *In the Matter of Peter Madsen and Mark Rafferty, Respondents* (Washington, DC: Securities and Exchange Commission, September 28, 1999).

46. Accounting and Auditing Enforcement Release No. 1044, *In the Matter of Thomas D. Leaper, CPA, William T. Wall III, CPA, Fred S. Flax, CPA and Kellogg & Andelson LLC, Respondents* (Washington, DC: Securities and Exchange Commission, June 17, 1998).

47. *The Wall Street Journal,* June 22, 1998, p. A4.

48. Accounting and Auditing Enforcement Release No. 1243.

49. *The Wall Street Journal,* December 30, 1998, p. B3.

50. Accounting and Auditing Enforcement Release No. 812.

51. Raytheon Co., annual report, December 1999. Information obtained from Disclosure, Inc., *Compact D/SEC.*

52. *The Wall Street Journal,* March 21, 2000, p. B1.

53. BJ's Wholesale Club, Inc., annual report, January 2000. Information obtained from Disclosure, Inc., *Compact D/SEC.*

54. Costco Wholesale Corp., annual report, August 1998. Information obtained from Disclosure, Inc., *Compact D/SEC.*

55. *The Wall Street Journal,* January 28, 1998, p. A4.

56. Ibid., February 6, 2001, p. C1.

57. EBay, Inc., annual report, December 1999. Information obtained from Disclosure, Inc., *Compact D/SEC.*

58. Emerging Issues Task Force Issue No. 99-19, *Reporting Revenue Gross as a Principal versus Net as an Agent,* (Norwalk, CT: Financial Accounting Standards Board, 1999).

59. *The Wall Street Journal,* February 28, 2000, C4.

60. For a more in-depth look at this subject, refer to E. Comiskey and C. Mulford, *Guide to Financial Reporting and Analysis* (New York: John Wiley & Sons, 2000), pp. 122–135.

61. SOP 81-1, *Accounting for Performance of Construction-Type and Certain Production-Type Contracts* (New York: Accounting Standards Executive Committee, American Institute of CPAs, July 1981).

62. Data obtained from *Accounting Trends and Techniques: Annual Survey of Accounting Practices Followed in 600 Stockholder' Reports* (New York: American Institute of CPAs, 1999).

63. Accounting and Auditing Enforcement Release No. 879, *In the Matter of William T. Manak, Respondent* (Washington, DC: Securities and Exchange Commission, February 6, 1997.)

64. Stirling Homex Corp., annual report, July 1971.

65. Staff Accounting Bulletin No. 101, *Revenue Recognition in Financial Statements* (Washington, DC: Securities and Exchange Commission, December 3, 1999).

66. Accounting and Auditing Enforcement Release No. 773, *Securities and Exchange Commission v. Stephen R.B. Bingham, Susan McKenna Grant, and William McClintock, Respondents* (Washington, DC: Securities and Exchange Commission, April 17, 1996).

67. *The Wall Street Journal,* November 4, 1998, p. S2. In 1999 the company changed its method of accounting, postponing revenue recognition until its client collects amounts due from the vendor.

68. Ibid., February 26, 1998, p. R1.

69. Profit Recovery International, Inc., Form 10-K annual report to the Securities and Exchange Commission, December 1998, p. 27.

70. *The Wall Street Journal,* November 4, 1998, p. S2. The Center for Financial Research and Analysis is a private research company specializing in identifying accounting and operational problems in public companies.

71. Revenue that has been collected in advance of being earned still can be recognized prematurely. However, such cases are the exception. Given the fact that the revenue has been collected, they are less of a problem than revenue that has not been collected.

72. For companies using contract accounting, increases in unbilled accounts receivable will accompany premature or fictitious revenue.

73. Accounting and Auditing Enforcement Release No. 1313, *In the Matter of Cylink Corporation, Respondent* (Washington, DC: Securities and Exchange Commission, September 27, 2000).

74. Refer to C. Mulford and E. Comiskey, *Financial Warnings* (New York: John Wiley & Sons, 1996), pp. 228–233. Also refer to Accounting and Auditing Enforcement Release No. 543, *In the Matter of Comptronix Corp., Respondent* (Washington, DC: Securities and Exchange Commission, March 29, 1994).

75. Refer also to C. Mulford and E. Comiskey, *Financial Warnings* (New York: John Wiley & Sons, 1996), pp. 224–225.

Aggressive Capitalization and Extended Amortization Policies

. . . if a company incorrectly calls an expense an asset for accounting purposes, it can provide a big boost to earnings, at least in the short term. And that is what critics say is happening at Pre-Paid Legal Services, Inc.[1]

. . . because of "aggressive accounting," expenses incurred in obtaining new food-service contracts were typically listed on the company's [Fine Host Corp.'s] balance sheet as assets to be depreciated over time. Instead, they should have appeared as a current expense against revenue. . . .[2]

Livent transferred preproduction costs for shows to fixed asset accounts such as the construction of theatres . . . and inflated profits by fraudulently amortizing preproduction costs over a much longer period of time.[3]

Unisys said it will take a $1.1 billion charge in its recently ended fourth quarter, much of it to write down goodwill still lingering on the books from the 1986 merger of Burroughs Corp. and Sperry Corp. that created Unisys.[4]

The four examples identified in the opening quotes capture the essence of the potential for accounting problems associated with capitalization and amortization policies. Through aggressive capitalization policies, companies report current-period expenses and/or losses as assets. As a result, expense recognition is postponed, boosting current-period earnings. These "assets" or deferred expenses are then amortized to expense over future reporting periods, burdening those periods with expenses that should have been recorded earlier.

For example, critics of Pre-Paid Legal Services, Inc., maintain that the company's policy of capitalizing the up-front commissions it pays its sales force, typically three years' worth for each policy sold, is aggressive and results in an overstatement of assets and earnings. Fine Host Corp. is a similar case, where the costs of obtaining new food-service contracts were capitalized and depreciated or amortized to expense over time.

When capitalized costs, even costs that have been properly capitalized, are amortized over extended periods, assets are carried beyond their useful lives. The net effect is to postpone expenses to future periods, boosting current-period earnings. Livent, Inc., is a case in point. The company was able to amortize its live-show preproduction costs, which include costs incurred in bringing a show to fruition, over extended periods by transferring those costs to fixed asset accounts. Fixed assets or property, plant, and equipment accounts typically carry much longer useful lives than preproduction costs, which include such soft expenditures as wages incurred and supplies purchased during preopening preparation and rehearsals.

Some also would argue that Pre-Paid Legal Services employs an extended amortization period for the sales commissions it capitalizes. The company amortizes these capitalized costs over a three-year period even though the life of an average policy is approximately two years. While not as blatant as the practices of Livent, Pre-Paid's policy could be viewed as postponing expense recognition.[5]

The fate befalling Unisys Corp. is common for companies that have boosted earnings with aggressive capitalization or extended amortization policies. Write-downs often ensue. In the case of Unisys, it was a write-down of goodwill that had become value-impaired. The company had chosen an amortization period that seemed appropriate at the time of the merger of Burroughs Corp. and Sperry Corp. In hindsight, however, that period was clearly too long, as it became apparent that the recorded asset had a shorter useful life than had been originally expected. It is hard to say whether the company could have anticipated this problem in an earlier period or not. There were undoubtedly signs that the previous merger had not created value whose life extended as long as had been originally anticipated. Certainly its stagnant sales and frequent losses in the years leading up to the write-down attested to the presence of potential problems.[6] Had these signs been heeded, the asset's useful life would have been reduced, resulting in higher recurring charges and a reduced need for a special one-time charge.

COST CAPITALIZATION

In 1996, America Online (AOL), Inc. announced that it was taking a special pretax charge of $385 million to write down subscriber acquisition costs that had been capitalized previously.[7] Those subscriber acquisition costs, which included the costs of manufacturing and distributing to prospective members millions of computer disks containing company software, had been capitalized on the premise that they would be recovered from new membership revenue. In effect, the company postponed expensing the costs in order to match them with that future revenue.

The Securities and Exchange Commission disagreed with the company's accounting treatment, likening the subscriber acquisition costs to advertising costs, which are generally expensed as incurred. The only exception to the expensing option, which would permit capitalization, was when persuasive historical evidence could be provided that would permit a reliable estimate of the future revenue that could be obtained from incremental advertising expenditures. According to the SEC, because AOL operated in a new, evolving, and unstable industry, it could not provide that kind of persuasive historical evidence. Expensing the subscriber acquisition costs was the only appropriate option.[8]

In 1996, AOL earned $62.3 million before income taxes on revenue of $1.1 billion. However, that year alone, the company capitalized subscriber acquisition costs of $363 million. Amortization that year of such costs capitalized in prior years totaled $126 million. Thus, the net effect of the company's capitalization policy was to boost pretax earnings in 1996 by a significant $237 million ($363 million minus $126 million).[9] Clearly the company would have lost money in 1996 if its policy had been to expense subscriber acquisition costs as incurred.

When Should Costs Be Capitalized?

The AOL example helps to showcase the judgment involved in, and potentially significant effects of, management decisions aimed at determining whether costs incurred should be capitalized or expensed. The principle guiding these decisions, known generally as the matching principle, is simple enough. The principle ties expense recognition to revenue recognition, dictating that efforts, as represented by expenses, be matched with accomplishments (i.e., revenue), whenever it is reasonable and practicable to do so.

For example, inventory costs are not charged to cost of goods sold when the inventory is purchased. Rather, those costs are charged to expense when the inventory is sold. That way the cost of the inventory and the revenue generated by its sale are reported on the income statement in the same time period. Similarly, a bonus paid a salesperson for completing a sale or the estimated cost of providing warranty repairs over an agreed-upon warranty period are expensed in the same time period that the related revenue is recognized. In this way, expenses incurred are matched with the recognized revenue.

Allocating Costs in a Rational and Systematic Manner

Most costs do not have such a clear association with revenue as can exist for inventory costs or a sales bonus or the estimated costs of a warranty repair. As a result, a systematic and rational allocation policy is used to approximate the matching principle. Thus, because a long-lived asset contributes toward the generation of revenue over several periods, the asset's cost must be allocated over those periods.

This reporting technique seems straightforward and works reasonably well for most expenditures. It is from this systematic and rational allocation approach that we get our current method of accounting for depreciation expense. Companies record assets purchased at their cost and then allocate that cost over the future periods that benefit. Consider the following example taken from the annual report of American Greetings Corp.:

> Property, plant and equipment are carried at cost. Depreciation and amortization of buildings, equipment and fixtures is computed principally by the straight-line method over the useful lives of the various assets.[10]

The company records property, plant, and equipment at cost and then employs the straight-line method as a systematic and rational method for allocating that cost over the assets' lives.

As seen with AOL, however, this systematic and rational allocation approach to matching is not always so straightforward. The method is particularly subjective when a transaction lacks a discrete purchase event as with property, plant, and equipment, and instead involves the incurrence of recurring expenditures over time. Management then is faced with the decision of whether to capitalize those recurring expenditures, reporting them as assets and later amortizing them, or expensing them when incurred.

AOL decided initially to capitalize its subscriber acquisition costs. However, highlighting the subjectivity of its decision, a disagreement arose with the SEC as to the extent to which those costs actually benefited future periods. It was the SEC's position that such future benefits were not sufficiently clear as to warrant capitalization. AOL eventually relented and wrote off the capitalized costs.

Examples of other costs for which there has been a recurring disagreement about the appropriateness of capitalization include software development and start-up costs.

Software Development Costs   The costs of developing new software applications are to be capitalized once technological feasibility is reached. Prior to that point, software development costs are expensed as incurred. Technological feasibility is defined as that point at which all of the necessary planning, designing, coding, and testing activities have been completed to the extent needed to establish that the software application can meet its design specifications. It is at that point that the software company has a more viable product and a higher likelihood of being able to realize its investment in the software through future revenue.[11] The following policy note provided by American Software, Inc., explains well how accounting for software development costs works:

> Costs incurred internally to create a computer software product or to develop an enhancement to an existing product are charged to expense when incurred as research and development expense until technological feasibility for the respective product is established. Thereafter, all software development costs are capitalized and reported at the lower of unamortized cost or net realizable value. Capitalization ceases when the product or enhancement is available for general release to customers.[12]

The definition of technological feasibility as requiring completion of the necessary planning, designing, coding, and testing to establish that the software application can meet its design specifications would seem to be rather late in the development of a new software product. In actuality, provided a software firm has a detailed program design, or a detailed step-by-step plan for completing the software, and has available the necessary skills and hardware and software technology to avoid insurmountable development obstacles, software costs can be capitalized once the detailed program design is complete and high-risk development issues have been resolved.

Clearly, management judgment plays a large role in determining when technological feasibility is reached and when capitalization should begin. In fact, one could reasonably argue that managements can raise or lower amounts capitalized by choice, raising or lowering earnings in the process.

For example, if a firm seeks to capitalize a significant amount of software costs incurred, it should develop a detailed program design and work out design bugs early in the development process. Consider the disclosure of software costs capitalized and expensed by American Software as provided in Exhibit 7.1.

As seen in the exhibit, the percentage of software development costs capitalized by American Software has increased to 51.9% in 2000 from 42.2% in 1998. Note how the amount of software costs expensed, reported as research and development expense in the exhibit, has declined during that same period from $12,112,000 in 1998 to $9,675,000 in 2000, even as total software development costs have remained relatively stable. Interestingly, in recent years the company has reduced significantly the percentages of software development costs capitalized. As recently as 1996 and 1997 the company capitalized 79.5% and 81.2%, respectively, of software costs incurred. However, in 1999 the company took a special charge of $24,152,000 to write down capitalized software development costs that had become value-impaired. Apparently the company capitalized more of the software costs incurred than could be realized through future software revenue.

Also reported in Exhibit 7.1 is the amount of capitalized software development costs that was amortized in each of the three years, 1998 to 2000. The company amortized $6,706,000, $6,104,000, and $3,632,000, respectively, in 1998, 1999, and 2000. As a result, the company's policy of capitalizing software development costs boosted pretax

Exhibit 7.1 Software Development Costs Capitalized and Expensed: American Software, Inc., Years Ending April 30, 1998–2000 (thousands of dollars, except percentages)

	1998	1999	2000
Total capitalized computer software development costs	$ 8,827	$ 10,902	$ 10,446
Total research and development expense[a]	12,112	11,511	9,675
Total research and development expense and capitalized computer software development costs	$ 20,939	$ 22,413	$ 20,121
Costs capitalized as percent of total costs incurred	42.2%	48.6%	51.9%
Total amortization of capitalized software development costs	$ 6,706	$ 6,104	$ 3,632

[a]Research and development expense refers to software development costs that were incurred and expensed prior to the achievement of technological feasibility.

Source: American Software, Inc., annual report, April 2000. Information obtained from Disclosure, Inc., *Compact D/SEC: Corporate Information on Public Companies Filing with the SEC* (Bethesda, MD: Disclosure, Inc., December 2000). The percentages were added to the company's annual report disclosures.

earnings by a net amount, calculated by subtracting the amount amortized from the amount capitalized, of $2,121,000, $4,798,000, and $6,814,000, in 1998, 1999, and 2000, respectively. If later it is determined that the costs capitalized are not realizable, or if they have not been amortized at a sufficiently rapid rate, additional write-downs, similar to the one taken in 1999, will be needed.

As a form of earnings management, some software firms may seek to minimize the amount of software development costs capitalized or even to expense all of such costs, capitalizing none. One way to achieve such an outcome in accordance with generally accepted accounting principles is to avoid the preparation of detailed program design. Capitalization must then wait until the necessary planning, designing, coding, and testing have been completed to establish that the software application can meet its design specifications. Because the amount of software development costs incurred beyond that point is likely immaterial, it may be sufficiently late in the development process to permit the expensing of all software development costs incurred.

For example, Microsoft Corp. provides this policy note for its software development expenditures:

> Research and development costs are expensed as incurred. Statement of Financial Accounting Standards (SFAS) 86, Accounting for the Costs of Computer Software to Be Sold, Leased, or Otherwise Marketed, does not materially affect the Company.[13]

Attesting to the significant effect on earnings that a company's software capitalization policy can have, consider again the case of American Software. If the company were to follow Microsoft's approach and expense all of its software development costs, cumulative pretax results across the three-year period 1998 through 2000 would have been lower by $13,733,000 (sum of annual amounts capitalized minus amounts amortized). Had it followed this approach, the company's reported cumulative pretax loss over the 1998 through 2000 time frame would have been much worse.

Many firms incur costs in developing software for their own internal use. Such costs are expensed currently until the preliminary development stage of the project is completed. After that point, essentially when a conceptual design for the software is completed, costs incurred on software are capitalized.[14] Consider this disclosure from the annual report of AbleAuctions.Com, Inc.:

> Computer software costs incurred in the preliminary development stage are expensed as incurred. Computer software costs incurred during the application development stage are capitalized and amortized over the software's estimated useful life.[15]

Start-up Costs   Accounting for start-up costs, which consist of costs related to such onetime activities as opening a new facility, introducing a new product or service, commencing activities in a new territory, pursuing a new class of customer, or initiating a new process in an existing or new facility, has changed markedly in recent years. Statement of Position 98-5, *Reporting on the Costs of Start-Up Activities,* now requires that all costs incurred related to start-up activities are to be expensed. Capitalization, no matter how strong an apparent link between current costs and future revenue might be, is no longer an option.[16]

Prior to the effective date in 1999 of SOP 98-5, companies did just about anything when accounting for start-up activities. Consider the following accounting policies for store preopening costs as reported in the annual reports of selected companies in 1996:

From the annual report of Filene's Basement Corp.:

Preopening costs are charged to expense within the fiscal year that a new store opens.[17]

From the annual report of Back Yard Burgers, Inc.:

Preopening costs consist of incremental amounts directly associated with opening a new restaurant. These costs, which principally include the initial hiring and training of employees, store supplies and other expendable items, are capitalized and amortized over the twelve-month period following the restaurant opening.[18]

From the annual report of Churchill Downs, Inc.:

Organizational costs and preopening costs are amortized over 24 months.[19]

From the annual report of Community Capital Corp.:

In accordance with the agreements with the organizers of the New Banks and subject to the New Banks being opened, the Company has agreed to include organizational and preopening costs in the initial capitalization of the New Banks. The total of the organizational and preopening costs is expected to range from $600,000 to $900,000 and will be amortized over a five-year period on a straight-line basis.[20]

At the time, all four companies—Filene's Basement, Back Yard Burgers, Churchill Downs, and Community Capital—were abiding by the matching principle when accounting for preopening costs. However, the disparity in the accounting policies selected, from an immediate expensing option to one of capitalization and amortization over a five-year period, is striking. Such diverse practices are what led the American Institute of CPAs to issue more specific guidance on the subject.

Even before SOP 98-5 was effective, the SEC was diligent in its pursuit of enforcement actions against companies that were abusing the option of capitalizing start-up costs. For example, by the end of 1984 Savin Corp. carried as deferred start-up costs $37 million of R&D costs that should have been expensed as incurred.[21] In a rather brazen act, Technology International, Ltd., capitalized approximately 80 percent of the general and administrative costs it incurred during the first three quarters of its fiscal year 1993. On its balance sheet, the company referred to these expenses as Pre-Operating and Deferred Costs.[22] Capitalization was clearly inappropriate. Similarly, as noted earlier, Livent capitalized its preproduction costs but grouped the costs with fixed assets to avail itself of a longer amortization period.[23]

There is no longer any equivocation when it comes to accounting for start-up costs. They should be expensed as incurred. Such clarity notwithstanding, however, some companies will still seek to capitalize such costs, possibly labeling them as something other than what they are.

Another item for which there is clarity in terms of capitalization policies is capitalized interest. Nonetheless, as seen below, capitalization still can lead to earnings difficulties.

Capitalized Interest Costs   In the United States, interest incurred on monies invested in an asset under construction is capitalized and added to the cost of the asset. Interest capitalization begins with the incurrence of construction costs and ceases when the asset is complete and ready for service. The amount of interest capitalized is actually "avoidable interest" and includes interest on monies borrowed specifically for the construction of the asset in question. In addition, interest on other borrowed funds that technically could have been repaid had available monies not been committed to the new construction project are also subject to capitalization.[24]

Capitalized interest is netted against interest expense reported on the income statement and, depending on the nature of the ongoing construction activity, is added either to the cost of property, plant, and equipment items under construction or to discrete inventory projects, such as homes, ships, and bridges. Amounts capitalized are amortized and included in depreciation expense as property, plant, and equipment items are used in operations. Interest capitalized to inventory projects is included in cost of goods sold when the inventory item is sold. Two examples follow that are consistent with these policies. In the first example, Ameristar Casinos, Inc., is capitalizing interest into the cost of property, plant, and equipment under construction:

> Costs related to the validation of new manufacturing facilities and equipment are capitalized prior to the assets being placed in service. In addition, interest is capitalized related to the construction of such assets. Such costs and capitalized interest are amortized over the estimated useful lives of the related assets.[25]

In the second example, Beazer Homes USA, Inc., capitalizes interest into its inventory of residential housing that is under construction:

> Inventory consists solely of residential real estate developments. Interest, real estate taxes and development costs are capitalized in inventory during the development and construction period.[26]

There are limits to the amount of interest that can be capitalized. For example, excluding limited exceptions for regulated utilities, the amount of interest capitalized cannot exceed the amount of interest incurred. In addition, capitalization cannot continue if it were to result in the cost of an asset exceeding its net realizable value, or the amount for which an asset could be sold less the costs of sale. This net realizable value rule, or NRV rule, provides a natural limit on the amount of interest that can be capitalized and helps to prevent overcapitalization.

After periods during which significant amounts of interest costs have been capitalized, a sudden decline in construction activity can lead to sharp increases in net interest expense and a reduction in earnings. For example, during a three-year period, interest capitalized by Domtar, Inc., declined from $20 million for the year ended December 1997 to $1 million in 1998 and $0 in 1999. At the same time, interest expense net of interest capitalized increased from $50 million in 1997 to $91 million in 1998 and $111 million in 1999.[27]

Construction delays and cost overruns also can lead to earnings problems for companies that capitalize interest. As costs for assets under construction accumulate, cost moves ever closer to net realizable value. Once NRV is reached, future interest cannot be capitalized. Even additional construction costs will need to be expensed to prevent carrying the asset at an amount greater than NRV. Moreover, as capitalized interest adds to the cost of assets, write-downs due to problems with assets becoming value-impaired will be greater.[28] For example, in 1999 U.S. Foodservice, Inc., a company with a long history of capitalizing interest on property, plant, and equipment items under construction, recorded a special charge to write down certain of these assets to net realizable value. Capitalized interest had increased the cost of these assets and added to the amount of the write-down. As noted by the company:

> The Company [U.S. Foodservice, Inc.] recognized a non-cash asset impairment charge of $35.5 million related to the Company's plan to consolidate and realign certain operating units and install new management information systems at each of the Company's operating units. These charges consist of write-downs to net realizable value of assets of operating units that are being consolidated or realigned.[29]

Other Capitalized Expenditures

A review of corporate annual reports turned up many other examples of expenditures that are being capitalized by various companies. A partial list of these capitalized expenditures is provided in Exhibit 7.2.

The amounts capitalized in the exhibit are expenditures that, according to the companies represented, will benefit future periods. For many, these future benefits can be seen readily, including Darling International's expenditures to prevent future environmental contamination; Hometown Auto's leasehold improvements; Lions Gate Entertainment's cost of producing film and television productions; RF Micro's costs of bringing its wafer fabrication facility to an operational state; and U.S. Aggregates' expenditures for development, renewals, and betterments of its quarries and gravel pits. Other capitalized expenditures, while not necessarily contrary to generally accepted accounting principles, are nonetheless more questionable. These capitalized amounts include About.Com's URL costs and deferred offering costs incurred in connection with an initial public offering and Gehl's costs incurred in conjunction with new indebtedness—an item that is commonly capitalized. Also included in the category of more questionable practices are InfoUSA's direct marketing costs associated with the mailing and printing of brochures and catalogs and J Jill Group's creative and production costs associated with the company's e-commerce web site. By capitalizing these more questionable amounts, the companies are reporting the expenditures as assets. Whether they represent what are traditionally considered to be assets is open to debate and will be discussed later in the chapter.

Two other items reported in Exhibit 7.2 that may, on the surface, appear to be questionable but are consistent with specific industry accounting standards are Miix Group's capitalization of policy acquisition costs and Forcenergy's capitalization of nonproductive petroleum exploration costs. Generally accepted accounting principles for insurance

---

Exhibit 7.2 Capitalized Expenditures

Company	Costs Capitalized
About.Com, Inc. (1999)	URL costs and deferred offering costs in connection with initial public offering (IPO)
Darling International, Inc. (1999)	Environmental expenditures incurred to mitigate or prevent environmental contamination that has yet to occur and that may result from future operations
Forcenergy, Inc. (1999)	Productive and nonproductive petroleum exploration, acquisition, and development costs (full-cost method)
Gehl Co. (1999)	Costs incurred in conjunction with new indebtedness
Hometown Auto Retailers, Inc. (1999)	Leasehold improvements
InfoUSA, Inc. (1999)	Direct marketing costs associated with the printing and mailing of brochures and catalogs
J Jill Group, Inc. (1999)	Creative and production costs associated with the company's e-commerce website
Lions Gate Entertainment Corp. (2000)	Costs of producing film and television productions
Miix Group, Inc. (1999)	Policy acquisition costs representing commissions and other selling expenses
RF Micro Devices, Inc. (2000)	Costs of bringing the company's first wafer fabrication facility to an operational state
U.S. Aggregates, Inc. (1999)	Expenditures for development, renewals, and betterments of quarries and gravel pits

Source: Disclosure, Inc., *Compact D/SEC: Corporate Information on Public Companies Filing with the SEC* (Bethesda, MD: Disclosure, Inc., December 2000). The year following each company name designates the specific annual report year end from which the data were compiled.

---

companies call for the capitalization of policy acquisition costs. These costs include expenditures on such items as selling commissions and expenses, premium taxes, and certain underwriting expenses.[30] In the petroleum industry, the so-called full-cost method permits capitalization of all petroleum exploration costs, including those leading to productive as well as nonproductive wells, along with the acquisition and development of productive wells. For petroleum companies, capitalization may continue as long as future revenue from all producing wells is expected to exceed total costs for exploration, acquisition, and development of producing and nonproducing wells.[31]

One last observation should be made in reference to Exhibit 7.2. While GAAP may permit or even require capitalization of certain expenditures, it does not automatically indicate that the values assigned to any resulting assets are beyond question. The analyst has a responsibility to evaluate the realizability of such assets and make adjustments when they are warranted.

Current Expensing

When no connection between costs and future-period revenue can be made, amounts incurred should be expensed currently. In such cases, the costs incurred do not benefit future periods and capitalization, which is tantamount to reporting current-period expenses as assets, is inappropriate. Included here would be general and administrative expenses and, in most cases, advertising and selling expenses.

Direct-Response Advertising   Direct-response advertising is an exception to the immediate expensing of selling expenses. The primary purpose of such advertising costs is to elicit sales to customers who can be shown to have responded specifically to the advertising in the past. Thus it can be demonstrated that such advertising will result in probable future economic benefits. Such costs can be capitalized when persuasive historical evidence permits formulation of a reliable estimate of the future revenue that can be obtained from incremental advertising expenditures.[32] Recall from an earlier example that the SEC determined that subscriber acquisition costs incurred by AOL did not fulfill the criteria for capitalization under guidelines for direct-response advertising.

Another firm that was found to be incorrectly capitalizing membership acquisition costs was CUC International, Inc., a predecessor company to Cendant Corp. In 1989, approximately 10 years prior to more celebrated problems at the firm, CUC International changed policies from amortizing membership acquisition costs over three years to one of amortizing those costs over a 12-month period.[33] In 1997, in response to an investigation by the SEC, the company changed it policy again and began expensing membership acquisition costs as incurred.[34]

Research and Development   Research and development costs, excluding expenditures on software development after technological feasibility is reached, also are expensed currently. One could reasonably argue that such expenditures will likely benefit future periods. Given the high-risk profile of such expenditures, however, and the uncertainty that future benefits will be derived from them, accounting standards require that such costs be expensed currently. Current expensing is a conservative approach that ensures consistency in practice across companies.[35]

Accounting guidelines calling for the current expensing of R&D costs notwithstanding, some companies have attempted to capitalize these expenditures. For example, during the years 1988 through 1991, American Aircraft Corp. improperly capitalized R&D costs as tooling. The company, which was developing an advanced helicopter design, maintained that it had progressed past the R&D phase and that capitalization of costs incurred as production tooling was appropriate. In actuality, the costs incurred were not tooling and should have been expensed as incurred.[36]

As another example, Twenty First Century Health, Inc., capitalized both R&D and organizational costs. In fact, between 1993 and 1995 these items were the largest "assets" on the company's balance sheet.[37]

As a final example consider Pinnacle Micro, Inc. During 1995 the company was developing a new optical disk drive. Certain of the nonrecurring engineering expenditures incurred during this development period were capitalized in the expectation that the costs would be matched against revenue when it commenced shipment of the disk drives. It seems rather clear that the costs incurred were actually R&D expenditures and should have been expensed. The company later reevaluated its position and expensed them.

Purchased In-Process Research and Development   Consistent with accounting for R&D costs incurred internally, purchased in-process R&D, paid as part of the price of the acquisition of a technology firm and having no alternative future use beyond the current R&D project, is expensed at the time of acquisition. The concern here is that the realizability of in-process R&D, like R&D generally, cannot be evaluated adequately to warrant capitalization. Of course, acquiring firms may like this treatment. It permits them to write off a significant amount of an acquisition price at the time of acquisition, freeing future earnings of amortization charges.

As an example, in 1998 Brooktrout, Inc., wrote off as purchased in-process R&D $9.8 million of a $30.5 million acquisition. For its $30.5 million, Brooktrout received only $7.9 million in tangible assets. Everything else, including the purchased in-process R&D, was intangible.

While most of these intangibles will be amortized against future earnings, the purchased in-process R&D was written off at the time of acquisition. In its annual report, the company provided the details of how the acquisition price was allocated. Details of that allocation are summarized in Exhibit 7.3. The company described the transaction, including the write-off, as follows:

> The Company recorded a one-time charge of $9.8 million ($5.9 million, net of tax benefits) in the fourth quarter of 1998 for the purchased research and development for seven projects that had not yet reached technological feasibility, had no alternative future use, and for which successful development was uncertain.[38]

As noted in Chapter 4, the SEC is concerned about what it sees as the abuse of creative acquisition accounting, including in-process R&D, in managing earnings to desirable levels. As the agency focuses attention on this activity, we are likely to see a more curtailed use of purchased in-process research and development in future years.

Patents and Licenses   Closely related to the topic of accounting for R&D expenditures is the topic of accounting for the patents and licenses that can be derived from successful R&D. Capitalization is permitted of costs incurred to register or successfully defend a patent. Such expenditures are not considered to be R&D costs. Also, patents as well as licenses purchased from others can be reported as assets at the purchase price. Whether arising from the capitalization of internal costs incurred or through purchases from others, patents and licenses are amortized over the shorter of their legal or economic useful lives.

One company that greatly abused accounting practices for patents and licenses was Comparator Systems Corp. In 1996, about a month after seeing the company's stock

---

Exhibit 7.3   Allocation of Acquisition Price: Brooktrout, Inc., Year Ending December 31, 1998

Cash paid	$ 29,400,000
Transaction costs	1,148,000
Total purchase price	$ 30,548,000
Allocated to tangible assets acquired	$ 7,915,000
Allocated to liabilities assumed	(1,863,000)
Purchased research and development	9,786,000
Existing technology	12,157,000
Customer base	1,276,000
Trademark	304,000
In-place workforce	973,000
Total	$ 30,548,000

Source: Brooktrout, Inc., annual report, December 1998. Information obtained from Disclosure, Inc., *Compact D/SEC: Corporate Information on Public Companies Filing with the SEC* (Bethesda, MD: Disclosure, Inc., December 2000).

---

price rise from only a few pennies to nearly $2 per share over the course of four days, the SEC filed suit against the company claiming that it defrauded investors by inflating assets and misrepresenting ownership of its technology. In question was a fingerprint recognition technology that company officials allegedly stole from a Scottish university. Those officials offered to market the technology in the United States and then refused to return it when requested by its rightful owners. The SEC's suit alleges that during 1994, 1995, and 1996, patents and licenses listed by the company as assets had no balance-sheet value. According to the SEC, serious questions of ownership surrounded some of these assets. For others, expiration dates had passed.[39]

Aggressive Cost Capitalization

Notwithstanding the specific guidance that exists for such costs as direct-response advertising, research and development, software development, interest during extended construction periods, and start-up activities, there remains much flexibility in applying the matching principle. Aggressive cost capitalization, like the aggressive application of accounting principles generally, occurs when companies ply this flexibility and stretch it beyond its intended limits. They do so to alter their financial results and financial position in order to, as noted earlier, create a potentially misleading impression of a firm's business performance.

For example, Chambers Development Co., Inc., capitalized the cost of developing new landfill sites. Capitalization of such costs is appropriate provided the costs are identifiable and segregated from ordinary operating expenses, provide a quantifiable benefit to future periods, and are recoverable from future revenue. Instead of following these practices, however, Chambers backed into the amount of landfill costs capitalized. That is, the company determined what it wanted its expenses to be using a predetermined percent of revenue. Any expenses incurred above these amounts were then capitalized. No real effort was made even to relate the costs capitalized to the actual landfill development activity. As a result of this activity, the company was able to maintain target profit margins.[40]

Among its many creative accounting practices, Sulcus Computer Corp. used aggressive capitalization to boost profitability during 1991 and 1992. The costs capitalized were considered to be components of acquisition costs paid in completing acquisitions of other companies. They should not have been capitalized. In one instance, the company capitalized what were clearly operating expenses, including salaries and employee housing. In another, severance pay on terminated employees was capitalized. With respect to this last example, in a memorandum written to company officials concerning his compensation, an officer of the company described his value as being increased because he had "[d]eveloped [the] concept of 'Acquisition Cost' which allowed the company to record an additional $300K in net income."[41]

In another rather blatant example of aggressive cost capitalization, Corrpro Companies, Inc., capitalized many miscellaneous operating expenses, referring to them as prepaid expenses. For example, the company improperly capitalized what was referred to as "Corporate Charge Expenses" and "Unemployment Tax Expenses." Also capitalized as prepaid expenses was a payment made to settle a lawsuit and the costs of completing a secondary offering of stock. In all of these examples, there were no future benefits to be obtained from the costs incurred.

DETECTING AGGRESSIVE COST CAPITALIZATION POLICIES

Given the direct effect on earnings and assets that aggressive capitalization can have, it is important to take steps to detect when such actions are being taken. Useful analytical tools include:

1. A review of the company's capitalization policies
2. A careful consideration of what the capitalized costs represent
3. A check to determine whether the company has been aggressive in its capitalization policies in the past
4. A check for costs capitalized in stealth

What Are the Company's Capitalization Policies?

The accounting policy note is an important note to review carefully. It is particularly important to compare the company's policies with those of competitors and others in the industry. Is the company in question capitalizing costs that other companies expense? Or is a more conservative approach being taken where the company expenses more?

Consider again expenditures incurred on direct-response advertising. While numerous companies that incur such advertising will capitalize such costs, not all firms will do so. For example, in the prepackaged software industry, companies such as Advantage Learning Systems, Inc., Elcom International, Inc., and Viza.Com, Inc., all capitalize direct-response advertising. In that same general industry, there are companies such as E Piphany, Inc., and Adept Technology, Inc., that do not capitalize such costs. Similarly, in the information retrieval services industry, GSV, Inc., Genesis Intermedia.Com, and E Universe, Inc., all capitalize direct-response advertising, while Digital Courier Technologies, Inc., and Audio Highway.Com, Inc. do not.

This is not to say that when a company capitalizes direct-response advertising it is necessarily being aggressive in its capitalization policy. Properly applied, the practice is in accordance with generally accepted accounting principles. The company is, however, capitalizing an expenditure that others in the industry have elected to expense. The net result is a near-term boost to earnings. Moreover, there are ample examples of firms that capitalized direct-response advertising in an ostensibly proper manner only to be forced by the SEC to discontinue that practice. As discussed earlier, AOL and Cendant Corp. are in this noteworthy group.

America Online and Cendant Corp. used capitalization guidelines for direct-response advertising to capitalize costs incurred in obtaining new subscribers or members. These so-called subscriber, member, or customer acquisition costs are properly capitalized in accordance with GAAP when, as noted earlier, persuasive historical evidence permits formulation of a reliable estimate of future benefits to be obtained.

Another company that capitalizes these expenditures is BCE, Inc., a Canadian provider of telecommunications and direct-to-home satellite broadcasting services. It describes its policy for customer acquisition costs as follows:

> BCE subsidizes the cost of the "Direct to Home" satellite hardware equipment sold to its customers. These subsidies are deferred and amortized over three years.[42]

The company is apparently installing satellite hardware equipment at a loss and capitalizing these losses as a component of its deferred subscriber acquisition costs.

Another interesting example and a twist on this whole area of subscriber, member, or customer acquisition costs is provided by Sciquest.Com, Inc. The company, a business-to-business marketplace for scientific and laboratory products, described its accounting for subscriber acquisition costs associated with a significant partnering relationship with key corporate users of its services in this way:

> The Company issued to these companies 5,035,180 warrants to purchase the Company's common stock at an exercise price of $0.01 per share. At December 31, 1999 the Company has recorded deferred customer acquisition costs of approximately $400,246,458 related to these warrants. In the event that the Company commits to issue additional warrants to purchase its common stock as more strategic relationships are formed, the Company will be required to record additional deferred customer acquisition costs equal to the difference between the fair value of the Company's common stock on the date the warrants are issued and the exercise price of the warrants of $0.01. The amount of deferred customer acquisi-

tion costs will be adjusted in future reporting periods based on changes in the fair value of the warrants until such date as the warrants are fully vested. Deferred customer acquisition costs will be amortized to operating expense over the term of the related contractual relationship, which in the case of the buyer agreements is three years and in the case of the supplier agreements is five years, using a cumulative catch-up method. The Company recognized $9,107,753 in stock based noncash customer acquisition expense during the fourth quarter of 1999 related to the amortization of deferred customer acquisition costs.[43]

For this transaction, Sciquest.Com recorded an increase in paid-in capital for $400,246,458—the difference between the market value of its stock and the $0.01 exercise price of the warrants issued to its partners. At the same time, the company netted deferred acquisition costs for the same amount against the increase in paid-in capital. Thus, the net effect of the issuance of the warrants was no change in paid-in capital. However, in future periods, the $400,246,458, adjusted for changes in the market value of the company's stock, will be amortized to customer acquisition expense. In fact, during the fourth quarter of 1999, the company recorded customer acquisition expense of $9,107,753.

For Sciquest.Com, a company that reported revenue of $3,882,000 in 1999, these are surprisingly large numbers. They could provide a potentially serious earnings drag going forward. Moreover, while the company is quick to point out that any expense related to its customer acquisition costs are noncash, these expenses are nonetheless very dilutive. Of course, a decline in the company's share price would reduce the amount of any remaining deferred customer acquisition costs. In fact, by September 2000, due to amortization and a decline in its share price, that amount had been reduced significantly to $24,361,135.[44]

What Do the Capitalized Costs Represent?

While it is a useful activity to compare a company's capitalization policies with those of other companies, it is possible that the companies chosen for comparison are also taking an aggressive approach. Accordingly, it is important to consider what the capitalized costs represent.

From a purely technical point of view, the costs may provide sufficient future benefits to warrant capitalization. However, when viewed separate and apart from the company, do the costs have a determinable market value? Or are they simply the product of a recorded journal entry whose value, if any, is tied to the company's fortunes?

For example, as seen in Exhibit 7.2, About.Com capitalized the costs incurred in connection with its initial public offering and Gehl capitalized the costs associated with issuing new debt. These so-called assets do not have a market value. They certainly do not represent something that can be sold. Also from that exhibit, the asset values of InfoUSA's direct-marketing costs associated with its printing and mailing of brochures and catalogs and J Jill Group's creative and production costs associated with its e-commerce web site can be questioned.

Earlier it was noted that accounting principles for insurance companies call for the capitalization of policy acquisition costs. Such a practice is followed by Pre-Paid Legal

Services, which sells what are effectively insurance policies against future legal fees. If one were simply to look at the company's accounting practice for acquiring new policy-holders, it would not appear to be out of line with general industry practice.

At the time a policy or membership, as the company refers to them, is sold, an advance is made to the sales agent (associate) for approximately three years' worth of commissions to be earned on the sale. The amount paid is capitalized as a commission advance and is amortized to expense over three years. If a policy is canceled, the company discontinues amortization of the commission advance and effectively treats it as a receivable from the sales agent to be collected from future commissions on other policies. The company, however, has no recourse in the event a sales agent stops selling policies.

The company describes its accounting practice as follows:

> Commission advances represent the unearned portion of commissions advanced to Associates on sales of Memberships. Commissions are earned as Membership fees are collected, usually on a monthly basis. The Company reduces Commission advances as Membership fees are paid and commissions earned. Unearned commission advances on lapsed Memberships are recovered through collection of fees on an associate's remaining active Memberships.[45]

Whether the company's practice is within generally accepted accounting principles or not, one must question the asset value of these commission advances. Certainly the company would have more trouble selling them than a piece of capital equipment or a patent. Moreover, unlike other receivables, a lender would be very unlikely to buy them in a factoring transaction. The fact that the company has no recourse against a sales agent who stops selling policies calls into question the ultimate collectibility of the advances.

In its defense, the company would argue that the commission advances represent a revenue stream to be earned over a membership period. However, even that is a tenuous argument considering the fact that the three-year amortization period exceeds the average two-year term that a new member keeps a policy.

A review of the Pre-Paid Legal's financial statements highlights the importance of its accounting policy for commission advances to its financial results and position. Consider the selected financial statement data provided in Exhibit 7.4.

As reported in the exhibit for the year ended December 1999, Pre-Paid Legal reported pretax earnings of $59,927,000. During that same year, total membership commission advances increased $38,703,000 ($120,588,000 less $81,885,000). Had the company expensed its membership commission advances as incurred, pretax earnings would have been reduced by $38,703,000 to $21,224,000 ($59,927,000 minus $38,703,000), or 65% less than the amount reported. Also, note that by the end of fiscal 1999, the total amount of membership commission advances of $120,588,000 actually exceeded its stockholders' equity of $114,464,000. The real essence of the company's financial position is captured in these capitalized commission advances.

One can quibble with Pre-Paid Legal's use of a three-year amortization period to expense commissions advanced on policies that have, on average, a two-year term. Beyond the amortization period, however, the company's policies may not be at odds with GAAP. That said, one must use reason and logic in reviewing the impact of its poli-

---

Exhibit 7.4   Selected Financial Statement Data: Pre-Paid Legal Services, Inc., Years Ending December 31, 1998 and 1999 (thousands of dollars)

Financial Statement Item	1998	1999
Income Statement Accounts:		
Revenue	$ 160,453	$ 196,240
Income before income taxes	41,332	59,927
Balance Sheet Accounts:		
Membership commission advances–current portion	21,224	32,760
Membership commission advances–noncurrent portion	60,661	87,828
Total membership commission advances	81,885	120,588
Stockholders' equity	101,304	114,464

Source: Pre-Paid Legal Services, Inc., Form 10-K annual report to the Securities and Exchange Commission (December 1999).

---

cies on the company's financial statements. In that light, the company's accounting practices appear to be aggressive.

There are numerous examples of other companies whose capitalized costs created assets of questionable value. For example, in 2000 Aurora Foods, Inc., restated results for 1998 and 1999, wiping out $81.6 million in pretax earnings for the two years. The primary culprit was capitalized promotional expense including price concessions offered to food stores to carry the company's products.[46] Another company carrying an asset of questionable value was Excel Communications, Inc. Using an accounting policy similar to that of Pre-Paid Legal, the company capitalized the cost of its sales commissions and amortized them over a 12-month period. In 1996 the company changed its policy to expense these costs as incurred.[47]

Other examples of companies reporting capitalized costs of questionable value include Ponder Industries, Inc., and Kahler Corp. Ponder Industries, an oil-services company, was having trouble with its operations in Azerbaijan. In fact, due to potential local government action there in 1992, the company was forced to stop work. During this work stoppage, which extended into 1993, the company continued to incur costs. However, rather than expense these costs, the company capitalized them, reporting them as assets.[48] They should have been expensed as incurred. During 1988 and 1989 Kahler Corp., a company that owned and managed hotels, carried one of its hotels as an asset held for sale. This accounting practice permitted the company to capitalize the operating losses from the hotel by adding them to the hotel's balance-sheet carrying value. As a result, those losses were excluded from the company's statement of operations. In 1990 the company reclassified the hotel as an operating property and began to amortize the property's book value. Certainly the capitalized losses of the hotel did not add to its market value.

Is There Evidence of Aggressive Capitalization Policies in the Past?

When there is evidence of aggressive capitalization policies in the past, it is not unreasonable to assume that a company may be continuing its aggressive ways. Experience would argue in favor of caution.

For example, as noted earlier, while in 1997 the celebrated problems of Cendant Corp. focused, among other things, on the company's aggressive capitalization of membership acquisition costs, that was not the first time the company found itself in trouble over its capitalization policies. As early as 1989, the company, then known as CUC International, Inc., sought to clean up its accounting for these same costs.

Evidence of aggressive capitalization behavior in prior years might be noted when a firm changes its accounting policies in response to the findings of the SEC. For example, while we have no reason at present to believe that AOL/Time Warner, Inc., is currently being aggressive in its capitalization policies, the change by AOL in response to a requirement by the SEC to begin expensing subscriber acquisition costs rather than capitalizing them is a reason for caution.

Numerous other examples of aggressive capitalization policies uncovered by the SEC have been provided here. They, too, provide reason to be suspect going forward.

However, even in the absence of a forced change in accounting by the SEC, one warning sign in particular suggests that a company has, in prior years, been aggressive in its capitalization policies. An analyst should be particularly wary of aggressive capitalization behavior when a company has taken a special charge to write down costs that were capitalized in prior years.

A good example to consider is American Software. Recall from Exhibit 7.1 that in 2000, the company capitalized 51.9% of its software development costs, up from 42.2% in 1998. Also recall that in 1999, after capitalizing as much as 81.2% of its software costs in 1997, the company took a special charge to, among other things, write down capitalized software costs. The existence of that special charge, taken because the realizability of software costs capitalized in prior years was in question, suggests that the company may have been aggressive in its capitalization policies. Accordingly, in future years, the company's capitalization policies should be examined carefully. The increase to 51.9% of software costs being capitalized in 2000, up from 42.2% in 1998, gives even more reason for caution.

Has the Company Capitalized Costs in Stealth?

It is not uncommon for companies that have been the most aggressive in capitalizing costs to take steps to hide their acts. For example, as noted earlier, Sulcus Computer Corp. was found by the SEC to have capitalized operating expenses as part of the costs of acquisitions. One would not expect to see the company state an accounting policy that specifies that operating expenses are capitalized as part of the costs of acquisitions. Rather, the company simply capitalized these expenses and left it to the financial statement reader to find them. Similarly, Corrpro Companies, which was found by the SEC to have improperly capitalized "Corporate Change Expenses" and "Unemployment Tax Expense," would not be expected to provide an accounting policy note disclosing these treatments. These costs were labeled as prepaid expenses on the company's balance sheet with no accompanying explanation.

Thus the reader of financial statements must be prepared to look beyond the stated accounting policies and beyond any accounts labeled as capitalized expenses to several other asset accounts reported on the balance sheet. Because they are more amenable to precise verification, cash and investments are unlikely to carry costs capitalized in an aggressive manner. Accounts receivable and inventory are possible hiding places for costs capitalized aggressively, as are other assets, including prepaid expenses, and property, plant, and equipment.

An example of a company that actually capitalized costs to accounts receivable and property, plant, and equipment was Sunrise Medical. The company capitalized miscellaneous operating expenses to accounts receivable, referring to the customer as "miscellaneous" on the accounts receivable subsidiary ledger. Operating expenses also were capitalized into property, plant, and equipment. These capitalized amounts were referred to as "soft goods" on the property, plant, and equipment subsidiary ledger. Audit tests ultimately uncovered the charade and earned the company an enforcement action by the SEC.[49]

An analysis of accounts receivable in conjunction with an examination of a company's revenue recognition practices will help determine if costs have been aggressively capitalized to that account. As to the other accounts mentioned and as discussed in Chapter 6, care should be taken in evaluating the relationship of each account to revenue and its rate of change relative to the rate of change in revenue. Calculated relationships with revenue should be compared with industry norms and amounts for competitors.

Additional comments about examining property, plant, and equipment are provided later in this chapter. Steps about evaluating accounts receivable and inventory are provided in Chapter 8.

AMORTIZING CAPITALIZED COSTS

Consistent with the matching principle, costs capitalized in one period because they benefit future periods are amortized to expense in those future periods. This process of amortization, or spreading costs over several reporting periods, is used to allocate costs in a prescribed rational and systematic manner.

While here the term *amortize* is used generally to refer to the systematic allocation of all capitalized costs, the term frequently is used to refer to an allocation over time of the cost of intangible assets. For example, as noted by Harrah's Entertainment, Inc.:

> We amortize goodwill and other intangibles, including trademarks, on a straight-line basis over periods up to 40 years.[50]

Depreciation, a form of amortization, is a term that typically is used to refer to an allocation of property, plant, and equipment accounts. As reported by A. Schulman, Inc.:

> It is the Company's policy to depreciate the cost of property, plant and equipment over the estimated useful lives.[51]

Notwithstanding technical differences between the terms *amortization* and *depreciation*, they are used interchangeably here.

Depletion, also a form of amortization, refers to an allocation of the costs of natural resources—oil reserves, gravel pits, rock quarries, and the like. As disclosed by Engelhard Corp.:

> Depletion of mineral deposits and mine development are provided under the units of production method.[52]

Extended Amortization Periods

Generally accepted accounting principles provide no specific guidance as to the appropriate period of amortization for long-lived assets. As a result, judgment is needed, providing management with much discretion over reported results. By increasing an amortization period, periodic expense is lowered, raising pretax earnings.

Judgment and Amortization Periods

Evidence of the effects of professional judgment and the differences that can arise in amortization periods can be seen in the accounting policy notes that follow. All of the companies operate within a single general industry group, the manufacture of semiconductors.

From the annual report of Cypress Semiconductor Corp.:

	Useful Lives in Years
Equipment	3 to 7
Buildings and leasehold improvements	7 to 10
Furniture and fixtures	5[53]

From the annual report of Dallas Semiconductor Corp.:

> Depreciation is calculated . . . over the estimated useful lives of the related assets, generally forty years for buildings, five to ten years on building improvements and two to nine years for computer hardware, software, and machinery and equipment.[54]

From the annual report of Diodes, Inc.:

> Property, plant and equipment are depreciated . . . the estimated useful lives, which range from 20 to 55 years for buildings and 1 to 10 years for machinery and equipment. Leasehold improvements are amortized using the straight-line method over 1 to 5 years.[55]

As seen in these disclosures, all three companies depreciate property, plant, and equipment accounts over different time periods. Buildings alone are depreciated over periods as short as seven to 10 years for Cypress Semiconductor to as many as 55 years for Diodes.

As another example, Vitesse Semiconductor Corp. reports that it depreciates property and equipment accounts over the relatively short period of three to five years, or approximately four years on average. Vitesse began its fiscal 2000 with machinery and equipment at cost of $98,913,000. At year-end, the company reported machinery and equipment at cost of $171,761,000.[56] Thus, during the year, the average cost of its machinery and equipment accounts was $135,337,000 (add the two amounts, $98,913,000 and $171,761,000, together and divide by 2). Using a four-year average depreciation period, the company would have depreciated the cost of its machinery and equipment by $33,834,000 ($135,337,000 divided by 4, assuming the straight-line method and no residual value). If the company were to extend the average useful lives of its equipment to six years, a period that is not out of line with other companies in the industry, depreciation would be reduced to $22,556,000 ($135,337,000 divided by 6), a reduction of $11,278,000, or 14% of pretax income of $81,678,000 for 2000. Amortization periods certainly can have a significant effect on reported income.

Similar differences exist for amortization periods assigned to intangibles. Consider the amortization periods primarily for intangibles provided below. The focus here is on intangibles other than goodwill. All of the companies are semiconductor manufacturers.

From the annual report of Analog Devices, Inc.:

	Amortization Lives
Goodwill	5–10 years
Other Intangibles	5–10 years[57]

From the annual report of LSI Logic Corp.:

. . . the excess of the purchase price over the fair value of assets acquired was allocated to existing technology, workforce in place, trademarks and residual goodwill, which are being amortized over a weighted average life of seven to eight years.[58]

From the annual report of Vitesse Semiconductor Corp.:

Goodwill and other intangibles are carried at cost less accumulated amortization, which is being provided on a straight-line basis over the economic useful lives of the respective assets, generally 5 to 15 years.[59]

As with property, plant, and equipment accounts, the amortization periods for intangibles can be diverse, ranging here from five to 15 years.

With much flexibility and discretion available to it, management may elect to employ an extended amortization period. Such a period is one that continues beyond a long-lived asset's economic useful life. When put in place, an extended amortization period minimizes amortization expense and boosts reported earnings.

A Prescription for Impairment Losses

The effects of the choice of amortization period or useful life on pretax earnings can be readily seen. Increasing amortization periods lowers amortization expense. What is less obvious, however, is that changes in amortization periods also affect asset book values. When amortization periods are lengthened, amortization expense is reduced, leaving greater asset book values on the balance sheet.

All long-lived assets, including property, plant, and equipment, intangibles, and good-will, are subject to write-down in the form of an impairment loss when their balance-sheet amounts are value-impaired. Generally such assets are value-impaired when their book values exceed the future cash flows expected to be received from their use. Impairment write-downs reduce overstated book value amounts to fair value.[60] Companies will have many names for such write-downs, including asset write-downs, special charges, and impairment losses.

In recent years, we have seen numerous examples of companies that have taken impairment losses. Rapid changes in business and technology combined with price dis-inflation or, in some cases, deflation have contributed to the need for companies to take these charges. Two recent examples of impairment losses include Aluminum Co. of America's charge in 1996 to write down manufacturing equipment taken out of service and a charge in 1998 by FPA Medical Management, Inc., to write down goodwill.[61] A third example is a series of restructuring charges taken by Eastman Kodak Co., most recently in 1999, that included write-downs of property, plant, and equipment.[62]

Because longer amortization periods permit larger book values to accumulate on the balance sheet than would be the case under shorter periods, the likelihood of an impairment-related write-down increases as amortization periods lengthen. This is not to say that all impairment losses are due to amortization periods that were chosen to be too long. For example, impairment losses might be more readily attributable to changes in general business conditions, changes in technology, declining market values, or changes in how a company employs its assets. However, it is not difficult to find examples of impairment losses that can be attributed, at least in part, to the use of amortization periods that were, in hindsight, too long. In this view, the impairment loss is really more of a catch-up amortization or depreciation charge.

For example, in 1998 Qualcomm, Inc. took a charge to write down leased equipment that had become obsolete.[63] Earlier, had the company factored an appropriate rate of obsolescence into its judgment of that equipment's useful life, such a charge may have been avoided. The same can be said about Unisys Corp., first noted in the opening quotes to this chapter. In 1998 the company took a $1.1 billion charge, primarily to write down goodwill that was "still lingering on the books from the 1986 merger of Burroughs Corp. and Sperry Corp. that created Unisys."[64] The company originally amortized this goodwill over a 40-year period.[65] Had the company chosen a 10-year period, for example, the goodwill would have been eliminated by the time of the special charge.

Waste Management, Inc., provides a particularly noteworthy example of how the use of an unrealistically long amortization period can lead to a charge for asset impairment. In 1997 the company took an impairment loss and restated its financial statements for the years ended December 1994, 1995, and 1996. The following reasons were provided for the adjustments:

> As a result of a comprehensive review begun in the third quarter of 1997, the Company determined that certain items of expense were incorrectly reported in previously issued financial statements. These principally relate to vehicle, equipment and container depreciation expense, capitalized interest and income taxes. With respect to depreciation, the Company determined that incorrect vehicle and container salvage values had been used, and

errors had been made in the expense calculations. Effective October 1, 1997, the Board of Directors approved a management recommendation to revise the Company's North American collection fleet management policy. Front-end loaders will be replaced after 8 years, and rear-end loaders and rolloff trucks after 10 years. The previous policy was to not replace front-end loaders before they were a minimum of 10 years old and other heavy collection vehicles before they were a minimum of 12 years old. As a result of this decision, the Company recognized an impairment writedown of $70.9 million in the fourth quarter of 1997 for those vehicles scheduled for replacement in the next two years under the new policy . . .

Depreciable lives have been adjusted commencing in the fourth quarter of 1997 to reflect the new policy. Also effective October 1, 1997, the Company reduced depreciable lives on containers from 15 and 20 years to 12 years, and ceased assigning salvage value in computing depreciation on North American collection vehicles or containers. These changes in estimates increased depreciation expense by $33.7 million in the fourth quarter of 1997.[66]

As described in the note, the company reduced the useful lives and residual values of its property, plant, and equipment. As a result of this decision, a special charge for asset impairment was needed. In addition, future depreciation expense will be increased by the shortened useful lives.

In addition to establishing asset useful lives that are unrealistically long, as seen in the Waste Management example, amortization charges also can be reduced by increasing asset residual values—the estimated market value of an amortized asset at the end of its useful life. Because assets are amortized to their estimated residual values, increases in residual values reduce the amount of amortization expense taken against an asset. The net result is the same as increasing asset useful lives—amortization expense is reduced and asset book values are increased.

A Closer Look at Restructuring Charges

Restructuring charges are closely related to charges taken for asset impairment. In fact, it is not uncommon for restructuring charges to include asset impairment losses as a component of their total. Restructuring charges typically are taken in conjunction with a consolidation or relocation of operations or the disposition or abandonment of operations or productive assets. Thus, it is easy to see how such charges would include impairment losses as well as other expenses, including write-downs of accounts receivable and inventory, and accruals of liabilities for so-called exit costs, including such expenses as lease terminations, closure costs, severance pay, benefits, and retraining.

Much of the official accounting guidance for restructuring charges comes in the form of an FASB Emerging Issues Task Force document, EITF 94-3, *Liability Recognition for Certain Employee Termination Benefits and Other Costs to Exit an Activity (including Certain Costs Incurred in a Restructuring)*. Supplementing EITF 94-3 is SEC Staff Accounting Bulletin 100, *Restructuring and Impairment Charges*. Generally, a restructuring charge cannot be recognized and a liability accrued until management at the proper level officially commits to a restructuring plan. For example, if the board of directors must approve a decision to close 50 stores, then a charge to close those stores cannot be recorded until board approval is obtained. Moreover, the specific stores slated for closure must be identified. If only 40 specific stores have been identified, then a charge to close only those stores may be recorded. Guidelines such as these are designed to prevent the accrual of broad and sweeping charges, so-called big bath charges, that are not backed by a specific plan of action and that might be used as an earnings management tool.

A useful footnote disclosure that now accompanies restructuring charges is a schedule that summarizes changes in any restructuring-related liability accounts. These liability or reserve accounts represent restructuring accruals that have yet to be settled. A separate liability account is reported for each restructuring activity. Disclosure of any activity in the liability accounts is made in each annual and quarterly filing with the SEC and, if material, is discussed in Management's Discussion and Analysis. An example is provided in Exhibit 7.5.

As can be seen from the exhibit, activity in the restructuring liability account provides useful information about the completion of the steps in the company's restructuring program. Only payments made to settle actual liabilities planned in the restructuring program are reported on the schedule along with other, immaterial adjustments. Thus it should now be more difficult for companies to charge recurring operating expenses against a restructuring reserve in an effort to boost operating earnings.

Exhibit 7.5 Restructuring Charge and Schedule of Activity in Restructuring Liability: Scientific Atlanta, Inc., Years Ending June 30, 1998, 1999, and 2000 (thousands of dollars)

3. Restructuring Charges

During fiscal year 1998, we announced a restructuring and consolidation of worldwide manufacturing operations for reduced cost, improved efficiency and better customer service . . .

During fiscal year 1998, we recorded restructuring charges of $23,412 which included $10,217 and $3,200 for assets to be abandoned and expenses related to the remaining contractual liabilities for canceled leases, respectively, as a result of the consolidation of operations, $5,173 for severance costs for approximately 500 employees primarily in manufacturing positions and $4,822 for the impairment of certain assets and other miscellaneous expenses. As of July 2, 1999, benefits paid and charged against the liability for severance totaled $6,360, and approximately 560 employees have actually been terminated. The restructuring plan was substantially completed during fiscal year 1999. As of June 30, 2000, $5,454 has been charged against the liability for contractual liabilities for canceled leases and other miscellaneous costs, and $1,381 remains in the liability which is expected to be utilized by 2002 for expenses related to contractual liabilities for canceled leases.

(continues)

Exhibit 7.5   *(Continued)*

The following reconciles the beginning restructuring charge to the liability at the end of fiscal years 1998, 1999, and 2000:

	Fixed Assets	Contractual Obligations under Canceled Leases	Severance	Other	Total
Restructuring charge	$ 10,217	$ 3,200	$ 5,173	$ 4,822	$ 23,412
Charges to the reserve and assets written off	(10,217)	—	(1,321)	(2,197)	(13,735)
Balance at June 28, 1998	—	3,200	3,852	2,625	9,677
Charges to the reserve	—	(927)	(5,039)	(2,111)	(8,077)
Reserve adjustments	—	(673)	1,187	(514)	—
Balance at July 2, 1999	—	1,600	—	—	1,600
Charges to the reserve	—	(219)	—	—	(219)
Balance at June 30, 2000	$ —	$ 1,381	$ —	$ —	$ 1,381

Source: Scientific Atlanta, Inc., annual report, June 2000. Information obtained from Disclosure, Inc., *Compact D/SEC: Corporate Information on Public Companies Filing with the SEC* (Bethesda, MD: Disclosure, Inc., March 2001).

DETECTING EXTENDED AMORTIZATION PERIODS

Two key steps are helpful in detecting extended amortization periods.

1. A calculation of the average amortization period for a company's depreciable asset base, and
2. A search for extended amortization periods in prior years.

Average Amortization Period

A direct approach in searching for extended amortization periods would be a check on a company's disclosed useful lives of long-term assets. Unfortunately, often this information is presented in a general fashion that is too vague to be useful in analysis. The Diodes example provided earlier is a case in point. The company indicates that buildings are depreciated over periods ranging from 20 to 55 years while machinery and equipment are depreciated over periods ranging from one to 10 years. It is hard to say from this information what amortization period is being used. Moreover, it is possible that the disclosed periods are not, in actuality, being used.

As an alternative, computation of an average amortization period or useful life of a company's collective depreciable asset base is recommended. To demonstrate the calculation, consider the detailed presentation of property, plant, and equipment information for Abercrombie and Fitch Co. provided in Exhibit 7.6.

Using the information provided in the exhibit, the company's overall average useful life can be calculated by first computing its depreciable asset base. This is the average cost of property, plant, and equipment accounts excluding the cost of land and construction in progress. At January 30, 1999 that figure was $149,890,000 ($152,618,000 less $2,728,000) and at January 29, 2000, the amount was $185,674,000 ($225,781,000 less $14,007,000 and $26,100,000). During 2000 the average depreciable cost was $167,782,000 ($149,890,000 plus $185,674,000, all divided by 2). Dividing the company's depreciation and amortization expense for 2000 of $27,261,000 by the calculated average depreciable cost of $167,782,000 yields a depreciation rate of 16.25%. Assuming the straight-line method and no residual value, the company is depreciating, or amortizing, 16.25% of its depreciable asset base per year. Dividing the 16.25% into 100% yields the number of years it would take to amortize 100% of the total—the average useful life for its collective depreciable base. It is 6.2 years in this example.

An average useful life of 6.2 years appears appropriate for a company that invests primarily in furniture, fixtures, equipment, and leasehold improvements. Also, the company's average useful life is a bit shorter than its industry average. For example, the Value Line Investment Survey reports a depreciation rate for specialty retailers of approximately 10%, indicating an average useful life of 10 years. Before making such a comparison, however, care should be taken to ensure that other companies in the industry do not have significant investments in buildings. Because buildings are depreciated

Exhibit 7.6   Property, Plant, and Equipment: Abercrombie and Fitch Co., Years Ending January 30, 1999, and January 29, 2000 (thousands of dollars)

	1999	2000
Land	$ —	$ 14,007
Furniture, fixtures, and equipment	126,091	158,753
Beneficial leaseholds	7,349	7,349
Leasehold improvements	16,450	19,572
Construction in progress	2,728	26,100
Total	$ 152,618	$ 225,781
Less: accumulated depreciation and amortization	63,060	79,378
Property and equipment, net	$ 89,558	$ 146,403
Depreciation and amortization expense	$ 20,946	$ 27,261

Source: Abercrombie and Fitch Co., annual report, January 29, 2000. Information obtained from Disclosure, Inc., *Compact D/SEC: Corporate Information on Public Companies Filing with the SEC* (Bethesda, MD: Disclosure, Inc., March 2001).

over much longer periods, their inclusion would bias any calculated industry average to a longer depreciation period. Because most retailers tend not to invest significantly in buildings, the comparison made here would appear to be valid.

Evidence of Extended Amortization Periods in Prior Years

In the search for extended amortization periods, it is also important to look for evidence of extended periods in prior years. The reasoning here is that the company in question may not have totally changed its practices, leaving itself open to future problems. Evidence of extended amortization periods in prior periods include charges for asset impairments or restatements that can be attributed, at least in part, to extended amortization periods in past years.

For example, as noted earlier, in 1997 Waste Management took a special charge and restated its results for 1994, 1995, and 1996. Among the reasons cited was a reduction in asset useful lives. Interestingly, in 1999, the company found it necessary to take additional charges for asset impairments. Whether extended amortization periods played a role in these additional charges is unclear from available information. However, it is not difficult to find a connection between extended amortization periods and increased amounts for the new asset-impairment charges.

Other Related Issues

While not directly related to extended amortization periods, the creative use of restructuring charges provides an ideal vehicle for managing earnings. A restructuring charge might be overstated in one period, creating a restructuring liability or reserve against which to charge future operating expenses. A careful examination of activity in the restructuring liability will help uncover such accounting machinations. In particular, one should examine and obtain explanations for significant reductions in the restructuring reserve during periods in which gross margin or selling, general, and administrative expense as a percentage of revenue unexpectedly improve. Expenditures on normal, recurring costs of goods sold or selling, general, and administrative expenses may have been charged to the restructuring reserve.

A firm also may have employed creative accounting practices by not recording an impairment charge when one was called for. Developing problems and an early sign of the need for an impairment charge can be found when the book value of an asset exceeds its market value. Unfortunately, it is difficult to obtain market value information against which to compare the book values of reported long-lived assets. Occasionally, however, such information is available or can be inferred from other available information. For example, at December 31, 2000, R.J. Reynolds Tobacco Holdings, Inc., reported goodwill of $7.4 billion related to prior-year acquisitions. At the same time, the company's entire market capitalization, including R.J. Reynolds and its acquired companies, was approximately $6.0 billion.[67] By early April 2001, the company's market capitalization had improved to approximately $7.6 billion. If the company were not able to maintain and increase its market value, a goodwill impairment charge might be needed.

CHECKLIST TO DETECT AGGRESSIVE CAPITALIZATION AND EXTENDED AMORTIZATION POLICIES

A checklist of items to consider in detecting aggressive capitalization and extended amortization policies is provided in Exhibit 7.7. In completing the checklist, the reader should refer to appropriate sections in the chapter to better evaluate the implications of the answers provided.

Exhibit 7.7   Checklist to Detect Aggressive Capitalization and Extended Amortization Policies

Detecting Aggressive Capitalization Policies

A. For cost capitalization generally:
  1. What are the company's policies with respect to cost capitalization?
    a. Is the company capitalizing costs that competitors or other companies in the industry expense?
    b. Does the company expense more, taking a more conservative approach?
    c. Are capitalized costs increasing faster than revenue over lengthy periods?
    d. What do capitalized costs represent?
      i.   An identifiable asset with an ascertainable market value?
      ii. Not an identifiable asset, whose market value, if any, is tied to the general fortunes of the company?
        1. Can the benefit to future periods be determined?
        2. What is the materiality of the asset to total assets and shareholders' equity?
  2. Do capitalized costs exceed market value?
B. For companies incurring software development costs:
  1. What proportion of software development costs incurred are being capitalized?
  2. How does this percentage compare with competitors or other companies in the industry?
C. For companies capitalizing interest costs:
  1. Should capitalization of interest costs be discontinued?
    a. Is the asset under construction complete and available for its intended use?
    b. Do costs incurred on the asset under construction give an indication of exceeding net realizable value?
      i.   Have there been construction delays?
      ii. Have there been cost overruns?
D. For companies capitalizing direct-response advertising and related expenditures such as customer acquisition or subscriber acquisition costs:
  1. Is persuasive historical evidence available that would permit formulation of a reliable estimate of future revenue to be obtained from incremental advertising or customer/subscriber acquisition expenditures?

(continues)

Exhibit 7.7 *(Continued)*

---

2. Is the company an insurance company that is properly capitalizing policy acquisition costs?

E. For companies incurring oil and gas exploration expenditures:

1. Does the company use the successful efforts method (expensing option) or the full cost method (capitalization option) to account for exploration expenditures?

2. Are petroleum prices declining, suggesting capitalized costs may be value impaired?

F. A policy of capitalizing the following costs should be considered at odds with generally accepted accounting principles:

1. Costs of start-up activities, including organizational costs and preopening costs

2. Advertising, marketing, and promotion costs, excluding direct-response advertising and general and administrative expenses

3. Costs incurred on internally conducted research and development activities and purchased in-process research and development

a. Software development is excluded and can be capitalized

i. For software written for sale or lease—capitalization begins after technological feasibility has been reached

ii. For software written for internal use—capitalization begins after the preliminary project stage is complete

G. Has the company shown evidence in the past of being aggressive in its capitalization policies?

1. Is there an example of a prior year write-down of capitalized costs that, in hindsight, should not have been capitalized?

2. Has a regulator, such as the SEC, forced a change in accounting policies in the past?

H. Has the company capitalized costs in stealth?

1. Examine unusual changes in and relationships with revenue of the following: accounts receivable, inventory, property, plant, and equipment, and other assets

Detecting Extended Amortization Policies

A. Has the company selected extended amortization and depreciation periods for capitalized costs?

1. As data permit, how does the calculated average amortization period for long-lived assets compare with competitors or other firms in the industry?

B. Be particularly alert for extended amortization periods in the following situations:

1. Company's industry is experiencing price deflation

2. Company is in an industry that is experiencing rapid technological change

3. Company has shown evidence in the past of employing extended amortization periods

a. Is there an example of a prior year write-down of assets that became value impaired?

C. For companies taking restructuring charges, examine activity in the restructuring liability or reserve account

1. Is there reason to believe that normal operating expenses are being charged to the reserve?

SUMMARY

Aggressive cost capitalization and extended amortization policies often are used by those who play the financial numbers game. Using examples taken from SEC enforcement actions, the financial press, and corporate annual reports, this chapter examines key issues of, and provides guidance on, how to detect such aggressive accounting behavior. Key points raised in the chapter include the following:

- Through guidance provided by the matching principle, costs incurred that benefit future periods should be capitalized and amortized to expense over the periods that benefit. Implementation of this standard provides considerable accounting flexibility.
- Costs that are properly capitalized include software development costs, capitalized interest, direct-response advertising, and policy acquisition costs.
- Costs that should not be capitalized include the costs of start-up activities, research and development, advertising and selling, and general and administrative expenses.
- Costs are capitalized in an aggressive manner when flexibility in accounting standards is stretched beyond intended limits. The net result is the reporting of assets for expenditures that do not benefit future periods.
- In detecting aggressive capitalization policies, one should:
  1. Carefully consider a company's capitalization policies
  2. Evaluate what capitalized costs represent
  3. Look for evidence of aggressive capitalization policies in the past
  4. Test for costs that have been capitalized in stealth
- Extended amortization periods carry beyond an asset's economic useful life.
- When assets are amortized over extended periods, the likelihood of an impairment loss increases because the assets' resulting book values are higher than they would be under more realistic periods.
- In detecting extended amortization periods, one should:
  1. Compare a calculated average amortization period for long-lived assets with competitors and other companies in the industry
  2. Look for evidence of the use of extended amortization periods in the past.
- Restructuring charges can be taken only when pursuant to an officially approved plan. The activity in a restructuring liability accrued for such costs as severance, benefits, and closure must be disclosed until a restructuring is complete.

GLOSSARY

Aggressive Cost Capitalization   Cost capitalization that stretches the flexibility within generally accepted accounting principles beyond its intended limits, resulting in reporting as assets items that more reasonably should have been expensed. The purpose of this activity is likely to alter financial results and financial position in order to create a potentially misleading impression of a firm's business performance or financial position.

Amortization   The systematic and rational allocation of capitalized costs over their useful lives. Refer also to *depreciation* and *depletion*.

Average Amortization Period   The average useful life of a company's collective amortizable asset base.

Capitalized Cost   An expenditure or accrual that is reported as an asset to be amortized against future-period revenue.

Capitalized Interest   Interest incurred during the construction period on monies invested in assets under construction that is added to the cost of the assets.

Costs Capitalized in Stealth   A particularly egregious form of aggressive cost capitalization where inappropriately capitalized costs are hidden within other unrelated account balances.

Customer, Member, or Subscriber Acquisition Costs   Promotion, advertising, and commission expenditures incurred in obtaining new customers, members, or subscribers for a company's products or services. Refer also to *policy acquisition costs*.

Depletion   The systematic and rational allocation of the cost of natural resources over their useful lives. Refer also to *amortization* and *depreciation*.

Depreciation   The systematic and rational allocation of the cost of property, plant, and equipment over their useful lives. Refer also to *amortization* and *depletion*.

Detailed Program Design   In software development, a detailed step-by-step plan for completing the software.

Direct-Response Advertising   Advertising designed to elicit sales to customers who can be shown to have responded specifically to the advertising in the past. Such costs can be capitalized when persuasive historical evidence permits formulation of a reliable estimate of the future revenue that can be obtained from incremental advertising expenditures.

Extended Amortization Period   An amortization period that continues beyond a long-lived asset's economic useful life.

Full-Cost Method   A method of accounting for petroleum exploration and development expenditures that permits capitalization of all such expenditures, including those leading to productive as well as nonproductive wells.

Impairment Loss   A special, nonrecurring charge taken to write down an asset with an overstated book value. Generally an asset is considered to be value-impaired when its book value exceeds the future net cash flows expected to be received from its use. An impairment write-down reduces an overstated book value to fair value.

Matching Principle   An accounting principle that ties expense recognition to revenue recognition, dictating that efforts, as represented by expenses, are to be matched with accomplishments, that is, revenue, whenever it is reasonable and practicable to do so.

Policy Acquisition Costs   Costs incurred by insurance companies in signing new policies, including expenditures on commissions and other selling expenses, promotion expenses, premium taxes, and certain underwriting expenses. Refer also to *customer, member,* or *subscriber acquisition costs*.

Preopening Costs   A form of start-up cost incurred in preparing for the opening of a new store or facility.

Purchased In-Process Research and Development   Unfinished research and development that is acquired from another firm.

Research and Development (R&D)   Planned search or critical investigation aimed at discovery of new knowledge and translation of those research findings or other knowledge into a plan or design for a new product or process or for a significant improvement to an existing product or process.

Restructuring Charge   A special, nonrecurring charge taken in conjunction with a consolidation or relocation of operations, or the disposition or abandonment of operations or productive assets. Such charges may include impairment losses as well as other expenses, such as writedowns of other assets including accounts receivable and inventory, and accruals of liabilities for so-called exit costs, including such expenses as lease terminations, closure costs, severance pay, benefits, and retraining.

Software Development Costs   Costs incurred in developing new software applications. Software development costs incurred in developing software for sale or lease are capitalized once technological feasibility is reached. Software development costs incurred in developing software for internal use are capitalized once the preliminary project stage is completed.

Start-up Costs   Costs related to such onetime activities as opening a new facility, introducing a new product or service, commencing activities in a new territory, pursuing a new class of customer, or initiating a new process in an existing or new facility.

Successful Efforts Method   A method of accounting for petroleum exploration and development expenditures that permits capitalization of expenditures only on successful projects.

Technological Feasibility   The point at which all of the necessary planning, designing, coding, and testing activities have been completed to the extent needed to establish that the software application in question can meet its design specifications

NOTES

1. *The Wall Street Journal,* January 17, 2001, p. C1.
2. Ibid., February 9, 1998, p. C17.
3. Accounting and Auditing Enforcement Release No. 1095, *In the Matter of Livent, Inc.* (Washington, DC: Securities and Exchange Commission, January 13, 1999), para. D1.
4. *The Wall Street Journal,* January 7, 1998, p. B12.
5. Ibid., January 17, 2001, p. C1. In its defense, Pre-Paid Legal maintains that any capitalized commissions remaining when a policy is canceled are treated as receivables from the sales staff, to be recovered from future policy sales. Moreover, according to the company, it has never incurred a loss due to unrecoverable commissions.
6. *The Wall Street Journal,* January 7, 1998, p. B12.
7. Ibid., October 30, 1996, p. A3.
8. Accounting and Auditing Enforcement Release No. 1257, *In the Matter of America Online, Inc., Respondent* (Washington, DC: Securities and Exchange Commission, May 15, 2000).
9. America Online, Inc., Form 10-K annual report to the Securities and Exchange Commission, September 1996, pp. F-3, F-4, and F-6.
10. America Greetings Corp., annual report, February 2000, p. 24.
11. Statement of Financial Accounting Standards No. 86, *Accounting for the Costs of Computer Software to be Sold, Leased, or Otherwise Marketed* (Norwalk, CT: Financial Accounting Standards Board, August 1985).
12. American Software, Inc., annual report, April 2000. Information obtained from Disclosure, Inc., *Compact D/SEC: Corporate Information on Public Companies Filing with the SEC* (Bethesda, MD: Disclosure, Inc., December 2000).

13. Microsoft Corp., Form 10-K annual report to the Securities and Exchange Commission, June 2000, Exhibit 13.4, p. 6.

14. Statement of Position 98-1, *Internally Developed Software* (New York: American Institute of CPAs, 1998).

15. AbleAuctions.Com, Inc. annual report, December 1999. Information obtained from Disclosure, Inc., *Compact D/SEC*, December 2000.

16. Statement of Position No. 98-5, *Reporting on the Costs of Start-Up Activities* (New York: American Institute of CPAs, 1998).

17. Filene's Basement Corp., annual report, February 1997. Information obtained from Disclosure, Inc., *Compact D/SEC*, September 1997.

18. Back Yard Burgers, Inc., annual report, December 1996. Information obtained from Disclosure, Inc., *Compact D/SEC*, September 1997.

19. Churchill Downs, Inc., annual report, December 1996. Information obtained from Disclosure, Inc., *Compact D/SEC*, September 1997.

20. Community Capital Corp., annual report, December 1996. Information obtained from Disclosure, Inc., *Compact D/SEC*, September 1997.

21. Accounting and Auditing Enforcement Release No. 871, *In the Matter of David J. Checkosky and Norman A. Aldrich* (Washington, DC: Securities and Exchange Commission, January 21, 1997).

22. Accounting and Auditing Enforcement Release No. 922, *Administrative Proceeding Instituted Against B. J. Thomas, CPA* (Washington, DC: Securities and Exchange Commission, June 10, 1997).

23. Accounting and Auditing Enforcement Release No. 1095.

24. Statement of Financial Accounting Standards No. 34, *Capitalization of Interest Cost* (Norwalk, CT: Financial Accounting Standards Board, October 1979).

25. Ameristar Casinos, Inc., annual report, December 1999. Information obtained from Disclosure, Inc., *Compact D/SEC*, December 2000.

26. Beazer Homes USA, Inc., annual report, September 1999. Information obtained from Disclosure, Inc., *Compact D/SEC*, December 2000.

27. Domtar, Inc. annual report, December 1999. Information obtained from Disclosure, Inc., *Compact D/SEC*, December 2000.

28. Statement of Financial Accounting Standards No. 121, *Accounting for the Impairment of Long-Lived Assets and for Long-Lived Assets to Be Disposed of* (Norwalk, CT: Financial Accounting Standards Board, March 1995).

29. U.S. Foodservice, Inc., annual report, July 1999. Information obtained from Disclosure, Inc., *Compact D/SEC*, December 2000.

30. Statement of Financial Accounting Standards No. 60, *Accounting and Reporting by Insurance Enterprises* (Norwalk, CT: Financial Accounting Standards Board, June 1982).

31. Statement of Financial Accounting Standards No. 19, *Financial Accounting and Reporting by Oil and Gas Producing Companies* (Norwalk, CT: Financial Accounting Standards Board, December 1977).

32. Statement of Position No. 93-7, *Reporting on Advertising Costs* (New York: American Institute of CPAs, 1993).

33. CUC International, Inc., annual report, January 1989, p. 22.

34. Cendant Corp., 10-K annual report to the Securities and Exchange Commission, December 1997, p. F-16.

35. Statement of Financial Accounting Standards No. 2, *Accounting for Research and Development Costs* (Norwalk, CT: Financial Accounting Standards Board, October 1974).

36. Accounting and Auditing Enforcement Release No. 751, *In the Matter of William F. Moody, Jr.* (Washington, DC: Securities and Exchange Commission, January 11, 1996).

37. Accounting and Auditing Enforcement Release No. 895, *In the Matter of Merle S. Finkel, CPA, Respondent* (Washington, DC: Securities and Exchange Commission, March 12, 1997).

38. Brooktrout, Inc., annual report, December 1999. Information obtained from Disclosure, Inc., *Compact D/SEC*, December 2000.

39. Accounting and Auditing Enforcement Release No. 786, *Securities and Exchange Commission v. Comparator Systems Corporation, Robert Reed Rogers, Scott Hitt and Gregory Armijo* (Washington, DC: Securities and Exchange Commission, May 31, 1996).

40. Accounting and Auditing Enforcement Release No. 764, *In the Matter of Richard A. Knight, CPA* (Washington, DC: Securities and Exchange Commission, February 27, 1996).

41. Accounting and Auditing Enforcement Release No. 778, *In the Matter of Sulcus Computer Corp., Jeffrey S. Ratner, and John Picardi, CPA* (Washington, DC: Securities and Exchange Commission, May 2, 1996), §III. B. 3. a. s.

42. BCE, Inc., annual report, December 1999. Information obtained from Disclosure, Inc., *Compact D/SEC*, March 2001.

43. Sciquest.Com, Inc., annual report, December 1999. Information obtained from Disclosure, Inc., *Compact D/SEC*, March 2001.

44. Sciquest.Com, Inc., Form 10-Q quarterly report to the Securities and Exchange Commission (September 2000), p. 3.

45. Pre-Paid Legal Services, Inc., annual report, December 1999. Information obtained from Disclosure, Inc., *Compact D/SEC*, March 2001.

46. *The Wall Street Journal,* February 22, 2000, p. A3.

47. Ibid., March 10, 1998, p. C1.

48. Accounting and Auditing Enforcement Release No. 938, *In the Matter of Ponder Industries, Inc., Mack Ponder, Charles E. Greenwood, and Michael A. Dupre, Respondents* (Washington, DC: Securities and Exchange Commission, July 22, 1997).

49. Accounting and Auditing Enforcement Release No. 1110, *In the Matter of Sunrise Medical, Inc.* (Washington, DC: Securities and Exchange Commission, not dated).

50. Harrah's Entertainment, Inc., annual report, December 1999. Information obtained from Disclosure, Inc., *Compact D/SEC*, March 2001.

51. A. Schulman, Inc., annual report, August 2000. Information obtained from Disclosure, Inc., *Compact D/SEC*, March 2001.

52. Engelhard Corp., annual report, December 1999. Information obtained from Disclosure, Inc., *Compact D/SEC*, March 2001.

53. Cypress Semiconductor Corp., annual report, January 2000. Information obtained from Disclosure, Inc., *Compact D/SEC*, March 2001.

54. Dallas Semiconductor Corp., annual report, December 2000. Information obtained from Disclosure, Inc., *Compact D/SEC*, March 2001.

55. Diodes, Inc., annual report, December 1999. Information obtained from Disclosure, Inc., *Compact D/SEC*, March 2001.

56. Vitesse Semiconductor Corp., annual report, September 2000. Information obtained from Disclosure, Inc., *Compact D/SEC*, March 2001.

57. Analog Devices, Inc., annual report, October 2000. Information obtained from Disclosure, Inc., *Compact D/SEC*, March 2001.

58. LSI Logic Corp., annual report, December 1999. Information obtained from Disclosure, Inc., *Compact D/SEC*, March 2001.

59. Vitesse Semiconductor Corp., annual report, September 2000. Information obtained from Disclosure, Inc., *Compact D/SEC*, March 2001.

60. Statement of Financial Accounting Standards No. 121, *Accounting for the Impairment of Long-Lived Assets* (Norwalk, CT: Financial Accounting Standards Board, March 1995).

61. *The Wall Street Journal,* September 30, 1996, p. B5 and May 18, 1998, p. B2, respectively.

62. Eastman Kodak Co., annual report, December 1999. Information obtained from Disclosure, Inc., *Compact D/SEC*, March 2001.

63. *The Wall Street Journal,* February 6, 1998, p. A6.

64. Ibid., January 7, 1998, p. B12.

65. Unisys Corp., annual report, December 1995. Information obtained from Disclosure, Inc., *Compact D/SEC*, September 1996.

66. Waste Management, Inc. annual report, December 1997. Information obtained from Disclosure, Inc., *Compact D/SEC*, September 1996.

67. Market capitalization includes the market value of equity plus the book value of the current portion and noncurrent portion of long-term debt.

CHAPTER EIGHT

Misreported Assets and Liabilities

Xerox Corp. said the Securities and Exchange Commission has begun an investigation into accounting problems at its Mexico unit, where the Company recently disclosed an internal probe involving issues of unpaid bills.[1]

Perry Drug Stores, Inc.'s valuation of physical inventory counts during the year generated results that were approximately $20 million less than the inventory carried on Perry's books . . . Had Perry followed its normal procedure of expensing inventory shrinkage to cost of sales, Perry would have reported a net loss of close to $6 million . . . instead of the net income of $8.3 million it originally reported.[2]

[A Division Controller at Guilford Mills, Inc.] made a series of false journal entries to . . . decrease a trade accounts payable account in a round-dollar amount ranging from $500,000, to $1,800,000, and credit a purchase account (cost of sales) in the same amount, which increased earnings.[3]

The claimed assets, which included up to 5,000,000 acres of undeveloped land, a $328,000 note and $3.4 million in artwork constituted between 78% and 96% of ANW, Inc.'s total holdings. These false and misleading financial statements were included in ANW, Inc.'s reports. . . .[4]

The valuation of assets and liabilities reported on the balance sheet provide a convenient method for playing the financial numbers game. As noted in the opening quotes, the assets and liabilities misstated might be common operating-related items such as accounts receivable, inventory, or accounts payable. Alternatively, the accounts misstated might be something a bit more unusual, such as undeveloped land or artwork. The net result is the same, however: a misstatement of earning power and financial position.

In most instances, assets are overvalued and/or liabilities are undervalued in an effort to communicate higher earning power and a stronger financial position. There is an exception, however, when, as part of a concerted effort to manage earnings, the balance sheet is reported in a conservative manner in an effort to store earnings for future years. Such tactics were discussed in Chapters 2 and 3.

LINK WITH REPORTED EARNINGS

As was seen in Chapter 7, a direct link exists between earnings and amounts reported as assets. When costs are capitalized, expenditures incurred are reported as assets on the balance sheet as opposed to expenses on the income statement. Current-period earnings are correspondingly higher.

A similar link exists between earnings and assets that are not subject to amortization, including such items as accounts receivable, inventory, and investments. When these assets are valued at amounts higher than can be realized through operations or sale, expenses or losses are postponed, inflating earnings.

For example, in 1992 Diagnostek, Inc., reported a $1.5 million receivable from United Parcel Service, Inc. (UPS), for lost or damaged shipments. Interestingly, this receivable was reported without having submitted a claim to UPS that would have helped to verify the amount due. Ultimately Diagnostek recovered only approximately $50,000 on the $1.5 million claim. By then a significant charge was needed to write down the UPS receivable. Earnings in prior years had been overstated.[5]

As another example, it is not difficult to see that special charges will be needed to address questions of collectibility concerning accounts receivable at Xerox Corp.'s Mexico unit, as noted in the opening quotes to this chapter.[6] Also, as noted in the opening quotes, consider Perry Drug Stores, Inc. The company did not record a $20 million shrinkage in inventory identified when a physical count was made. Instead, the company carried the missing inventory in a suspense account known simply as "Store 100" inventory and included it within its consolidated inventory. The net result was the postponement of an after-tax charge of approximately $14.3 million.[7]

As another example that demonstrates how an overvaluation of assets will postpone expenses and losses and overstate earnings, consider Presidential Life Corp. The company carried at cost its investments in the debt securities of several below-investment-grade issuers. Because of financial difficulties, the market value of these securities had declined precipitously and was not expected to recover. Presidential Life, however, continued to carry the investments at cost. By postponing a write-down, the company effectively reported the unrealized losses on its investments as assets.[8]

An undervaluation of liabilities also will inflate earnings temporarily. Liabilities of particular concern are obligations arising from operations, including accounts payable, accrued expenses payable, tax-related obligations, and contingent obligations such as liabilities for environmental and litigation problems. These amounts might be undervalued until true amounts owed are acknowledged and recorded.

For example, at Material Sciences Corp. not only was finished goods inventory fictitiously increased, reducing cost of goods sold, but false entries also were used to reduce accounts payable and lower cost of goods sold. By reducing cost of goods sold as inventory was increased and accounts payable were reduced, the company's earnings were correspondingly increased.[9]

In a similar scheme, as noted in the opening quotes, a division controller at Guilford Mills, Inc., would routinely adjust accounts payable and cost of goods sold downward by round amounts ranging from $500,000 to $1,800,000. Across three quarters, the net result was an overstatement of operating income by a cumulative $3,134,000.[10]

To overstate income, employees at Micro Warehouse, Inc. employed a slight variation on the same scheme. When inventory was received that had not yet been invoiced, the proper accounting procedure was to increase inventory and a corresponding liability account, referred to as accrued inventory, for amounts ultimately due. For some shipments, however, rather than increasing the liability account, cost of goods sold was reduced instead. The net effect was a direct increase in earnings.[11]

While Material Sciences, Guilford Mills, and Micro Warehouse all boosted earnings by openly reducing a liability and an expense account, earnings also can be boosted by neglecting to accrue a liability for expenses incurred. For example, as one of its many accounting irregularities, Miniscribe, Inc., did not sufficiently accrue obligations for outstanding warranties. Reported accrued liabilities for warranties declined even as sales grew. Related warranty expense was correspondingly understated.[12]

Also overstating earnings by understating a liability was Lee Pharmaceuticals, Inc. Although it learned as early as 1987 that it had contributed to high levels of contamination in the soil and groundwater beneath and surrounding its facilities, and that it had an estimable obligation to effect a cleanup, as late as 1996 the company had not accrued a liability for estimated amounts due.[13]

Autodesk, Inc., and Tesoro Petroleum Corp. show clearly the link between accrued liabilities and income. In its fiscal 1999 annual report, Autodesk made the following disclosure:

> Autodesk reversed $18.6 million of accruals associated with litigation matters. Of the amount, $18.2 million related to final adjudication of a claim involving a trade-secret misappropriation brought by Vermont Microsystems, Inc.[14]

In a similar disclosure in 1988, Tesoro Petroleum Corp. announced the "receipt" of $21 million in pretax income that "was held as a contingency reserve for potential litigation. . . . [the Company] said the contingency reserve is no longer needed."[15] In both cases, Autodesk and Tesoro Petroleum had accrued a contingent liability for litigation that ultimately did not result in loss. As a result, the companies were in a position to reverse, or add to, income amounts that had been accrued previously.

BOOSTING SHAREHOLDERS' EQUITY

As seen here, an overstatement of assets or understatement of liabilities can be directly linked to an increase in earnings. As earnings are increased, so are retained earnings, leading to a direct increment to shareholders' equity.

On some occasions, companies that play the financial numbers game will overstate the value of assets received for the issue of stock. While bypassing the income statement, the net effect is still an increase in shareholders' equity. The company appears to be more financially sound. Only when the overvalued asset is written down or sold for a loss will the fictitious increase in shareholders' equity be reversed.

For example, in 1989 Members Service Corp. issued stock to acquire certain oil and gas properties. A valuation of approximately $3.3 million was assigned to the stock and interests acquired. Unfortunately, the properties acquired were nearly worthless. Worse, in 1991, even after losing its ownership interest in the properties through litigation, Members Service Corp. reported a $2.1 million valuation for these same oil and gas interests.[16]

As another example, in 1992 Bion Environmental Technologies, Inc., issued 250,000 shares of company stock in exchange for a note receivable. The valuation assigned to the stock issued was $748,798. This was a wildly optimistic valuation and had no relation to the market value of the company's stock, which at the time was hardly worth even one cent per share. Even worse was the company's chosen method of accounting for the note received in the transaction. When stock is issued for a note to be paid at a later date, generally accepted accounting principles call for the note to be subtracted from shareholders' equity rather than being reported separately as an asset. The net effect is no change in assets or shareholders' equity. However, in an effort to boost assets and shareholders' equity, Bion Environmental did, in fact, report the note receivable as an asset. As a result, the company's shareholders' equity increased from less than $10,000 to over $750,000.[17]

Finally, as noted in the opening quotes, up to 96% of ANW, Inc., assets and shareholders' equity were overstated. Among its reported assets were up to 5,000,000 acres of undeveloped land, a $328,000 note receivable, and $3.4 million in artwork. According to the SEC, the amounts reported were false and misleading.[18]

Having demonstrated the link between earnings and shareholders' equity of misstated assets and liabilities, attention now turns to a more careful examination of selected accounts. The overvaluation of assets that are not subject to periodic amortization—in particular, accounts receivable, inventory, and investments—is examined first. A detailed look at undervalued liabilities—in particular, accounts payable, accrued expenses payable, tax-related obligations, and contingent liabilities—follows.

OVERVALUED ASSETS

Accounts Receivable

As seen in Chapter 6, accounts receivable play a key role in detecting premature or fictitious revenue. Such improperly recognized revenue leads to an uncollectible buildup in accounts receivable. As a result, the account grows faster than revenue, and accounts receivable days (A/R days), the number of days it would take to collect the ending balance in accounts receivable at the year's average rate of revenue per day, increase to a level that is higher than normal for the company and above that of competitors and the company's industry in general. However, even when revenue is recognized properly, earnings can be boosted, at least temporarily, by improperly valuing accounts receivable.

Accounts receivable are reported at net realizable value, the net amount expected to be received on collection. An estimate of uncollectible accounts, also known as the allowance or reserve for doubtful accounts, is subtracted from the total amount due to derive net realizable value. The allowance or reserve for doubtful accounts arises with the recording of an expense, the provision for doubtful accounts. When facts indicate that some or all of a particular account receivable is uncollectible, the uncollectible portion is charged against the allowance for doubtful accounts. That is, the actual loss, when it is known, is charged against the balance-sheet account, the allowance or reserve for doubtful accounts. The expense effect of the loss, the provision for doubtful accounts, was recorded earlier as an estimate.

A company that chooses to boost earnings temporarily can do so by minimizing the expense recorded as the provision for doubtful accounts. This, in turn, will understate the allowance or reserve for doubtful accounts and overstate the net realizable value of accounts receivable. Only later, often in subsequent years, when the allowance or reserve for doubtful accounts proves inadequate to handle actual uncollectible accounts, will the problem surface. Then an additional provision or expense must be recorded to accommodate the additional uncollectible accounts. Worse, the problem may not come to light for even longer periods if actual uncollectible accounts are not written off and instead are carried as collectible claims. Either way, the net realizable value of accounts receivable will be overstated.

While there is no reason to expect a conscious decision to minimize the provision for doubtful accounts in prior periods, in 1999 Advocat, Inc., found its allowance or reserve for doubtful accounts to be inadequate. As a result, an additional provision was needed, as reported in this disclosure:

> The provision for doubtful accounts was $7.0 million in 1999 as compared with $2.4 million in 1998, an increase of $4.6 million. The increase in the provision for doubtful accounts in 1999 was the result of additional deterioration of past due amounts, increased write-offs for denied claims and additional reserves for potential uncollectible accounts receivable.[19]

As is the case when earnings are boosted with premature or fictitious revenue, when accounts receivable are overvalued by consciously minimizing estimates of uncollectible accounts, accounts receivable, net of the allowance for doubtful accounts, can be expected to increase faster than revenue. Also, A/R days will increase to a level that is historically high for the company and above the levels of competitors and other companies in the industry. A key difference, however, is that revenue typically is rising when a company reports premature or fictitious revenue. While revenue also may be increasing when a company consciously reports overstated accounts receivable, a financial statement reader should be particularly on guard for overvalued accounts receivable in the presence of flat to declining revenue. Declining revenue indicates declining demand for a company's products and services and possible inroads by competitors. There also may be overall economic or industry-specific weakness that is affecting not only the company but its customers, affecting their ability to pay. In addition, the company may be selling to less creditworthy customers in an attempt to maintain previous revenue levels. All such factors lead to the reduced collectibility of accounts receivable and to a heightened risk that they are overvalued.

Many of these problems were being experienced by Springs Industries in 1998. An earnings shortfall in the second quarter of that year was blamed "on a larger-than-expected provision for bad debts and 'disappointing' sales of bedding."[20] One analyst saw the company's earnings warning as a sign that "Springs was losing market share in bedding to WestPoint Stevens, Inc., Dan River, Inc. and Pillowtex Corp."[22] Clearly, sales problems were showing up not only in declining revenue but in collection problems as well.

Collection problems also pestered Ikon Office Solutions, Inc., in 1998. In the company's quarter ended June 1998, a pretax charge of $94 million was recorded, largely to reflect "increased reserves for customer defaults."[22] Sales that quarter were slightly higher, rising 6 percent over the same quarter in 1997.

Simply because a company records a special provision or charge for uncollectible accounts receivable does not necessarily mean that a conscious effort had been made in prior periods to boost earnings artificially. Even a best estimate of uncollectible accounts can prove inadequate as circumstances change. Nonetheless, the impact of a special charge to adjust for a large unexpected increase in uncollectible accounts will have the same effect on earnings—a precipitous decline. Moreover, the company's earning power implied by reported profits in prior years was, whether consciously or not, overstated. Accordingly, a financial statement reader must be attuned to the risk of overvalued accounts receivable, whether the overvaluation is a purposeful act or not. Consider, for example, the cases of Planetcad, Inc., and Earthgrains Co.

Planetcad, Inc.

In its 1999 annual report, Planetcad, Inc., a software firm, made this disclosure about problem receivables:

> General and administrative expense increased 14% to $2.4 million in 1999 from $2.1 million reported in 1998. Increased general and administrative expense for 1999 versus 1998 was primarily due to increased bad debt expense. Bad debt expense in 1999 was $569,000 as compared to $85,000 in 1998, as the Company recognized the expense related to a few large balance accounts. The Company believes future charges will not be at the level incurred in 1999.[23]

According to its note, in 1999 the company recorded an outsize increase to bad debt expense, or provision for doubtful accounts as it is referred to here, to account for a few questionable receivables. While the company had been profitable in 1998, reporting pretax income of $598,000 on revenue of $14,350,000, the additional provision for doubtful accounts, along with other problems, pushed the company into a loss position in 1999. That year the company reported a pretax loss of $2,754,000 on revenue of $14,900,000.

It is instructive to look at the company's revenue and accounts receivable balances in the years leading up to the special charge for uncollectible accounts in 1999. Amounts for the years 1996 through 1999 are reported in Exhibit 8.1.

Exhibit 8.1   Revenue and Accounts Receivable with Related Statistics: Planetcad, Inc., Years Ending December 31, 1996–1999 (thousands of dollars, except percentages and A/R days)

	1996	1997	1998	1999
Revenue	$10,630	$10,884	$14,350	$14,900
Percent increase from prior year	—	2.4%	31.8%	3.8%
Accounts receivable, net	$1,542	$2,732	$3,981	$4,156
Percent increase from prior year	—	77.2%	45.7%	4.4%
A/R days[a]	52.9	91.6	101.3	101.8

[a]A/R days calculated by dividing accounts receivable by revenue per day, where revenue per day is revenue divided by 365.

Source: Data obtained from Disclosure, Inc., *Compact D/SEC: Corporate Information on Public Companies Filing with the SEC* (Bethesda, MD: Disclosure, Inc., March 2001).

In examining the exhibit, it is clear that over the course of the period reviewed, the company had a chronic and worsening collection problem. Across the period, accounts receivable, net of the allowance for doubtful accounts, continued to increase at rates higher than that of revenue. As a result, the company's A/R days continued to grow. By 1999, A/R days were up to 101.8 days. By then it was taking nearly twice as long as it did in 1996 to collect amounts due.

In reviewing the data in the exhibit, it can be seen that evidence of collection problems and an impending write-down were available well before the actual event in 1999. In the periods preceding 1999, the company's estimate of its uncollectible accounts was optimistic and unrealistically low. Expectations of earning power formed over those years would likely have been optimistic as well.

Earthgrains Co.

In its fiscal year ended March 2000, Earthgrains Co. also recorded a special charge for problem accounts receivable. In this instance, however, the problem was attributed to a single customer, as relayed in this disclosure:

Marketing, distribution and administrative expenses increased in 2000 to 39.4% from 38.0% on a percentage-of-sales basis. The increase is a result of the one-time, $5.4 million accounts receivable write-off related to a customer bankruptcy filing, increased goodwill amortization, and inflationary cost pressures, including increases in employee-related costs, and other expenses, including fuel.[24]

While the company attributed the collection problem to a single customer, the allowance for doubtful accounts should have been large enough to handle that customer's problems. The company's revenue and receivable figures for the years leading up to 2000 provide some insight into the problem. Consider the figures reported in Exhibit 8.2.

Exhibit 8.2   Revenue and Accounts Receivable with Related Statistics: Earthgrains Co., Years Ending March 25, 1997, March 31, 1998, March 30, 1999, and March 28, 2000 (thousands of dollars, except percentages and A/R days)

	1997	1998	1999	2000
Revenue	$1,662,600	$1,719,000	$1,925,200	$2,039,300
Percent increase from prior year	—	3.4%	12.0%	5.9%
Accounts receivable, net	$141,500	$156,500	$184,500	$261,300
Percent increase from prior year	—	10.6%	17.9%	41.6%
A/R days[a]	31.1	33.2	35.0	46.8

[a]A/R days calculated by dividing accounts receivable by revenue per day, where revenue per day is revenue divided by 365.

Source: Data obtained from Disclosure, Inc., *Compact D/SEC: Corporate Information on Public Companies Filing with the SEC* (Bethesda, MD: Disclosure, Inc., March 2001).

As can be seen in the exhibit, accounts receivable at Earthgrains Co. increased faster than revenue for each of the years 1998, 1999, and 2000. The year 2000 was particularly troublesome, with accounts receivable increasing 41.6% on a 5.9% increase in revenue. As a result, A/R days increased to 46.8 days in 2000 from 35.0 days in 1999 and 31.1 days in 1997. This information indicates that the company appeared to be experiencing collection problems.

A review of quarterly statistics for the fourth quarter of the company's year ending March 2000 and for the first three quarters of the year ended March 2001 indicate that the company was beginning to gain control of its problems. Data are provided in Exhibit 8.3.

In reviewing this exhibit, it can be seen that using quarterly revenue figures, A/R days were nearly 50 days in the quarter ended March 28, 2000, the last quarter of the fiscal year. In the quarters that followed, however, both through write-offs and increased collection efforts, the company's A/R days gradually declined, returning to 30.3 days in the quarter ended January 2, 2001.

At both Planetcad and Earthgrains Co., accounts receivable were overvalued. It cannot be known for sure whether this overvaluation was the result of a conscious effort to report higher earnings in prior years or simply due to a miscalculation of the collectibility of accounts receivable. Either way, however, earnings were temporarily overstated and subject to decline as each company came to grips with its collection problems.

Inventory

Inventory represents the cost of unsold goods on the balance sheet. When those goods are in fact sold, their cost is transferred to the income statement and reported as cost of

---

Exhibit 8.3   Revenue and Accounts Receivable with Related Statistics: Earthgrains Co., Quarters Ending March 28, 2000, June 20, 2000, September 12, 2000, and January 2, 2001 (thousands of dollars, except A/R days)

	March '00	June '00	Sept. '00	Jan. '01
Revenue	$477,500	$599,600	$603,200	$782,100
Accounts receivable	261,300	265,200	270,000	259,300
A/R days[a]	49.9	40.4	40.8	30.3

[a]Quarterly A/R days calculated by dividing accounts receivable by quarterly revenue per day, where quarterly revenue per day is quarterly revenue divided by 91.25.

Source: Data obtained from Disclosure, Inc., *Compact D/SEC: Corporate Information on Public Companies Filing with the SEC* (Bethesda, MD: Disclosure, Inc., March 2001).

---

goods sold, known also as cost of sales. An overvaluation of inventory will understate cost of goods sold and, correspondingly, overstate net income.

There are many approaches available to a company intent on overvaluing inventory. For example, a very direct approach is simply to overstate the physical quantity of items included in inventory. Such an approach may employ the use of fictitious counts for fake goods or the reporting as valid inventory merchandise that should be considered as scrap or defective. As a second approach, a company simply may increase the reported valuation of inventory without changing its physical count. This approach entails the simple step of valuing the inventory on hand at a higher amount. As a third method, a company may overvalue inventory by postponing a needed write-down for value-impaired goods that are obsolete or slow-moving.

All three approaches for overvaluing inventory are detailed below. They are followed with a close look at the last-in, first-out (LIFO) method of inventory and how it can be employed as a creative accounting practice.

Overstating Physical Counts

The act of overstating the physical quantity of inventory held is a rather brazen act of creative accounting. Unfortunately, there are many examples available of companies that have attempted to overvalue their inventory in this manner.

Consider, for example, Centennial Technologies, Inc. According to the SEC, management at the company altered inventory tags used by counters as they counted inventory on hand in an effort to overstate quantities reported.[25]

Also consider Bre-X Minterals, Ltd. Acts of fraudulent inventory reporting do not get much worse than this. The company reported a significant gold find in the jungles of Indonesia. A flurry of public announcements, including press releases and television appearances, each pointing to increased amounts of discovered gold reserves, created excitement and a buying frenzy in the company's stock. Heads turned and questions began to surface, however, when, at the height of activity and excitement, the company's geologist committed suicide by "jumping" from a company helicopter. Ultimately it was determined that Bre-X personnel had "salted," or added gold to, core test samples. In reality, as the facts of the case unfolded, the company owned little if any gold. That revelation was, of course, after investors had lost millions of investment dollars.[26]

Another gold company, International Nesmot Industrial Corp., was accused by the SEC of engaging "in a deliberate scheme to overstate the company's income and inflate its reported assets by including in inventory fake gold materials. . . ."[27] According to the SEC, the company made up brass bars to look like gold bars. The only likely real use for such fake gold bars would be in the making of a movie.

At Perry Drug Stores, Inc., an accurate physical count was in fact taken. Unfortunately, as noted in the opening quotes to this chapter, the company did not record a noted $20 million shrinkage in inventory as a reduction in reported inventory and an addition to cost of goods sold.[28] A similar physical inventory shortfall was noted at Fabri-Centers of America, Inc. Here, too, a valid physical count was taken, but once again, a noted shortfall was not recorded, leading to an overstatement of inventory.[29]

Taking an alternative tack to overstate inventory, Miniscribe Corp., a computer disk-drive manufacturer, actually packaged as good inventory scrap items that had little or no value.[30] Once properly packaged, of course, the goods appeared to be valid inventory. It was only when those packages were opened that the true value of their contents was seen.

A similar approach was used at Craig Consumer Electronics, Inc. The company's credit line was secured by its inventory. Borrowings were permitted against new goods and, to a lesser extent, refurbished ones. In an effort to boost inventory levels that were used to secure the company's line of credit, managers transferred defective goods into the new and refurbished categories. This tactic, at least temporarily, permitted the company to exceed its credit limit by a significant amount.[31]

Increasing Reported Valuation

A company need not change the physical count of its inventory to boost its reported valuation. A journal entry designed to increase inventory and reduce cost of goods sold will achieve the same effect. The impact, however, like a fast-acting drug, is immediate. As inventory is increased, so are current assets and the company's apparent liquidity. By reducing cost of goods sold, the company's gross profit margin, or gross profit divided by revenue, benefits along with net income.[32] Retained earnings are also increased, adding to shareholders' equity.

Inventory fraud was only one component of the elaborate financial fraud carried out at the electronics manufacturer Comptronix Corp. in the late 1980s. In a regular, almost routine fashion, approximately once per month management simply journalized an increase to inventory and a reduction in cost of goods sold. Aware that an unexplained increase in inventory would likely be a warning sign to some analysts, some of the bogus inventory was periodically transferred to property, plant, and equipment. The reasoning was that the falsely recorded amounts would be less apparent if carried in property, plant, and equipment. Fake invoices for equipment purchases were prepared to make it appear as though equipment additions were actually being made.[33] Of course, using the steps outlined in Chapter 7, in particular, a careful review of the relationship between revenue and property, plant, and equipment, a financial statement reader would be attuned to potential problems.

The value of inventory on hand was also overstated at Leslie Fay Companies, Inc. The method used, however, was a bit more covert than simply journalizing an increase to inventory. What the women's apparel maker did was to overstate the number of garments manufactured, effectively reducing the manufacturing cost of each one. Then as garments were sold, a smaller cost was recorded in cost of goods sold, leaving more of the manufacturing cost in ending inventory.[34] It was an interesting scheme, although one that would be picked up by an accurate physical inventory count and price extension.

Delaying an Inventory Write-down

Inventory write-downs are a routine occurrence. Inventory is reported at cost, or, if the cost to replace inventory on hand is lower, at that lower replacement cost. When goods become obsolete or slow-moving, replacement cost is likely to decline. Replacement cost also can be expected to decrease in the presence of general price declines. Either way, a write-down is needed.

The conscious postponement of an inventory write-down is a form of creative accounting. The company has reported earnings and financial position that convey a perception of business performance that is contrary to reality. An inventory write-down, however, is not prima facie evidence that inventory has been consciously overvalued in prior periods. Conditions and circumstances change, sometimes quickly. As they do, management periodically must evaluate its inventory levels, mix, and valuation in light of changes in such factors as demand, customer tastes, and technology. With this evaluation comes the need for professional judgment to determine whether a write-down is, in fact, necessary.

Whether a write-down is due to a conscious decision to overvalue inventory in prior periods or due to a valid judgment call, it is important to remember that an overly optimistic assessment of earning power has been conveyed by amounts reported in prior periods. The write-down serves as a jolt back to reality and signals the need for a sober reappraisal of business prospects.

Consider the case of Cisco Systems, Inc. As late as November 2000, orders at the company were reportedly growing at rates approaching 70% per annum. In fact, the biggest problem the company expected to face was having sufficient inventory to meet its burgeoning demand. Accordingly, the company took steps to increase its supply line of parts for manufacture. It made commitments to buy components months before they were expected to be needed.

In December 2000, the company hit a wall as orders declined precipitously in a delayed reaction to the burst of the Internet bubble and a shriveling in the investments made by its telecommunications equipment customers. Commenting on its swift reversal of fortune, John Chambers, the company's CEO, noted, "I don't know anybody that can adjust to that."[35] In fact, the company's business seemed to change virtually overnight from revenue growth that averaged in the 60% to 70% range in late 2000 to a decline in revenue expected to be as much as 30% in mid 2001. As a result, the company found itself with more inventory than it needed, forcing it to take a write-down of $2.5 billion in April 2001. That write-down was a sobering jolt indeed.

Note that there is no evidence of a conscious effort to overvalue inventory at Cisco Systems. The write-down was due to a rapid change in business conditions that arguably could not have been anticipated earlier. Nonetheless, the write-down is still painful, and it serves as a reminder that the company's prospects are not what they were as recently as six months earlier.

It is interesting to look at selected financial statement accounts and statistics from the company's quarterly reports in the periods leading up to its inventory write-down. The inventory buildup is certainly apparent. Consider the data provided in Exhibit 8.4.

In reviewing the exhibit, it can be seen that inventory is growing much faster than revenue. For every quarter examined, inventory increased more than 25%, with increases of 40.3% and 58.8% in the June-to-July 2000 and September-to-October 2000 quarters, respectively. During the period under review, inventory days, or the number of days it would take to sell the ending balance in inventory at the quarter's average rate of cost of goods sold per day, increased to 89.6 days in the January 2001 quarter. This was up from as little as 41.3 days in January 2000. In one year the company's supply of inventory relative to sales had more than doubled.

Exhibit 8.4 Revenue, Cost of Goods Sold, and Inventory with Related Statistics: Cisco Systems, Inc., Quarters Ending January 29, 2000, April 29, 2000, July 29, 2000, October 28, 2000, and January 27, 2001 (millions of dollars, except percentages and inventory days)

	Jan. '00	April '00	July '00	Oct. '00	Jan. '01
Revenue	$4,350	$4,919	$5,782	$6,519	$6,748
Percent increase from prior quarter	—	13.1%	17.5%	12.7%	3.5%
Cost of goods sold	$1,536	$1,748	$2,098	$2,378	$2,581
Inventory	$695	$878	$1,232	$1,956	$2,533
Percent increase from prior quarter	—	26.3%	40.3%	58.8%	29.5%
Inventory days[a]	41.3	45.8	53.6	75.1	89.6

[a]Quarterly inventory days calculated by dividing inventory by quarterly cost of goods sold per day, where quarterly cost of goods sold per day is quarterly cost of goods sold divided by 91.25.

Source: Data obtained from Disclosure, Inc., *Compact D/SEC: Corporate Information on Public Companies Filing with the SEC* (Bethesda, MD: Disclosure, Inc., March 2001), and from Cisco Systems, Inc., Form 10-Q quarterly report to the Securities and Exchange Commission, January, 2001, pp. 3–4.

According to the company, the inventory buildup was to ensure that it had the parts on hand it needed to fill expected future orders of its manufactured goods and was not the result of slowing demand. There was evidence of slowing revenue growth in the January 2001 quarter, as evidenced by an unexpectedly small increase in revenue of 3.5%. The company's inventory mix, however, attested to its views that future orders would be higher and parts were needed to fill them.

At fiscal year end July 2000, the company reported raw materials and finished goods inventory levels at 11.8% and 49.9% of total inventory, respectively. At the end of the second quarter in January 2001, raw materials and finished goods inventory were at 37.2% and 27.2% of total inventory, respectively.

When a company faces an expected decline in orders, it will slow purchases of raw materials in an effort to limit the amount of goods put into the manufacturing pipeline. Such an action will help prevent an unwanted buildup in finished goods inventory. In the Cisco Systems example, much of the inventory growth was in the raw materials category, consistent with an expectation of increased orders. It was when those orders did not materialize by April 2001 that the company found it necessary to write down its inventory.

LIFO Method

LIFO, the last-in, first-out method of inventory cost calculation, assumes that inventory costs included in cost of goods sold were of the last units purchased during a year. Inventory reported on the balance sheet thus consists of older purchase costs. The primary alternative to LIFO, the FIFO, or first-in, first-out method, includes older costs in cost of goods sold and leaves more recent purchase costs on the balance sheet.[36]

When inventory costs are rising, the LIFO method will result in lower earnings than the FIFO method. However, as a benefit, a LIFO company's taxable income and the amount of income taxes paid are reduced. When costs are rising, FIFO will report higher income and provide a higher inventory valuation than LIFO.

Statistics indicate that in 1999, about one-third of large, public companies used the LIFO method for at least part of their inventories while about 44% of them used the FIFO method. For companies that do not wish to select one extreme or the other, the average-cost method provides results that are somewhat between the LIFO/FIFO extremes. In 1999 the average-cost method was used by about 19% of large, public companies with other miscellaneous inventory cost methods being used by the remaining firms.[37]

LIFO and Interim Results While the LIFO method would not be expected to be a vehicle for misstating inventory and cost of goods sold, for interim financial statements, it can be used to do just that. Companies that report using the LIFO method typically maintain their internal books and accounts on a FIFO basis and adjust to LIFO for reporting purposes. This provides them with access to current cost or FIFO cost data for internal decision making and also provides a ready source of information for fulfilling SEC disclosure requirements of the current cost of their inventory. Thus, at the end of a reporting period a company will adjust amounts for inventory and cost of goods sold from their FIFO internal account valuations to LIFO amounts. For example, in order to incorporate the inflationary effects of rising costs, inventory will be reduced and cost of goods sold will be increased to adjust them from FIFO to LIFO.

The LIFO method is, however, an annual inventory cost approach. That is, the official adjustment to LIFO is made at the end of the year after all actual purchase information and price change data for the full year are known. What that means is that for interim periods, companies must adjust to LIFO for estimates of what they think the annual rate of price change in inventory will be. The effects of any errors in estimation are corrected after the end of the year and reflected in the fourth quarter's results.

Consider the selected interim results for Winn-Dixie Stores, Inc., a grocery chain, for the year ended June 30, 1999, presented in Exhibit 8.5.

The quarterly data presented in the exhibit indicate that in 1999, Winn-Dixie estimated that inflation's after-tax effect on inventory and cost of goods sold was $2,444,000 in the September 1998 and January 1999 quarters. Note how the company reported a net LIFO charge, or increase to expense and reduction in earnings, for $2,444,000 net of tax in each of the first two quarters of the year. Apparently, by the March 1999 quarter, price increases were seen to be moderating; the inflation adjustment for that quarter was only $1,833,000. By the end of the year, the company became aware that it had overstated inflation's effect on inventory and cost of goods sold. As a result, a credit and increase to earnings of $4,030,000 was needed to counter the excessive estimates of inflation and accompanying adjustments made earlier in the year. To the extent that earlier interim results were relied on, expectations about the year's performance would have been somewhat pessimistic.

Accompanying the information provided in Exhibit 8.5 was this disclosure made by the company:

> During 1999, the fourth quarter results reflect a change from the estimate of inflation used in the calculation of LIFO inventory to the actual rate experienced by the Company of 1.1% to 0.3%.[38]

In other words, early in the year the company estimated the year's inflation rate to be 1.1% for 1999, and by the end of the year the actual rate of inflation was a more moderate 0.3%. Interestingly, in 2000 the company's estimate was very close to the actual inflation rate. That year the company's estimate for inflation was 1.0%; by the end of the year the actual rate of inflation was 1.1%.

Thus, while Winn-Dixie overestimated inflation's effects during the year, a company that wished to report higher earnings during a year could purposefully underestimate inflation's effect. Such a benefit would be short-lived, however. Assuming the company wished to adjust back to actual price changes by year-end, the fourth quarter's results would need to include an addition to expense and reduction in earnings.

While the LIFO interim adjustment is not a particularly troublesome amount to derive for well-established companies like Winn-Dixie, with experienced accounting staffs, it can pose a problem to smaller, younger companies. With a less sophisticated accounting staff, such companies may make only a rough guess at the effects of price changes on LIFO amounts during interim periods. Such a step is not inconceivable given that interim

Exhibit 8.5 Selected Quarterly Data: Winn-Dixie Stores, Inc., Quarters Ending September 16, 1998, January 6, 1999, March 31, 1999, and June 30, 1999 (thousands of dollars)

	Sept. '98	Jan. '99	Mar. '99	June '99
Net sales	$3,190,755	$4,264,207	$3,203,524	$3,478,017
Gross profit on sales	841,275	1,156,000	872,659	930,979
Net earnings	14,550	52,349	58,818	56,608
Net LIFO charge (credit)	2,444	2,444	1,833	(4,030)

Source: Winn-Dixie Stores, Inc. 10-K annual report to the Securities and Exchange Commission, June 30, 1999, p. F-30.

results are not audited, even for public companies. Worse, some companies may leave any needed LIFO adjustments to the auditors to be effected at year-end. This is a problem particularly for nonpublic companies. For such companies that have only partially adjusted or that have not adjusted to LIFO during interim periods, the income statement will effectively be on a basis that approximates FIFO, being adjusted to LIFO only at year-end.

To detect whether a complete adjustment to LIFO has been effected, the interim gross profit margin should be compared with the prior year's annual gross profit margin. The premise here is that the prior year's annual gross profit margin will include the effects of a complete adjustment to LIFO. If the current year's interim results have not been adjusted to LIFO, then to the extent they reflect FIFO amounts, the interim gross profit margin will exceed the prior year's annual gross profit margin. This comparison assumes a constant inventory sales mix. If the mix has changed, then adjustments for the anticipated effects on gross profit of that change must be taken into account before a meaningful comparison of gross profit margins can be made.

LIFO Liquidations A reduction in inventory quantities by a company that uses the LIFO method is termed a LIFO liquidation. Here, current-period purchases or production of inventory fall behind sales. As a result, older LIFO inventory costs will be reflected in cost of goods sold. Assuming rising prices, these older LIFO costs will be lower than current purchase or production costs, leading to a reduction in cost of goods sold and an increase in net income. Consider this disclosure of a LIFO liquidation provided by Tesoro Petroleum Corp.:

> During 1999, certain inventory quantities were reduced, resulting in a liquidation of applicable LIFO inventory quantities carried at lower costs prevailing in previous years. This LIFO liquidation resulted in a decrease in cost of sales of $8.4 million and an increase in earnings from continuing operations of approximately $5.3 million aftertax ($0.16 per share) during 1999.[39]

Many business reasons justify a reduction in inventory quantity. Two such reasons include a move toward just-in-time inventory practices and a concerted effort to outsource more of a firm's production needs. It is possible, however, that a company may effect a LIFO liquidation in an effort simply to report higher income. It should be apparent that such income is not sustainable and will disappear when older inventories are replaced at higher costs.

A decline in LIFO inventory is evidence of a LIFO liquidation. The earnings effect of that liquidation, however, must be obtained elsewhere. Public companies are required to disclose that information and typically will do so in the footnotes, as was the case with Tesoro Petroleum Corp.[40] This disclosure should be examined carefully to determine the extent of the liquidation's effect on earnings. Unfortunately, for nonpublic companies, such a disclosure may not be available. In such cases, an improvement in gross margin over a prior year may be the result of the liquidation. If the improvement is significant, management should be questioned regarding the role, if any, played by the LIFO liquidation.

Detecting Overvalued Inventory

Whether inventory is overvalued due to an overstated physical count, an increase in the value assigned to inventory on hand, or a delayed write-down of obsolete or slow-moving goods, the same steps can be used for detection. As a result of these inventory misdeeds, there will be an unexplained increase in inventory that is outsize relative to an observed increase in revenue. Moreover, inventory days will rise and reach levels that are higher than the statistic for key competitors and other companies in the industry. An inventory that is fictitiously increased will also result in an unexpected improvement in gross profit margin. This is, of course, not to say that an improvement in gross profit margin is a sign of inventory fraud. The point is that gross profit margin benefits from steps taken to overstate inventory improperly. However, a decline in gross profit margin associated with business difficulties, which include obsolete or slow-moving merchandise, likely will offset any improvement that may be derived from an overvaluation of inventory arising from a conscious decision to delay an inventory write-down.

Consider again the case of Cisco Systems and the data reported in Exhibit 8.4. The company's inventory was increasing at a rate that was much faster than revenue. With this increase in inventory came an increase in inventory days that reflected the bloat the company was experiencing.

Also refer to the case of Perry Drug Stores introduced earlier in the chapter. At Perry Drug, an accurate physical count of inventory on hand at its fiscal year end in 1992 was taken. The problem was, however, that the company did not record an inventory shrinkage of approximately $20 million that was discovered with the count. Thus, after the physical count, the company carried inventory on its balance sheet at $20 million greater than the amount of inventory known to be physically on hand. Exhibit 8.6 presents selected data for Perry Drug Stores for a five-year period surrounding 1992, the year in question.

In reviewing the exhibit, it can be seen that revenue grew slightly over the period 1989 through 1993. Inventory, however, grew rapidly, particularly in 1992, the year in ques-

Exhibit 8.6   Revenue, Cost of Goods Sold, and Inventory, with Related Statistics: Perry Drug Stores, Inc., Years Ending October 31, 1989, 1990, 1991, 1992, and 1993 (thousands of dollars, except percentages and inventory days)

	1989	1990	1991	1992	1993
Revenue	$645,209	$633,207	$640,821	$674,431	$698,432
Percent increase (decrease) from prior year	—	(1.9%)	1.2%	5.2%	3.6%
Cost of goods sold	$468,460	$459,795	$464,454	$494,314	$544,029
Inventory	$124,934	$121,351	$123,674	$140,202	$111,263
Percent increase (decrease) from prior year	—	(2.9%)	1.9%	13.4%	(20.6%)
Inventory days[a]	97.3	96.3	97.2	103.5	74.6

[a]Inventory days calculated by dividing inventory by cost of goods sold per day, where cost of goods sold per day is cost of goods sold divided by 365.

Source: Data obtained from Disclosure, Inc., *Compact D/SEC: Corporate Information on Public Companies Filing with the SEC* (Bethesda, MD: Disclosure, Inc., September 1994).

tion. In fact, after remaining around $120 million for the years 1989 through 1991, inventory jumped suddenly to $140 million in 1992, an increase of 13.4% on a revenue increase of 5.2%. Inventory days, which had remained at 96 to 97 days in the 1989 to 1991 period, jumped suddenly to 103.5 days in 1992. Recall that it was at year-end 1992 that the company's physical count came in approximately $20 million less than what was reported on its books. The $20 million overstatement of inventory is especially evident in examining the data provided in Exhibit 8.6. In fact, if $20 million were subtracted from the $140,202,000 in inventory reported at year-end 1992 and added to the cost of goods sold, inventory days would be reduced to 85 days, which is more in line with amounts reported in previous periods. Note that by the end of 1993, the company had come to grips with its inventory difficulties and was now carrying only $111,263,000 in inventory, or 74.6 days' worth.

Investments

The range of investments available to a company is wide and includes debt securities, such as commercial paper, treasury bills and notes, and both corporate and treasury bonds, and equity securities, such as common and preferred stock. Companies also may invest in certain financial derivatives, such as options to purchase or sell stock or commodities, warrants to purchase stock, commodity futures and forwards, and certain swap agreements. The focus here is on the use of creative accounting practices for more traditional investments in debt and equity securities. Investments in financial derivatives are beyond the chapter's scope.[41]

Investments in Debt Securities

Investments in debt securities, including both short-term and long-term fixed-income investments, can be held as trading instruments, held to maturity, or carried as available for sale. The classification affects how the investments are reported.[42]

Investments in debt securities that are made with the intention of selling within a short period of time are considered to be debt securities held for trading purposes. Trading entails the frequent buying and selling of securities in an effort to generate profits from short-term changes in price. Holding periods likely are to be measured in terms of months or less and may even be as short as several days or even several hours.

Debt securities held for trading purposes are reported at fair market value. Unrealized holding gains and losses arising from periodic changes in fair market value are included in income as they arise.

The intent with investments in debt securities held to maturity is to hold the investments until the scheduled maturity date. The sole purpose of the investment is to generate interest income over the holding period. Such investments are carried at amortized cost, that is, cost net of any unamortized discount or plus any unamortized premium. Interest income, consisting of cash interest plus any amortized discount, or less any amortized premium, is included in income as it accrues. No adjustment is made to fair value unless that value has declined below cost and is not expected to recover. In such cases, where the decline in fair value is considered to be an other-than-temporary decline, the investment is written down to fair value and the decline is reported in earnings as a loss. That fair value becomes the investment's new cost basis.

Investments in debt securities that are held as available for sale do not meet the criteria as trading securities or as debt securities held to maturity. The securities are not expected to be held until maturity, but neither is the holding period expected to be as short as what is typical of a trading position. The classification available for sale is effectively a default category for investments in debt securities that cannot be classified as either trading or held to maturity.

Investments in available-for-sale debt instruments are reported at fair value. Unrealized holding gains and losses arising from changes in fair value are not reported in earnings but rather as part of accumulated other comprehensive income, a component of shareholders' equity. Like debt securities that are classified as held to maturity, an other-than-temporary decline in the fair value of an available-for-sale debt security would be recorded and included in earnings as a loss.

ABC Bancorp reports investments in held-to-maturity and available-for-sale debt securities. Consider this statement regarding the company's classification of its investments:

> Securities are classified based on management's intention on the date of purchase. Securities which management has the intent and ability to hold to maturity are classified as held to maturity and reported at amortized cost. All other debt securities are classified as available for sale and carried at fair value with net unrealized gains and losses included in stockholders' equity, net of tax.[43]

Investments in Equity Securities

Investments in equity securities, including common and preferred stock, can be held as trading securities or as available for sale. With the exception of redeemable preferred stock, which has a scheduled redemption date, the held-to-maturity classification is not available for equity securities.

Investments in equity securities that are considered to be either trading or available for sale are accounted for like debt securities. That is, such investments are reported at fair market value. Unrealized gains and losses arising from changes in fair market value are reported in earnings for trading securities and in accumulated other comprehensive income, a component of shareholders' equity, for equity securities held as available for sale. In addition, an investment in an equity security that is considered to be available for sale whose fair market value declines in a manner that is considered to be other than temporary would be written down to that lower fair market value amount. A loss for the market value decline would be reported in earnings.

Corning, Inc., is quite succinct in its description of its accounting for equity securities. Consider this note:

> Corning's marketable securities consist of equity securities classified as available-for-sale which are stated at estimated fair value based primarily upon market quotes. Unrealized gains and losses, net of tax, are computed on the basis of specific identification and are reported as a separate component of accumulated other comprehensive income in shareholders' equity until realized. A decline in the value of any marketable security below cost that is deemed other than temporary is charged to earnings, resulting in a new cost basis for the security.[44]

Investments in equity securities that are not readily marketable are reported at cost. Such investments are not adjusted for perceived changes in estimated market value unless an apparent decline in market value is experienced that is considered to be an other-than-temporary decline. In such instances, the investment is written down to the estimate of market value, which becomes the investment's new cost basis. The accompanying loss is included in earnings.

Investments in equity securities that give the investor sufficient ownership interest to exert significant influence over the operating, investing, and financing activities of the investee are accounted for using the equity method. Typically, an ownership position of 20% or more is considered sufficient to provide the investor with such significant influence.[45] Here the investor records in earnings and as an increase in the investment carrying value its share of the investee's reported net income. Dividends are reported as a reduction in the investment amount. No adjustments are made for changes in an equity-method investment's fair value unless a decline in fair value is considered to be other than temporary. In such a case, the investment would be written down and a loss recorded on the income statement. Boeing Co. describes the equity method as follows:

> Investments in joint ventures in which the Company does not have control, but has the ability to exercise significant influence over the operating and financial policies, are accounted for under the equity method. Accordingly, the Company's share of net earnings and losses from these ventures is included in the consolidated statements of operations.[46]

Creative Accounting Practices and Investments in Debt and Equity Securities

Creative accounting practices employed in the reporting for investments in debt and equity securities may come in the classification of an investment as trading, held to maturity, or available for sale, in the determination of whether a decline in market value is other than temporary, or in the accounting for realized gains and losses on sale.

Classifying Investments Accounting principles permit the use of management judgment in the classification of investments into trading, held-to-maturity, or available-for-sale categories. Classification is to be made at the time of acquisition but can be altered for changes in such circumstances as a deterioration in an issuer's creditworthiness, changes in tax law, changes in regulations, or changes due to business combinations or dispositions. The appropriateness of classifications made is to be reassessed at each reporting date.

When investments are moved between categories, they must be adjusted to fair value. For investments moved to the trading category, any adjustment to fair value would be reflected in earnings. Investments moved from the trading category would already have been adjusted to fair value. For investments moved to the available-for-sale category from the held-to-maturity classification, any adjustment to fair value is reported in accumulated other comprehensive income, a component of shareholders' equity. For investments moved to the held-to-maturity category from the available-for-sale classification, any unrealized gain or loss will continue to be carried in accumulated other comprehensive income but henceforth will be amortized to interest income over the remaining period to maturity.

Because investments classified as trading securities must be marked to market value with resulting gains and losses reflected in income, that classification provides little opportunity to apply creative accounting practices. Accordingly, the creative use of accounting guidelines for the classification of investments would more likely be in the classification of debt securities as either held to maturity or available for sale.

For example, classification of an investment in debt securities as held to maturity would permit postponement of the recognition in accumulated other comprehensive income of any temporary decline in fair value. As another possibility, the transfer of investments in debt securities to the available-for-sale classification from held to maturity would permit the recognition in accumulated other comprehensive income of gains that previously had gone unrecognized. While the amounts involved are small, in 1999 ABC Bancorp completed just such a transfer. It was reported as follows:

> . . . .the Company elected on December 31, 1999, to transfer all debt securities classified as securities held to maturity to securities available for sale. Upon election, the Company transferred debt securities with a market value of $15,420,000 to securities available for sale. These securities were marked to fair value resulting in a net unrealized gain of $90,000 which was included in stockholders' equity at $59,000, net of related taxes of $31,000.[47]

AFLAC, Inc., also transferred investments in debt securities between classifications. In 1998 the company transferred investments from the available-for-sale classification to held to maturity. The company reported the transfer in this way:

During the fourth quarter of 1998, we revised our investment management policy regarding the holding-period intent for certain of our private placement debt securities. Our past practice was to hold these securities to their contractual or economic maturity dates. We have now made this our formal policy. Accordingly, debt securities carried at a fair value of $6.4 billion were reclassified as of October 1, 1998, from the category "available for sale" to "held to maturity." The related unrealized gain of $1.1 billion as of October 1, 1998, on these securities is being amortized from other comprehensive income into investment income over the remaining term of the securities.[48]

The transfer will permit the recognition in income of unrealized investment gains totaling $1.1 billion over the holding periods of the investments. However, there should be no net effect on earnings. After the investments are written up to reflect the gains, they will be carried at a premium. That premium must be amortized against interest income over the investments' holding period, offsetting recognition of the investment gains.

Accounting for Unrealized Declines in Fair Market Value   Deciding when a decline in the fair market value of debt or equity securities is other than temporary requires the application of professional judgment. The decision is more art than science. There is always hope that market value will recover, even in the presence of disappointing news. Such hope leads many to postpone recognition of growing investment losses.

Because judgment must be employed in determining when a market value decline is other than temporary, there is much room for postponing loss recognition. In 1994 Quaker Oats Co. paid $1.7 billion for its Snapple brand of juice and iced tea business. In 1997 the company agreed to sell the business for $300 million, resulting in the need for a $1.4 billion pretax charge. It is likely that the company knew that the value of its interest was impaired well before 1997. Presumably, the company was not prepared to acknowledge such a loss prior to that date.[49]

Loss recognition was also postponed at Presidential Life Corp. The company's investments in debt securities included such poor credit risks as Circle K Corp., Eastern Airlines, Inc., and Southland Corp. The fair values of these investments had declined significantly. Any chance of recovery was extremely remote. It was the SEC that forced the company to acknowledge its losses and write these investments down.[50]

Laidlaw, Inc., employs the equity method to account for its 44% ownership position in Safety-Kleen Corp. In 2000 Laidlaw wrote down its holding in Safety-Kleen by $560 million as a result of the disclosure of possible accounting irregularities at the company and Laidlaw's decision to suspend Safety-Kleen's CEO and two other top officers.[51] Presumably Laidlaw determined that the decline in Safety-Kleen's market value was other than temporary, necessitating the write-down. Had Laidlaw chosen to postpone the loss, it would have needed to argue that the decline in Safety-Kleen's market value was a temporary event and that it had the intent and resources needed to hold the investment until its market value recovered.

Accounting for Realized Gains and Losses on Sale   Except for write-downs for declines in investment value that are considered to be other than temporary and investments that are carried as trading positions, an actual sale is required before a gain or loss on an investment position is recognized in earnings. Because the recognition of a gain or loss requires a sale, companies can "cherry pick" their investments planned for sale, deciding which ones are to be sold depending on whether gains or losses are desired.

Consider again the case of IBM first noted in Chapter 1. Recall that in its third quarter report for 1999, the company netted $4 billion in gains on the sale of its Global Network against selling, general, and administrative expense.[52] As a result, the company imparted an impression that recurring operating expenses were being reduced, giving a big boost to operating profit. While the timing of the company's sale was presumably based on an evaluation of the investment's economics and not one of managing the quarter's and year's financial results, that latter explanation cannot be completely ruled out.

When it first released its earnings report for the third quarter of 1999, First Union Corp. met Wall Street's forecasts. That was an important development as, prior to that, the company had disappointed investors for several periods. Later it was determined that the company was able to make its numbers only after the inclusion of a one-time gain of $23 million from the sale of 14 branch banks. Without the gain, the company would have missed its forecasts for the quarter by two cents per share.[53] As with IBM, the timing of the sale was presumably a function of factors other than making Wall Street's estimates. Nonetheless, the sale and the method by which it originally was reported raises questions about the real motivation.

Detecting Investment-Related Creative Accounting Practices

It is important to know, or have a general appreciation for, the fair market values of a company's investments. For investments carried in a trading account and for available-for-sale securities, market value is the proper balance-sheet valuation. While unrealized gains and losses on the trading securities are included in earnings, the gains and losses on the available-for-sale securities are recorded in accumulated other comprehensive income, a component of shareholders' equity. Thus any gains or losses that are accumulated here ultimately will be reported in earnings, either when they are sold or through a write-down for an other-than-temporary decline. If losses on such investments are accumulating, it is possible the company is consciously avoiding a write-down. An objective assessment should be made as to whether a turnaround in fair value is possible or whether a sale of the investment is, in fact, imminent.

Investments in debt securities that are classified as held to maturity and nonmarketable equity securities are reported at cost. In the case of held-to-maturity securities, cost is adjusted for any unamortized discount or premium. Investments reported under the equity method also are accounted for at cost, adjusted for the investor's share of any undistributed earnings or losses of the investee. Here an estimate of the investment's fair value is important to determine the extent to which the recognition of any losses may have been postponed. If a decline in fair value is significant and is not expected to be recovered, the company may be avoiding a write-down. Here again an assessment should be made as to whether a recovery in market value is possible or whether a sale is imminent.

The effects of any gains or losses on the sale of investments should be removed from earnings before evaluating a company's financial performance. Such gains and losses are inherently nonrecurring and should not be considered part of a company's core operations.[54]

UNDERVALUED LIABILITIES

Liabilities are probable future sacrifices of corporate resources or services made to settle present obligations. When properly valued, they are reported at the present value of the resources or services to be provided in their settlement. An undervalued liability is one that is reported at an amount less than the present value of the underlying obligation.[55] A loss or expense will result when the liability is either settled or adjusted to present value. Accordingly, earnings expectations formed without giving full consideration to an undervalued liability will be overly optimistic.

Because their effect on earnings is more direct and their amounts are more subject to manipulation, the focus here is on operations-related liabilities, such as accrued expenses payable and accounts payable, as opposed to financing-related obligations, such as notes and bonds payable. In particular, we look at creative accounting practices as they relate to accrued expenses payable, accounts payable, tax-related obligations, and contingent liabilities. Steps for detecting each type of undervalued obligation are provided in each of the respective sections.

Accrued Expenses Payable

Accrued expenses payable are expenses that have been recognized or accrued but that have not been paid. As a result, the unpaid amount is reported as a liability on the balance sheet. Examples include amounts due for unpaid selling, general, and administrative expense and unpaid research and development expense. Unpaid expenses can include wages and benefits, warranties, utilities, and insurance.

When operations-related expenses are underaccrued, future earnings will be subject to higher than normal expense levels. These additional expenses will be recorded when an underaccrued liability is increased or when a payment is made to settle an obligation for which no liability had been accrued. Reported earnings will decline.

For example, in 1998 General Electric Co. underaccrued its warranty obligations for a particular series of gas-fired turbines used in power plants. Because of design flaws, the turbines cracked, leading to a very expensive product recall. The costs of the recall and repair were expected to run over $100 million more than had been accrued for just such potential problems. It became necessary for the company to record a special charge to increase its accrued liability sufficiently to handle the recall and repair claims.[56]

As another example, consider Centuri, Inc. The case of Centuri entailed more active steps to misstate results in an effort to mislead investors than was the case at GE. As a way to boost earnings, Centuri did not accrue employee vacation expense, certain employee payroll taxes and medical expenses, and real estate taxes. As a result, accrued liabilities were understated by $912,679.[57]

A search for underaccrued expenses should include a careful review of the trend in accrued expenses payable. A decline in that liability over time indicates that payments exceed new expense accruals. While this may happen over short periods of time and may accompany, for example, a scaling back of operations, as a company grows a general increasing trend in accrued expenses payable should be expected.

A useful means for evaluating the trend in accrued expenses payable is to compare the percent change in that balance-sheet account with the percent change in revenue. If revenue increases faster than accrued expenses payable, the implication is that accrued expenses payable may be undervalued. Care should be taken in making such comparisons, however, because certain factors may cause the trend in accrued expenses payable to depart from the trend in revenue. For example, revenue might increase but, through efficiencies gained, operating expenses may not increase as the same rate. In addition, the number of days for which wages are unpaid at the end of a reporting period likely will change between accounting periods, causing increases or decreases in accrued expenses payable that are unrelated to changes in revenue.

As another test, compare selling, general, and administrative expense as a percentage of revenue with prior periods. Consider whether an improvement in that expense ratio reflects true operating efficiencies or a failure to accrue operating expenses properly.

Selected accrued expenses payable were understated at MiniScribe Corp. In 1986 the company's revenue increased 62% to $184.9 million. That same year accrued warranty expense payable actually declined from $2,083,000 to $1,374,000.[58] One must question a decline in the warranty liability account, especially in the presence of a significant increase in revenue. As was later learned, in the case of MiniScribe, the decline in the warranty obligation was only one part of a widespread accounting fraud.[59]

Accounts Payable

While accrued expenses payable arise as the result of unpaid expenses, increases in accounts payable are typically due to purchases of inventory for which payment has not been made. When accounts payable are understated, inventory purchases often are understated as well. An understatement of inventory purchases combined with an accurate beginning inventory valuation will result in an understatement of the cost of goods available for sale. Subtracting a properly valued ending inventory from an understated cost of goods available for sale will result in an understatement of cost of goods sold. Thus, an understatement of accounts payable can be linked to an understatement of cost of goods sold and, correspondingly, an overstatement of net income. Later, when unrecorded inventory purchases are discovered and recorded, a charge to income will be needed, or, if the unrecorded purchases relate to prior years, a charge must be taken to retained earnings as prior-year results are restated.

The case of Guilford Mills, referred to earlier, demonstrates well the close link between accounts payable and cost of goods sold. A division controller at the company routinely, typically at the end of each month, adjusted accounts payable and cost of goods sold downward by fictitious amounts, boosting operating income.[60]

Accounts payable days (A/P days), the number of days it would take to pay the ending balance in accounts payable at the year's average rate of cost of goods sold per day, is a useful statistic for detecting unusual or unexpected changes in accounts payable. The measure is calculated by dividing accounts payable by cost of goods sold per day, or cost of goods sold divided by 365. An unexpected improvement in gross profit margin also may be an indicator that an inappropriate adjustment was made to accounts payable and cost of goods sold.

It is important to note, however, that a misstatement of inventory purchases and accounts payable may be of insufficient magnitude to have a sufficient effect on gross margin or A/P days to be noticeable. A more sensitive indicator employs the relation that exists between inventory and accounts payable.

As noted, most accounts payable transactions are for the purchase of inventory. Thus, changes in accounts payable should closely track, in percentage terms, changes in inventory. As an example, consider the data for Guilford Mills presented in Exhibit 8.7.

The quarter ended December 28, 1997, was the first quarter identified by the SEC as containing misreported amounts. It was during that quarter that the division controller began making adjustments to reduce inventory purchases and accounts payable. Interestingly, around that same time the company discontinued reporting accounts payable in its quarterly financial statements and instead combined accounts payable with accrued expenses payable, reporting the total as other current liabilities. Accounts payable was the larger of the two amounts included in the subtotal. Whether there was an ulterior motive for this reporting change is unknown.

Because the company did not report accounts payable, A/P days could not be computed. Nonetheless, other data provided in Exhibit 8.7 merit note. In particular, as

Exhibit 8.7 Selected Income Statement and Balance Sheet Amounts with Related Statistics: Guilford Mills, Inc., Quarters Ending December 29, 1996, March 30, 1997, June 29, 1997, September 28, 1997, and December 28, 1997 (thousands of dollars, except percentages)

	Dec. '96	Mar. '97	June '97	Sept. '97	Dec. '97
Revenue	$210,863	$219,144	$238,358	$226,344	$213,377
Cost of goods sold	173,014	178,097	187,248	174,784	173,066
Gross profit	37,849	41,047	51,110	51,560	40,311
Gross profit margin	17.9%	18.7%	21.4%	22.8%	18.9%
Inventory	144,736	148,251	144,052	141,898	159,095
Percent increase (decrease) from prior quarter	—	2.4%	(2.8%)	(1.5%)	12.1%
Other current liabilities[a]	110,942	100,354	107,279	115,424	97,786
Percent increase (decrease) from prior quarter	—	(9.5%)	6.9%	7.6%	(15.3%)

[a]Accounts payable plus accrued expenses payable.

Source: Data obtained from Disclosure, Inc., *Compact D/SEC: Corporate Information on Public Companies Filing with the SEC* (Bethesda, MD: Disclosure, Inc., June 1998).

inventory grew by 12.1% in the December 1997 quarter, other current liabilities, including accounts payable, actually declined by 15.3%. At that point, other current liabilities had declined to an amount that was well below the $110,942,000 amount where it stood at the end of the same quarter in the previous year. This decline occurred even though inventory increased to $159,095,000 from $144,736,000 at the end of the same quarter in the previous year. In addition, while gross margin declined to 18.9% in the December 1997 quarter from 22.8% in the September 1997 quarter, gross margin was still higher in the December 1997 quarter than the 17.9% reported in the December 1996 quarter. While these statistics do not point unequivocally to improper adjustments to inventory purchases and accounts payable, they do merit closer scrutiny and a possible questioning of management.

Tax-Related Obligations

A complete treatment of the tax topic is beyond the scope of this book and chapter. However, even in an abbreviated look at the topic, key items can be identified that should be examined closely.[61]

Income tax expense is accrued on all taxable earnings in the year those earnings are reported on the income statement. Accrued income tax expense that is currently due and payable to a taxing authority is referred to as current income tax expense and results either in an actual cash outlay for taxes or in an increase in income taxes payable for which a cash outlay will occur in the very near term. Accrued income tax expense that is not currently due and payable is referred to as deferred income tax expense. The sum of the two—current income tax expense plus deferred income tax expense, equals total income tax expense—which is reported as the income tax provision on the income statement.

Consider the case of The Lubrizol Corp. For the years ended December 1998, 1999, and 2000, the company reported on its income statement an income tax provision of $47,614,000, $72,358,000, and $52,339,000, respectively, on pretax income of $118,814,000, $195,350,000, and $170,348,000. The components of the tax provision for each of the three years were provided in a footnote to the company's financial statement. Excerpts from that footnote are provided in Exhibit 8.8.

In the exhibit, Lubrizol reports that for 2000, its income tax provision of $52,339,000 was comprised of current tax expense, the amount that is currently due and payable, of $44,540,000, and deferred tax expense, which resulted in an increase in net deferred tax liabilities, that is, deferred tax liabilities net of deferred tax assets, of $7,799,000.

Deferred income tax expense arises primarily because of temporary differences between the amount of pretax earnings reported on the income statement for a reporting period (referred to as book income) and the amount of taxable income, on which current income tax expense is calculated, reported on the tax return for that same period. Temporary differences between income on the income statement and tax return arise as the result of differences between generally accepted accounting principles that guide the calculation of income for the income statement and the Internal Revenue Code, which guides the calculation of taxable income.

Exhibit 8.8   Components of the Provision for Income Taxes, The Lubrizol Corp., Years Ending December 31, 1998, 1999, and 2000 (thousands of dollars)

	1998	1999	2000
Current:			
United States	$16,649	$46,983	$14,679
Foreign	25,233	24,063	29,861
	41,882	71,046	44,540
Deferred:			
United States	3,385	(3,467)	6,613
Foreign	2,347	4,779	1,186
	5,732	1,312	7,799
Total	$47,614	$72,358	$52,339

Source: The Lubrizol Corp., Annual Report, December 2000, p. 32.

For example, in calculating taxable income, the Internal Revenue Code permits use of accelerated depreciation methods. Accelerated depreciation permits a company to depreciate its property, plant, and equipment items more quickly in the early years, allowing for a larger deduction against taxable income and, in effect, a tax subsidy to encourage investment. However, in computing book income, these same companies typically will use straight-line depreciation. Straight-line depreciation is considered to be more consistent with the manner in which an asset is used over its useful life and more appropriate for the calculation of depreciation expense for financial reporting purposes. Accordingly, in the early years of a depreciable asset's useful life, depreciation expense is higher on the tax return than on the income statement and taxable income will be less than book income. As a result, total income tax expense will exceed current income tax expense and deferred tax expense will be recorded, leading to an increase in a deferred tax liability.

A deferred tax liability is effectively an income tax obligation that will be paid later, when the asset's depreciation deduction on the tax return falls below that on the income statement. The timing of that event is a function of the asset's useful life. For example, for assets with extended useful lives, a company may not have to begin paying down a deferred tax liability for several years. In the meantime, if new purchases of long-lived assets are made, adding to the deferred tax liability balance, tax payment can be deferred even longer, effectively resulting in a near-permanent postponement of tax payment.

Depreciation expense is referred to as a temporary difference between taxable and book income because it causes a difference between them that is only temporary.

Cumulative depreciation expense reported on the tax return and on the income statement will be the same over a depreciated asset's useful life. It is different, however, in each of the intervening years. In the early years of the asset's life, depreciation expense on the tax return exceeds that reported on the income statement. Then, in later years, depreciation expense is higher on the income statement than on the tax return.

Depreciation is only one type of temporary difference creating initially higher book income than taxable income. Other items creating deferred tax liabilities include unrealized investment gains, the taxable portion of undistributed investee income, and the amortization of intangibles at a rate slower when calculating book income than when calculating taxable income.

In the early years for some temporary differences, taxable income actually will exceed book income. For example, as part of the matching principle, in calculating book income, a company must accrue warranty expense at the time a sale is made. That company, however, will not receive a tax deduction for its warranty expense until an actual repair expenditure is made. Such an expenditure may not occur until a subsequent year. Here current tax expense will exceed total tax expense. A reduction in deferred tax expense will be recorded, leading to an increase in a deferred tax asset, which effectively represents income taxes that have been paid currently but that will not be recovered until a future date when the actual warranty deduction is taken for tax purposes.

Other popular examples of temporary differences that create deferred tax assets include restructuring charges and asset write-downs. Both expenses are recorded on the income statement, reducing book income. Tax deductions are not provided for them, however, until associated losses are realized. As a result, taxable income will exceed book income and current tax expense will exceed total tax expense, resulting in a reduction in deferred tax expense and the creation of a deferred tax asset.

As deferred tax assets represent the tax savings to be derived from future tax deductions, there is always the possibility that recovery does not happen. For example, a tax deduction for a future warranty expense or restructuring charge creates a tax savings only if the company reports taxable income in that future period. If it does not, any resulting taxable loss can be carried back for two years to obtain a refund of taxes paid in those earlier years. If taxes were not paid in the two prior years, the resulting taxable loss can be carried forward for 20 years to be used as a deduction against future taxable income. Even with such an extended carryforward period, realization is not assured and companies must record a valuation allowance against deferred tax assets when it is more likely than not that some portion of the deferred tax asset will not be realized. Increases in a valuation allowance are recorded by increasing deferred tax expense, leading to an increase in total tax expense. As realization becomes more likely, the valuation allowance can be reduced, leading to a decrease in deferred tax expense and total tax expense.

Returning to the case of Lubrizol, as seen in Exhibit 8.8, in 2000 the company recorded a higher total income tax provision, $52,339,000, than its current tax expense, $44,540,000. The difference was deferred income tax expense, $7,799,000, which led to an increase in the company's net deferred tax liabilities during the year. The largest contributor to the increase in the company's net deferred tax liabilities (deferred tax liabilities minus deferred tax assets) during the year was a decline in its deferred tax assets, indicating that the company was deducting for tax purposes expenses and losses that had previously been recorded for book purposes. As deferred tax assets declined, net deferred tax liabilities increased.

Creative Accounting and Tax-Related Obligations   Because taxes must be accrued on all taxable earnings in the year those earnings are reported on the income statement, it is not unreasonable to expect that pretax income will be taxed at a rate that is approximately equal to the federal statutory income tax rate, 35%, plus a state tax rate net of any federal benefit for state taxes. Currently, the combined tax rate should be in the 35% to 40% range for a U.S. company. A company's effective tax rate, calculated by dividing total tax expense as reported on the income statement by pretax income, can be expected to fall in that range. It might be slightly higher due, for example, to higher state taxes or local income taxes, or because of higher foreign rates than the 35% U.S. federal income tax rate. Alternatively, it may be lower due to earnings generated in a foreign country with lower tax rates or due to nontaxable earnings such as municipal bond interest or the nontaxable portion of corporate dividends.

When a company's effective tax rate departs significantly from that 35% to 40% range, reasons for the departure should be noted. In particular, care should be taken to determine whether the tax rate can be expected to revert back to the 35% to 40% range in the near future, having a potentially significant effect on earnings. In addition, regardless of the level of an effective tax rate, reasons for any changes in that rate should be examined carefully to determine whether or not the new rate will continue.

It is hard to overstate the importance of a company's effective tax rate on its reported results. Slight reductions in the rate can raise earnings and sometimes can raise them sufficiently to change what would have been a poor or mediocre earnings report into something more spectacular. Consider the release by Hewlett Packard Co. of its earnings for the third quarter of 1999. The company beat Wall Street's expectations by two cents per share, and the market rewarded it with a $17 billion increase in its market value. Quite a feat! However, as noted by Barron's:

> Glancing through the earnings report itself, we happened to notice that all of the gain in profits in the October quarter came from lower taxes. Earnings from continuing operations before taxes were actually a tad lower this year than last.[62]

In fact, the company's effective tax rate declined in the quarter in question by one-half of 1%. That was enough, however, to add approximately $5 million to net income.

Generally accepted accounting principles require that public companies provide a reconciliation of the statutory federal income tax rate to the effective income tax rate on income from continuing operations. Alternatively, a reconciliation can be provided of the statutory federal income tax expense calculated on reported pretax income from continuing operations to actual income tax expense.[63] Such a disclosure provides insight into why a company's effective tax rate or actual tax expense may have varied from the statutory rate or tax and why it may have changed from previous periods. Of particular concern are reductions in the effective tax rate or actual tax that cannot be continued.

Examples include short-lived tax holidays provided by foreign tax jurisdictions, tax credits that are expected to expire or that may not be available in future periods, loss carryforwards that are expected to stop in the near term, or adjustments to the valuation allowance on deferred tax assets. A reduction in income taxes that is caused by any of these or other nonrecurring items will lead to a corresponding increase in net income that cannot be sustained.

In 2000, Cleveland-Cliffs, Inc., reported income before income taxes of $16.6 million. That same year, the company's income tax expense was actually a benefit of $1.5 million, which, when added to income before income taxes, resulted in net income of $18.1 million. The company's reconciliation of the statutory to its actual income tax expense is provided in Exhibit 8.9.

In reviewing the exhibit, it can be seen that in 2000, Cleveland-Cliffs reduced its actual income tax expense from a statutory tax of $5.8 million to an actual credit of $1.5 million. The primary contributing factors to the decline in income tax expense was $2.6 million for percentage depletion in excess of cost depletion, a permitted item in the tax code that is expected to continue, and $4.9 million for prior-year tax adjustments. This item relates to audits of prior-year tax returns and, although similar benefits were received in 1998 and 1999, cannot be expected to continue in future years. Accordingly, this item should be viewed as a nonrecurring reduction in the company's income tax expense that boosted net income temporarily.

As another example, in 2000, LaCrosse Footwear, Inc., reported a pretax loss of $5,675,000. That year, the company reduced its pretax loss with a tax benefit of $906,000, an amount that is considerably less than would be expected if a 35% rate were

---

Exhibit 8.9   Reconciliation of Statutory to Actual Income Tax Expense, Cleveland-Cliffs, Inc., Years Ending December 31, 1998, 1999, and 2000 (millions of dollars)

	1998	1999	2000
Tax at statutory rate of 35 percent	$25.1	$1.7	$5.8
Increase (decrease) due to:			
Percentage depletion in excess of cost depletion	(5.9)	(1.8)	(2.6)
Effect of foreign taxes	—	.2	(.2)
Prior years' tax adjustments	(4.7)	(.3)	(4.9)
Other items—net	(.1)	.1	.4
Income tax expense (credit)	$14.4	$(.1)	$(1.5)

Source: Cleveland-Cliffs, Inc., Annual Report, December 2000, p. 32.

Exhibit 8.10   Reconciliation of Statutory to Effective Income Tax Rate, LaCrosse Footwear, Inc., Years Ending December 31, 1998, 1999, and 2000

	1998	1999	2000
Statutory federal tax rate	35%	(35%)	(35%)
State taxes, net of federal tax benefit and other	4.2	(4.0)	(3.7)
Valuation allowance	—	—	22.7
Effective tax rate	39.2%	(39%)	(16%)

Source: LaCrosse Footwear, Inc., Annual Report, December 2000, p. 14.

applied to the pretax loss. The company provided a reconciliation of the statutory federal income tax rate to its effective tax rate. The reconciliation is presented in Exhibit 8.10.

As seen in the exhibit, in 2000 LaCrosse reported that a statutory benefit of 35% was expected when a pretax loss was reported. Losses on company state tax returns increased the expected benefit further. That year, however, the company increased the valuation allowance on its deferred tax assets, a majority of which was associated with the company's operating loss carryforwards. In the opinion of company management, it was more likely than not that a portion of the future tax deductions (mainly the operating loss carryforwards) represented by the deferred tax assets would not be realized. The valuation allowance was increased to accommodate this uncertainty, leading to higher income tax expense or, in this example, a lower tax benefit. In future years, as uncertainty surrounding the deferred tax assets is resolved, the company may be in a position to reduce the valuation allowance (reducing income tax expense) and increase net income.

Income tax expense plays a significant role in the calculation of reported net income. In both the Cleveland-Cliffs and LaCrosse Footwear examples, it is clear that changes in income tax expense, both down and up, can give temporary boosts or reductions to net income. If a company is so inclined, income tax expense can be a convenient vehicle for employing creative accounting practices, although this is not to say that either Cleveland-Cliffs or LaCrosse has adjusted income tax expense to manage earnings.

Contingent Liabilities

A contingent liability is an obligation that is dependent on the occurrence or nonoccurrence of one or more future events to confirm the existence of an obligation, the amount owed, the payee, or the date payable. Such liabilities are accrued only when it is deemed probable that a liability has been incurred and the amount of any obligation can be reasonably estimated. If both of these conditions are not met, the contingent liability will not be recorded, although subject to standard materiality thresholds, it should be reported in a footnote.[64] Examples of contingent liabilities that are likely to be recorded include a warranty obligation and an anticipated litigation loss from a judgment entered by the courts. The cost of cleaning up environmental damage caused by a company is another example, where before completion the total cost of a cleanup cannot be known with certainty.

Failure to accrue a contingent liability that is both probable and subject to reasonable estimation would result in the understatement of a liability and the overstatement or net income and shareholders' equity. Consider again the example of Lee Pharmaceuticals mentioned earlier. Management at the company had become aware of high levels of contamination in its soil and groundwater as early as 1987. Consultants hired by the company confirmed the company's role in the contamination in 1989. Estimates of the cost to clean up the property that ranged from $465,200 to $700,000 were available to management of the company by 1991. Given the probable nature of the obligation for cleanup and the availability of a reasonable estimate of the cost, the company should have accrued a loss. In accordance with GAAP, the amount accrued would have been the lower amount of the estimated loss range. Yet the company made no such loss accrual through 1996, significantly overstating its financial results and position.

For all companies, a careful reading of the footnotes is necessary to determine whether or not certain unrecognized contingent liabilities exist. This reading should be coupled with a careful understanding of a company's business dealings, which will provide added insight into the possible existence of unrecognized contingencies.

CHECKLIST TO DETECT MISREPORTED ASSETS AND LIABILITIES

A checklist of items to consider in detecting misreported assets and liabilities is provided in Exhibit 8.11. In completing the checklist, the reader should refer to appropriate sections in the chapter to better evaluate the implications of the answers provided.

Exhibit 8.11   Checklist to Detect Misreported Assets and Liabilities

---

Detecting Overvalued Assets

A. Accounts receivable

  1. Compare the percentage rate of change in accounts receivable with the percentage rate of change in revenue for each of the last four to six quarters.

    a. What are the implications of differences in the rates of change?

  2. Is the allowance for doubtful accounts sufficient to cover future collection problems?

    a. Compute A/R days for each of the last four to six quarters

      i. Is the trend steady, improving, or worsening?

(continues)

Exhibit 8.11 *(Continued)*

      ii. Is the overall level high when compared with competitors or other firms in the industry?

  3. Have economic conditions for the company's customers worsened recently?

    a. Are company sales declining?

    b. Are there other general economic reasons to expect that customers are, or may be, having difficulties?

  4. Are sales growing rapidly?

    a. Has the company changed its credit policy?

      i. Is credit being granted to less creditworthy customers?

    b. Have payment terms been extended?

B. Inventory

  1. Are inventories overstated due to inclusion of nonexistent inventories or by the reporting of true quantities on hand at amounts that exceed replacement cost?

    a. Compute gross margin and inventory days for the last four to six quarters

      i. Is the trend steady, worsening, or improving?

      ii. How do the statistics compare with competitors and other firms in the industry?

        1. Before making comparisons with competitors, make sure that the same inventory methods (LIFO, FIFO, etc.) are being used

    b. Do ongoing company events and fortunes suggest problems with slackening demand for the company's products?

      i. Are sales declining?

      ii. Have raw materials inventories declined markedly as a percentage of total inventory?

    c. Are prices falling, suggesting general industry weakness and an increased chance that inventory cost may not be recoverable?

    d. Is the company in an industry that is experiencing rapid technological change, increasing the risk of inventory obsolescence?

    e. Has the company shown evidence in the past of inventory overvaluation?

      i. Is there an example of a prior year write-down of inventory that became value impaired?

  2. Does the company use the FIFO method?

    a. Companies that use FIFO run a greater risk that inventory costs may exceed replacement costs

  3. Does the company employ the LIFO inventory method for at least a portion of its inventory?

    a. Are LIFO adjustments being made for interim periods?

      i. Has the LIFO reserve account remained unchanged during interim periods?

      ii. If the LIFO reserve account has been adjusted during interim periods, does the estimate of inflation used appear reasonable?

(continues)

Exhibit 8.11 *(Continued)*

---

      iii. How does gross margin for interim periods compare with prior years' annual results?

   b. Was there a decline in LIFO inventory?

      i.   Have the effects of a LIFO liquidation been disclosed?

      ii. What were the effects on gross profit and net income?

4. What is the nature of the company's environment with respect to inventory controls?

   a. Do controls to guard against theft seem adequate?

   b. When a physical inventory is taken, how does the amount compare with the books?

      i.   Do the books consistently exceed the physical count by a significant amount?

      ii. Are the books adjusted or are differences dismissed as errors in taking the physical inventory?

C. Investments

   1. For debt securities held until maturity, and nonmarketable equity securities:

     a. Is there evidence of a nontemporary decline in fair value?

   2. For debt securities and marketable equity securities that are available for sale:

     a. Are investment losses included in stockholders' equity that might be taken to income in the future?

        i.   Might the designation of these losses be changed to other-than-temporary?

        ii. Is sale of one or more investments imminent?

     b. Has stockholders' equity been buoyed by substantial write-ups to market value that may disappear in a market decline?

   3. For investments accounted for under the equity method:

     a. Is there evidence of a nontemporary decline in fair value?

Detecting Undervalued Liabilities

A. Accrued expenses payable

   1. What is the trend in accrued expenses payable?

   2. Compare the percentage rate of change in accrued expenses payable with the percentage rate of change in revenue for each of the last four to six quarters.

     a. What are the implications of differences in the rates of change?

   3. Does an improvement in selling, general, and administrative expense as a percentage of revenue reflect true operating efficiencies?

B. Accounts payable

   1. Compute A/P days for each of the last four to six quarters

     a. Is the trend steady, worsening, or improving?

     b. How does the statistic compare with competitors' and other firms in the industry?

   2. Was there an unexpected improvement in gross profit margin?

Exhibit 8.11 *(Continued)*

   3. How does the percent change in accounts payable compare with the percent change in inventory?

C. Tax-Related Obligations

   1. What is the effective tax rate and how does it compare to the statutory tax rate?

     a. Review the reconciliation of the statutory to the effective tax rate or statutory to actual tax expense and identify nonrecurring items

   2. What is the valuation allowance, if any, for deferred tax assets?

     a. Does it seem reasonable after carefully considering the prospects for future taxable income?

D. Contingent Liabilities

   1. What unrecognized contingencies are noted in a careful reading of the footnotes?

   2. Given an understanding of the company's business dealings, is there reason to believe that an unrecognized contingent liability exists?

[1] *The Wall Street Journal,* June 30, 2000, p. B6.

SUMMARY

Assets and liabilities may be misstated, giving an altered impression of a firm's financial results and position. This chapter looks at operations-related assets and liabilities that often are misstated by companies intent on playing the financial numbers game and provides guidance on detecting misreported amounts. Key points raised in the chapter include the following:

- Because of a direct link between the balance sheet and income statement, misreported assets and liabilities also result in a misstatement of net income and shareholders' equity.

- Accounts receivable may be overvalued due to the recognition of premature or fictitious revenue or as a result of an improper assessment of future collectibility.

- Inventory may be misreported through an overstatement of a physical count, through an overvaluation of actual inventory on hand, or through a postponement of a needed write-down for value-impaired goods that are obsolete or slow-moving.

- There are special issues to consider for firms reporting inventory on the last-in, first-out (LIFO) method. In particular, fourth-quarter results for LIFO firms may include material catch-up adjustments for inflation effects not accounted for earlier in the year. In addition, LIFO liquidations may boost reported results temporarily by charging to cost of goods sold older, lower-cost purchases.

- Creative accounting practices employed in the reporting of investments in debt and equity securities may result from the manner in which investments are classified as trading, held to maturity, or available for sale, in the determination of whether a decline in market value is other than temporary, or in the accounting for realized gains and losses on sale.

- Underreported operating expenses lead to understated accrued expenses payable. Future earnings will be subject to higher than normal expense levels when an under-accrued liability is increased or when a payment is made to settle an obligation for which no liability had been accrued.
- An understatement of accounts payable typically is tied to an understatement of inventory purchases and cost of goods sold.
- Potential evidence of a below-normal income tax accrual will be suggested by a below-normal effective income tax rate.
- Contingent liabilities are accrued when it is probable that an obligation has been incurred and the amount of the obligation can be reasonably estimated. Footnote disclosure is appropriate for contingencies not meeting these criteria.

GLOSSARY

Accounts Payable   Amounts due to vendors for purchases on open account, that is, not evidenced by a signed note.

Accounts Payable Days (A/P Days)   The number of days it would take to pay the ending balance in accounts payable at the average rate of cost of goods sold per day. Calculated by dividing accounts payable by cost of goods sold per day, which is cost of goods sold divided by 365.

Accounts Receivable   Amounts due from customers for sales on open account, not evidenced by a signed note.

Accounts Receivable Days (A/R Days)   The number of days it would take to collect the ending balance in accounts receivable at the year's average rate of revenue per day. Calculated by dividing accounts receivable by revenue per day, which is revenue divided by 365.

Accrued Expenses Payable   Expenses that have been recognized or accrued but have not been paid.

Accumulated Other Comprehensive Income   Cumulative gains or losses reported in shareholders' equity that arise from changes in the fair value of available-for-sale securities, from the effects of changes in foreign-currency exchange rates on consolidated foreign-currency financial statements, certain gains and losses on financial derivatives, and from adjustments for underfunded pension plans.

Allowance for Doubtful Accounts   An estimate of the uncollectible portion of accounts receivable that is subtracted from the gross amount of accounts receivable to arrive at the estimated collectible amount.

Amortized Cost   Cost of a security adjusted for the amortization of any purchase premium or discount.

Asset   Probable future economic benefit that is obtained or controlled by an entity as a result of a past transaction or event.

Available-for-Sale Security   A debt or equity security not classified as a held-to-maturity security or a trading security. Can be classified as a current or noncurrent investment depending on the intended holding period.

Average-Cost Inventory Method   The inventory cost-flow assumption that assigns the average cost of beginning inventory and inventory purchases during a period to cost of goods sold and ending inventory.

Book Income   Pretax income reported on the income statement.

Cherry Picking   Selecting specific assets for sale so as to record desired gains or losses.

Common Stock   That part of the capital stock of a corporation that carries voting rights and represents the last claim on assets and dividends.

Contingent Liability   An obligation that is dependent on the occurrence or nonoccurrence of one or more future events to confirm the existence of an obligation, the amount owed, the payee, or the date payable.

Cost of Goods Sold   The cost incurred for goods sold during a period, including all purchase and/or production costs.

Cost of Sales   See *cost of goods sold*.

Current Income Tax Expense   That portion of the total income tax provision that is based on taxable income.

Debt Security   A security representing a debt relationship with an enterprise, including a government security, municipal security, corporate bond, convertible debt issue, and commercial paper.

Deferred Income Tax Expense   That portion of the total income tax provision that is the result of current-period originations and reversals of temporary differences.

Deferred Tax Asset   Future tax benefit that results from (1) the origination of a temporary difference that causes pretax book income to be less than taxable income or (2) a loss, credit, or other carryforward. Future tax benefits are realized on the reversal of deductible temporary differences or the offsetting of a loss carryforward against taxable income or a tax-credit carryforward against the current tax provision.

Deferred Tax Liability   Future tax obligation that results from the origination of a temporary difference that causes pretax book income to exceed taxable income.

Effective Tax Rate   The total tax provision divided by pretax book income from continuing operations.

Equity Method   Accounting method for an equity security in cases where the investor has sufficient voting interest to have significant influence over the operating and financial policies of an investee.

Equity Security   An ownership interest in an enterprise, including preferred and common stock.

Fair Market Value   See *market value*.

Fair Value   The amount at which an asset could be purchased or sold or a liability incurred or settled in a current transaction between willing and informed parties. When a quoted market price is available, fair value is the product of the number of units in question times that market price. That product also is referred to as the item's market value. For traded securities, the terms *fair value* and *market value* are synonymous. When no quoted market price is available for the item in question, fair value must be estimated.

First-In, First-Out (FIFO) Inventory Method   The inventory cost-flow assumption that assigns the earliest inventory acquisition costs to cost of goods sold. The most recent inventory acquisition costs are assumed to remain in ending inventory.

Gross Profit   Revenue less cost of goods sold.

Gross Profit Margin   Gross profit divided by revenue.

Held-to-Maturity Security   A debt security for which the investing entity has both the positive intent and the ability to hold until maturity.

Income Tax Expense   See *income tax provision.*

Income Tax Provision   The expense deduction from pretax book income reported on the income statement. It consists of both current income tax expense and deferred income tax expense. The terms *income tax expense* and *income tax provision* are used interchangeably.

Inventory   The cost of unsold goods that are held for sale in the ordinary course of business or that will be used or consumed in the production of goods to be sold.

Inventory Days   The number of days it would take to sell the ending balance in inventory at the average rate of cost of goods sold per day. Calculated by dividing inventory by cost of goods sold per day, which is cost of goods sold divided by 365.

Inventory Shrinkage   A shortfall between inventory based on actual physical counts and inventory based on book records. This shortfall may be due to such factors as theft, breakage, loss, or poor recordkeeping.

Last-In, First-Out (LIFO) Inventory Method   The inventory cost-flow assumption that assigns the most recent inventory acquisition costs to cost of goods sold. The earliest inventory acquisition costs are assumed to remain in ending inventory.

Liability   A probable future sacrifice of economic benefits arising from present obligations of a particular entity to transfer assets or provide services to other entities in the future as a result of past transactions or events.

LIFO Liquidation   A reduction in the physical quantity of an inventory that is accounted for using the LIFO inventory method.

Market Value   A quoted market price per unit times the number of units being valued. Synonymous with fair value for financial instruments when a quoted market price is available.

Nonmarketable Security   A debt or equity security for which there is no posted price or bid-and-ask quotation available on a securities exchange or over-the-counter market.

Other-than-Temporary Decline in Market Value   The standard used to describe a decline in market value that is not expected to recover. The use of the other-than-temporary description as opposed to describing a loss as permanent stresses the fact that the burden of proof is on the investor who believes a decline is only temporary. That investor must have the intent and financial ability to hold the investment until its market value recovers. In the absence of an ability to demonstrate that a decline is temporary, the conclusion must be that a decline in value is other than temporary, in which case the decline in value must be recognized in income.

Percentage Depletion   A deduction against taxable income permitted companies in the natural resources industry equal to a percentage of gross income generated by a property. The deduction is permitted even if it results cumulatively in more than 100% of the cost of the property being deducted over time. Thus, percentage depletion can create a permanent difference between book income and taxable income.

Preferred Stock   Stock that has a claim on assets and dividends of a corporation that are prior to that of common stock. Preferred stock typically does not carry the right to vote.

Present Value   The amount due on an obligation less any interest on that obligation that would be expected to accrue under market interest-rate conditions over the period prior to settlement. On an interest-bearing liability, the amount owed on the liability, the principal, is its present value. Interest is paid in addition to that present value amount. On a noninterest-bearing liability, the amount owed is considered to include interest. To calculate present value, the liability must be discounted to remove that interest. The liability amount, excluding interest, would be the noninterest-bearing liability's present value.

Provision for Doubtful Accounts   An operating expense recorded when the allowance for doubtful accounts is increased to accommodate an increase in uncollectible accounts receivable.

Realized Gains and Losses   Increases or decreases in the fair value of an asset or a liability that are realized through sale or settlement.

Redeemable Preferred Stock   A preferred stock issue that must be redeemed by the issuing enterprise or is redeemable at the option of the investor. Considered a debt security for accounting purposes.

Reserve for Doubtful Accounts   See *allowance for doubtful accounts*.

Security   A share or an interest in a property or an enterprise such as a stock certificate or a bond.

Shareholders' Equity   The residual interest or owners' claims on the assets of a corporation that remain after deducting its liabilities.

Significant Influence   The extent of influence of an investor over the operating and financial policies of an investee. Typically implied when an investor has a voting interest of between 20% and 50% of an investee's voting shares. However, can be implied as a result of such factors as board representation, participation in management, material intercompany transactions, and technological dependency.

Statutory Tax Rate   The income tax rate that is stated in income tax law. It is applied to taxable income reported in income tax returns. The U.S. Federal statutory corporate income tax rate starts out at 15% for taxable income up to $50,000 and rises quickly to 35%.

Taxable Income   Income subject to income tax as reported on the tax return.

Temporary Difference   A difference between pretax book income and taxable income that results from the recognition of revenues or gains and expenses or losses in different periods in the determination of pretax book and taxable income. Temporary differences give rise to either deferred tax assets or liabilities.

Trading Security   A debt or equity security bought and held for sale in the near term to generate income on short-term price changes.

Unrealized Gains and Losses   Increases or decreases in the fair value of an asset or a liability that have not been realized through sale or settlement.

Valuation Allowance   A contra- or reduction account to deferred tax assets. The valuation allowance represents that portion of total deferred tax assets that the firm judges is unlikely to be realized. The probability threshold applied in evaluating realization is 50%. That is, if it is more than 50% likely that some or all of a deferred tax asset will not be realized, then a valuation allowance must be set off against part or all of the deferred tax asset.

Write-Down   A reduction in the balance-sheet valuation of an asset with an accompanying expense or loss recorded in earnings.

NOTES

1. *The Wall Street Journal,* June 30, 2000, p. B6.
2. Accounting and Auditing Enforcement Release No. 1037, *In the Matter of Richard Valade, CPA, Respondent* (Washington, DC: Securities and Exchange Commission, May 19, 1998), §B.

3. Accounting and Auditing Enforcement Release No. 1287, *In the Matter of Guilford Mills, Inc., Respondent* (Washington, DC: Securities and Exchange Commission, July 24, 2000), § A.4.

4. Accounting and Auditing Enforcement Release No. 789, *Securities and Exchange Commission v. ANW, Inc., et al.* (Washington, DC: Securities and Exchange Commission, June 3, 1996), para. 2.

5. Accounting and Auditing Enforcement Release No. 762, *In the Matter of Diagnostek, Inc., Joseph Sanginiti, and Dennis Evans, CPA* (Washington, DC: Securities and Exchange Commission, February 23, 1996).

6. *The Wall Street Journal,* June 30, 2000, B6.

7. Accounting and Auditing Enforcement Release No. 1037.

8. *The Wall Street Journal,* March 2, 1993, p. B3.

9. Accounting and Auditing Enforcement Release No. 1176, *In the Matter of Material Sciences Corp., Respondent* (Washington, DC: Securities and Exchange Commission, September 28, 1999).

10. Accounting and Auditing Enforcement Release No. 1287.

11. Accounting and Auditing Enforcement Release No. 1144, *In the Matter of Micro Warehouse, Inc., Respondent* (Washington, DC: Securities and Exchange Commission, July 28, 1999).

12. MiniScribe Corp., annual report, December 1986.

13. Accounting and Auditing Enforcement Release No. 1023, *In the Matter of Lee Pharmaceuticals, Henry L. Lee, Jr., Ronald G. Lee, Michael L. Agresti, CPA, Respondents,* (Washington, DC: Securities and Exchange Commission, April 9, 1998).

14. Autodesk, Inc., annual report, January 2000. Information obtained from Disclosure, Inc., *Compact D/SEC: Corporate Information on Public Companies Filing with the SEC* (Bethesda, MD: Disclosure, Inc., September 2000).

15. Tesoro Petroleum Corp., annual report, December 1998. Information obtained from Disclosure, Inc., *Compact D/SEC: Corporate Information on Public Companies Filing with the SEC* (Bethesda, MD: Disclosure, Inc., September 1999).

16. Accounting and Auditing Enforcement Release No. 983, *In the Matter of George Christopher Bleier, CPA, Respondent* (Washington, DC: Securities and Exchange Commission, November 7, 1997).

17. Accounting and Auditing Enforcement Release No. 768, *In the Matter of Louis R. Weiss, CPA* (Washington, DC: Securities and Exchange Commission, March 11, 1996).

18. Accounting and Auditing Enforcement Release No. 789, para. 2.

19. Advocat, Inc., annual report, December 1999. Information obtained from Disclosure, Inc., *Compact D/SEC: Corporate Information on Public Companies Filing with the SEC* (Bethesda, MD: Disclosure, Inc., March 2001).

20. *The Wall Street Journal,* June 17, 1998, p. B4.

21. Ibid.

22. Ibid., August 17, 1998, p. C22.

23. Planetcad, Inc., annual report, December 1999. Information obtained from Disclosure, Inc., *Compact D/SEC*, March 2001.

24. Earthgrains Co., annual report, March 2000. Information obtained from Disclosure, Inc., *Compact D/SEC*, March 2001.

25. Accounting and Auditing Enforcement Release No. 883, *Securities and Exchange Commission v. Emanuel Pinez* (Washington, DC: Securities and Exchange Commission, February 14, 1997).

26. *The Wall Street Journal,* February 19, 1998, p. A8.

27. Accounting and Auditing Enforcement Release No. 940, *Securities and Exchange Commission v. Alexandra Elizabeth Montgomery, Willia Kenneth Nestor, Frederick Burgess, and Harriet Gluck* (Washington, DC: Securities and Exchange Commission, July 24, 1997), para. 2.

28. Accounting and Auditing Enforcement Release No. 1037, §B.

29. Accounting and Auditing Enforcement Release No. 885, *In the Matter of Alan D. Rosskamm, Respondent* (Washington, DC: Securities and Exchange Commission, February 18, 1997).

30. Accounting and Auditing Enforcement Release No. 1050, *In the Matter of Owen D. Taranta, CPA, Respondent* (Washington, DC: Securities and Exchange Commission, August 11, 1999).

31. Accounting and Auditing Enforcement Release No. 1326, *Securities and Exchange Commission v. Richard I. Berger and Donna M. Richardson* (Washington, DC: Securities and Exchange Commission, September 27, 2000).

32. Gross profit is revenue less cost of goods sold.

33. *The Wall Street Journal,* December 14, 1992, p. B4.

34. Ibid., February 23, 1993, p. A1.

35. Ibid., April 18, 2001, p. A8.

36. For a more complete treatment of the LIFO and FIFO inventory methods, refer to E. Comiskey and C. Mulford, *Guide to Financial Reporting and Analysis* (New York: John Wiley & Sons, 2000), chapter 4, "Topics in Revenue Recognition and Matching."

37. Statistics obtained from *Accounting Trends and Techniques: Annual Survey of Accounting Practices Followed in 600 Stockholders' Reports* (New York: American Institute of CPAs, 2000).

38. Winn-Dixie Stores, Inc. Form 10-K annual report to the Securities and Exchange Commission, June 30, 1999, p. F-30.

39. Tesoro Petroleum Corp., annual report, December 1999. Information obtained from Disclosure, Inc., *Compact D/SEC*, March 2001.

40. Companies will do this in different ways. Disclosures may include the effects on cost of goods sold, on operating profit, on net income or earnings per share, or any combination of these measures.

41. The reader is referred to Comiskey and Mulford, *Guide to Financial Reporting and Analysis.* Chapter 6, "Financial Derivatives," is devoted to the topic of recent developments in accounting for financial derivatives.

42. Statement of Financial Accounting Standards No. 115, *Accounting for Certain Investments in Debt and Equity Securities* (Norwalk, CT: Financial Accounting Standards Board, May 1993).

43. ABC Bancorp, annual report, December 1999. Information obtained from Disclosure, Inc., *Compact D/SEC*, March 2001.

44. Corning, Inc., annual report, December 1999. Information obtained from Disclosure, Inc., *Compact D/SEC*, March 2001.

45. In some instances, such as when an investor has sufficient representation on the investee's

board of directors, ownership positions of less than 20% may give the investor significant influence. Refer to Accounting Principles Board Opinion No. 18, *The Equity Method of Accounting for Investments in Common Stock* (New York: Accounting Principles Board, March, 1971).

46. Boeing Co., annual report, December 1999. Information obtained from Disclosure, Inc., *Compact D/SEC*, March 2001.

47. ABC Bancorp, annual report, December 1999. Information obtained from Disclosure, Inc., *Compact D/SEC*, March 2001.

48. AFLAC, Inc., annual report, December 1999. Information obtained from Disclosure, Inc., *Compact D/SEC*, March 2001.

49. *The Wall Street Journal,* March 28, 1997, p. A3.

50. Ibid., March 2, 1993, p. B3.

51. Ibid., April 28, 2000, p. A4.

52. Ibid., November 24, 1999, p. C1.

53. Ibid., November 22, 1999, p. A4.

54. The exception is a company, including many financial institutions, that has an established trading desk where investment gains and losses are a key part of operations.

55. Present value is the amount due on an obligation less any interest on that obligation that would be expected to accrue under market interest-rate conditions over the period prior to settlement. On an interest-bearing loan, the amount owed on the loan, the loan principal, is the present value of the loan. Interest is paid in addition to that present value amount. On a non–interest-bearing liability, the amount owed is considered to include interest. To calculate present value, the liability must be discounted to remove that interest. The liability amount, excluding interest, would be the non–interest-bearing liability's present value. It should be noted, however, that because the amount of interest is considered to be immaterial, the present value of a non–interest-bearing obligation that is due within one year is, for practical purposes, said to be equal to the total amount due. Thus, obligations such as accounts payable and accrued expenses payable are not discounted when reported on the balance sheet.

56. *The Wall Street Journal,* March 4, 1998, p. B4.

57. Accounting and Auditing Enforcement Release No. 774, *In the Matter or Charles W. Wallin, CPA* (Washington, DC: Securities and Exchange Commission, April 19, 1996).

58. MiniScribe Corp., annual report, December 1986.

59. Accounting and Auditing Enforcement Release No. 1150, *In the Matter of Owen D. Taranta, CPA, Respondent* (Washington, DC: Securities and Exchange Commission, August 11, 1999).

60. The controller's adjustment was actually to reduce inventory purchases, which reduced cost of goods sold. Accounting and Auditing Enforcement Release No. 1287.

61. For a careful treatment of the tax subject, refer to chapter 5, "Income Tax Reporting and Analysis," in E. Comiskey and C. Mulford *Guide to Financial Reporting and Analysis.*

62. *Barron's,* November 22, 1999, p. 6.

63. Statement of Financial Accounting Standards No. 109, *Accounting for Income Taxes* (Norwalk, CT: Financial Accounting Standards Board, February 1992).

64. Statement of Financial Accounting Standards No. 5, *Accounting for Contingencies* (Norwalk, CT: Financial Accounting Standards Board, March 1975).

CHAPTER NINE

Getting Creative with the Income Statement: Classification and Disclosure

The appropriate classification of amounts within the income statement can be as important as the appropriate measurement or recognition of such amounts.[1]

Operating income is often more important to investors than net income, and widely regarded as an indicator of how well management is running the shop.[2]

The top line is the bottom line for investors lately.[3]

The quotes suggest some of the motivation for this chapter as well as its content. The traditional prominence accorded the bottom line of the income statement is being challenged by a variety of intermediate income statement subtotals. The past decade has witnessed an exceptional degree of attention being focused on the layers or subtotals that make up the income statement. With this emphasis on subtotals, as opposed to a single bottom line, the classification of items within the income statement takes on greater importance. This chapter reviews the current structure and classification of items within the income statement. The opportunistic use of income statement classification to alter apparent earnings performance is also considered.

The financial numbers game is played principally by accelerating or decelerating the recognition of revenue or gains and expenses or losses. That is, earnings are shifted among different periods in the interperiod version of the game. However, an intraperiod form of the numbers game is also possible. Here alterations in the apparent financial performance of a firm are achieved through variations in the summarization, classification, labeling, and disclosure of items within the income statement of a single period. The very plausible assumption underlying this approach is that earnings performance is judged by more than simply the bottom line of the conventional income statement.

If earnings performance were assessed somewhat exclusively by net income—that is, the bottom line of the income statement—then simply moving items up or down within the income statement, in a form of intra–income statement creativity, would be fruitless. However, in the past decade we have seen a strong shift away from a primary emphasis on the bottom line of the income statement. In the extreme case, especially for the "new" economy companies, the "bottom line" becomes the "top line." That is, growth in sales or total revenue is accorded a stature previously reserved for net income. Gross profit, the excess of sales or revenue over cost of goods sold, also known as cost of sales or cost of revenue, enjoys an elevated status as well.

Some income statement creativity goes beyond simply moving up the income statement to measures such as operating income, gross profits, or sales. Selected pro-forma measures of performance are increasingly common. These measures usually are computed by beginning with net income and then making selected additions and subtractions to arrive at a new pro-forma measure. For example, real estate investment trusts (REITs) provide an alternative performance measure called funds from operations (FFO). This pro-forma measure starts out with net income, and then real estate–related depreciation is added back. The effects of gains and losses on the sale of real estate assets also are removed. Some firms also report pro-forma measures of earnings that remove selected noncash expenses as well as nonrecurring or nonoperating gains or losses. Recently, pay-roll taxes paid by firms upon the exercise of executive stock options have been added back to net income in arriving at pro-forma earnings. A careful consideration of these pro-forma measures is the subject of Chapter 10.

Just as with interperiod techniques, which shift revenue or gains and expenses or losses among periods, intrastatement (within the income statement) creativity also can be employed to alter a financial statement reader's impression of a firm's financial performance.[4] Again, the effectiveness of intrastatement techniques is based on the plausible assumption that the bottom line, as a measure of financial performance, is not dominant.

This chapter is organized around identifying and illustrating selected creative income statement practices. To provide essential background for the discussion, an overview of current generally accepted accounting principles (GAAP) requirements for income statement structure and classification is provided. It is within the framework of these requirements that the income statement creativity of the financial numbers game is exercised.

CURRENT INCOME STATEMENT REQUIREMENTS AND PRACTICES

Under current practice and GAAP requirements, the income statement takes on two basic formats: single step and multistep. The single-step statement involves limited subtotals and basically provides a summary listing of all revenue and all expenses. In the simplest cases, the only intervening subtotal is income before income taxes. With the multistep format, subtotals are provided for items such as gross profit, operating income, and other income and expense. Examples of the single-step and multistep formats are provided in Exhibits 9.1 and 9.2, respectively.

Exhibit 9.1 Single-Step Income Statement Format: Callon Petroleum Co., Consolidated Statements of Operations, Years Ending December 31, 1998, 1999, and 2000 (thousands of dollars)

	1998	1999	2000
Revenues:			
Oil and gas sales	$35,624	$37,140	$56,310
Interest and other	2,094	1,853	1,767
Total revenues	37,718	38,993	58,077
Costs and expenses:			
Lease operating expenses	7,817	7,536	9,339
Depreciation, depletion, and amortization	19,284	16,727	17,153
General and administrative	5,285	4,575	4,155
Interest	1,925	6,175	8,420
Accelerated vesting and retirement benefits	5,761	—	—
Impairment of oil and gas properties	43,500	—	—
Total costs and expenses	83,572	35,013	39,067
Income (loss) from operations	(45,854)	3,980	19,010
Income tax expense (benefit)	(15,100)	1,353	6,463
Net income (loss)	$(30,754)	$2,627	$12,547

Source: Callon Petroleum Co., Form 10-K Annual Report to the Securities and Exchange Commission, December 2000, p. 35. Earnings per share and preferred dividend information, provided as part of the income statement, is omitted from the above.

Alternative Income Statement Formats

The single-step income statement of Callon Petroleum Company, in Exhibit 9.1, is presented by about 28% of companies—based on an annual survey of 600 companies taken by the American Institute of Certified Public Accountants.[5] Notice that, while they are disclosed on separate line items, significant nonrecurring items of Callon Petroleum are simply listed with the other recurring expense items.

The multistep income statement of Colonial Commercial Co., in Exhibit 9.2, is presented by about 72% of firms, based on the AICPA survey. About one-half of firms using the multistep income statement present gross profit (sales minus cost of sales) or operating income (sales minus operating expenses), with an undisclosed number disclosing both gross profit and operating income.[6]

The Colonial Commercial income statement provides measures of both gross profit and operating profit. Gross profit margins are widely used by analysts in analyzing current and prospective firm profitability. The separation of operating from nonoperating

Exhibit 9.2   Multistep Income Statement Format: Colonial Commercial
Corp., Consolidated Statements of Income, Years Ending December 31, 1998,
1999, and 2000 (thousands of dollars)

	1998	1999	2000
Sales	$25,234	$42,259	$58,320
Cost of sales	18,558	30,409	42,224
Gross profit	6,676	11,850	16,096
Selling, general and administrative expenses, net	5,769	10,070	15,352
Operating income	907	1,780	744
Gain on sale of Monroc, Inc. stock	2,102	—	—
Gain on land sale	827	—	—
Interest income	181	173	60
Other income	114	153	221
Interest expense	(200)	(516)	(1,204)
Income (loss) from continuing operations before income taxes	$3,931	$1,590	$(179)
Income taxes	79	683	910
Income (loss) from continuing operations	3,852	907	(1,089)
Discontinued operations			
Loss from operations of discontinued segment	—	—	(3,212)
Loss on disposal of discontinued operation	—	—	(3,732)
Loss on discontinued operations	—	—	(6,944)
Net income (loss)	$3,852	$907	$(8,033)

Source: Colonial Commercial Corp., Form 10-K Annual Report to the Securities and Exchange
Commission, December 2000, p. 24. Earnings per share information, provided as part of the income
statement, is omitted from the above as well as a note on discontinued operations.

items may help to explain the dominance of the multistep format. That is, the development of the operating-income category requires companies to separate operating and nonoperating items. This is not a feature of the single-step format.

The single- and multi-step income statements presented in Exhibits 9.1 and 9.2 included only a single *special* income statement classification, that is, the loss on discontinued operation of Colonial Commercial.[7] Special income statement classifications are discussed and illustrated next.

Special Income Statement Classifications

Generally accepted accounting principles require that selected items be classified below income from continuing operations in the income statement. This standard income state-

---

Exhibit 9.3   Income Statement Format with Special Items

Income or loss from continuing operations	$XXX
Income or loss from discontinued operations	XXX
Extraordinary gains and losses	XXX
Cumulative effect of accounting changes	XXX
Net income or loss	$XXX

Source: Key guidance is found in Accounting Principles Board Opinion No. 30, *Reporting the Results of Operations* (New York: American Institute of Certified Public Accountants, June 1973).

---

ment format is presented in Exhibit 9.3. Each of the elements in the exhibit is presented net of any associated income tax effect.

The categories for discontinued operations and for extraordinary gains and losses involve a degree of judgment, and its creative employment in the case of discontinued operations will be discussed later. There is less flexibility in the cases of the extraordinary classification and with accounting changes.

Extraordinary Items

To be classified as extraordinary, an item of revenue or gain and expense or loss must be judged to be both unusual and nonrecurring. Given the requirements of this test, very few items are classified as extraordinary. In recent years, the annual survey conducted by the AICPA has located, on average, only about three extraordinary items per year out of 600 companies surveyed. This excludes extraordinary gains and losses on debt retirement.

Gains and losses realized on debt retirement are the single most common extraordinary item. This is not because these items satisfy the joint test of unusual and nonrecurring. Rather, Statement of Financial Accounting Standard No. 4, *Reporting Gains and Losses on the Extinguishment of Debt*, simply requires extraordinary classification.[8]

SFAS No. 4 was issued at a time (1975) when it was increasingly common for firms to repurchase their own debt at a discount. There was concern that the associated gains were not being disclosed in a very forthright manner. Investors could misjudge the operating performance of firms if they were unaware of the contribution made to earnings by these transactions.[9] While the FASB response could be seen as somewhat extreme, requiring extraordinary treatment for these gains and losses ensures that they are not overlooked by investors. Some examples of the rare breed of extraordinary items, exclusive of gains and losses on debt retirements, are found in Exhibit 9.4.

There may not seem to be much of a pattern to the extraordinary classification decision based on the limited number of available cases. However, it is common for this classification to be applied to gains and losses resulting from natural disasters, the effects of government regulation, and the expropriation of assets by a foreign government—usually during war or comparable disruptions. The cases of Avoca, Inc., Noble Drilling Corp., and Phillips Petroleum Co. are consistent with these conditions, that is, wars and government

---

Exhibit 9.4   Some Examples of Extraordinary Items

Item or Event	Company
Gain on insurance settlement due to damage from the San Francisco earthquake to a building	American Building Maintenance, Inc. (1989)
Insurance proceeds resulting from destruction of a building by fire	Avoca, Inc. (1995)
Loss on an interest rate swap termination; swap hedged floating rate debt	Berlitz International, Inc. (1999)
Settlement of a lawsuit	BLC Financial Services, Inc. (1998)
Costs of canceled business acquisition agreement	Bria Communications Corp. (1996)
Gain on sale of residential mortgage loan servicing operations	KeyCorp (1995)
Gains on the disposition of assets following a pooling of interests	Kimberly-Clark Corp. (1997)
Insurance settlement due to deprivation of use of logistics and drilling equipment abandoned in Somalia due to civil unrest	Noble Drilling Corp. (1991)
Gain from settlement with the government of Iran over the expropriation of Phillip's oil production interests	Phillips Petroleum Co. (1990)
Write-off of unamortized balance of intrastate operating rights	Schwerman Trucking Co. (1995)
Gain on the sale of the company's consumer credit card portfolio	SunTrust Banks, Inc. (1999)

Sources: Companies' annual reports. The year following each company name designates the annual report from which each example was drawn. Information obtained from Disclosure, Inc., *Compact D/SEC: Corporate Information on Public Companies Filing with the SEC* (Bethesda, MD: Disclosure, Inc., June 2000).

---

actions. While not listed in the exhibit, gains and losses associated with the 1989 earthquake in the Bay area of San Francisco typically were classified as extraordinary.

Some classification diversity can be observed by contrasting some of the extraordinary items in Exhibit 9.4 with comparable items that were not so classified. BellSouth Corporation (1993) did not classify as extraordinary costs associated with damages from Hurricane Andrew. In contrast, American Building Maintenance classified as extraordinary an insurance gain due to earthquake damage. Moreover, Sun Company (1992) did not treat as extraordinary a recovery from the government of Iran from an expropriation of properties. However, Phillips Petroleum classified the same item as extraordinary.

Other high-profile cases in which the extraordinary classification was not applied include the release of toxic chemicals by Union Carbide Corp. (1984) in Bophal, India, and the oil spill by an Exxon Corp. (1989) (now Exxon Mobil Corp.) tanker in Valdez, Alaska. The position taken by Union Carbide and Exxon, respectively, must have been that the chemical release and oil spill were risks inherent in the operation of their respective businesses. They may have been nonrecurring, at least in terms of magnitude, but they also could not be considered unusual. Classification as extraordinary requires that the gain or loss be both unusual and nonrecurring.

To the extent that analysts are interested in identifying nonrecurring items as part of their earnings analysis, the extraordinary classification is of limited value given the rarity of nonrecurring items being so classified. Rather, analysts will need to review income statement details, the cash flow statement, financial statement notes, and management's discussion and analysis in their efforts to locate nonrecurring items. Moreover, the rarity of extraordinary items, along with the prominence of their disclosure in the income statement, make them unlikely tools to use in the financial numbers game.

Discontinued Operations

A discontinued operation involves the disposition of a business segment. A business segment traditionally has been held to be a complete and separate business activity and not simply a product line. The current segment reporting standard, SFAS No. 131, *Disclosures about Segments of an Enterprise and Related Information*, identifies the following three characteristics of a segment:

1. It engages in business activities from which it may earn revenues and incur expenses (including revenues and expenses relating to transactions with other components of the same enterprise).
2. Its operating results are regularly reviewed by the enterprise's chief operating decision maker to make decisions about resources to be allocated to the segment and assess its performance.
3. Discrete financial information is available.[10]

Both the gain and loss from the disposition of the discontinued operation, as well as the operating results of the discontinued operation, are disclosed separately in the income statement. Separate classification of discontinued operations is designed to make the income statements of successive periods more informative. If the income statement of 2000 contained one collection of business segments and 2001 a smaller set, it would be difficult to judge the financial performance of the continuing businesses. Removing the results of a discontinued business from the results of continuing operations for 2000 preserves the interpretive value of the operating results of 2001 compared to 2000.

A selection of discontinued operations is found in Exhibit 9.5. A careful examination of these examples suggests that making this classification decision often involves some close calls. As with many areas of judgment in financial reporting, there is a gray area when it comes to classifying discontinued operations as segments.

The discontinued operation classification of A.O. Smith Corp. in the exhibit appears quite plausible in that it disposed of its storage tank and fiberglass pipe business. These businesses appear to be quite different from A.O. Smith's remaining motors and gener-

Exhibit 9.5   Some Examples of Discontinued Items

Company	Principal Business	Discontinued Operation
Atlantic American Corp. (1999)	Insurance	Furniture company
Ball Corp. (1996)	Packaging, aerospace and technologies	Glass containers
Barringer Laboratories, Inc. (1999)	Analytical environmental testing services	Mineralogical and geochemical testing
Bestfoods, Inc. (1999)	Food preparations	Corn refining
Cabot Corp. (2000)	Liquefied natural gas and microelectronics	Carbon black, fumed metal oxides, tantalum and cesium formate
Colonial Commercial Corp. (2000)	Door and doorframe manufacturing	Doors, door hardware, and HVAC distribution
The Cooper Companies, Inc. (1999)	Specialty healthcare: vision and women's healthcare markets	Psychiatric services
Dean Foods Co. (1999)	Food processor	Vegetables segment
Green Mountain Coffee Inc. (1999)	Coffee roaster	Company-owned retail store operations
Kinark Corp. (2000)	Hot dip galvanizing	Bulk liquids terminal and public warehousing
Olin Corp. (1999)	Chlor Alkali products and metals	Specialty chemicals
Per-Se Technologies, Inc. (2000)	Hospital services	Physician services, software, and e-health
A.O. Smith Corp. (1999)	Motors and generators	Storage tank and fiberglass pipe markets
Smurfit-Stone Container Corp. (2000)	Newsprint business	Paper and packaging

Sources: Companies' annual reports. The year following each company name designates the annual report from which each example was drawn.

ators business. The same would be true of Ball Corp.'s disposition of its containers business. However, some of the others appear less obvious.

Barringer Laboratories, Inc., provides testing services and treated its mineralogical and geochemical testing as a discontinued operation. Auto companies typically have reported only two segments, auto manufacturing and finance. However, Ford Motor Co. currently reports four segments: (1) Automotive, (2) Visteon, (3) Ford Credit, and (4) Hertz.[11] Could a case be made that sport utility vehicles and compact cars should be two different segments? Would this be consistent with Barringer's classification of its different testing services as separate segments? The classification of vegetables as a separate segment by Dean Foods Co. also may seem to be surprising.

Like most GAAP, the guidance for classification of discontinued operations is somewhat general in nature. It leaves room for the exercise of some judgment in making this classification decision. However, the additions made to segment GAAP by SFAS 131 added some criteria that should make it clearer whether a unit should be considered to be a segment. It should be possible to establish whether:

1. Operating results are reviewed by the enterprise's chief operating decision maker
2. Discrete financial information is available for units

However, a recent speech by the Chief Accountant of the Division of Corporation Finance of the SEC reveals unhappiness with the application of the new segment standard:

> Let me warn you that our patience with deficient segment disclosure has been exhausted. Expect the staff to request an amendment, rather than suggest compliance in future filings, if components regularly reviewed by the chief operating decision maker are not presented separately.[12]

There is some evidence, to be discussed later, that this flexibility in the classification of segments has been exploited in the past in an intra-income-statement version of the numbers game.

Accounting Changes

Accounting changes fall into three primary categories:

1. Changes in accounting principle
2. Changes in estimates
3. Changes in reporting entities[13]

Change in Accounting Principle   A change in accounting principle is reported using either the cumulative-effect (catch-up) or retroactive restatement methods. The accounting treatment applied to an accounting change is increasingly determined as a part of the standard-setting process. The cumulative-effect method is the most common, and it includes the cumulative effect of the switch to the new method in the income statement for the year of the change. This cumulative total represents the amount by which prior year results would have been higher or lower if the new method had been in use. Unlike the cumulative effect, which relates to prior years, the effect of the change in accounting principle on income from continuing operations for the year of the change is not set out separately in the income statement. Rather, normally it is disclosed as part of the note describing the accounting change. Under the retroactive restatement method, financial statements of previous years are recast to reflect the application of the new accounting principle.[14]

Examples of changes in accounting principles would be a change from accelerated to straight-line depreciation, a change from the LIFO to average-cost inventory method, or a change from the completed-contract to percentage-of-completion method of accounting for long-term contracts. Each of these changes would be considered discretionary in nature because they do not result from the issuance of a new accounting standard by, for example, the Financial Accounting Standards Board.[15]

Although these changes are characterized as discretionary, this does not mean that they can simply be adopted at will in order to achieve a desired effect on net income. Rather, the new accounting principle should be *preferable* to the old. For example, the new accounting principle might result in a better measure of net income by improving the matching of revenue and expenses. Moreover, a change in accounting principle calls for a reference in the auditor's report. However, no such reference is required in the case of a change in estimate. The following reference to a change in accounting principle from the auditor's report of Corn Products International, Inc., is typical:

> As discussed in note 3 to the consolidated financial statements, the Company changed its inventory costing method in the United States in 2000.[16]

Nondiscretionary changes in accounting principle are the most common. These result from the issuance of new accounting standards that must be adopted. In recent years, nondiscretionary changes have dominated reported changes in accounting principle. For example, in 1999 there were only 29 discretionary accounting changes involving inventory, depreciation, and other items disclosed in the annual survey by the AICPA. Changes were considered discretionary if they were not associated with an identified new GAAP requirement. These 29 discretionary changes were out of a total of 107 accounting changes, of which most were changes in accounting principles.[17] Some examples of recent changes in accounting principle are provided in Exhibit 9.6.

Virtually all of the changes in the exhibit could be justified on the basis of improvements in the process of revenue recognition and matching. Some will increase and some will reduce near-term earnings.

AK Steel Holding Corp.'s earnings will be increased because their change accelerated the recognition of previously unrecognized pension-related gains. Dow Chemical Co.'s shift to straight-line depreciation typically will boost earnings, as will the changes of Johns Manville Corp. and Rock Tenn Co. The switch by Brown & Sharpe Manufacturing Co. to the completed-contract reporting generally will decrease its earnings by delaying the recognition of contract profits. For Profit Recovery Group International, Inc., its change also will delay revenue recognition.[19] The near-term profit implications of the changes made by Robert Mondavi Co. and Knight-Ridder, Inc., are uncertain. However, the Mondavi switch to FIFO should be positive for profits if inventory replacement costs increase, but negative if they decrease.[20]

Changes in Accounting Estimates   The accounting for changes in estimates is handled on a prospective basis. To illustrate, assume that an airline extends the expected useful life of some of its aircraft to 25 from 20 years. The prospective treatment simply calls for spreading the remaining undepreciated cost of the aircraft, net of its residual value, over

---

Exhibit 9.6   Examples of Changes in Accounting Principle

Company	Accounting Change
AK Steel Holding Corp. (1999)	Changed its policy for recognizing previously unrecognized actuarial gains related to pensions
Brown & Sharpe (1998) Manufacturing Co.	Changed from the percentage-of-completion to the completed-contract method
Dow Chemical Co. (1997)	Changed from accelerated to a straight-line depreciation
The Goodyear Tire & Rubber Co. (2000)	Changed from the LIFO to FIFO inventory method
Johns Manville Corp. (1998)	Changed from the allowance to the capitalization method of accounting for furnace rebuild costs
Knight-Ridder, Inc. (1998)	Changed the method used to determine the market-related value of pension plan assets
Profit Recovery Group International, Inc. (1999)	Changed point of revenue recognition from the time at which overpayment claims were presented to the invoicing date[18]
Robert Mondavi Co. (2000)	Changed its inventory method from LIFO to FIFO
Rock Tenn Co. (1997)	Changed its depreciation method from 150 percent declining balance to straight-line

Sources: Companies' annual reports. The year following each company name designates the annual report from which each example was drawn. Information obtained from Disclosure, Inc., *Compact D/SEC: Corporate Information on Public Companies Filing with the SEC* (Bethesda, MD: Disclosure, Inc., June 2000).

---

five additional years. This reduces future annual depreciation amounts and raises earnings. The change is handled prospectively, that is, it affects only the results of current or future and not prior periods.

Estimates are a pervasive feature of financial reporting, and they must be made in a wide range of areas. For example, estimates are required in order to gauge the stage of completion of contracts when the percentage-of-completion method of contract reporting is used. Maintaining proper allowances for uncollectible accounts receivable and for warranty obligations requires considerable estimation. Moreover, estimates are required to ensure that assets are not carried forward at amounts greater than what can be recovered from their use in future operations.

Some examples of changes in accounting estimates are provided in Exhibit 9.7. The planned installation of its latest model product caused Advance Technologies, Inc., to reduce the remaining lives of the older-model installed units. In retrospect, the original useful-life estimate was too long. America Online, Inc., came under pressure over its practice of carrying subscriber acquisition costs on the balance sheet as an asset. As a result, it switched to the policy of expensing these costs as incurred. This resulted in the

---

Exhibit 9.7   Examples of Changes in Accounting Estimates

Company	Change in Estimate
Advance Technologies, Inc. (1998)	Reduced the remaining useful lives on the shopper calculators that were installed at Wal-Mart Supercenters
America Online, Inc. (1998)	Changed to immediate expensing of subscriber acquisition costs from capitalization and amortization over 24 months
Coca-Cola Enterprises, Inc. (1999)	Revised the estimated useful lives as well as residual values of vehicles and cold drink equipment
Cover All Technologies, Inc. (1999)	Independent actuarial valuations indicated the need to increase deferred contract revenues, resulting in a reduction of insurance services revenues
Delta and Pine Land Co. (1999)	An additional provision for seed returns was necessary because returns were greater in the fourth quarter than the levels anticipated at the end of the third quarter
Evans & Sutherland Computer Corp. (1999)	Revised its estimate of the carrying value of inventory and recorded a write-down of $13.3 million for obsolete, excess, and overvalued inventories
Infocure Corp. (1999)	Reduced the amortization period of its goodwill to three years from 15 years
The Manitowoc Co. (1999)	Eliminated a deferred tax valuation allowance because of improved prospects for the utilization of net operating loss carryforwards
Southwest Airlines, Inc. (1999)	Increased the useful life of its 737–300 and 737–500 aircraft from 20 to 23 years

Sources: Companies' annual reports. The year following each company name designates the annual report from which each example was drawn. Information obtained from Disclosure, Inc., *Compact D/SEC: Corporate Information on Public Companies Filing with the SEC* (Bethesda, MD: Disclosure, Inc., June 2000).

immediate write-off of a $385 million balance of deferred subscriber acquisition costs. In this case, the prospective approach to accounting for a change in estimate required the immediate write-off of the unamortized balance.[21] The same situation is found in the case of Cover All Technologies, Inc., and the need for an immediate increase in deferred revenues.

The revisions in depreciation and amortization periods by Coca-Cola Enterprises, Inc., and Infocure Corp. also illustrate the prospective accounting for changes in estimates. For Coca-Cola Enterprises, the effect of the change was a prospective decrease in year 2000 depreciation of $160 million. The reduction in the write-off period for goodwill increased Infocure's future annual amortization expense. Delta and Pine Land Co. underestimated seed returns; the magnitude of the change in estimate actually reduced fourth-quarter revenue to a negative number. Manitowoc Co. identified some tax-planning strategies that increased the likelihood that its loss carryforwards would be utilized, which in turn reduced its income tax provision.

Disclosing the Effects of Changes in Accounting Principle versus Accounting Estimates
As seen in Exhibit 9.3, most changes in accounting principle are highlighted in the income statement because the cumulative effect of the change is disclosed separately in the statement. The cumulative adjustment represents the effect of the new policy on the earnings of prior years. However, investors also are interested in the earnings effects of the changes for the year of the change. That is, what is the effect of the change on income from continuing operations for the year of the change?

Also, in the case of some accounting changes, the results of previous years are restated, and no cumulative-effect adjustment is reported in the income statement in the year of change. For example, Goodyear Tire and Rubber changed from the LIFO to FIFO inventory method for 2000. Goodyear presented the three most recent income statements on the new FIFO basis and then adjusted opening retained earnings for 1998 for the remaining effect of the accounting change.

Moreover, in the case of a change in estimate, the prospective treatment of the change results in no cumulative-effect adjustment in the income statement in the year of the change. Nevertheless, investors should be interested in the extent to which a change in earnings for the current year is a product of the change in estimate.

The current-year effects of both changes in accounting principles and accounting estimates must be disclosed. Typically, this disclosure is found in a footnote describing the nature of the change and its effect on earnings and earnings per share for the year of the change. Moreover, for most changes in accounting principle, the cumulative effect of the change is displayed on a separate line in the income statement. The following disclosures of a change in estimate and two changes in accounting principle are typical.

Disclosure of a Change in an Estimate: Southwest Airlines, Inc.
Effective January 1, 1999, the Company revised the estimated useful lives of its 737–300 and –500 aircraft from 20 to 23 years. This change is the result of the Company's assessment of the remaining useful lives of the aircraft based on the manufacturer's design lives, the Company's increased average aircraft stage (trip) length, and the Company's previous experience. The effect of this change was to reduce depreciation expense approximately $25.7 million and increase net income $.03 per diluted share for the year ended December 31, 1999.[22]

Change in Accounting Principle, Cumulative-Effect Method: AK Steel Corp.
Effective January 1, 1998, the Company conformed the AK Steel and Armco methods of amortizing unrecognized net gains and losses related to obligations for pensions and other

postretirement benefits and conformed the measurement dates for actuarial valuations. In 1998, the Company recognized net of tax income of $133.9 million, or $1.33 per share, as a cumulative effect of this accounting change.

Adoption of the new method increased 1998 income from continuing operations by approximately $11.2 million or $0.11 per share, and decreased 1999 income from continuing operations by approximately $7.0 million, or $.07 per share.[23]

Change in Accounting Principle, Retroactive Restatement: The Goodyear Tire and Rubber Co.

During the fourth quarter of 2000, the Company changed its method of inventory costing from last-in first-out (LIFO) to first-in first-out (FIFO) for domestic inventories. Prior periods have been restated to reflect this change. The method was changed in part to achieve a better matching of revenues and expenses. The change increased net income in 2000 by $44.4 million ($.28 per basic and diluted share), and increased retained earnings for years prior to 1998 by $218.2 million.[24]

Change in Entity Sometimes the scope of the reporting entity is changed. The most common example has been when a business combination is accounted for as a pooling of interests. The scope of the reporting entity is expanded to include the two combining companies. In this circumstance, the financial statements that are presented must be restated to reflect the combined companies—that is, the new reporting entity. This requirement preserves the interpretative value of the new time series of financial statements.

REPORTING COMPREHENSIVE INCOME

The scope of income measurement was expanded with the issuance of SFAS No. 130, *Reporting Comprehensive Income*.[25] Comprehensive income includes traditional realized net income as well as other changes in net assets (owners' equity) that do not result from investments by or distributions to owners. These new income elements are collectively labeled *other comprehensive income*.

Other Comprehensive Income

Other comprehensive income (OCI) includes several items that, prior to the issuance of SFAS No. 130, bypassed the income statement and were reported directly in shareholders' equity. The characteristic generally shared by each is that, while they do represent changes in net assets from nonowner sources, they are not realized items. Currently, the primary components of other comprehensive income are:

- Unrealized gains and losses on available for sale investments
- Foreign currency translation adjustments
- Minimum pension liability adjustments
- Gains and losses on financial derivatives used in certain hedging applications

When recognized as part of comprehensive income, each of these items is presented net of its separate income tax effect, if any.

Each element of other comprehensive income has the potential to be quite volatile. Unrealized investment gains and losses move with the changing values of securities. The extent of pension underfunding also is tied to changing security prices because funded status is measured by the relationship between pension assets, mainly traded securities, and pension obligations. Foreign currency translation gains and losses move with fluctuations in currency values. Finally, gains and losses on financial derivatives fluctuate based on changes in the underlying prices and rates that determine the values of the derivatives.

Alternative Reporting Formats for Comprehensive Income

SFAS No. 130 provides three different methods by which comprehensive income may be reported. Two involve presenting comprehensive income in an income statement format, and the third permits the summarization of comprehensive income as part of the statement of stockholders' equity.

The three alternative methods of reporting comprehensive income can be summarized as follows:

1. Other comprehensive income (or loss) is included as a separate section at the bottom of a conventional income statement. Other comprehensive income simply is added to realized net income (or loss), and the result is comprehensive income. There is a single income statement, with comprehensive income as the bottom line.
2. A second income statement is developed. This statement begins with realized net income from the conventional income statement. Then other comprehensive income is added to the conventional net income, and comprehensive income is the result.
3. All comprehensive income information is summarized and reported in the statement of shareholders' equity. Comprehensive income (conventional net income plus other comprehensive income), other comprehensive income, and accumulated other comprehensive income are all reported in the statement of shareholders' equity.

In the stock market of this new century, firms and investors have a strong aversion to accounting treatments that increase earnings volatility. As noted above, each element of other comprehensive income has the potential to be very volatile. If volatility of other comprehensive income is joined with the market's aversion to income volatility, then it becomes rather easy to predict that firms would avoid either of the income statement options of reporting comprehensive income. In fact, only about one in six firms use either of the income-statement options (options 1 and 2 above).[26] The method of choice relegates comprehensive income information to the statement of shareholders, option 3. An example of this third reporting option is presented in the next section.

Reporting Comprehensive Income

When shareholders' equity is used to report other comprehensive income, the statement of shareholders' equity will include an opening balance for accumulated other comprehensive income plus the current-period comprehensive income items as well as comprehensive income for the year. Typically, there is a column in the statement of shareholders' equity where this information is displayed. As an example, the relevant

Exhibit 9.8 Reporting Comprehensive Income: The Timken Company, Partial Consolidated Statement of Shareholders' Equity, for the Year Ended December 31, 1999 (thousands of dollars)

Balances	Total Shareholders' Equity	Accumulated Other Comprehensive Income (Loss)
Balance at December 31, 1998	$1,056,081	$(49,716)
Net income	62,624	
Year ended December 31, 1999:		
Foreign currency translation adjustment (net of income tax of $2,829)	(13,952)	(13,952)
Minimum pension liability adjustment (net of income tax of $274)	(466)	(466)
Total comprehensive income	48,206	(14,418)
Dividends	(44,502)	
Purchase of treasury shares	(14,271)	
Issuance of treasury shares	467	
Balance at December 31, 1999	$1,045,981	$(64,134)

Note: Columns for common stock, retained earnings, and treasury stock have been omitted from this abridged Timken statement of shareholders' equity.

Source: The Timken Co., annual report, December 1999, p. 24.

portion of the statement of shareholders' equity of The Timken Company is provided in Exhibit 9.8. The same current-period other-comprehensive-income information is presented in the statement of shareholders' equity as would have been presented in either of the two income statement options. In addition, the accumulated other comprehensive income balance is disclosed as part of total shareholders' equity.

The display of other comprehensive income items in a statement of shareholders' equity does not provide the same level of visibility as their presentation in one of the income statement formats. Some recent experimental evidence suggests that analysts are less likely to detect creative accounting in cases where gains on the sale of securities are disclosed as part of other comprehensive income in a statement of shareholders' equity.[27]

There is scant evidence at this point that investors find the new presentation requirements for other comprehensive income to be useful. Earnings-per-share numbers continue to be computed based on realized net income, not comprehensive income. Analysts forecast conventional net income, exclusive of nonrecurring items, not comprehensive income. Also, the statement of cash flows continues to employ realized net income and not comprehensive income.[28]

CREATIVE INCOME STATEMENT CLASSIFICATIONS

The potential importance of classification creativity within the income statement was highlighted in one of the quotations that opened this chapter: "The appropriate classification of amounts within the income statement can be as important as the appropriate measurement or recognition of such amounts."[29]

Classificatory creativity within the income statement mainly involves moving individual income statement items around within the income statement. This is done in order to alter key income statement subtotals as well as the reader's perception of financial performance. Three examples will be discussed:

1. Moving income statement items either into or out of the scope of operating income, producing either an increase or a decrease in operating income
2. Moving expenses from cost of sales to the selling, general, and administrative expense category, producing an increase in gross profit
3. Moving operations out of the discontinued operations classification when they are sold at gains but into discontinued operations when sold at losses, producing higher levels of income from continuing operations

Getting Creative with Operating Income

Operating income is a common element of the multistep income statement format (see Exhibit 9.2). It is an important income statement subtotal because it includes mainly the revenue, gains, expenses, and losses that are associated with the basic operating activities of the firm. Therefore, operating income should be useful in judging basic operating performance.

However, as with the pro-forma measures of net income discussed in the following chapter, the determination of operating income permits a degree of flexibility. Operating income is not strictly defined under GAAP. Accordingly, the items that are classified into this element of the multistep income statement are open to the exercise of considerable judgment. Such judgment permits the use of classification creativity.

Relevant GAAP, Accounting Principles Board Opinion No. 30, *Reporting the Results of Operations*, requires the following:

> A material event or transaction that is unusual in nature or occurs infrequently but not both, and therefore does not meet both criteria for classification as an extraordinary item, should be reported as a separate component of income from continuing operations. The nature and financial effects of each event and transaction should be disclosed on the face of the income statement or, alternatively, in notes to the financial statements.[30]

Notice that this statement is silent on the classification of items within or outside of operating income. The reference is simply to their inclusion within income from continuing operations (see Exhibit 9.3).

Nonrecurring Items Classified Within and Outside of Operating Income

The exercise of classification creativity could involve any item of revenue, gain, expense, or loss. However, nonrecurring items are some of the most likely targets. A substantial listing of mainly nonrecurring items, some within and others outside of operating income, is provided in Exhibit 9.9. An effort was made to include items that reflect their frequency of appearance either within or outside of operating income. A review of these disclosures does suggest some patterns.

Exhibit 9.9   Nonrecurring Items Within and Outside of Operating Income

Company	Nonrecurring Items
Within Operating Income	
Adolph Coors Co. (2000)	Special charges
Advanced Micro Devices, Inc. (1999)	Restructuring and other special charges
Amazon.Com, Inc. (1999)	Stock-based compensation
American Homestar Corp. (2000)	Asset impairment and acquisition costs
Amgen, Inc. (1998)	Legal assessments and awards
Applebee's International, Inc. (2000)	Loss on disposition of restaurants and equipment
Armstrong World Industries, Inc. (1999)	Charge for asbestos liability
Avon Products, Inc. (2000)	Special charges
Brooktrout Technologies, Inc. (1998)	Merger-related charges
Burlington Resources, Inc. (1999)	Impairment of oil and gas properties
Chemed Corp. (2000)	Acquisition expenses
Cisco Systems, Inc. (1999)	Charge for purchased research and development
Colonial Commercial Corp. (1999)	Costs of abandoned acquisition
Detection Systems, Inc. (2000)	Shareholder class action litigation settlement
Escalon Medical Corp. (2000)	Write-down of patents and goodwill
The Fairchild Corp. (2000)	Gains on sales of subsidiaries and affiliates
Hasbro, Inc. (2000)	Loss on sale of business units
Holly Corp. (2000)	Voluntary early retirement costs
Kulicke and Soffa Industries, Inc. (1999)	Resizing costs
Lufkin Industries, Inc. (1999)	LIFO liquidation benefit
North American Scientific, Inc. (2000)	Charge for in-process research and development
PetsMart, Inc. (2000)	Loss on disposal of subsidiary
National Steel Corp. (1999)	Unusual credit (property tax settlement)
Office Depot, Inc. (2000)	Store closure and relocation costs

Exhibit 9.9 *(Continued)*

Company	Nonrecurring Items
Omnicare, Inc. (1999)	Legal and related costs
Papa John's International, Inc. (2000)	Advertising litigation expenses
Praxair, Inc. (1999)	Hedge gain in Brazil and net income hedge gains
Raven Industries, Inc. (2000)	Gain on sale of Glassite
Silicon Valley Group, Inc. (1999)	Inventory write-downs
Tubescope, Inc. (1998)	Write-off of Italian operations
Wegener Corp. (1999)	Write-down of capitalized software

Outside of Operating Income

Advanced Micro Devices, Inc. (1999)	Litigation settlement charge
Bell Microproducts, Inc. (1999)	Foreign currency remeasurement gain
Brown & Co., Inc. (1999)	Gain on sale of subsidiary
Chemed Corp. (1999)	Unrealized gains and losses on investments
Cisco Systems, Inc. (1999)	Realized gains on sales of investments
Colonial Commercial Corp. (1999)	Gain on land sale
Delta Air Lines, Inc. (2000)	Fair value adjustments of SFAS 133 derivatives
Escalon Medical Corp. (2000)	Gain on sale of silicone oil product line
Fairchild Corp. (2000)	Investment income (loss); nonrecurring gain
Galy & Lord, Inc. (1998)	Loss on foreign currency hedges
Gannett Co., Inc. (1999)	Gain on sale of five remaining radio stations
Gerber Scientific, Inc. (2000)	Litigation benefit
Micron Technology, Inc. (2000)	Gain on issuance of subsidiary stock
National Steel Corp. (1999)	Gain on disposal of non-core assets
Newmont Mining Corp. (2000)	Unrealized mark-to-market gain on call options
Nova Chemicals Corp. (1999)	Losses on hedges of former economic exposures
Omnicare, Inc. (1999)	Write-off of related-party note receivable
Raven Industries, Inc. (1999)	Gain on sale of investment in affiliate
Saucony, Inc. (1999)	Foreign currency gains and losses
The Sherwin-Williams Company (1999)	Provisions for disposition/termination of operations
Video Display Corp. (2000)	Gain on sale of subsidiary
Young Broadcasting, Inc. (2000)	Gain on sale of station

Sources: Companies' annual reports. The year following each company name designates the annual report from which each example was drawn.

Restructuring, asset impairment, and special charges typically are included within operating income. Investment-related gains are more likely to be excluded from operating income. Litigation and related costs appear both within and outside of operating income, but most appear to be within operating income. Charges related to the acquisition of other entities, merger, and integration costs also are included within operating income, as are various asset write-downs. Not surprisingly, most of the items included within operating income are operations-related, that is, they are not unusual. However, in some cases the operations relationship is rather tenuous.

Foreign currency items usually are classified outside the scope of operating income. This is a bit odd since exchange gains and losses are typically a product of operations that incur currency risk. However, note that Praxair, Inc., did include a foreign currency hedge gain within operating income.

Classifying investment gains outside of operating income could be designed to avoid an unreasonable elevation of expectations about the sustainability of operating income. Alternatively, investment-related losses seem more likely to be included in operating income: acquisition costs (American Homestar Corp.), loss on disposition of restaurants (Applebee's International, Inc.), merger-related charges (Brooktrout Technologies, Inc.), charge for purchased research and development (Cisco Systems, Inc.), and loss on disposal of subsidiary (PetsMart, Inc.). Classification of such losses within the scope of operating income will cause earnings growth in the subsequent period to appear to be more dramatic.

Gains and losses on investments, and related assets, appear both within and outside of operating income. Within operating income: loss on disposition of restaurants and equipment (Applebee's), loss on disposal of a subsidiary (PetsMart), gains on the sale of subsidiaries and affiliates (Fairchild Corp.), gain on the sale of Glassite (Raven Industries, Inc.), and write-off of Italian operations (Tubescope). Outside of operating income: gain on sale of subsidiary (Brown & Co, Inc. and Video Display Corp.), realized and unrealized gains on investments (Chemed Corp. and Cisco Systems), gain on silicone oil product line (Escalon Medical Corp.), gain on sale of five remaining radio stations (Gannett Co.), and gain on sale of investment in affiliate (Raven Industries).

There are some interesting contrasts with some companies that classify similar items both inside and outside the scope of operating income. Raven Industries includes a gain on the sale of Glassite, an apparent subsidiary of Raven, in operating income, but it excludes a gain on the sale of an affiliate—a company in which an ownership position of between 20% and 50% is held. Litigation-related items are both included in and excluded from operating income.

The items included in the exhibit are representative of the range of items gleaned from a review of several hundred annual reports of companies presenting a multistep income statement. The listed items are a representative sample of the much larger number of items actually located. In addition, those included were only those judged to be more or less nonrecurring in character.

Operating Income and the Potential for Income Statement Creativity

With the emphasis in the marketplace on the generation of recurring or sustainable earnings, there may be an incentive to make classification decisions that are designed to influence the level of operating income. This assumes that statement users focus on operating income as providing a good initial representation of sustainable earnings performance.[31] While it may include nonrecurring items, operating income may be viewed as a better indicator of sustainable earnings than subtotals farther down the income statement.

Statement users need to be aware of the incentive for companies to classify nonrecurring items opportunistically so as to achieve a desired operating income result. The similarity of the items classified within and outside of operating income suggests very real potential for the exercise of income statement creativity in this section of the multistep income statement. Users need to examine the items both within and outside of operating income and make their own judgments about the appropriateness of the classifications.

Getting Creative with Sales and Gross Profit

Widespread disenchantment with the bottom line, and a focus on alternative indicators of financial performance, is not a recent development. However, the past decade has witnessed a sharp increase in the attention devoted to other measures of financial performance.[32] The ultimate development in this process is to substitute sales, the top line, for net income, the bottom line. Or, as noted in one of the quotes opening this chapter: "The top line is the bottom line for investors lately." A focus on gross margin or gross profit (sales or revenue minus cost of sales or cost of revenues, respectively) is only one notch below revenue in this evolution of performance assessment.

Creativity in Reporting Sales and Revenue

The Emerging Issues Task Force (EITF) of the FASB highlighted the importance of how sales or revenue are measured with this observation:

> How companies report revenue for the goods and services they offer has become an increasingly important issue because some investors may value certain companies on a multiple of revenues rather than a multiple of gross profit or earnings.[33]

If the position of the EITF is well founded, then there would be incentives to maximize reported sales or revenue, even when net income would be the same under alternative approaches to the measurement of sales and revenue. That is, whether an item of revenue or expense is included in the computation of revenue, cost of sales, or selling, general, and administrative expenses (SG&A), the bottom line remains the same.

Reporting Revenue as a Principal versus an Agent   A key focus of the EITF has been the circumstances under which revenue should be reported based on the gross amount billed to a customer or the net amount retained. The gross amount billed is properly recognized as revenue if the company has earned revenue from the sale of goods or services. Alternatively, only the amount billed to the customer, less the amount paid to the supplier, should be recognized as revenue if the company has simply earned a fee or commission.

The EITF has outlined indicators of gross revenue reporting and net revenue reporting, respectively. These indicators are summarized in Exhibit 9.10. The EITF stressed that no one of the indicators in the exhibit normally would be determinative of whether gross or net revenue should be reported: "None of the indicators should be considered presumptive or determinative; however, the relative strength of each indicator should be considered."[34] The EITF indicators call for the exercise of a good deal of judgment, judgment that could be used to recognize revenue at gross versus net if this would be expected to have a positive effect on share valuation.

Revenue Measurement and Shipping and Handling Costs   The treatment of customer billings for shipping and handling costs also has been engaged by the EITF. Sales and revenue obviously are increased if billings for shipping and handling are treated as part of sales or revenue. The EITF managed to reach a consensus that calls for the inclusion of billings for shipping and handling in sales and revenue. However, consensus was not reached on the classification of the associated shipping and handling costs in the income statement.

To the extent that both sales and gross margin are key performance indicators, firms will not be indifferent to the classification of shipping and handling costs. Gross margin obviously will be improved if shipping and handling costs are pushed down into the selling, general, and administrative expense category. This is considered further in the next section where gross margin is the focus.

Exhibit 9.10   Indicators of Gross versus Net Revenue Reporting

Gross-Revenue Reporting Indicators
- The company is the primary obligor in the arrangement.
- The company has a general inventory risk (before customer order is placed or upon customer return).
- The company has latitude in establishing price.
- The company adds meaningful value to the product or service.
- The company has discretion in supplier selection.
- The company is involved in the determination of product or service specifications.
- The company has physical loss inventory risk (after customer order or during shipping).
- The company has credit risk.

Net-Revenue Reporting Indicators
- The supplier (not the company) is the primary obligor in the arrangement.
- The amount the company earns is fixed.
- The supplier (and not the company) has credit risk.

Source: Emerging Issues Task Force, EITF Issue 99-19, *Reporting Revenue as a Principle versus Net as an Agent*, Issue Summary No. 1, Supplement No. 3, pp. 15–18.

Creativity in the Measurement of Gross Margin

The range of flexibility in the measurement of sales and gross margin is somewhat limited compared to the case of operating income discussed earlier. A focus of contention in this area has been the gross margin measurement practices of some Internet retailers. One position is that certain customer costs should be classified as part of cost of sales as opposed to being moved down to the selling, general, and administrative expense category. Pushing these costs down to SG&A improves the gross margin percentage. However, net income is unchanged.

As noted, the EITF reached a consensus on the treatment of amounts billed to customers for shipping and handling costs: They are to be classified as revenue in the income statement.[35] However, the treatment of shipping and handling costs within the seller's income statement is not yet resolved. Some members of the EITF felt that it would be better to address this issue as part of an overall project on income statement classification. Moreover, the EITF observed that there was no general agreement on what should be included in shipping and handling costs.

In the face of a lack of a consensus on the classification of shipping and handling costs, the staff of the FASB drafted a possible consensus for consideration by the EITF. This draft reveals a preference for classification within cost of sales or cost of revenue:

> The classification of shipping and handling costs is an accounting policy decision that should be disclosed pursuant to APB 22. A company may adopt a policy of including shipping and handling costs in cost of sales. If shipping and handling costs are significant and are not included in cost of sales, a company should disclose both the amount of such costs and which line item on the income statement includes that amount.[36]

Under current practice, there are differences among firms in the treatment of shipping and handling or fulfillment costs. Some include such costs in cost of sales, while others push them down into SG&A. With a strong focus on gross margin within the investment community, there is an incentive for firms to classify costs outside of cost of sales and by so doing to increase gross margin.

In the meantime, there remains room for the exercise of income statement creativity, and there also will remain a lack of comparability in gross margins of affected companies. Even if all firms were to classify shipping and handling in cost of sales, a lack of comparability could remain because of differences in what are considered to be shipping and handling costs.

Some examples of the classification of shipping and handling (fulfillment) costs are provided in Exhibit 9.11. These disclosures reveal some sharp differences in the determination of cost of sales and, as a result, in gross margin.

The policies applied to fulfillment costs appear to be quite similar. Each of the five Internet retailers includes only a narrow set of costs, beyond the basic cost of the goods sold, in the cost of sales classification. The most consistent items included are inbound and outbound shipping costs and packaging materials. However, notice that Etoys, Inc., adds handling costs to the more standard litany of inbound and outbound shipping. Amazon.com, Inc., classifies shipping charges to customers as revenue, in line with the consensus reached by the Emerging Issues Task Force. FogDog, Inc., adds credit card

---

Exhibit 9.11 Classification of Shipping and Handling (Fulfillment) Costs

Company	Classification
Amazon.com, Inc. (2000)	The company already classified shipping charges to customers as revenue. The company classifies inbound and outbound shipping costs and the cost of tangible supplies used to package product for shipment to customers as cost of sales. The company does not currently impose separate handling charges on customers and classifies costs incurred in operating and staffing distribution and customer centers (including costs attributable to receiving, inspecting, and warehousing inventories; picking, packaging, and preparing customers' orders for shipment; and responding to inquiries from customers) and credit card fees as marketing, sales, and fulfillment expenses.
B&N.com, Inc. (1999)	Gross profit is net sales less the cost of sales, which consists of the cost of merchandise sold to customers, and outbound and inbound shipping costs.
	All fulfillment costs, including the cost of operating and staffing distribution centers and customer service, are included in marketing and sale expense.
Drugstore.com, Inc. (1999)	Cost of sales consists primarily of the cost of products sold to our customers, including allowances for shrinkage and slow moving and expired inventory, as well as outbound and inbound shipping costs.
EToys, Inc. (1999)	Gross profit is net sales less cost of sales, which consists of the costs of products sold to customers, outbound and inbound shipping and handling costs, and gift-wrapping costs.
FogDog, Inc. (1999)	Costs of merchandise revenue consist of product costs, shipping and handling costs, credit card processing fees, and in fiscal 1999 included out-bound freight costs and certain promotional expenses.

Sources: Companies' annual reports. The year following each company name designates the annual report from which each example was drawn. The information for Amazon.Com was from its 10-Q Report to the Securities and Exchange Commission for the second quarter, 2000.

---

processing fees and, beginning in fiscal 1999, outbound freight and certain promotional expenses.

The gross or net reporting of revenues and the treatment of the shipping and handling costs affect the measurement of sales and gross profit. They are representative of a broader range of related issues, such as the treatment of coupons, rebates, and discounts as well as barter transactions. Some degree of classification creativity currently exists and will continue to call for careful scrutiny. Moreover, additional issues will emerge as firms continue to develop complex new ways of doing business.

Getting Creative in Classifying Extraordinary Items and Discontinued Operations

There has been some evidence in the past of opportunistic decisions in the classification of items as extraordinary or as discontinued operations. The motivation is to influence the amount or trend in an income statement subtotal. As noted earlier, the SEC recently has emphasized the significance of such classification issues:

> The appropriate classification of amounts within the income statement or balance sheet can be as important as the appropriate measurement or recognition of such amounts. Recently, financial statement users have placed greater importance and reliance on individual income statement captions and subtotals such as revenues, gross profit, marketing expense, research and development expense, and operating income.[37]

The desire to achieve a target level of income from continuing operations could influence the classification of a gain or loss as extraordinary. An early study suggested that management behavior was consistent with classification decisions being made to achieve earnings objectives.[38] That is, items were moved into or out of the extraordinary classification based on the goals of management for income from continuing operations. If income from continuing operations was below target, then an income item was less likely to be classified as extraordinary. Just the opposite was true if income from continuing operations was above target levels.

Similar results were developed in the case of classification decisions associated with gains and losses of potentially discontinued operations.[39] A sample of companies that reported gains and losses on the disposition of components of their businesses was studied. The study findings indicated that a "significantly greater proportion of gains on the disposal of components were included in income from continuing operations and a greater proportion of losses were disclosed below-the-line."[40] Below-the-line treatment means that gains and losses were treated as discontinued operations. Above-the-line treatment would include the gains and losses in income from continuing operations. These results are consistent with firms using a form of classification creativity to achieve a desired earnings outcome.

The current scrutiny of income statements, and the disclosure expectations for material nonrecurring gains and losses, would seem to limit the role of these classification decisions in achieving specific earnings objectives. To be effective, it would be necessary to obscure the results of such classificatory maneuvers, a difficult but not impossible task. Moreover, the range of items that can be properly classified as extraordinary has narrowed substantially over the past two decades. Classification flexibility in this area is now very limited. Also, with a new segment-reporting standard, there may be less flexibility in the classification of gains and losses associated with the disposal of business components.[41]

CREATIVITY WITH OTHER ASPECTS OF THE INCOME STATEMENT

The primary area of income statement creativity discussed above is the opportunistic classification of revenue, gains, expenses, and losses within different sections or line items of the income statement. Three other topics that do not involve classification also may be considered income statement creativity. The first involves the summarization of disparate items of other income and expense as part of a possible effort to obscure non-recurring items. The second involves the practice of creativity in the use of terminology. This entails the use of terms with a view towards creating an impression that may not be consistent with underlying reality. The third involves application of the concept of materiality to lower the prominence of selected items in order to achieve a desired income statement outcome.

Combining Disparate Income Statement Balances

It is a common practice to net miscellaneous items of nonoperating revenue, gain, expense, and loss. This reporting may increase the likelihood that important information is overlooked in assessing financial performance. Typically, the net balance of these various miscellaneous items is simply presented on the face of the income statement. Moreover, note references often are not identified with this line item, even in cases where a specific note detailing the composition of the line item does exist.

It is common for analysts to scan across income statements looking for line items with significant changes. (This point was made repeatedly in the survey results reported in Chapter 5.) Analysts then will make a note to follow-up and attempt to determine the composition of the line item. However, if disparate—that is, recurring and nonrecurring—items offset each other, then the absence of a line-item change will reduce the likelihood of a search for the composition of the line item.

The other income and expense note of The Sherwin-Williams Co. is provided in Exhibit 9.12. Notice that there is a relatively modest increase in the net balance of this line-item category between 1997 and 1999. In the absence of sharp changes in this line item, an analyst would be less inclined to seek out its detailed composition. There was no reference on this line item to the note presented in the exhibit. However, there was, at the bottom of the income statement, the standard boilerplate advisory to "See notes to consolidated financial statements."

An examination of the Sherwin-Williams "Other income and expense" note reveals that offsetting movements in the "Provisions for environmental matters" and "Foreign currency transaction losses" explain most of the stability in the net balance. It is quite common to treat a provision for environmental matters as nonrecurring but to treat foreign currency losses as recurring.[42] The modest change in the net balance of "Other income and expense" might result in an analyst not seeking out the composition of this line item.

Failure to explore the composition of the balance could result in missing a significant increase across the period in the environmental provision, a clear nonrecurring item. It would be important to consider the role of this significant nonrecurring item in evaluating earnings for both 1999 as well as 2000. The absence of a comparable provision in

Exhibit 9.12   Composition of an Other Income and Expense Note: The Sherwin-Williams Co., Years Ended December 31, 1997, 1998, and 1999 (thousands of dollars)

	1997	1998	1999
Dividend and royalty income	$(3,361)	$(3,069)	$(4,692)
Net expense of financing and investing activities	3,688	2,542	7,084
Provisions for environmental matters—net	107	695	15,402
Provisions for disposition and termination of operations	4,152	12,290	3,830
Foreign currency transaction losses	15,580	11,773	3,333
Miscellaneous	3,199	1,815	4,583
	$23,365	$26,046	$29,540

Note: Note references included by Sherwin-Williams in this schedule have been omitted.

Source: The Sherwin-Williams Company annual report, December 31, 1999, p. 30.

2000 will result in an increase in 2000 earnings, other things being equal. However, this increase should not be interpreted as an improvement in operating performance because it would simply be the result of the presence of a nonrecurring charge in 1999. That is, earnings in 1999 were marginally understated by the nonrecurring environmental charge.

In fact, the 2000 annual report of Sherwin-Williams disclosed no "provision for environmental matters." The separate effect of the disappearance of this charge, which was $15 million in 1999, was to increase pretax results by $15 million.

In a highly summarized income statement, Archer Daniels Midland Co. (ADM) included a line item for "Other expense" that decreased by about $26 million between 1999 and 2000. As with Sherwin-Williams, there was no reference on the other expense line item to a numbered note that detailed the composition of this line item. The ADM "Other expense" note is presented in Exhibit 9.13.

Given the size of the numbers in the ADM income statement—year 2000 net income of $301 million—the $26 million decrease in "Other expense, net" might not have prompted further scrutiny. However, as with the case of Sherwin-Williams, the net balance is the sum of offsetting balances, some of which are recurring and some nonrecurring.

Notice that a $65 million increase in nonrecurring gains on marketable securities in 1999 is virtually offset by the net changes in the other, largely recurring, elements of other expense.[43] A similar situation exists in 2000, where the $91 million decline in nonrecurring gains on marketable securities is more than offset by the net change in the other, again largely recurring, elements of other expense.

With the size of, and fluctuations in, the Other expense balance, it would be helpful to statement users if the securities gains were set out on a separate line, just below earnings

Exhibit 9.13   Composition of an Other Expense Note: Archer Daniels Midland Company, Years Ended June 30, 1998, 1999, and 2000 (thousands of dollars)

	1998	1999	2000
Investment income	$123,729	$118,720	$136,317
Interest expense	(293,220)	(326,207)	(377,404)
Net gains on marketable securities	36,544	101,319	10,103
Equity in earnings (losses) of affiliates	20,364	(4,273)	88,206
Other	2,327	(680)	5,798
	$(110,256)	$(111,121)	$(136,980)

Source: Archer Daniels Midland Company, Annual Report, June 30, 2000, p. 31.

from operations, in ADM's multistep income statement. The blending of recurring and nonrecurring items in income statement balances makes it more difficult for statement users to judge financial performance. Adding a line or two for the more material of such items would be a relatively low-cost change in the disclosure practices of ADM.

The lesson for statement users is always to look for the detailing of other income and expense notes, even in cases where the net balances are either small or relatively stable. The discussion of the cases of Sherwin-Williams and Archer Daniels Midland is designed simply to illustrate how information on the composition of other income and expense could be important in understanding changes in profitability. There is no suggestion that either company was in any way attempting to obscure relevant information about its performance.

Use of Creative Income-Statement Terminology

The *American College Dictionary* defines the word euphemism as "the substitution of mild, indirect, or vague expression for a harsh or blunt one."[44] Consider the real meaning of the change in an analyst's recommendation on a stock to a "source of funds." The appropriate blunt word is, of course, sell! The fields of finance and accounting have fervently embraced the use of euphemisms to create the illusion that something bad may actually be something good.[45] Some of the most creative terminology deployed in the income statement is found in cases where firms decide that their business must be scaled back, reorganized, or restructured.

Restructurings and Creative Income Statement Terminology

Restructuring is the most common prefix applied to nonrecurring charges associated with reorganizations of various forms. It is interesting to note that most of the terms employed in these descriptions begin with the letter "r." Some examples of these "r" words would include:

- Restructure
- Realign
- Redeploy
- Reconfigure
- Resize

- Right-size
- Rationalize
- Reposition
- Reengineer
- Reorganize

It is a common feature of human behavior to put the best face on adversity and reversals of fortunes. For the past decade, it has been popular to engage in a range of organizational changes and to summarize their cost consequences under the rubric of restructuring. The popularity of this label grew when the market appeared to applaud the announcement of restructurings, along with their associated costs, by sending the company's stock price up.

A positive market response is not surprising if it is assumed that the announcement is both news and that the restructuring shows the promise of improving a firm's future performance. However, with the passage of time, it appeared that firms were overdoing a good thing by reaching out and bringing a wide range of costs under the restructuring-cost umbrella. In some cases future operating costs were included as well as the costs of very tentative plans.

A case of overreaching appears to be provided by AmeriServe Food Distribution, Inc. A court-appointed examiner for the federal bankruptcy court in Wilmington, Delaware, reported that AmeriServe had classified operating expenses as restructuring charges. The effect of this misclassification was seen to mask a deteriorating financial circumstance.[46]

A review of the financial statements of firms using the wide range of "r" words would show an equally broad set of charges. A selection of items listed under the restructuring charge label is provided in Exhibit 9.14.

The term *restructuring* was used in connection with each of the entries in the exhibit. The labels represent a blend of activities and types of income statement charges. Recording special warranty and repossession accruals, as in the case of American Homestar Corp., simply identifies a type of charge and not a restructuring activity as such. Terms such as *severance obligations* (American Homestar, The Quaker Oats Co., and York International Corp.) both describe the character of an income statement charge and imply an associated activity. The range of items listed in the exhibit, while for only five different firms, is fairly representative of the items associated with the use of the term *restructuring charge* in income statements.

As noted earlier, the reporting of restructuring charges has been associated with positive share-price effects. This reaction would seem to be appropriate if the activities associated with the restructuring improve future profit prospects, by in some cases reducing future costs or avoiding losses. Occasionally, firms disclose information about cost savings expected to result from restructurings. The following is an example of such a disclosure provided by The Quaker Oats Co.:

> This project is expected to significantly lower operating costs by removing inefficient assets, building operating scale in key product lines, and integrating foods and beverages

---

Exhibit 9.14 Composition of Restructuring Charges

Company	Detail of Charges
American Homestar Corp. (1999)	• Special warranty and repossession accruals • Inventory write-downs, idled and closed plants • Severance obligations • Fair value adjustment to asset held for sale • Unfavorable operating leases for centers subject to the restructuring plan
Crown Cork & Seal, Inc. (2000)	• Employee termination benefits • Asset write-downs • Exit costs
Petsmart, Inc. (1999)	• Closing or relocating stores • Discontinuing Discovery Center in superstores • Write-down and write-off of fixtures • Consolidation of distribution centers • Impaired investments
The Quaker Oats Company (1999)	• Severance and termination benefits • Asset write-offs • Losses on leases and shutdown costs
York International Corp. (1999)	• Fixed asset write-downs • Inventory write-downs • Severance costs • Contractual obligations

Sources: Companies' annual reports. The year following each company name designates the annual report from which each example was drawn.

---

warehousing. Actions will include plant closures, line consolidations and selective outsourcing of product manufacturing and logistics. Targeted savings for the project are in the range of $40 million to $50 million in 2001, rising to $60 million to $70 million beginning in 2002 and going forward.[47]

A review of disclosures associated with a range of labels, restructuring as well as the other "r" words, suggests a great deal of similarity in both the types of charges and the activities. As suggested, there appears to be a certain amount of euphemistic use of these labels, which may be designed to obscure the fact that mistakes may have been made and losses incurred. In other cases, especially where material net benefits are expected, positive labels and positive market reactions are reasonable.

The concern is that positive labels are applied in cases that simply represent a cleanup activity resulting from, ex post, poor choices. The best strategy for investors and other statement users would be to ignore the labels and carefully examine the character of the underlying charges and, if any, the associated activities. Charges, in the absence of a set of planned activities, are unlikely to be positive for firm valuation.

Emphasizing the Noncash Nature of Nonrecurring Charges

It is very common for firms to characterize certain nonrecurring charges, including portions of restructuring charges, as noncash. This could be seen as simply aimed at helping the reader to understand the implications of certain events for a firm's cash flow. However, it also may be designed to suggest that the charge is not as bad as it might have been if a cash outflow were required.

Use of the noncash label is the most problematic in cases where obligations have been accrued but simply have not yet been paid. The associated costs are only noncash from the very narrow perspective of not entailing a cash outlay in the period in which they were recorded. In truth, with the exception of assets being originally acquired or liabilities discharged in noncash transactions, almost all restructuring and related charges are cash items. However, the actual cash outlay may take place in periods prior to the charge, during the period of the charge, or in periods after the charge was recorded.

Materiality and Income Statement Creativity

As with other tactics discussed, firms may make opportunistic use of the concept of materiality to alter reported results and the transparency associated with these results. As a case in point, during the 1980s a major commercial bank reported interim results that included a gain on debt retirement. This item was not set out separately in the reported results. Subsequently, analysts argued that the gain should have been set out in the income statement as an extraordinary item—as GAAP requires.[48]

The bank responded that GAAP applied only to transactions that were material. The gain amounted to approximately 7% of net income for the interim period. While relatively small, the gain represented a major portion of the growth in profits for this interim period. The bank subsequently restated its quarterly filing with the SEC.

The analyst community clearly believed that this bank was using the materiality concept to avoid highlighting the gain and its material contribution to the growth in profits during the period. As the gain was nonrecurring, it inflated the bank's sustainable earnings.

As a matter of practice and tradition, rules of thumb have been employed in deciding whether an item is material or not. A common materiality threshold is identified in a recent SEC Staff Accounting Bulletin:

> One rule of thumb in particular suggests that the misstatement or omission of an item that falls under a 5% threshold is not material in the absence of particularly egregious circumstances, such as self-dealing or misappropriation by senior management.[49]

The SEC rejects the idea that materiality can be assessed simply on the basis of an ad hoc numerical threshold. As stated in the SAB on materiality:

The staff has no objection to such a *rule of thumb* (reference is to the 5% threshold) as an initial step in assessing materiality. But quantifying, in percentage terms, the magnitude of a misstatement is only the beginning of an analysis of materiality; it cannot appropriately be used as a substitute for a full analysis of all relevant considerations.[50]

The implication of this is that, depending on the particular circumstances, relatively small dollar amounts could be held to be material. The SEC recently has provided guidance on the factors that might cause a relatively small item to be considered material. These factors are presented in Exhibit 9.15.

The creative application of the materiality standard in the construction of the income statement and associated disclosures could take a number of avenues. The invocation of lack of materiality could be used to justify not correcting a so-called immaterial error or other form of misstatement. Further, it could be used as the basis for failing to disclose a so-called immaterial item of nonrecurring revenue, gain, expense, or loss, depending on what a firm wanted readers to believe about a firm's performance.

Some of the items in Exhibit 9.15 represent very powerful incentives to exploit the application of the materiality concept. Meeting or exceeding consensus analyst forecasts

---

Exhibit 9.15   When Is Small Material? SEC Guidance

Relevant Considerations

1. Whether the misstatement arises from an item capable of precise measurement or whether it arises from an estimate and, if so, the degree of imprecision inherent in the estimate.
2. Whether the misstatement masks a change in earnings or other trends.
3. Whether the misstatement hides a failure to meet analysts' consensus expectations for the enterprise.
4. Whether the misstatement changes a loss into income or vice versa.
5. Whether the misstatement concerns a segment or other portion of the registrant's business that has been identified as playing a significant role in the registrant's operations or profitability.
6. Whether the misstatement affects the registrant's compliance with regulatory requirements.
7. Whether the misstatement affects the registrant's compliance with loan covenants or other contractual requirements.
8. Whether the misstatement has the effect of increasing management's compensation— for example, by satisfying requirements for the award of bonuses or other forms of incentive compensation.
9. Whether the misstatement involves concealment of an unlawful transaction.

Source: Securities and Exchange Commission, Staff Accounting Bulletin No. 99, *Materiality,* August 12, 1999, p. 4. This Staff Accounting Bulletin is available on the SEC web site: *www.sec.gov/rules/acctreps/sab99.htm.*[52]

---

has become an important requirement in the marketplace, especially for firms whose earnings are valued at lofty price-to-earnings (P/E) relationships. The presence of far more small profits than small losses suggests the potential influence of consideration 4 in the exhibit. Both experience and available research testify to the influence of considerations 7 and 8 on judgments about materiality.[51]

The exploitation of materiality is more insidious than most of the other examples of income statement creativity discussed in this chapter. After all, if provided with the details of how an earnings number has been developed, a reader can accept, reject, or modify the measure. However, there is no opportunity to assess the implications of a number that is simply not included or that is included but not separately disclosed.

SUMMARY

The income statement is the premier playground for those who engage in the financial numbers game. The goal of this chapter has been to outline the key features of the GAAP-basis income statement. Then, based on this foundation, the manner in which the flexibility underlying its design and construction might be utilized is discussed and illustrated. Key points made in the chapter include the following:

- The traditional preeminence of the income statement's bottom line as a measure of financial performance is under attack, and a variety of alternatives have been deployed.
- The income statement follows two basic designs: single-step and multistep. The multistep format is used most frequently, and its inclusion of subtotals for both gross profit and operating income are its distinguishing features and strengths. The single-step format does not include these potentially informative subtotals.
- Beyond income from continuing operations, special income statement categories are provided for discontinued operations, extraordinary items, and the cumulative effects of accounting changes. These items normally are treated as nonrecurring for purposes of analysis and are routinely excluded from net income in developing pro-forma measures of performance. There is only limited flexibility in determining the classification of items into these categories, and, as a result, they play only a minor role in the financial numbers game.
- Items termed other comprehensive income (OCI) are fairly recent additions to the measurement of income. Under previous GAAP, the unrealized nature of items caused them to be included in shareholders' equity until they were realized. Currently the primary elements of other comprehensive income are certain unrealized gains and losses on investments, foreign currency translation adjustments, adjustments for underfunded pension plans, and selected gains and losses on financial derivatives used for hedging purposes.
- Three alternatives are available in reporting other comprehensive income. Two involve reporting the elements of OCI in an income statement format. The third, the alternative elected by most firms, reports these items in shareholders' equity only. We

expect that the financial numbers game will continue to be played with conventional net income as the key input and not the new, augmented comprehensive income.

- Beyond the development of alternatives to net income, the financial numbers game can involve the creative movement of items between income statement classifications. As the focus of users has moved away from the bottom line, these alternative amounts and subtotals become fertile numbers-game turf. In the multistep GAAP income statement, there are incentives to move items, especially items of revenue or gain, up into the measurement of operating income. Similarly, there are incentives to move costs or expenses out of cost of sales and into operating expenses so as to increase gross profit margins. Of course, none of this activity changes the size of the bottom line.

- There is some evidence that firms have used the judgmental dimension of the classifications of extraordinary items and discontinued operations to move gains and losses either into or out of income from continuing operations.

- Merging an offsetting recurring and nonrecurring item within the other income and expense line item may obscure the presence of nonrecurring items.

- The creative use of terminology for items in the income statement may make it possible to create the sense that something bad is in fact good.

- Errors or misstatements may remain uncorrected if materiality standards are not applied properly.

GLOSSARY

Abusive Earnings Management The use of various forms of gimmickry to distort a company's true financial performance in order to achieve a desired result.[53]

Change in Accounting Principle A change in the basic accounting treatment applied in a unique area of accounting. Examples would be a change from accelerated to straight-line depreciation for fixed assets, a change from completed-contract to percentage-of-completion accounting for long-term contracts, and a change from the capitalization and amortization of overhaul costs to one of immediate expensing.

Core Earnings A measure of earnings that includes only the results of the primary operating activities of the firm. It is most common to see the measure used by financial firms.

Change in Reporting Entity A change in the scope of the entities included in a set of, typically, consolidated financial statements.

Change in Accounting Estimate A change in the implementation of an existing accounting policy. A common example would be extending the useful life or changing the expected residual value of a fixed asset. Another would be making any necessary adjustments to allowances for uncollectible accounts, warranty obligations, and reserves for inventory obsolescence.

Cumulative Effect of Accounting Change The change in earnings of previous years assuming that the newly adopted accounting principle had previously been in use.

Discontinued Operations Net income and the gain or loss on disposal of a business segment whose assets and operations are clearly distinguishable from the other assets and operations of an entity.

Emerging Issues Task Force (EITF) A special committee of the Financial Accounting Standards Board established to reach consensus on how to account for new and unusual financial transactions that have the potential to create differing financial reporting practices.

Extraordinary Gain or Loss   Gains and losses that are judged to be both unusual and non-recurring.

Financial Covenant   A feature of a debt or credit agreement that is designed to protect the lender or creditor. It is common to characterize covenants as either positive or negative covenants. A positive covenant might require that the debtor maintain a minimum amount of working capital. A negative covenant might limit dividend payments that may be made.

Materiality   "The omission or misstatement of an item in a financial report is material if, in the light of surrounding circumstances, the magnitude of the item is such that it is probable that the judgment of a reasonable person relying upon the report would have been changed or influenced by the inclusion or correction of the item."[54]

Nonrecurring Items   Items that do not appear with any regularity but are not considered to be unusual. If an item is judged to be both nonrecurring and unusual, then it should be classified as extraordinary.

Operating Earnings   A measure that is comparable to adjusted earnings. While it may appear very close to operating income, it is not a GAAP measure, as is true of operating income. Operating income is a line item that may appear in a multistep, GAAP-basis income statement. Operating earnings is an after-tax measure that is normally produced by making a variety of adjustments to net income.

Operating Income   A measure of results produced by the core operations of a firm. It is common for both recurring and nonrecurring items that are associated with operations to be included in this measure. Operating income is typically found in multistep income statements and is a pretax measure.

Opportunistic Behavior   Using the flexibility inherent in GAAP to alter earnings so as to achieve desired outcomes.

Permanent Earnings   Reported earnings that have had the after-tax effects of all items of nonrecurring revenues, gains, expenses, and losses removed. Used interchangeably with *sustainable earnings*.

Pro-forma Earnings   Measures of earnings that are derived by making adjustments to net income or loss found in the GAAP income statement. Also see *operating earnings*.

Restructuring Charge   Costs associated with restructuring activities, including the consolidation and/or relocation of operations or the disposition or abandonment of operations or productive assets. Such charges may be incurred in connection with a business combination, a change in an enterprise's strategic plan, or a managerial response to declines in demand, increasing costs, or other environmental factors.

Special Items   A term that is used interchangeably with *nonrecurring items*.

Staff Accounting Bulletins   Interpretations and practices followed by the Division of Corporate Finance and Office of the Chief Accountant in administering the disclosure requirements of the federal securities laws.

Sustainable Earnings   Reported earnings that have had the after-tax effects of all material items of nonrecurring revenue or gain and expense or loss removed.

Transparency   The full and fair disclosure of all material items that have implications for the analysis of both earnings and financial position.

NOTES

1. Securities and Exchange Commission, *Letter: 2000 Audit Risk Alert to the Amercan Institute of Certified Public Accountants* (Washington, D.C.: Securities and Exchange Commission, October 13, 2000), p. 3.

2. *The Wall Street Journal*, November 24, 1999, p. C1.

3. Ibid., September 25, 2000, p. C1.

4. Decades ago an interstatement version of the financial numbers game was common. Here the focus was on shifting selected gains and losses between the income statement and the balance sheet. That is, there was flexibility that permitted a gain or loss to be included in net income or retained earnings. The popular view was that gains tended to be included in the income statement, while losses went directly to retained earnings.

5. *Accounting Trends and Techniques* (New York: American Institute of Certified Public Accountants, 2000), p. 311. The longer-term trend has been for more firms to use the multistep format. The 1980 edition of *Accounting Trends and Techniques* (p. 254) disclosed that only about 40% of the sample firms used the multistep method in 1979, versus about 72 percent in 1999. This is consistent with a general trend toward improvements in financial statement disclosures.

6. The term *operating earnings* sometimes is used to represent income after taxes but before selected nonrecurring and noncash items of revenue or gain and expense or loss. As such, it is a common example of a pro-forma earnings measure.

7. The very low effective tax rate of Colonial Commercial in 1998 was due to the use of a capital loss carryover to eliminate the tax that otherwise would be due from the gain on the Monroc, Inc., investment. The tax provision in 2000, in the face of a pretax loss, resulted from an increase in the valuation allowance of Colonial's deferred tax assets. The likelihood of realizing the tax benefits underlying the Colonial deferred tax assets declined in 2000.

8. SFAS No. 4, *Reporting Gains and Losses on the Extinguishment of Debt* (Norwalk, CT: Financial Accounting Standards Board, March 1975).

9. A recent controversy over the earnings performance of Fannie Mae centered on the treatment of extraordinary gains on debt retirement. Fannie Mae met the consensus analyst forecast for earnings in the second quarter of 2000, but only if extraordinary gains were included in its results. Thompson Financial/First Call, a firm that accumulates and makes available analyst earnings forecasts, surveyed analysts who had provided earnings forecasts on Fannie Mae. Out of 11 analysts, nine believed that the extraordinary gain should be included in earnings and two felt that it should not. Fannie Mae felt that the extraordinary gains should be included in its results for purposes of determining whether it had met the consensus forecast. Fannie Mae considered these items to be part of its continuing operations and noted that it had reported extraordinary gains and losses on debt retirements in 27 of the last 40 quarters. For more relevant discussion: *The Wall Street Journal*, July 14, 2000, p. A2.

10. SFAS No. 131, *Disclosures about Segments of an Enterprise and Related Information* (Norwalk, CT: Financial Accounting Standards Board, June 1997), para. 10.

11. Ford Motor Company, annual report, December 1999, pp. 26 and 71. Visteon is a supplier to vehicle manufacturers, automotive components suppliers, automotive aftermarket suppliers, and various nonautomotive companies. In 1999, 88% of its revenue was derived from Ford Motor Company.

12. R. Bayless, *Financial Reporting Issues in 2001* (Washington, D.C.: Securities and Exchange Commission, March 2001), p. 1. This is a speech given by the chief accountant of the Division of Corporation Finance of the SEC. It is available at: *www.sec.gov/speech/spch464.htm*.

13. Relevant GAAP guidance is found in Accounting Principles Board Opinion No. 20, *Accounting Changes* (New York: Accounting Principles Board, July 1971).

14. The retroactive adjustment method of accounting for a change in accounting principle is principally applied to the following: (1) a change from the LIFO inventory method, (2) a change

in accounting for long-term contracts, and (3) a change to or from the full cost method of accounting, which is used in the extractive industries.

15. Certain pronouncements from the American Institute of Certified Public Accountants and the Securities and Exchange Commission also may prompt changes in accounting principles.

16. Corn Products International, Inc., annual report, December 2000, p. 16.

17. *Accounting Trends and Techniques*, p. 78. We assume that the accounting changes listed as "Other" were discretionary.

18. A substantial number of changes in revenue recognition policies have been associated with the SEC's issuance of Staff Accounting Bulletin Number 101, *Revenue Recognition in Financial Statements* (Washington, DC: Securities and Exchange Commission, December 3, 1999).

19. These accounting changes may cause profits for some years to be either smaller or larger than under the old methods. For example, profits under the percentage-of-completion method generally will be higher than those under the completed-contract method. However, the opposite could be the case in certain years because of the concentration of profits in a single year under the completed-contract method.

20. For a complete discussion of the effects of LIFO versus FIFO, see E. Comiskey and C. Mulford, *Guide to Financial Reporting and Analysis* (New York: John Wiley & Sons, 2000), pp. 136–154.

21. A case can be made for the previous practice of capitalizing and amortizing subscriber acquisition costs over the future periods that are benefited. However, this change was made in 1996 when the financial prospects of America Online were more uncertain. This high level of uncertainty was the basis for the switch to immediate write-off of these costs.

22. Southwest Airlines Co., annual report, December 1999, p. F14.

23. AK Steel Holding Co., annual report, December 1999, p. 35. Only the key aspects of the note describing this change in estimate have been included.

24. The Goodyear Tire and Rubber Co., annual report, December 31, 2000, p. 42.

25. SFAS No. 130, *Reporting Other Comprehensive Income* (Norwalk, CT: Financial Accounting Standards Board, June 1997).

26. The annual survey by the American Institute of Certified Public Accountants identified 497 companies that presented a statement reporting comprehensive income. This is out of a sample of 600 companies. Of these, 26 did so in a combined statement of income and comprehensive income, 65 did so in a separate statement of comprehensive income, and 406 did so in a statement of changes in shareholders' equity. *Accounting Trends and Techniques*, p. 429.

27. D. Hirst and P. Hopkins, "Comprehensive Income Reporting and Analysts' Valuation Judgments," *Journal of Accounting Research* (Supplement Issue, 1998), pp. 47–84.

28. If the statement of cash flows were to start out with comprehensive income, then most of the other comprehensive income elements would need to be adjusted out because of their non-cash character.

29. Securities and Exchange Commission, *Letter: 2000 Audit Risk Alert to the American Institute of Certified Public Accountants* (Washington, D.C.: Securities and Exchange Commission, October 13, 2000), p. 3.

30. Ibid, para. 26.

31. This element in the income statement comes, of course, before the inclusion of nonoperating items of income and expense as well as interest and income taxes.

32. A related development is a growing interest in nonfinancial measures of performance.

33. Emerging Issues Task Force, EITF Issue 99-19, *Reporting Revenue as a Principle versus Net as an Agent*, Issue Summary No. 1, Supplement No. 3, p. 15.

34. Ibid.

35. Emerging Issues Task Force, Issue No. 00-10, *Accounting for Shipping and Handling Fees and Costs* (Norwalk, CT: Financial Accounting Standards Board, July 2000).

36. Emerging Issues Task Force, Issue No. 00-10, *Accounting for Shipping and Handling Fees and Costs*, Issue Summary No. 1, Supplement No. 2 (Norwark, CT: Financial Accounting Standards Board, September 6, 2000), p. 1

37. SEC, *Letter: 2000 Audit Risk Alert*, p. 3.

38. A. Barnea, J. Ronen, and S. Sadan, "The Implementation of Accounting Objectives: An Application to Extraordinary Items," *The Accounting Review*, January 1973, pp. 110–122.

39. D. Rapaccioli and A. Schiff, "Reporting Sales of Segments Under APB Opinion No. 30," *Accounting Horizons*, December 1991, pp. 53–59.

40. Ibid., p. 58.

41. Statement of Financial Accounting Standards No. 131, *Reporting Disaggregated Information About a Business* (Norwalk, CT: FASB, June 1997).

42. Given the frequently volatile nature of foreign currency gains and losses, we sometimes treat these items as nonrecurring in our efforts to development measures of sustainable earnings. See chapter 3, "Analyzing Business Earnings II: Calculating Sustainable Earnings Base," in Comiskey and Mulford, *Guide to Financial Reporting and Analysis*.

43. In the absence of other information, it is not possible to establish whether the sharp increase in equity earnings is recurring or not. The equity earnings line item would not generally be treated as nonrecurring.

44. *American College Dictionary* (New York: Harper & Brothers Publishers, 1953), p. 414.

45. For more finance and investing examples, see *The Wall Street Journal*, November 14, 2000, p. C1.

46. See ibid., July 3, 2000, p. C17.

47. The Quaker Oats Co. annual report, December 1999, pp. 52–53.

48. SFAS No. 4.

49. Securities and Exchange Commission, Staff Accounting Bulletin No. 99, *Materiality* (Washington, D.C.: Securities and Exchange Commission, August 12, 1999), p. 2.

50. Ibid., p. 2.

51. Documentation, in the form of references to relevant research literature, is provided in Chapter 3.

52. Staff Accounting Bulletins are not rules or interpretations of the commission, nor are they published as bearing the commission's official approval. They represent interpretations and practices followed by the Division of Corporate Finance and Office of the Chief Accountant in administering the disclosure requirements of the federal securities laws.

53. Securities and Exchange Commission, *1999 Annual Report* (Washington, D.C.: Securities and Exchange Commission, 2000), p. 84.

54. FASB, Statement of Financial Accounting Concepts No. 2, *Qualitative Characteristics of Accounting Information* (Norwalk, CT: Financial Accounting Standards Board, 1980), see "Glossary of Terms—Materiality."

Getting Creative with the Income Statement: Pro-Forma Measures of Earnings

Pro forma information is a tool that companies have invented to disseminate an idealized version of their performance. It may exclude any cost or expense the company wants, yet it is presented in a form that suggests reliability and soundness.[1]

Cash flow, by the way, is not EBITDA. EBITDA is the biggest joke of the 1990s.[2]

Are GAAP net earnings on the endangered species list? Pro forma per-share figures in earnings announcements, a number derived after removing an expanding list of items and sometimes real cash expenses, seem to be crowding out traditional net earnings in many industries.[3]

Operating income . . . is often more important to investors than net income, and widely regarded as an indicator of how well management is running the shop.[4]

The previous chapter laid out the GAAP requirements surrounding the income statement and also outlined how the financial numbers game could be played by creative classifications within the GAAP-basis income statement. Pro-forma creativity develops measures of financial performance that employ GAAP information, but they are decidedly non-GAAP measures. A common justification for one such pro-forma measure (sustainable or core earnings) is illustrated by this statement from the Corning, Inc. annual report:

Corning believes comparing its operating results excluding non-recurring items, a measure that is not in accordance with generally accepted accounting principles (GAAP) and may not be consistent with measures used by other companies, provides a better understanding of the changes in its operating results.[5]

Corning's pro-forma measure is GAAP net income adjusted for the effects of a number of charges and gains that it judged to be nonrecurring. In practice, it is common to discuss results after the exclusion of selected nonrecurring items. Corning simply refers to this pro-forma measure as "operating results excluding non-recurring items." By adjusting only for nonrecurring items, the scope of Corning's restatement is rather limited. The range of adjustments made to GAAP net income is greater in the case of some of the other pro-forma measures of performance. These measures often adjust GAAP earnings for noncash items as well as selected recurring and nonrecurring items of revenue, gain, expense, and loss. However, they all share a common feature: They employ GAAP-based information in the creation of alternative, non-GAAP measures of performance.

The first two of the chapter-opening quotes are clearly critical of pro-forma measures of financial performance. Lynn Turner, chief accountant of the Corporation Finance Division of the SEC, has characterized some of these measures by referring to them as EBBS, or "earnings before the bad stuff."[6] Such criticisms have led the Financial Executives International (FEI), an organization made up mainly of company financial officers, and The National Investor Relations (NIRI) Institute to release "best practice" guidelines for firms that release pro-forma measures of financial performance in earnings press releases.[7] A key feature of these recommendations is found in the following:

> GAAP results provide a critical framework for pro-forma results, although the pro-forma results may be more analytically useful. The order in which reported or pro-forma results are presented in the release is not as important as their context. Pro-forma results should always be accompanied by a clearly described reconciliation to GAAP results; this reconciliation is often provided in tabular form.[8]

The FEI/NIRI guidelines do not explicitly criticize pro-forma measures of financial performance. However, the absence of their recommended reconciliation of the pro-forma to GAAP numbers represents a clear weakness in most of the current presentations of pro-forma data.

This chapter builds on the discussion in Chapter 9 and presents a review and analysis of pro-forma measures of financial performance. The computation of these pro-forma measures is considered along with their motivation, characterization, and disclosure. Their role in the financial numbers game is also explored.

RECASTING THE BOTTOM LINE: PRO-FORMA EARNINGS MEASURES

Adaptations of net income are generically referred to as pro-forma earnings.[9] Other labels include EBITDA (earnings before interest, taxes, depreciation, and amortization), sustainable earnings, core earnings, and operating earnings.[10] The *Random House Unabridged Dictionary of the English Language* provides an accounting-oriented definition of "pro-forma":

Indicating hypothetical financial figures based on previous business operations for estimate purposes.[11]

Some pro-forma earnings numbers are quite consistent with the Random House definition of pro-forma. This is especially true when pro-forma earnings have been developed, at least in part, to provide a better baseline for forecasting earnings. This is often the case when net income is adjusted so as to eliminate the effects of nonrecurring items. It is less true in cases where adjustments to reported net income are designed to derive a joint cash flow and sustainable earnings measure. Pro-forma earnings typically involve adjustments to net income for items that are either noncash or nonrecurring or both.

The two most common pro-forma numbers, which fall within the spirit of income statement creativity, are (1) earnings before interest, taxes, depreciation, and amortization (EBITDA) and (2) adjusted or sustainable earnings. EBITDA is well known and widely used in the business and financial community. It is also common for sustainable earnings to be labeled adjusted earnings. Whether called adjusted or sustainable earnings, the exclusion of nonrecurring items is the key feature of these measures.

Earnings before Interest, Taxes, Depreciation, and Amortization

EBITDA represents part of a movement up the income statement from the bottom line. EBITDA is predated by and probably evolved from earnings before interest and taxes (EBIT). EBIT is positioned farther down the income statement, below the point at which depreciation and amortization would have been deducted. EBIT is one of the early income statement adaptations. It is designed mainly to gauge the extent to which fixed charges are covered by earnings.[12] EBIT has been a common financial covenant in debt and other credit agreements for decades.

EBITDA has a shorter history, with its widespread use extending back only into the early 1980s. EBITDA was used early on in leveraged buyouts (LBOs) on the premise that there would be no replacement of fixed assets until later while the LBO company was run and debt was serviced. It has long been common to require firms to maintain a specified minimum EBIT coverage ratio as part of a debt or credit agreement. As interest is deductible before the computation of income taxes, it is logical to add back both income taxes as well as interest. In more recent years, it has become even more common for fixed-charge and debt-limit covenants to be based on EBITDA.[13] While the measurement of EBITDA would seem to be dictated by the underlying words, in practice the measurement of EBITDA is often more extensive. Frequently a variety of adjustments are made beyond simply those for interest, taxes, depreciation, and amortization.

Measurement of EBITDA

As noted, it is common for firms to measure EBITDA by including additional adjustments. In this sense, most measures of EBITDA should be viewed as adjusted EBITDA, a term that is sometimes used to describe expanded measures of EBITDA. A review of some of the additional adjustments made in arriving at adjusted EBITDA provides additional insight into the character of this alternative measure of financial performance.

The process of moving up from the bottom line of the income statement and selectively jettisoning items of revenue, gain, expense, and loss is an exercise in income statement creativity. Exhibit 10.1 contains examples of some of the additional adjustments made to arrive at EBITDA. It is far more common to observe items of loss or

---

Exhibit 10.1 EBITDA Adjustment Items

Company	EBITDA Adjustments
ACG Holdings, Inc. (1998)	EBITDA is defined as earnings before interest expense, income taxes, depreciation, amortization, other special charges related to asset write-offs and write-downs, other income (expense), discontinued operations and extraordinary items.
Boca Resorts, Inc. (1998)	Adjusted EBITDA represents EBITDA plus the annual change in Premier Club net deferred income.
The Carbide/Graphite Group, Inc. (1999)	EBITDA is defined as operating income before depreciation and amortization, early retirement/severance charges, and other expense.
Coast Resorts, Inc. (1999)	EBITDA means earnings before interest, taxes, depreciation, amortization, deferred (noncash) rent expense and certain nonrecurring items, including preopening expenses.
Lifestyle Furnishings International, Ltd. (1999)	Adjusted EBITDA for 1998 excludes transition costs related to the restructuring and reengineering initiative costs related to the development and implementation of year 2000 compliance costs related to computer system implementation.
News Communications, Inc. (1999)	EBITDA, excluding three one-time expenses: hiring costs associated with a new president, an increase in the reserve for uncollected receivables, and an adjustment to the accrual for unpaid commissions.
Sunrise Medical, Inc. (1998)	EBITDA excludes reengineering expenses, merger costs, and unusual items.
Teletouch Communications, Inc. (1998)	EBITDA for fiscal 1998 excludes the gain on sale of assets.

Sources: Companies' annual reports. The year following each company name designates the annual report from which each example was drawn. Information obtained from Disclosure, Inc., *Compact D/SEC: Corporate Information on Public Companies Filing with the SEC* (Bethesda, MD: Disclosure, Inc., June 2000).

expense as opposed to revenue or gain being adjusted from net income to arrive at EBITDA. This may simply reflect the fact that the former items tend to be more numerous. Beyond this, one or more of three characteristics are typically associated with the additional adjustments: (1) nonrecurring, (2) noncash, and (3) nonoperating.

An examination of the entries in the exhibit reveals a mix of adjustments that reflect one or more of the above characteristics. The motivation for adding back depreciation and amortization is usually its noncash character. Alternatively, it sometimes reflects the sentiment that depreciation and the amortization of intangibles are not real expenses. That is, in spite of the traditional GAAP requirement to depreciate fixed assets and to amortize intangibles, many feel that these assets often do not decline in value and that over time they actually may appreciate in value.

An example of the rejection of depreciation is found in the measure used to judge the financial performance of real estate firms, especially real estate investment trusts (REITs). Depreciation is added back to net income, along with adjustments for other selected nonrecurring items, to arrive at a pro-forma measure termed *funds from operations* (FFO). The case for rejecting depreciation in measuring financial performance is illustrated by the next excerpt from a document that supports adding real estate depreciation back to the earnings of REITs:

> GAAP historical cost depreciation of real estate assets is generally not correlated with changes in the value of those assets, whose value does not diminish predictably over time, as historical cost depreciation implies. For this reason, comparisons of the operating results of REITs that rely on net income have been less than satisfactory.[14]

Similar arguments have been made in the case of some intangible assets. Goodwill is a common example. Interestingly, a new standard issued by the Financial Accounting Standards Board no longer requires the routine amortization of goodwill. Rather, goodwill will be written down only if it is judged to be impaired.[14a]

Interest and taxes are the standard add-backs to develop measures for determining the coverage of fixed charges. Additional adjustments for the growth in deferred income by Boca Resorts, Inc., and of deferred rent by Coast Resorts, Inc., reflect the cash-flow dimension of EBITDA. That is, the growth in these balances represents an inflow of cash that has not yet been included in net income (Boca Resorts) and an expense that has not yet required a cash outflow (Coast Resorts). Hence, these increases are added to net income in order to produce a measure that is closer to cash flow.

The adjustments for write-offs (ACG Holdings, Inc.), severance charges (The Carbide/ Graphite Group, Inc.), certain nonrecurring items (Coast Resorts), transition costs (Lifestyle Furnishings International, Inc.), adjustments to the accrual for commissions (News Communications, Inc.), and gain on sale of assets (Teletouch Communications, Inc.), are all consistent with developing a measure of sustainable financial performance. The adjustments for some of the nonrecurring items, for example, other income and other expenses, reflects the effort to develop a measure that is based on operating items.

The determination of what items should be adjusted out of EBITDA, where the key consideration is their nonrecurring character, is difficult. Nonrecurring items are not specifically defined under GAAP.

It is common for EBITDA measures to be developed with additional adjustments for nonrecurring and nonoperating revenue, gains, expenses, and losses. These all entail the exercise of considerable judgment. A strict version of EBITDA requires the exercise of little or no judgment. However, the dominance of adjusted EBITDA measures means that there is abundant room for the exercise of creativity. This also means that it is very difficult to compare EBITDA performance among different firms. Doing so is somewhat akin to trying to compare the weights of different people when they all make a number of unique adjustments to their scales. There is a clear problem with the comparability of EBITDA measures among firms.

Comparability of EBITDA among Firms

EBITDA combines adjustments for noncash, nonrecurring, and nonoperating items in an effort to create a revised measure that is a combined operating cash flow and sustainable earnings statistic. The adjustments that are prompted by the noncash feature are reasonably nonjudgmental.[15] However, the specification of nonrecurring items for adjustment introduces the potential for the creation of EBITDA measures that are not comparable between different firms. This potential for a lack of comparability among firms is cited frequently in discussions of EBITDA disclosures. The following commentary is typical:

> All companies do not calculate EBITDA in the same manner. As a result, EBITDA as presented here may not be comparable to the similarly titled measure presented by other companies.[16]
>
> Our calculation of EBITDA may be different from the calculation used by other companies and, therefore, comparability may be limited.[17]

It is worth noting that the lack of comparability introduced by adjusted EBITDA measures simply adds to the lack of comparability that already exists due to differences among firms in accounting policies followed as well as variations in accounting estimates. Also, the judgments that go into the computation of EBITDA affect both interyear and interfirm comparability. That is, EBITDA may be measured differently among firms as well as differently by individual firms across different years.

Company Characterizations of EBITDA

The characterizations of EBITDA provided by companies help to clarify some of the motivations for the creation of this measure. Some examples of EBITDA characterizations are provided in Exhibit 10.2. The information in the exhibit as well as the results of a review of about 200 companies was used to identify a number of recurring themes in these EBITDA characterizations. EBITDA is held to be:

- Useful in evaluating operating performance
- Helpful in judging the ability to meet future cash requirements
- Useful as a measure of operating cash flow
- Helpful in evaluating financial condition, results of operations, and cash flow

Exhibit 10.2   Characterizations of EBITDA

Company	Characterization of EBITDA
Ameriking, Inc. (1999)	EBITDA is included to provide additional information with respect to the ability of the Company to meet its future debt service, capital expenditure and working capital requirements.
The Carbide/Graphite Group, Inc. (1999)	Management believes that EBITDA is an appropriate measure of the Company's ability to service its cash requirements. EBITDA is an important measure in assessing the performance of the business segments.
Lightbridge, Inc. (1999)	Lightbridge considers EBITDA to be meaningful given the impact on operating income from non-cash expenses.
Metro Goldwyn Mayer, Inc. (1999)	Management considers EBITDA to be an important measure of comparative operating performance. It should be considered in addition to, but not as a substitute for or superior to, operating income, net earnings, cash flow and other GAAP measures. The items excluded from EBITDA are significant components in assessing financial performance.
News Communications, Inc. (1999)	EBITDA is used in this report because management believes that it is an effective way of monitoring our operating performance and is widely used among media related businesses.
Niagara Mohawk, Inc. (1999)	EBITDA is a non-GAAP measure of cash flows and is presented to provide additional information about Niagara Mohawks' ability to meet its future requirements for debt service.
Stimsonite Corp. (1998)	EBITDA, a measure of operating cash flow, increased to $16.1 million from $14.3 million in 1997.

Note: The above entries are abridgements of the actual language used by the listed companies.

Sources: Companies' annual reports. The year following each company name designates the annual report from which each example was drawn. Information obtained from Disclosure, Inc., *Compact D/SEC: Corporate Information on Public Companies Filing with the SEC* (Bethesda, MD: Disclosure, Inc., June 2000).

- Widely accepted as an indicator of funds available to service debt
- Useful in measuring operating performance, liquidity, and leverage

EBITDA as a measure of cash flow is one of the more common themes. It is obviously not a GAAP measure of cash flow, and companies often make this point as part of an effort to distinguish EBITDA from GAAP cash-flow measures. Yet, companies repeatedly refer to EBITDA as a measure of cash flow, often presenting any qualifying language at some other location in the financial statements or notes.

The evaluation of operating performance is another common EBITDA application. This is clearly facilitated by the adjustments that remove nonrecurring or nonoperating revenue, gains, expenses, and losses. These adjustments provide better indicators of sustainable performance and better predictors of future results.[18]

Because of its prevalence and its representation as a measure of cash flow and operating performance, it is not surprising to observe EBITDA being employed in financial covenants found in debit and credit agreements. The problem of comparability can be dealt with in this setting because the credit agreement can include the specific definition of EBITDA to be used in measuring compliance with the EBITDA covenant.

Use of EBITDA in Financial Covenants

Financial covenants are used so that lenders and other creditors will have more control over the likelihood of their ultimate repayment. Financial covenants provide some capacity to monitor and influence the behavior of the debtor. Exhibit 10.3 provides some representative uses of EBITDA in financial covenants. The EBITDA-based covenants are of three types:

1. Coverage covenant: requires a minimum ratio of EBITDA to fixed charges
2. Leverage covenant: permits a maximum ratio of debt to EBITDA
3. Level covenant: requires maintenance of a minimum level of EBITDA

The common use of EBITDA by lenders in financial covenants is evidence that they find it to be a useful device in helping to monitor their borrowers and to ensure the eventual repayment of their funds.[19]

While based on GAAP-based income statement data, EBITDA rearranges and removes certain income statement data in the creative effort to develop alternative measures of financial performance and cash flows. As a cautionary measure, and with a nudge from the Securities and Exchange Commission, some companies that include EBITDA information in their annual reports highlight its non-GAAP character.

Cautionary Comments about Non-GAAP EBITDA Information

EBITDA incorporates only information that is present in the GAAP-basis income statement. Providing cautionary or qualifying commentary in conjunction with EBITDA data is consistent with SEC guidance.[20] Examples of cautionary or qualifying language are found in Exhibit 10.4.

Exhibit 10.3   EBITDA-Based Financial Covenants

Company	Financial Covenant
ABR Information Services, Inc. (1998)	Requires a funded debt-to-EBITDA ratio maximum of 2.5 to 1
Abercrombie & Fitch Co. (1999)	A financial covenant requires a minimum EBITDAR to interest expense and minimum rent
Foodarama Supermarkets, Inc. (1999)	Requires the maintenance of certain levels of EBITDA
Marine Drilling Companies, Inc. (1999)	Calls for a maximum ratio of debt to EBITDA of 4 to 1
Packaging Corp. of America (1999)	Must not exceed a leverage ratio (indebtedness divided by EBITDA) of 6.75 at December 31, 1999, decreasing per the guidelines set forth in the Credit Agreement to 4.00 as of March 31, 2006
Roanoke Electric Steel (1999)	Funded debt cannot be greater than 3 times consolidated EBITDA, and the ratio of EBITDA to the sum of current maturities of long-term debt and consolidated interest expense must equal at least 1.5.

Sources: Companies' annual reports. The year following each company name designates the annual report from which each example was drawn. Information obtained from Disclosure, Inc., *Compact D/SEC: Corporate Information on Public Companies Filing with the SEC* (Bethesda, MD: Disclosure, Inc., June 2000).

Despite the many cautionary notes provided about EBITDA, the manner in which it is presented and characterized implies, contrary to SEC guidance, its superiority to GAAP-based earnings and cash-flow data.

EBITDA as Income Statement Creativity

EBITDA involves a creative rearrangement of selected income statement data. While the EBITDA acronym suggests a simple alternative measure developed in a quite mechani cal manner, this is usually not the case. Rather, most measures of EBITDA go beyond the acronym and involve the selective exclusion of GAAP-basis income statement data. Terms like *special charges* and *nonrecurring items* are common labels applied to these exclusions. However, as noted earlier, these terms are not well defined in practice or in GAAP. Their identification entails a good deal of judgment, and this results in much flexibility in developing EBITDA measures. EBITDA is truly a creative income statement-based measure. However, this effort to develop an alternative measure of cash flow and financial performance brings with it some new problems and continues some old.

Exhibit 10.4   Qualifying EBITDA

Company	Qualifying Language
Browning Ferris Industries, Inc. (1997)	EBITDA, which is not a measure of financial performance under generally accepted accounting principles, is included because the company understands that such information is used by certain investors when analyzing the company's financial condition and performance.
Lifestyle Furnishings, Ltd. (1997)	Adjusted EBITDA should not be considered as an alternative to net income, cash flow from operations or operating profit as determined by generally accepted accounting principles, and does not necessarily indicate that cash flow will be sufficient to meet cash requirements.
St. Mary Land & Exploration Co. (2000)	EBITDA is a financial measure commonly used for St. Mary's industry and should not be considered in isolation or as a substitute for net income, cash flow provided by operating activities or other income or cash flow data prepared in accordance with generally accepted accounting principles or as a measure of a company's profitability or liquidity. Because EBITDA excludes some, but not all, items that affect net income and may vary among companies, the EBITDA presented above may not be comparable to similarly titled measures of other companies.
Unidigital, Inc. (1999)	EBITDA does not represent and should not be considered as an alternative to net income or operating income as determined by generally accepted accounting principles.

Sources: Companies' annual reports. The year following each company name designates the annual report from which each example was drawn. Information obtained from Disclosure, Inc., *Compact D/SEC: Corporate Information on Public Companies Filing with the SEC* (Bethesda, MD: Disclosure, Inc., June 2000). Information on St. Mary Land and Exploration Co. is from its annual report, December 2000, p. 26.

Interfirm Comparability   The flexibility associated with the development of EBITDA results in a lack of interfirm comparability. It is common for EBITDA firms to point out the comparability issue as part of their EBITDA disclosures.[21] For example, Lightbridge, Inc., takes the position that EBITDA enhances comparability because it eliminates the effects of differences in depreciation and amortization policy among telecommunications companies.[22] American West Holding Corp. makes a similar point:

> The Company believes that EBITDAR margin, which is a non-GAAP measurement, is the best measure of relative airline operating performance. EBITDAR measures operating performance before depreciation and aircraft rentals. By excluding both rentals and depreciation, differences in the method of financing aircraft acquisitions are eliminated. Cash earnings are distorted by differences in financing aircraft as depreciation attributable to owned-aircraft (including those acquired through finance leases) is added back to cash earnings while operating lease rentals are deducted.[23]

A lack of comparability among firms is not a unique weakness of EBITDA. It also afflicts GAAP-based measures of performance, notably net income. However, the measure of net income is laid out quite clearly in the income statement. Moreover, the accounting policies used to develop net income are disclosed. There is usually no comparable presentation of the development of EBITDA. Rather, one must simply rely on statements concerning the measurement or definition of EBITDA, such as those presented in Exhibit 10.1. Efforts to reproduce disclosed EBITDA numbers from the combination of company definitions and their financial statements can be difficult.

If EBITDA is going to compete with net income, then in the interests of clarity and transparency a schedule that details the computation of EBITDA should be provided. Moreover, this information should be presented in the same location with any qualifying commentary or other key EBITDA disclosures.

Pitting EBITDA against Net Income   Occasionally the SEC has felt the need to comment on the use by firms of alternatives to GAAP net income and GAAP cash flow from operating activities. On the matter of earnings, the SEC has declared that "Such measures [alternatives to GAAP net income] should not be presented in a manner that gives them greater authority or prominence than conventionally computed earnings."[24]

A review of EBITDA disclosures would suggest that the SEC's guidance is ignored on occasion. A study of the presentation of information on EBITDA reveals that it is often reported ahead of net income. This appears to be most common in the case of the EBITDA references in the president's letter to shareholders.[25] A sampling of EBITDA disclosures in the president's letter revealed the following average order of presentation of sales (or revenue), net income, and EBITDA: Revenue, 1.20; EBITDA, 2.20; and Net Income, 2.30.[26] EBITDA and Net Income are basically tied for being the second measure of financial performance presented in the president's letter. However, EBITDA either is presented before earnings or is presented in cases where earnings are not presented at all in 25 out of the 40 cases examined. That is, by being presented first, EBITDA is given greater prominence than earnings, something that the SEC advised against.

The Grubb & Ellis Company's annual report states:

> Fiscal 1998 revenue grew 24 percent to $282.8 million, exceeding our goal of 20 percent revenue growth. *EBITDA*, before non-recurring items for fiscal 1998, totaled $19.1 million, compared with $17.6 million in 1997. Net income was $21.5 million, or $0.98 per share, an increase over $19.0 million, or $.97 per share, last year.[27]

The Mindspring Enterprises, Inc., annual report says:

Our revenue increased by 118% to $114,673,000. Our customer base grew by 149% to 693,000. EBITDA increased 365% to $23,013,000. Earnings per share increased 328% from a loss of $(0.18) per share in 1997 to a profit of $0.41 per diluted share in 1998.[28]

Beyond the issue of order of presentation, a further questionable practice involves reporting EBITDA margins. The most common margin disclosures are of gross margin—gross profit divided by sales—and net margin—net income divided by sales. Presentation of EBITDA margins implies that EBITDA is a measure of profitability. It is not a GAAP profitability measure, and its use in place of GAAP-basis margins would also seem to be inconsistent with SEC guidance.

EBITDA as Cash Flow   It is common for company disclosures to characterize EBITDA as cash flow. As discussed earlier, EBITDA has aspects of both a cash flow and sustainable earnings measure. Noncash items are added back to earnings, but nonrecurring items of revenue, gain, expense, and loss are also typical adjustments. Some representations of EBITDA as cash flow are provided in Exhibit 10.5.

EBITDA is clearly not operating cash flow as it is defined under GAAP. Firms frequently make this point in their EBITDA disclosures. The following is a typical disclosure of the non-GAAP character of EBITDA as a cash-flow measure:

Exhibit 10.5   EBITDA as a Cash Flow Measure

Company	Cash Flow Language
Aztar Corp. (1999)	In 1999, our consolidated operating cash flow, as measured by earnings before interest, taxes, depreciation, amortization and rent (EBITDAR), grew to $160.6 million.
Brown-Forman Corp. (2000)	EBITDA represents a measure of the company's cash flow.
Dole Foods Company, Inc. (1999)	Cash flow from operations (EBITDA) grew to $372 million, an increase of 10% over prior years.
Mandalay Resort Group (1999)	Companies frequently refer to operating cash flow, or EBITDA, as a benchmark of earning power.
SI Technologies, Inc. (1999)	Sales and cash flow, as measured by EBITDA, increased to record levels.

Sources: Companies' annual reports. The year following each company name designates the annual report from which each example was drawn. Information obtained from Disclosure, Inc., *Compact D/SEC: Corporate Information on Public Companies Filing with the SEC* (Bethesda, MD: Disclosure, Inc., June 2000).

> EBITDA does not represent net income or cash flows from operations as those terms are defined by generally accepted accounting principles and does not necessarily indicate whether cash flows will be sufficient to fund cash needs.[29]

The addition of depreciation and amortization to net income in computing EBITDA is typically based on their noncash character. However, in some cases their addition reflects the view that the underlying assets being depreciated or amortized either will not require replacement or are not declining in value.

The failure to include working capital requirements and the adding back of both interest expense and taxes are the key differences between EBITDA and cash flow from operating activities under GAAP.[30]

As should be clear by now, EBITDA is a non-GAAP measure, but it is derived from the GAAP-basis income statement and associated GAAP data. It involves a creative rearrangement of income statement data. It has become a very popular measure by which management represents its financial performance. Moreover, it is widely used by bankers and other providers of debt capital to gauge and monitor the ongoing ability to service debt.

As financial statistics go, EBITDA is neither fish nor fowl. Rather, it is a blend of adjustments to GAAP income statement data that produce a blended measure of cash flow and sustainable earnings. As a measure of cash flow it is incomplete, mainly because of the failure to include working capital requirements. Moreover, in the typical case, the adjustments for nonrecurring items are also selective. Comparability becomes a key weakness of EBITDA as a result of the variability in the adjustments made to net income in arriving at EBITDA.

A related pro-forma measure, which also employs considerable income statement creativity, is sustainable earnings. This measure is also referred to as core or adjusted earnings.

Adjusted or Sustainable Earnings

EBITDA is a non-GAAP, pro-forma financial measure that begins with net income or loss and then recasts earnings in order to develop an alternative measure of performance. The adjustments to net income or loss are of three basic types: (1) noncash, (2) nonrecurring, and (3) nonoperating. Sustainable earnings is an additional pro-forma measure, which also begins with net income or loss, but it makes adjustments only for nonrecurring items of revenue, gain, expense, and loss. The goal is to develop a measure of financial performance that complies with investors' need for "information about that portion of a company's reported earnings that is stable or recurring and that provides a basis for estimating sustainable earnings."[31] In the spirit of this quote, Harbinger Corporation states that the adjusted earnings are provided "In order to facilitate comparison of operating results year over year."[32]

Developing a measure of sustainable earnings is not required by GAAP. Moreover, a sustainable earnings series, developed by performing a comprehensive restatement of reported earnings, is not provided by most companies. However, it is common for firms to provide some information on the effects of selected nonrecurring items and to indicate what results would have been in the absence of these items. In addition to being part of earnings releases, such information sometimes is provided in Management's Discussion and Analysis of Financial Condition and Results of Operations (MD&A) and in selected notes to the financial statements. A SEC disclosure requirement that relates specifically to the disclosure of nonrecurring (unusual or infrequent) items is found in this passage:

> Describe any unusual or infrequent events or transactions or any significant economic changes that materially affected the amount of reported income from continuing operations and, in each case, indicate the extent to which income was so affected. In addition, describe any other significant components of revenues and expenses that, in the registrant's judgment, should be described in order to understand the registrant's results of operations.[33]

Disclosures of Nonrecurring Items and Adjusted Earnings

A sampling of disclosures of nonrecurring items and their effects on adjusted earnings is provided in Exhibit 10.6. These disclosures are from both the MD&A and notes to the financial statements. These pro-forma data are an additional form of income statement creativity. They involve the recasting of information that is already a part of the GAAP-based income statement. Providing information on earnings, after the exclusion of non-recurring items of revenue, gain, expense and loss, should result in an earnings series that is both more stable and of greater value in making estimates of sustainable earnings.[34]

However, this creativity could be used somewhat selectively so as to play the financial numbers game. As with EBITDA, these pro-forma summaries are not GAAP statements. Nonrecurring is the key quality of adjustment items that are added to or deducted from GAAP net income. However, the precise meaning of nonrecurring is not well defined. Companies have considerable capacity to be opportunistic in making decisions about what items are adjusted out of reported earnings in arriving at adjusted earnings. This is a common characteristic of pro-forma measures, as was also pointed out in the case of EBITDA.

Notice that some of the exhibit disclosures enumerate the specific nonrecurring items (C.R. Bard, Inc. and Cisco Systems, Inc.) that have been adjusted out of earnings, while others simply characterize the nature of the adjustment items (Vishay Intertechnology, Inc.). However, elsewhere in its annual report Vishay does detail its nonrecurring items.

The disclosures in the exhibit are fairly typical. That is, where the effects on earnings are enumerated, it is usually in a textual format and not in a schedule. More frequently, nonrecurring items are disclosed without summarizing their effects on earnings. This is the least effective approach to dealing with nonrecurring items. A more effective presentation provides a detailed statement that summarizes the effect of nonrecurring items on adjusted earnings.

Summary Disclosures of Nonrecurring Items   The least helpful disclosures of nonrecurring items simply enumerate their amount and presence, usually in the MD&A section, but do not summarize their effects on net income. The disclosures in Exhibit 10.6 are an improvement on this practice because they do indicate the effect of the nonrecurring items on net income. However, a potential limitation of these disclosures, especially

---

Exhibit 10.6   Adjusting Earnings for the Effects of Nonrecurring Items

Company	Disclosures
C. R. Bard, Inc. (1999)	In 1999, Bard reported net income of $118.1 million, or diluted earnings per share of $2.28. Excluding the impact of the after-tax gain on the sale of the cardiopulmonary business of $0.12 and the after-tax impact of the fourth quarter write-down of impaired assets of ($0.11), diluted earnings per share was $2.27.
Cisco Systems, Inc. (1999)	Net income and net income per share include purchased research and development expenses of $471 million and acquisition-related costs of $16 million. Pro-forma net income and diluted net income per share, excluding these nonrecurring items net of tax, would have been $2,548 million and $0.75, respectively.
Phillips Petroleum Co. (1999)	Phillips' net income was $609 million in 1999, up 157 percent from net income of $237 million in 1998. Special items benefited 1999 net income by $61 million, while reducing net income in 1998 by $138 million. After excluding these items, net operating income for 1999 was $548 million, a 46 percent increase over $375 million in 1998.
Vishay Intertechnology, Inc. (1999)	Net earnings, before special charges, for the year ended December 31, 1999 were $97,799,000 or $1.14 per share. After special charges of $14,562,000 or $0.17 per share, net earnings were $0.97 per share.

Sources: Companies' annual reports. The year following each company name designates the annual report from which each example was drawn.

---

when the nonrecurring items are not listed separately, is that they may not be comprehensive. That is, some items that are arguably nonrecurring may not have been removed from net income in arriving at adjusted earnings.

The disclosures of nonrecurring items by Mason Dixon Bancshares, Inc., in Exhibit 10.7 are both comprehensive and presented in a user-friendly schedule, as opposed to being embedded in textual material.

The term *core net income* is common among financial firms. The report by the Special Committee on Financial Reporting of the American Institute of Certified Public Accountants recommended that core earnings be presented in income statements. It provided the following description of core earnings:

Exhibit 10.7   Comprehensive Revision of Earnings: Mason Dixon Bancshares, Inc., Consolidated Income Statement, Year Ending December 31, 1998 (thousands of dollars)

Reported net income	$10,811
Adjustments, add (deduct), for nonrecurring items:	
Gain on sale of branches	(6,717)
Special loan provision for loans with Year 2000 risk	918
Special loan provision for change in charge-off policy	2,000
Reorganization costs	465
Year 2000 costs	700
Impairment loss on mortgage sub-servicing rights	841
Income tax expense on the nonrecurring items above	1,128
Core (adjusted) net income	$10,146

Source: Mason Dixon Bancshares, Inc., Annual Report, December 1998. Information obtained from Disclosure, Inc., *Compact D/SEC: Corporate Information on Public Companies Filing with the SEC* (Bethesda, MD: Disclosure, Inc., June 2000).

A company's core activities are usual or recurring activities, transactions, and events. Usual means the activity is ordinary and typical for a particular company. Recurring means the activity, transaction, or event is expected to occur again after an interval. Core activities include usual or recurring operations and recurring non-operating gains and losses. Conversely, non-core activities, transactions, and events are unusual (not typical for a particular company) or non-recurring (not expected to occur again in the foreseeable future or before a specified interval).[35]

Mason Dixon's earnings revision is quite comprehensive. However, two items remain in core (adjusted) net income that could be candidates for adjustment: gain on sale of securities of $792,000 and gain on sale of mortgage loans of $2,140,000. Such transactions no doubt fit within the concept of Mason Dixon's core earnings. In a nonfinancial firm, the gain on the sale of securities would be a prime candidate for exclusion in moving toward adjusted net income. However, another financial firm, Emerald Financial Corporation, excluded gains on the sale of loans in a comparable revision of earnings.[36] As with EBITDA, comparability of adjusted earnings must be considered a potential weakness of this pro-forma information.

In Exhibit 10.8, the income statement of Cooper Industries, Inc., displays information on nonrecurring items within the body of the GAAP-basis income statement. Doing this has the virtue of not requiring the reader to look to some other location for information on the presence of nonrecurring items and their effects on earnings.

The presentation of nonrecurring items within the body of the Cooper income statement is generally consistent with the recommendation of the Special Committee on

Exhibit 10.8   Adjusted Earnings within the Income Statement: Cooper Industries, Inc., Consolidated Income Statements, Year Ending December 31, 1998–2000 (millions of dollars)

	1998	1998	2000
Revenues	$3,651.2	$3,868.9	$4,459.9
Cost of sales	2,447.1	2,603.4	3,018.3
Selling and administrative expenses	616.4	640.9	732.9
Goodwill amortization	43.8	47.1	58.5
Operating earnings before nonrecurring items	543.9	577.5	650.2
Nonrecurring gains	(135.2)	—	—
Nonrecurring charges	53.6	3.7	—
Operating earnings after nonrecurring items	625.5	573.8	650.2
Interest expense, net	101.9	55.2	100.3
Income before income taxes	523.6	518.6	549.9
Income taxes	187.7	186.7	192.5
Income from continuing operations	335.9	331.9	357.4
Income from discontinued operations, net of income taxes	87.1	—	—
Net Income	$ 423.0	$ 331.9	$ 357.4

Note: Earnings per share data, included with the Cooper income statement, are not reproduced above.

Source: Cooper Industries, Inc., annual report, December 2000, p. 20.

Financial Reporting of the AICPA.[37] The other major nonrecurring item in Cooper's income statement, Discontinued Operations, is placed below Operating earnings after nonrecurring items. A fully adjusted net income measure also would require the deduction of the income from discontinued operations. However, this is easy to accomplish with the information as presented.

Notice the difference between the trend in Cooper's performance as represented by the income series that excludes the nonrecurring items. Only modest growth is suggested by Operating earnings after nonrecurring items for the period 1998 to 2000. However, substantial earnings growth is indicated for the same period by Operating earnings before nonrecurring items. Getting a reliable reading on trends, if any, in underlying operating performance is a key benefit of the income statement creativity represented by the development of adjusted earnings.

In addition to the summary income statement disclosures of nonrecurring items, Cooper provided detailed notes on nonrecurring and unusual items. Some of these items are quite small: a $2.8 million gain on a litigation settlement and a $0.8 million insurance recovery based upon an unsuccessful offer for another company in 1999. Nonrecurring items in 1998 included charges of $5.8 million for a voluntary severance program and $1.5 for other severance and closure costs. Others are very large: a $132.7 million gain on an exchange of securities and a $53.6 million restructuring charge, both in 1998.

The presentation of adjusted or pro-forma earnings numbers within the GAAP income statement is uncommon. Supplemental disclosures of this information are the norm. However, even with the absence of detail on the nonrecurring items on the face of the income statement, Cooper's disclosures provide an opportunity to present an alternative measure of operating performance within the framework of the GAAP-basis income statement. It is decidedly user friendly.

The reliability of alternative measures of financial performance, such as that presented by Cooper Industries, turns on the classification of items of revenue, gain, expense, and loss as recurring versus nonrecurring. The treatment of individually small nonrecurring items also could have a significant influence on the message conveyed by the adjusted earnings. Some attention was given to the issue of materiality in Chapter 9. Some examples of the classification of items as nonrecurring are presented in the next section.

Nonrecurring Classification Decision

The classification of items as nonrecurring is the key to developing adjusted earnings. No definition can remove the need for judgment in identifying nonrecurring items. However, some further insight into this classification decision can be gained by reviewing the range of items removed from net income in arriving at the pro-forma earnings. A sampling of these items is presented in Exhibit 10.9.

Some of the labels applied to these pro-forma earnings numbers by the companies were: underlying results (Johns Manville Corp. and Phillip Morris Cos.), core operating results (Area Bancshares Corp.), pro-forma results (Schnitzer Steel Industries, Inc.), adjusted net income (Beringer Wine Estates, Inc. and Air Canada), and normalized net earnings (Curtiss-Wright Corp).

The listing in the exhibit includes more nonrecurring charges than gains. This simply reflects the typical excess of nonrecurring charges over nonrecurring gains. A review of 1,100 third-quarter earnings reports for 2000 showed 18 nonrecurring charges per 100 companies against only eight nonrecurring gains per 100 companies.[38]

Pro-forma, or adjusted, income measures are presented by many firms, but these presentations are found most frequently among firms with numerous nonrecurring items. With the growth in the frequency of nonrecurring items, adjusted earnings are essential in order to determine the trends, if any, in basic operating profitability. The presence of numerous nonrecurring items may mask developing profitability trends. There is some evidence that earnings purged of nonrecurring items have more predictive value and information content, and are more closely associated with firm value than as-reported earnings.[39]

However, adjusted earnings are not developed with the level of formal guidance associated with GAAP net income. The limited number of adjustments reported with adjusted net earnings and the absence of detailed summaries of the nonrecurring items

---

Exhibit 10.9   Adjustments for Pro-Forma Earnings

Company	Nonrecurring Items
Nonrecurring Losses or Expenses	
Air Canada (1998)	Estimated impact of strike
American Standard Cos., Inc. (1999)	Asset impairment charges
ATI Technologies, Inc. (1999)	Purchased in-process research and development
BEA Systems, Inc. (2000)	Payroll taxes on gains from employee options
Beringer Wine Estates, Inc. (1999)	Charge from inventory step-up
Compaq Computer Corp. (1999)	Restructuring and related charges
Cone Mills Corp. (1999)	Operating losses of businesses exited
Crown Cork & Seal Co., Inc. (1999)	Charges due to an earthquake in Turkey
Federal Mogul Corp. (1999)	Reengineering and integration costs
Johns Manville Corp. (1999)	Shutdown, demolition and site restoration
Micron Electronics, Inc. (2000)	e-commerce infrastructure development
Nova Chemicals Corp. (1999)	Loss on hedges of currency exposures
Pall Corp. (2000)	Charge for increase in environmental reserve
Phillip Morris Cos, Inc. (1999)	Beer asset write-downs
Schnitzer Steel Industries, Inc. (2000)	Inventory write-down
Stewart & Stevenson Services, Inc. (1999)	Change in estimated profit on a contract
Toys "R" Us, Inc. (1999)	Costs to establish internet subsidiary
Nonrecurring Gains or Revenues	
Air Canada (1998)	Fuel excise tax rebate
Airtran Holdings, Inc. (1999)	Gain on litigation settlement
Area Bancshares Corp. (1999)	Securities gains
C. R. Bard, Inc. (1999)	Gain on settlement of patent infringement claims
Cameco Corp. (1999)	Sale of uranium property interests
Cisco Systems, Inc. (2000)	Sale of minority stock investment
Curtiss-Wright Corp. (1999)	Environmental insurance settlements
Federal Mogul, Inc. (1999)	Gain on currency option
Phillips Petroleum Co. (1999)	Kenai tax settlement benefit
Quaker Chemical Corp. (1999)	Reversal of repositioning and integration charges
Supervalue, Inc. (2000)	Sale of Hazelwood Farms Bakeries

Sources: Companies' annual reports. The year following each company name designates the annual report from which each example was drawn.

make it unclear how comprehensively earnings have been adjusted. Ample room remains for firms to be creative with the income statement data that are the grist for adjusted earnings. A process that should be prompted by the desire to reveal what might otherwise be obscured could, instead, be used to do the opposite.

Interim Pro-forma Earnings Releases

The examples of adjusted earnings are drawn mainly from information found in formal financial statement disclosures in company annual reports. However, the initial announcements of interim and annual earnings usually include relatively limited disclosures. More complete information often is available only later, when the more formal interim reports on Form 10-Q or the annual report on Form 10-K are filed or the annual reports to shareholders are released. In the case of interim reports on Form 10-Q, note disclosures are far less extensive than in the annual report. It is quite common for limited-disclosure earnings releases to include pro-forma measures of earnings, with their prominence often greater than that accorded to GAAP-based net income or loss. The degree to which these pro-forma measures are explained varies.

The earnings release of Amazon.Com, Inc., for its 2001 first-quarter results is more detailed than the earnings releases of many other companies.[40] The release provides a useful example of the adjustments made to arrive at pro-forma results and includes disclosures that reconcile actual results under GAAP to the pro-forma results.

In its release, Amazon initially presents information on sales and gross profit growth, and then follows immediately with a disclosure of a pro-forma operating loss of $49. A pro-forma net loss of $76 million is presented next. The pro-forma net loss makes additional adjustments for the effects of noncash gains and losses, equity in losses of equity method investees, and cumulative effect of a change in accounting principle. The net loss on a GAAP basis of $234 million is presented last.

The Amazon earnings release includes comments on both the nature and role of the pro-forma information:

> Pro-forma information regarding Amazon.com's results from operations is provided as a complement to results provided in accordance with accounting principles generally accepted in the United States (GAAP). Pro-forma *operating loss* excludes stock-based compensation costs, amortization of goodwill and other intangibles, and impairment-related and other costs (including restructuring and other charges). Management measures the progress of the business using this pro-forma information.
>
> Pro-forma *net loss* excludes stock-based compensation costs, amortization of goodwill and other intangibles, impairment-related and other costs (including restructuring and other charges), non-cash gains and losses, equity in losses of equity-method investees, and the cumulative effect of change in accounting principle. [41]

Amazon.Com places an emphasis on pro-forma as opposed to GAAP numbers when it comes to judging their financial performance. This is consistent with the declaration that "Management measures the progress of the business using this pro-forma information." In a listing of "Highlights of First Quarter Results," seven items are listed, beginning with the growth in sales, gross profit, and customers. These three disclosures are followed by the pro-forma loss from operations and the pro-forma net loss. The net loss on a GAAP basis and the ending balance of cash and marketable securities are listed sixth and seventh.

In contrast to the above ordering of information, the financial statements provided with the earnings release present the GAAP-basis income statement first. These GAAP-basis statements are followed immediately by pro-forma income statements. These disclosures provide an explicit reconciliation of GAAP and pro-forma results. The pro-forma statement of operations for the three months ended March 31, 2001 is presented in Exhibit 10.10.

Amazon.com also presented pro-forma measures in its 2000 annual report to the SEC on Form 10-K, along with the following qualifier:

> The pro-forma information is not presented in accordance with accounting principles generally accepted in the United States and may not necessarily be useful in analyzing our results.[42]

The Amazon.Com pro-forma measures are not showcased in the 10-K report, for the year ending December 31, 2000, to the extent that they are in the 2001 interim earnings releases. The high profile of the pro-forma results in the earnings release may be due to the fact that such releases are not subject to SEC regulation.[43]

Amazon's disclosures appear to conform to the recent recommendations made by the combined efforts of Financial Executives International and the National Investor Relations Institute (FEI/NIRI).[44] The recommendations included the requirement that pro-forma "results should always be accompanied by a clearly described reconciliation to GAAP results." In addition, the report stated that the "order in which reported or pro-forma results are presented in the release is not as important as their context." Therefore, Amazon's presentation of pro-forma results before actual results does not represent a problem, according to the FEI/NIRI report.

Amazon does balance, to some extent, the prominence given the pro-forma results in the opening paragraph of its earnings release by presenting the GAAP-basis income statement before presenting the reconciliation of GAAP-basis and pro-forma results shown in Exhibit 10.10.

The adjustments made to arrive at pro-forma results, such as those disclosed in the exhibit, share much the same blend of noncash and nonrecurring features that were discussed in connection with adjustments made in arriving at EBITDA. Adjustments for nonrecurring items are probably the easiest to support, and analysts routinely remove such items from reported earnings in assessing ongoing performance. The potential difficulty with these adjustments is that considerable discretion may be employed in deciding just what is and is not considered to be nonrecurring. Moreover, these calculations are devoid of any GAAP guidance, and the Securities and Exchange Commission has not made any move to restrain this activity.

The adjustment for noncash items is more difficult to justify, unless the central objective of the pro-forma measures is to represent cash flow. However, the adjustment for nonrecurring items, some of which are associated with current cash flows, suggests that cash flow is not the central objective of pro-forma measures of results.

Exhibit 10.10   GAAP-Basis and Pro-Forma Earnings: Amazon.Com Inc., Consolidated Statements of Operations, for the Three Months Ended March 31, 2001 (thousands of dollars)

	As Reported	Pro-Forma Adjustments	Pro Forma
Net sales	$ 700,356	—	$700,356
Cost of sales	517,759	—	517,759
Gross profit	182,597	—	182,597
Operating expenses:			
Fulfillment	98,248	—	98,248
Marketing	36,638	—	36,638
Technology and content	70,284	—	70,284
General and administrative	26,028	—	26,028
Stock-based compensation	2,916	(2,916)	—
Amortization of goodwill and other intangibles	50,831	(50,831)	—
Impairment-related and other	114,260	(114,260)	—
Total operating expenses	399,205	(168,007)	231,198
Loss from operations	(216,608)	168,007	(48,601)
Interest income	9,950	—	9,950
Interest expense	(33,748)	—	(33,748)
Other expense, net	(3,884)	—	(3,884)
Non-cash gains and losses, net	33,857	(33,857)	—
Net interest expense and other	6,175	(33,857)	(27,682)
Loss before equity in losses of equity-method investees	(210,433)	134,150	(76,283)
Equity in losses of equity-method investees	(13,175)	13,175	—
Net loss before change in accounting principle	(223,608)	147,325	(76,283)
Cumulative effect of change in accounting principle	(10,523)	10,523	—
Net loss	$(234,131)	$ 157,848	$(76,283)

Note: Earnings per share date were provided with the income statement but are not included above.

Source: Amazon.Com, first-quarter earnings release, April 24, 2001, pp. 5–6

There is something quite peculiar about a reporting and disclosure system that requires a strict adherence to GAAP in developing the required measures of performance but then permits the virtually unfettered production of competitors to GAAP. Moreover, when these competitive measures are presented along with GAAP measures, it is common for them to be given equal or greater prominence.

Pro-forma measures of earnings, especially when they are featured in a company's earnings release, provide maximum freedom to exercise income statement creativity and play the financial numbers game. With the exception of pro-forma earnings that involve only adjustments for nonrecurring items, these pro-forma measures should be seen as the equivalent of home remedies that have not had to meet the rigors of FDA testing in order to demonstrate their efficacy. They should be examined carefully and used with caution.

SUMMARY

The income statement is the premier playground of those who engage in the financial numbers game. The goal of this chapter has been to analyze selected measures of financial performance that are GAAP based but that are not GAAP measures. Key points made in the chapter include the following:

- The traditional preeminence of the income statement's bottom line as a measure of financial performance is under attack, and a variety of alternatives have been developed. Virtually all of the competitors to net income are not measures that are part of the body of GAAP. These non-GAAP alternatives normally use information that is part of the conventional income statement. However, these alternative, pro-forma measures rearrange this information and use only a subset of the information in the income statement.

- Pro-forma measures of financial performance are developed by removing selected nonrecurring or noncash revenues, gains, expenses, and losses from GAAP net income. The resulting measure of financial performance then is characterized either as being superior to net income as an indicator of financial performance or as being demanded by statement users.

- EBITDA (earnings before interest, taxes, depreciation, and amortization) is a popular pro-forma measure of financial performance. EBITDA often is presented prior to net income as a measure of a firm's financial performance. It is common for the calculation of EBITDA to include adjustments for nonrecurring items as well as ITDA (interest, taxes, depreciation, and amortization). EBITDA is a blended measure of cash flow and sustainable earnings. While often represented as a measure of cash flow from operations, its failure to include working capital requirements as well as interest and taxes, clearly operating cash flow items, leaves it open to substantial criticism.

- Adjusted earnings is an even more dominant concept than EBITDA. Somewhat informal and incomplete adjusted earnings data are presented virtually every time earnings are released. If there are any material nonrecurring items, then their effect on earnings will be discussed. Some versions of adjusted earnings continue to be developed by removing only the effects of nonrecurring items. However, in more recent years, selected noncash items have been removed from net income as well. Both EBITDA and adjusted (pro-forma) earnings started out with a narrow focus. EBITDA simply moved up the income statement to a location before interest and taxes and then added back depreciation and amortization. Adjusted earnings simply removed nonrecurring items of revenue, gain, expense, and loss. The computation of both EBITDA and adjusted earnings now involves adjustments based on selected items that are seen to be nonrecurring or noncash. A unifying concept of why these measures should be seen to be as preferable to GAAP-based measures is yet to be articulated. Companies presenting these measures make little or no effort to defend their use.

- Selected adjustments to the bottom line can provide a measure of earnings that is a better indicator of sustainable financial performance. This is especially true if the adjustments represent nonrecurring items of revenue, gain, expense, and loss. However, these adjusted or pro-forma measures currently are provided in an unregulated environment that lacks any standards to guide their development and use. Some of these adjusted or pro-forma measures lack adequate justification, and at times they seem driven simply to improve the apparent financial performance of firms. At a minimum, firms should justify these measures, detail their computation, and reconcile them to conventional bottom-line net income or loss. In the meantime, like an unapproved therapy or drug, they should be used with caution.

GLOSSARY

Abusive Earnings Management   The use of various forms of gimmickry to distort a company's true financial performance in order to achieve a desired result.[45]

Adjusted Earnings   Net income adjusted to exclude selected nonrecurring and noncash items of reserve, gain, expense, and loss.

Adjusted EBITDA   Conventional earnings before interest, taxes, depreciation, and amortization (EBITDA) revised to exclude the effects of mainly nonrecurring items of revenue or gain and expense or loss.

Core Earnings   A measure of earnings that includes only the results of the primary operating activities of the firm. It is most common to see the measure used by financial firms.

EBBS   Earnings before the bad stuff. An acronym attributed to a member of the Securities and Exchange Commission staff. The reference is to earnings that have been heavily adjusted to remove a wide range of nonrecurring, nonoperating, and noncash items.

EBDDT   Earnings before depreciation and deferred taxes. This measure is used principally by firms in the real estate industry, with the exception of real estate investment trusts, which typically do not pay taxes.

Defined EBITDA   A measure of EBITDA that is outlined or defined in a debt or credit agreement. Also see *adjusted EBITDA* and *recurring EBITDA*.

EBIT   Earnings before interest and taxes. The measure often is used to gauge coverage of fixed charges.

EBITA   Earnings before interest, taxes, and amortization expense.

EBITDA   Earnings before interest, taxes, depreciation, and amortization.

EBITDA Margin   EBITDA divided by total sales or total revenue.

EBITDAR   Earnings before interest, taxes, deprecation, amortization, and rents.

Financial Covenant   A feature of a debt or credit agreement that is designed to protect the lender or creditor. It is common to characterize covenants as either positive or negative covenants. A positive covenant might require that the debtor maintain a minimum amount of working capital. A negative covenant might limit dividend payments that may be made.

Nonrecurring Items   Items that do not appear with any regularity but are not considered to be unusual. If an item is judged to be both nonrecurring and unusual, then it would properly be classified as extraordinary.

Operating Earnings   An after-tax measure of performance that selectively excludes items of nonrecurring and sometimes noncash revenue, gain, expense, and loss. It may be used interchangeably with adjusted earnings.

Operating Income   A measure of results produced by the core operations of a firm. It usually is found in multistep income statements and is a pretax measure. The term *operating earnings* is sometimes used interchangeably with operating income. However, operating income is a GAAP measure, and operating earnings is a pro-forma, non-GAAP measure of performance.

Opportunistic Behavior   Using the flexibility inherent in GAAP to alter earnings so as to achieve desired outcomes.

Permanent Earnings   Reported earnings that have had the after-tax effects of all items of nonrecurring revenues, gains, expenses, and losses removed. Used interchangeably with *sustainable earnings*.

Pro-forma Earnings   Measures of earnings that are derived by making adjustments to the net income or loss found in the GAAP income statement.

Recurring EBITDA   The standard EBITDA with the effects of nonrecurring items removed. Comparable to *adjusted EBITDA*.

Restructuring Charge   Costs associated with restructuring activities, including the consolidation and/or relocation of operations or the disposition or abandonment operations or productive assets. Such charges may be incurred in connection with a business combination, a change in an enterprise's strategic plan, or a managerial response to declines in demand, increasing costs, or other environmental factors.

Special Items   A term that is used interchangeably with *nonrecurring items*.

Sustainable Earnings   Reported earnings that have had the after-tax effects of all material items of nonrecurring revenue or gain and expense or loss removed.

NOTES

1. From a speech by Laura S. Unger, acting chairman of the SEC, given to the Philadelphia Bar Association on March 30, 2001. The speech is titled "Protecting the Integrity of Financial Information in Today's Marketplace," and the quote is from p. 4. The speech is available at: *www.sec.gov/news/speech/spch474js.htm.*

2. Interview with Robert Olstein, of New York–based Olstein & Associates, *Barrons*, October 5, 1998.

3. George Donnelly, "Pro Forma Performances," *CFO Magazine*, November 27, 2000, p. 1.

4. *The Wall Street Journal*, November 24, 1999, p. C1.

5. Corning, Inc., annual report, December 1999, p. 41.

6. *The Wall Street Journal*, April 27, 2002, p. C16.

7. FEI/NIRI, "Earnings Press Release Guidelines," April 26, 2002. Available at: *www.fei.org/news/FEI-NIRI-EPRGuidelines-4-26-2001.cfm*.

8. Ibid., p. 1.

9. *Pro-forma earnings* is sometimes used to describe the results of a restatement of prior-year income statements to show what net income would have been if a newly adopted accounting principle had been in effect. The expression also is used to describe earnings that would have resulted if the estimated values of stock options had been amortized as expense over the option-vesting period.

10. The use of the terms *operating profit* or *operating income*, in the pro-forma setting, should be distinguished from their use in the multistep income statement to identify the excess of operating revenue and gains over operating expenses and losses.

11. *Random House Dictionary of the English Language*, 2nd unabridged ed. (New York: Random House, 1987), p. 1545.

12. Fixed charges are not always confined to interest. It is common to include rental payments as an additional fixed charge element.

13. A word or term search of a data source that includes about 11,000 public companies located 80 references to EBIT and 1,004 to EBITDA. Not every reference to either EBIT or EBITDA would necessarily indicate an EBIT or EBITDA coverage covenant. However, these data suggest the relative frequency of their use. Information was obtained from Disclosure, Inc., *Compact D/SEC: Corporate Information on Public Companies Filing with the SEC* (Bethesda, MD: Disclosure, Inc., June 2000).

14. National Association of Real Estate Investment Trusts (NAREIT), *White Paper on Funds from Operations*, October 1999, p. 1.

14a. SFAS No. 142, *Goodwill and Other Intangible Assets* (Norwalk, CT: FASB, June 2001).

15. The authors were consulted once on the treatment of LIFO reserve adjustments in the computation of EBITDA. The pressure came from bank clients who had credit-agreement covenants based on EBITDA. Their argument with the bank was that an increase in a LIFO reserve put a noncash component into cost of sales. In a sense, it was strictly analogous to depreciation and amortization. After some discussion, the bank agreed that its clients could add back LIFO reserve charges to net income in arriving at EBITDA.

16. Coast Resorts, Inc., annual report, December 1999. Information obtained from Disclosure, Inc., *Compact D/SEC*.

17. Metro Goldwyn Mayer, Inc., December 1999. Information obtained from Disclosure, Inc., *Compact D/SEC*.

18. L. Brown and K. Sivakumar, "Comparing the Usefulness of Three Proxies for Quarterly Income: 'The Street versus Two Income Numbers Obtained from Financial Statements," ms., October 19, 2000, pp. 17–22.

19. In a related EBITDA application, it is common to find borrowing costs tied to EBITDA. The following, from the 2000 annual report of Papa Johns International, Inc., is illustrative: "The increment [in the interest rate] over LIBOR and the commitment fee are determined quarterly based upon the ratio of total indebtedness to EBITDA." Papa Johns International, Inc., annual report, December 2000, p. 47.

20. Securities and Exchange Commission, *Accounting Series Release No. 142*. Included in *SEC Accounting Guide* (Chicago: Commerce Clearing House, June 1, 1989), pp. 3584–3587.

21. Examples of firms citing the comparability issue: Advantica Restaurant Group, Inc., Coast Resorts, Inc., and The New York Times Co.

22. Lightbridge, Inc., annual report, December 1999. Information obtained from Disclosure, Inc., *Compact D/SEC*.

23. America West Holding, Corp., annual report, December 1999. Information obtained from Disclosure, Inc., *Compact D/SEC*. For clarity, note that depreciation is deducted in arriving at earnings but is added back to earnings in deriving EBITDA. Lease rentals are deducted in arriving at earnings but typically are not added back in deriving EBITDA. The *R* in the company's use of *EBITDAR* refers to lease rentals.

24. SEC, *Accounting Series Release No. 142*, p. 3585.

25. Cautionary comments on the non-GAAP nature of EBITDA are seldom provided in the president's letter in those cases in which EBITDA is disclosed in this location.

26. These averages are based on a review of about 100 EBITDA disclosures, of which 40 included EBITDA disclosures in the president's letter.

27. Grubb & Ellis Company, annual report, December 1999. Information obtained from Disclosure, Inc., *Compact D/SEC* (emphasis added).

28. Mindspring Enterprises, Inc., annual report, December 1998. Information obtained from Disclosure, Inc., *Compact D/SEC*.

29. Marvel Enterprises, Inc., annual report, December 1999. Information obtained from Disclosure, Inc., *Compact D/SEC*.

30. GAAP cash flow requirements are found in Statement of Financial Accounting Standards No. 95: *Statement of Cash Flows* (Norwalk, CT: Financial Accounting Standards Board, November 1987).

31. Special Committee on Financial Reporting, *The Information Needs of Investors and Creditors* (New York: American Institute of Certified Public Accountants, November 1993), p. 4. Notice how this measure and its associated role or purpose conforms to the definition of pro-forma provided earlier: hypothetical financial figures based on previous business operations for estimation purposes.

32. Harbinger Corporation, GA, annual report, December 1999. Information obtained from Disclosure, Inc., *Compact D/SEC*.

33. Securities and Exchange Commission, *Regulation S-K*, Subpart 229.300, Item 303(a)(3)(i).

34. L. Brown and K. Sivakumar, "Comparing the Usefulness of Three Proxies for Quarterly Income: The Street versus Two Income Numbers Obtained from Financial Statements," Unpublished Manuscript, October 19, 2000, pp. 17–22. An improvement in the predictive value of an earnings series when nonrecurring items have been removed is one of the findings of this study.

35. Special Committee on Financial Reporting, *Improving Business Reporting—A Customer Focus* (New York: American Institute of Certified Public Accountants, 1994), p. 81.

36. Emerald Financial Corporation, annual report, December 1998. Information obtained from Disclosure, Inc., *Compact D/SEC*.

37. Ibid., p. 81.

38. These earnings reports were included in *The Wall Street Journal* in issues from the first week of November, 2000.

39. Brown and Sivakumar, "Comparing the Usefulness of Three Proxies."

40. Amazon.Com, "Release of 2001 First Quarter Results," April 24, 2001.

41. Ibid., p. 5, (emphasis added).

42. Amazon.Com, Inc., annual report on Form 10-K to the Securities and Exchange Commission, December 2000, p. 26.

43. A recent article in *CFO Magazine* quotes SEC spokesman John Heine, on pro-forma earnings disclosures, as follows: "The rule that governs is the antifraud provision." Mr. Heine went on to add that "Communications can't be misleading or false or omit information that makes them misleading or false." See: George Donnelly, "Pro Forma Performance," *CFO Magazine*, November 27, 2000, pp. 1–2.

44. FEI/NIRI, "Earnings Press Release Guidelines."

45. Securities and Exchange Commission, *1999 Annual Report* (Washington, DC: Securities and Exchange Commission, 2000), p. 84.

CHAPTER ELEVEN

Problems with Cash Flow Reporting

Signs of trouble at FPA Medical Management, Inc., which filed for bankruptcy-court protection Sunday, actually emerged months before the acquisitive company gave the first details in May of a cash crunch. . . . There was an inconsistency between cash flows and earnings, reported a Wall Street analyst last October.[1]

There's no foolproof standard for tracking how revenue growth is consistently translating into earnings. But one yardstick clearly comes closest: cash flow from operations, that is, the amount of money that the ongoing business throws off. Why? Because that measure is least subject to accounting distortions.[2]

VandenBerg, in his capacity as CFO, treated Goodfriend's uncashed check as a cash and cash equivalent item, instead of a receivable from a related party, for financial reporting purposes.[3]

The importance of sustainable cash flow for both equity investors and creditors is paramount and well documented. As has been noted throughout this book, investors seek out and ultimately pay higher prices for corporate earning power—a company's ability to generate a sustainable and likely growing stream of earnings that provides cash flow. If not provided currently, investors must have an expectation that cash flow will be provided in future years. It is this stream of cash flow that investors discount in assigning a valuation to equity securities. For creditors, a sustainable cash-flow stream is sought as a primary source of debt service, providing the cash needed to pay the interest and principal on granted loans.

There is general agreement that cash provided by operating activities, often referred to simply as operating cash flow, as reported in financial statements prepared in accordance with generally accepted accounting principles, is a key measure of a company's ability to generate sustainable cash flow. Investors and creditors might adjust this operating cash-flow amount to incorporate their own views of what constitutes sustainable cash flow. For example, investors may subtract replacement capital expenditures and dividends to derive what is often referred to as "free cash flow"—discretionary cash flow that is available for equity claims while maintaining a company's productive capacity. Creditors might add back amounts paid for interest to compute what is often referred to as "net cash after operations"—cash flow that is available for debt service. Nonetheless, even these specially calculated cash-flow figures are founded on, or closely associated with, the GAAP definition of cash provided by operating activities.

There is also general agreement that GAAP-defined operating cash flow is not subject to the kinds of creative accounting practices that often befall accrual-based earnings. The thinking here is that while managements can use the flexibility in GAAP to boost or reduce earnings as needed, when measuring cash flow it is a different matter. Because cash flow must be deposited, providing a form of objective verification, it must be accurate. The second quote that opens this chapter is representative of this point of view. While noting that there is no foolproof performance yardstick, it commends operating cash flow, "Because that measure is least subject to accounting distortions."[4]

Yet, as will be seen in this chapter, while providing less flexibility than is available in the measurement and reporting of earnings, measurement and reporting of cash flow offers a surprising amount of flexibility. Companies may exploit this flexibility, particularly when separating total cash flow into its operating, investing, and financing components. For example, a company might classify an operating expenditure as an investing or financing item. Similarly, an investing or financing inflow might be classified as an operating item. Such steps will not alter the total change in cash. Because of the importance of operating cash flow to assessments of earning power, companies can improve on their apparent operating performance and potentially gain some of the rewards of the financial numbers game, which are described in Chapter 1, by taking steps to boost operating cash flow even in the absence of changes in total cash flow.

Before proceeding, it should be noted that instead of traditional operating cash flow, many investors and creditors use earnings before interest, taxes, depreciation, and amortization as a preferred measure of "cash flow." Both groups see it as a crude measure, but one that is easy to compute and that provides a generous and liberal definition of cash flow. Informed users of the measure understand that EBITDA is not cash flow per se but rather a measure of working capital or funds provided by operations, calculated before interest and taxes.

Because EBITDA is based on earnings and does not remove changes in accrued working capital accounts in its calculation, it is subject to the same creative accounting practices that plague reported earnings. Accordingly, comments made in earlier chapters about creative accounting practices that apply to earnings computed under accrual-based accounting practices apply rather equally to EBITDA. There are, however, some important exceptions. In particular, because it is calculated before taxes, depreciation, and amortization, creative accounting practices that apply to those topics are generally not applicable to EBITDA. See Chapter 10 for more discussion of EBITDA.

REPORTING CASH FLOW

Generally accepted accounting principles are very focused on the measurement and reporting of accrual-based earnings. The vast majority of all accounting standards released deal in one way or another with accrual-accounting concepts. That is not to diminish the importance to GAAP of cash-flow reporting. It is just that, in the view of the Financial Accounting Standards Board, information about accrual-based earnings and not cash flow per se is more useful to investors and creditors in assessing an investment's cash-flow prospects. As noted by the FASB:

> The primary focus of financial reporting is information about an enterprise's performance provided by measures of earnings and its components. Investors, creditors, and others who are concerned with assessing the prospects for enterprise net cash inflows are especially interested in that information.[5]

Thus, in the view of the FASB, the purpose of the statement of cash flow is one of support for the other accrual-based statements. The statement is designed to provide confirmation that accrual-based earnings ultimately are resulting in cash flow and to provide information on the sources and uses of that cash flow. It is not designed to be a predictor of cash flow. If earnings are not resulting in cash flow, then the statement of cash flow should aid investors and creditors in determining why.

While there have been some minor modifications since its original release, primary guidance in the area of cash-flow reporting comes from a single accounting standard, Statement of Financial Accounting Standard No. 95, *Statement of Cash Flows*.[6] Although on the surface the statement appears to be very specific in its prescriptions for the measurement and reporting of cash flow, many differences appear to exist. In fact, in our review of numerous cash-flow statements in preparation to write this chapter, we noted many examples of measurement and reporting differences across companies that gave differing or, in some cases, unexpected cash-flow signals. For most of these, fault could be placed with the reporting companies. In some, however, even more specific guidance from the FASB would have been helpful.

Preparing the Cash Flow Statement

According to the FASB, the cash-flow metric to be used in preparation of cash-flow statements is cash and cash equivalents. Cash includes currency on hand and demand deposits. Cash equivalents are highly liquid debt instruments with original maturities of three months or less that can be viewed as essentially the same as cash.

An example cash-flow statement for Orthodontic Centers of America, Inc., is provided in Exhibit 11.1. The company's cash-flow statement demonstrates the use of cash and cash equivalents.

This cash-flow statement is prepared in what is known as the indirect-method format. That is, it starts with net income and reconciles to cash provided by operating activities, deriving that cash-flow metric indirectly from net income.[7]

Exhibit 11.1   Consolidated Statements of Cash Flows: Orthodontic Centers of America, Inc., Years Ending December 31, 1998–2000 (thousands of dollars)

	1998	1999	2000
Operating Activities			
Net Income (loss)	$33,813	$45,836	$(2,854)
Adjustments to reconcile net income (loss) to net cash provided by operating activities:			
Provision for bad debt expense	2,295	2,079	373
Depreciation and amortization	9,124	12,238	15,175
Deferred income taxes	(2,767)	1,273	(7,792)
Cumulative effect of changes in accounting principles	—	678	50,576
Changes in operating assets and liabilities:			
Service fee receivables	(22,733)	(27,491)	(13,549)
Supplies inventory	(2,663)	(2,305)	889
Prepaid expenses and other	228	(1,342)	(2,309)
Advances to/amounts payable to orthodontic entities	(1,756)	(2,420)	(8,233)
Accounts payable and other current liabilities	6,568	(5,199)	7,368
Net cash provided by operating activities	22,109	23,347	39,644
Investing Activities			
Purchases of property, equipment and improvements	(17,638)	(22,520)	(20,271)
Proceeds from (sales of) available-for-sale investments	19,674	204	(16)
Intangible assets acquired	(42,216)	(17,178)	(28,246)
Advances to orthodontic entities	(4,906)	(3,951)	—
Payments from orthodontic entities	1,927	370	—
Net cash used in investing activities	(43,159)	(43,075)	(48,533)
Financing Activities			
Repayment of notes payable and long-term debt	(7,864)	(6,742)	(6,530)
Proceeds from long-term debt	20,055	30,577	7,483
Repayment of loans from key employee program	—	—	2,632
Issuance of common stock	595	114	4,299
Net cash provided by financing activities	12,786	23,949	7,884
Foreign currency translation adjustment	—	—	(127)
Change in cash and cash equivalents	(8,264)	4,221	(1,132)
Cash and cash equivalents at beginning of year	9,865	1,601	5,822
Cash and cash equivalents at end of year	$ 1,601	$ 5,822	$ 4,690

Exhibit 11.1 *(Continued)*

	1998	1999	2000
Supplemental Cash Flow Information			
Cash paid during the year for:			
Interest	$ 337	$ 2,499	$ 4,271
Income taxes	$ 19,287	$ 33,931	$ 31,568
Noncash Investing and Financing Activities			
Notes payable and common stock issued			
to obtain service agreements	$ 13,609	$ 4,512	$ 5,974

Source: Orthodontic Centers of America, Inc. Form 10-K Annual Report to the Securities and Exchange Commission, December 2000, p. 24.

The indirect-method format is used by most reporting companies. Few companies use an alternative format, the direct-method format. Rather than deriving cash provided by operating activities indirectly from net income, direct-method format cash-flow statements present actual operating inflows and outflows of cash. For example, likely captions on a direct-method format cash-flow statement include such inflows as cash collected from customers and interest and dividends received. Cash outflows include cash paid to employees and other suppliers and income taxes paid.

Many companies would argue that their accounting systems are not designed to capture the kind of cash-flow information needed for a direct-method format cash-flow statement. Accordingly, they opt for the indirect-method format. Moreover, because companies that employ the direct-method format for their cash-flow statements also must provide a reconciliation of net income to cash provided by operating activities, most companies elect to provide an indirect-method statement instead and forgo preparation of a direct-method format statement.

In reconciling net income to cash provided by operating activities, Orthodontic Centers adds to net income such noncash expenses as the provision for bad debts, depreciation and amortization, and deferred income taxes. The noncash cumulative loss on a change in accounting principles also was added back to net income.

Other adjustments to net income in computing cash provided by operating activities consist of changes in operations-related assets and liabilities, such as receivables, inventory, prepaid expenses, and accounts payable and other current liabilities. The balances in these asset and liability accounts are increased and decreased as accrual-based revenue and expenses are recorded. As they are the result of noncash revenue and expense accruals—items that increase or decrease net income without providing or using cash—changes in their balances must be adjusted out of net income in calculating cash provided by operating activities.

Following the operating section of the statement of cash flow are sections detailing the cash flow associated with the company's investing and financing activities. The cash-flow information in these sections is presented in a direct-method format, that is, they present actual cash inflows and outflows. For example, the company reports cash used for purchases of property, equipment, and improvements and cash proceeds from long-term debt. A closer look at how cash flow is separated into operating, investing, and financing activities is provided in separate sections of this chapter.

After the company's cash flow is divided into three key sections—operating, investing, and financing—and after an adjustment for the effects of changes in foreign-currency exchange rates on cash, the cash-flow statement sums to the change in cash and cash equivalents. This is the actual change in cash and cash equivalents as reported on the balance sheet. Demonstrating how the change in cash and cash equivalents links the beginning and ending balance sheets, the company adds cash and cash equivalents at the beginning of the year to the change in cash and cash equivalents to yield the year-ending balances.

Following the cash-flow activity are supplemental disclosures, as required by generally accepted accounting principles, of cash paid for interest and income taxes and of noncash investing and financing activities. Because the statement of cash flow is just that—a statement of cash flow—significant noncash investing and financing transactions entered into during the reporting period are excluded. To ensure that the financial statement reader is aware of these transactions, GAAP requires that they be disclosed as supplemental information to the cash-flow statement. Orthodontic Centers discloses a single such item, the purchase of service agreements, an investing activity, which was paid for by issuing notes payable and common stock, a financing activity.

Cash Flow Provided by Operating Activities

Cash provided by operating activities or operating cash flow consists of the cash effects of transactions that enter into the determination of net income, such as cash receipts from sales of goods and services and cash payments to suppliers and employees for acquisitions of inventory and operating expenses and to lenders for interest expense. Generally, cash flow provided by operating activities is the cash-flow counterpart of accrual-based income from continuing operations. There are, however, some important exceptions.

For example, gains and losses from the sale of investments or items of property, plant, and equipment are included in accrual-based income from continuing operations. The proceeds from sale of these assets are reported as cash flow provided or used from investing activities. The cash flow associated with the purchase and sale of investments classified as trading securities are included in cash provided by operating activities. Any gains or losses on sale also would be included in income from continuing operations.[8]

As another example, all income taxes paid are included with cash flow provided by operating activities. However, on the income statement, income taxes on such items as the operating income component and gains or losses on the disposal of discontinued operations, on extraordinary items, and on the cumulative effect of changes in accounting principles are reported with their respective items and excluded from income from continuing operations.

In addition, any cash flow associated with the operating income or loss component of discontinued operations is included with cash flow provided by operating activities but is excluded from income from continuing operations. Gains and losses on the disposal of discontinued operations are excluded from cash provided by operating activities, being reported instead as investing activities, and are similarly excluded from income from continuing operations.

Gains and losses considered to be extraordinary items are excluded from income from continuing operations. Whether the cash flow associated with such items is excluded from cash provided by operating activities depends on the nature of the underlying extraordinary item. For example, the cash-flow effects of extraordinary items related to the disposal of assets would be reported as investing actions. The cash-flow effects of an early debt retirement would be reported as a financing action. Other extraordinary events that are not considered to be investing or financing activities would be included with cash provided by operating activities.

The cumulative effects of changes in accounting principles are excluded from income from continuing operations. Such changes are inherently noncash events and accordingly do not impact cash provided by operating activities.[9]

As with accrual-based income from continuing operations, cash provided by operating activities is defined from the viewpoint of the shareholder. That is, income from continuing operations is considered to be income available for shareholders after the prior claims of lenders, in the form of interest expense, have been deducted. Similarly, the statement of cash flows reports operating cash flow that is available for shareholders. Here again, the prior claims of lenders in the form of interest paid have been deducted. Dividends, however, are a distribution to shareholders and are not deducted in calculating income from continuing operations or cash provided by operating activities.

Cash Flow from Investing Activities

Cash provided or used by investing activities consists of changes in cash and cash equivalents from making and collecting loans; from acquiring and disposing of debt or equity investments, except for trading securities; and from purchases and sales of items of property, plant, and equipment or other productive assets. Investments in and sales of securities that are held for trading purposes are reported with operating activities.

Thus, while the cash expended to invest in assets is reported in the investing section of the statement of cash flow, any income generated by that investment is reported in the operating section. For example, an investment in stock or bonds would be reported in the investing section of the statement of cash flow. The cash dividends or interest generated by those investments would be reported in the operating section. The sale of that investment at a gain would necessitate the subtraction of the gain from net income in calculating cash provided by operating activities. Because the indirect-method format cash-flow statement starts with net income in calculating operating cash flow, the gain, which is included in net income, must be subtracted. The proceeds from the investment's sale will be reported as a cash inflow in the investing section of the statement of cash flow.

Cash Flow from Financing Activities

Financing cash flows consist of changes in cash and cash equivalents by obtaining resources from owners and providing them with a return on, and a return of, their investment, and from borrowing money and repaying amounts borrowed. Thus, cash raised from stock issues and debt financing are financing activities. Dividends paid on equity are also a financing activity. However, as explained earlier, interest paid on debt is reported as an operating item.

The repayment of debt at an early repayment premium would result in a loss for the difference between the repayment amount and the debt's book value. Under GAAP, that loss would be included in net income as an extraordinary item. Note that because the loss is considered an extraordinary item, it would be excluded from income from continuing operations. In calculating operating cash flow, the loss would need to be removed from net income by adding its effects back to net income. The debt repayment amount, which includes the effects of the loss, would be reported as a cash outflow in the financing section of the cash-flow statement.

A summary of how inflows and outflows of cash are classified in the statement of cash flows is provided in Exhibit 11.2. More information on how items of income are classified on the income statement into such captions as income from continuing operations, discontinued operations, extraordinary items, and changes in accounting principle is available in Chapter 9.

Importance of Operating Cash Flow

For any company, cash provided by operating activities or operating cash flow is a key measure of performance. As noted earlier, investors seek earning power, which focuses on a company's ability to generate a sustainable and likely growing stream of earnings that provides cash flow. The ability to generate positive operating cash flow provides evidence of a company's ability to provide the cash flow that investors seek. Operating cash flow serves as a foundation for corporate valuation, the concern of equity investors, and for sustained debt service, the focus of creditors.

Operating cash flow is more likely to be sustained than other sources of cash that may be provided from investing activities or financing activities. For example, cash provided by investing activities would include cash provided from the sale of an investment or an item of property, plant, and equipment. The cash received from such a sale cannot be expected to continue. Also, cash received from the issue of stock or debt, referred to as cash provided by financing activities, is not recurring cash flow. Sales of assets and issues of stock or debt are inherently nonrecurring events and often, as with the issue of stock or debt, may carry the expectation of a future cash payment.

Investors and creditors can take confidence in a company's ability to generate operating cash flow as it indicates a measure of success in corporate performance. Corporations make cash investments with the expectation of earning returns on those investments. When a company is able to generate positive operating cash flow, it indicates that the company has made investments that are, in fact, providing cash returns.

This is not to say that an inability to generate operating cash flow is inherently bad or unacceptable. Start-up companies, and even profitable companies that are growing rapidly, may have temporary difficulties in generating positive operating cash flow.

Exhibit 11.2   Classification of Inflows and Outflows of Cash within the Statement of Cash Flows

Cash Provided by Operating Activities

Includes:

Receipts from sale of goods or services

Interest and dividends received

Payments to employees and other suppliers

Payments of interest

Payments of taxes

Payments for or proceeds from operating income of discontinued operations prior to disposition

Purchase of and proceeds from sale of trading securities

Calculated using indirect-method format as follows:

Start with net income

Remove noncash expenses:

    Provision for uncollectible accounts

    Depreciation and amortization

    Deferred income tax expense

Remove items included in net income related to investing activities:

    Gains and losses on sales of investments, except for trading securities

    Gains and losses on sales of property, plant, and equipment

    Gains and losses on dispositions of discontinued operations

Remove items included in net income related to financing activities:

    Extraordinary items related to gains and losses on early retirement of debt

Remove cumulative effect of change in accounting principle

Remove changes in operations-related assets and liabilities:

    Accounts receivable

    Inventory

    Prepaid expenses

    Tax-refund receivable

    Accounts payable

    Accrued expenses payable

    Income taxes payable

Cash from Investing Activities

Purchase of and proceeds from collection of principal of loans and other debt instruments

Purchase of and proceeds from sale of equity investments, excluding trading securities

Purchase of and proceeds from sale of property, plant, and equipment

Cash from Financing Activities

Issues and repurchases of debt

Issues and repurchases of equity

Dividend payments

However, as their businesses mature, these firms need to be able to begin generating positive operating cash flow or ultimately they will find it difficult to secure additional financing.

Given the importance of cash provided by operating activities to investors and creditors, both groups focus very carefully on this performance metric. As they do, they tend to accept it as an accurately measured amount and less subject to manipulation than reported earnings. Unfortunately, cash flow, especially operating cash flow, is not immune to the creative practices of the financial numbers game. Moreover, even in the absence of attempts by some managements to mislead, unexpected vagaries in the manner in which operating cash flow is defined can be misleading.

PROBLEMS WITH REPORTED OPERATING CASH FLOW

Certain of the GAAP-based requirements for the calculation of cash provided by operating activities are quite esoteric and may be unknown to many investors and creditors. For example, some may be surprised to learn that operating cash flow includes all income taxes, regardless of the item that gave rise to the taxable event and whether the item itself is reported in operating cash flow or not. As another example, operating cash flow includes the operating component of operations that are being discontinued. Unaware of rules such as these, and others, for reporting operating cash flow, financial statement users may by be misled by the signals gleaned from a careful analysis of that metric.

In addition, while accounting standards have attempted to eliminate flexibility in the reporting of operating cash flow, managements intent on "managing" their operating cash flow in an intended direction still have leeway. For example, consider a company whose operating cash flow is higher, for whatever reason, than expected for a reporting period. A reduction in inventory, the unexpected collection of certain receivables, or an amount of nonrecurring income might be the cause. Such a company might temper that cash-flow surplus by purchasing securities classified as trading. In a subsequent period, the sale of those same securities would bolster operating cash flow. As another example, most companies, but not all, report expenditures on capitalized software costs as investing activities. Expenditures on software costs that are expensed as incurred are included with operating cash flow. Thus, not only are earnings increased by increases in amounts capitalized, but operating cash flow is boosted as well. Further, while amortization of capitalized software will reduce income from continuing operations, because it is a noncash expense, that amortization will not reduce cash provided by operating activities.

In this section, we look collectively at what we refer to as problems with reported operating cash flow. The section consists of a collection of examples that deal with issues that have the potential to generate misleading or unexpected signals regarding operating cash flow. Some of the examples deal with the GAAP-based rules for reporting operating cash flow. Others focus on how managements use flexibility in the reporting rules for operating cash flow to potentially mislead investors and creditors in their assessments of earning power.

Operating Income Component of Discontinued Operations

As discussed in Chapter 9, on the income statement, income from discontinued operations is reported separately from income from continuing operations. Income from discontinued operations includes operating income of the discontinued segment for the period prior to the point in time at which a decision was made to dispose of the segment and any gain or loss on the ultimate sale of that segment. On the cash-flow statement, however, operating cash flow consists of cash provided by all operating activities, including continuing operations and any cash flow associated with the operating income of the discontinued segment. Thus, cash provided by operating activities, which sounds as if it consists exclusively of recurring elements, may contain certain cash flow that is inherently nonrecurring—that is, cash flow associated with discontinued operations.

Nothing in the accounting standards precludes the separate disclosure of cash provided by continuing operations and discontinued operations. It is just that separate disclosure is not required.

Consider, for example, CytRx Corp. On its income statement in 2000, the company reported income from discontinued operations of approximately $799,000. In a footnote, the company noted that the discontinued operations were the result of the sale of a drug used in research animals together with a related business, which the company referred to collectively as Titermax[R], for $750,000. The purchase price was paid with $100,000 in cash and a note receivable for $650,000. The company went on to note:

> Net income associated with the Titermax activities included in income (loss) from discontinued operations was approximately $119,000 . . . for 2000. A gain related to the sale of $680,000 was recorded in the second quarter of 2000 and is also classified as discontinued operations.[10]

Thus the company was properly including the operating income of the discontinued operations of $119,000 with the $680,000 gain on sale and reporting their total, $799,000, as discontinued operations.

On the company's statement of cash flow, in computing operating cash flow, the gain of $680,000 was subtracted from the net loss for the year. The $100,000 received on the sale of the discontinued segment was reported in the investing section of the cash-flow statement.

Note that by subtracting from the net loss only the gain on sale of the discontinued segment, any cash associated with the $119,000 operating income of the discontinued segment remained within operating cash flow. Assuming no changes in operating-related assets and liabilities for the discontinued segment, the net result would be a boost to operating cash flow of $119,000. Such a boost to operating cash flow would have resulted in a net reduction in the reported cash used in operating activities by approximately 11% ($119,000 as a percentage of cash used by operating activities excluding the $119,000, of $1,121,020).

Separate Disclosure of Operating Cash Flow from Discontinued Operations   The statement of cash flow for CytRx Corp. made no mention of the operating cash flow provided by discontinued operations. Without a careful reading of the footnotes, it would appear that cash used in operating activities for 2000 was the reported amount of the cash-flow drain from continuing operations. In fact, the continuing cash drain was higher than the amount reported because of the inclusion in operating cash flow of the cash provided by discontinued operations.

While not required, many companies will disclose separately on their statements of cash flow the cash provided or used by discontinued operations. Such disclosure is very useful and highlights the amount of cash flow provided or used by this inherently non-recurring item.

For example, in the notes to its annual report for the year ended May 30, 1999, Dean Foods Co. described the sale of Agrilink Foods, Inc. as follows:

> On September 23, 1998, the Company sold the stock of Dean Foods Vegetable Company to Agrilink Foods, Inc. ("Agrilink") for $378.2 million in cash, a $30.0 million Agrilink subordinated note and Agrilink's aseptic foods business, which has been valued at $80.2 million. . . . The Company recorded an after-tax gain on the sale of the Vegetables segment of $83.8 million ($2.07 per diluted share). Accordingly, Vegetables segment results are presented as discontinued operations.[11]

The company's statement of cash flow for the three years ended May 30, 1997, 1998, and 1999 reported cash provided by continuing operations of $147,264,000, $162,710,000, and $163,918,000, respectively. Note that the company reported cash provided by continuing operations and not simply cash provided by operations. On a separate line on the statement of cash flow, the company reported cash provided by discontinued operations for the three years ended May 30, 1997, 1998, and 1999 of $39,525,000, $38,169,000, and $297,552,000, respectively.

It is unclear from the company's disclosures the portion of the disclosed cash provided by discontinued operations that was related to the proceeds from sale of the discontinued segment and the portion that was related to the operations of the discontinued segment. For the years 1997 and 1998, the cash provided by discontinued operations would consist entirely of cash provided by operations of the discontinued segment. However, for the year of sale, 1999, the sale proceeds apparently are included with cash provided by operations of the discontinued segment. Nonetheless, by disclosing separately the cash flow provided by discontinued operations, Dean Foods has reported an operating cash flow amount, referred to as cash provided by continuing operations, that is inherently a recurring source of cash flow.

Adjusting Operating Cash Flow for Discontinued Operations   Not all companies will separate cash flow provided by discontinued operations from cash provided by continuing operations. When evidence of discontinued operations appears on the income statement, the financial statement reader should be aware that if there is no separate disclosure of cash provided by discontinued operations, then cash provided by the operating component of the discontinued segment will be included with cash provided by operations reported on the statement of cash flow.

Either the income statement or the footnotes, or both, will disclose the after-tax operating income component of the discontinued segment. This amount can be used as a proxy for the operating cash flow provided by the discontinued segment. If material, it should be removed from cash provided by operating activities to obtain a more reliable and meaningful measure of cash provided by operations.

Income Taxes Paid

As noted, all income taxes paid are included with operating cash flow. Amounts paid and reported with operating cash flow include taxes on operating income as well as income taxes on transactions classified as investing activities or financing activities, including taxes on discontinued operations, extraordinary items, and taxes, if any, on changes in accounting principles.

During the deliberation phase of SFAS No. 95, *The Statement of Cash Flows*, the Financial Accounting Standards Board considered allocating income taxes paid to investing and financing transactions.[12] The board decided, however, that such an allocation scheme would be so complex and arbitrary that the costs involved would exceed the possible benefit.

The FASB may be correct in its assessment. However, we are left with measures of operating cash flow that, from the standpoint of taxes, may give misleading information.

Consider, for example, the case of Lands End, Inc. In the footnotes to its annual report for the year ended January 28, 2000, the company made this disclosure:

> During the first quarter of fiscal 1998, the company sold its majority interest in The Territory Ahead to The International Cornerstone Group, Inc. of Boston, Massachusetts, resulting in an after-tax gain of $4.9 million. The after-tax gain was recorded in the first quarter of fiscal 1998.[13]

The company's income statement reported the gain on sale as a pretax item in the amount of $7,805,000. The statement of cash flow subtracted a "Pre-tax gain on sale of subsidiary" for the same amount from net income in computing cash used by operating activities. The proceeds from the sale of the subsidiary, $12,350,000, were reported as cash provided from investing activities. Thus, the tax on the gain on sale of the subsidiary, a cash payment of approximately $2.9 million (calculated as the pretax gain of $7.8 million less the after-tax gain of $4.9 million), was left in cash used by operating activities. That tax, which arguably belonged in the investing section of the cash-flow statement, reduced operating cash flow. In this case, it increased the amount of cash used in operations by approximately 12% ($2.9 million as a percentage of cash used by operating activities, excluding the $2.9 million taxes paid, of $24.0 million).

In December 1998 IBM announced that it would sell its Global Network to AT&T Corp. for $5.0 billion. IBM closed the deal in 1999 and reported a pretax gain of $4.1 billion, which was reported to be $2.5 billion after tax. On the company's statement of cash flow for 1999, the entire pretax gain was subtracted from net income in calculating cash provided by operations. The cash proceeds from the sale received that year, $4.9 billion, were reported in the investing section of the cash-flow statement.[14]

In its year ended December 31, 1999, IBM reported operating cash flow of $10.1 billion, up from $9.3 billion in 1998 and $8.9 billion in 1997. However, reducing operating cash flow in 1999 were income taxes on the gain from the sale of the Global Network of $1.6 billion ($4.1 billion pretax gain less $2.5 billion after-tax gain). Had those taxes been reported in the investing section of the cash-flow statement, operating cash flow in 1999 would have been $11.7 billion, or 16% higher than the $10.1 billion reported.

Excluded from this discussion of the tax effects of the gain on sale is the fact that operating cash flow for the years 1997, 1998, and 1999 actually include the cash provided by operations of the divested unit. The amount of operating cash flow generated by that company prior to its disposal was not disclosed in the IBM annual report. In the absence of such a disclosure, calculating it would not be practical.

When gains are reported on transactions that are not part of operations, operating cash flow is reduced by any income taxes paid on the gains. The situation is reversed when losses are recognized on nonoperating transactions. Here income tax benefits serve to bolster operating cash flow.

For example, a loss on the sale of investments or fixed assets would be removed from net income on a pretax basis in calculating operating cash flow. The proceeds from sale would be included with cash flow from investing activities. The tax savings from the loss would increase operating cash flow by reducing income taxes paid.

In 1999 Federal Mogul Corp. recorded an after-tax loss on the early retirement of debt in the amount of $38.2 million. That year, the company correctly reported the loss as an extraordinary item on its income statement. On its statement of cash flow, the pretax loss was added back to net income in calculating cash provided by operating activities. That pretax loss, $58.1 million, indicates that the debt retirement transaction saved the company $19.9 million in income taxes paid during the year ($58.1 million pretax gain less $38.2 million after-tax gain). That $19.9 million in income tax savings boosted operating cash flow for the year by approximately 7% ($19.9 million in tax savings as a percentage of operating cash flow before the tax savings of $305.6 million).[15]

Adjusting Operating Cash Flow for Income Taxes Paid   For a meaningful measure of operating cash flow, one that can be compared with prior years, only income taxes on continuing operations should be included. The tax effects of gains or losses on transactions classified as investing or financing items should be removed. Since the underlying investing and financing items tend to be nonrecurring, their tax effects should also be considered as nonrecurring.

A careful examination of the cash-flow statement will highlight the existence of any such gains or losses. For example, pretax gains on the sale of investments or property, plant, and equipment items will be subtracted from net income in calculating operating cash flow. The tax effects of these gains should be added back to operating cash flow. Similarly, pretax losses will be added to net income in computing operating cash flow. The tax effects of these items should be subtracted from operating cash flow.

In computing operating cash flow, net income also will be adjusted for the pretax effects of extraordinary items. If these items are considered to be part of investing or financing activities, their tax effects should be removed from operating cash flow. For example, an extraordinary loss on early debt retirement will be added to net income in computing operating cash flow. Debt retirement is considered to be a financing transaction. The cash disbursed to settle the debt obligation will be reported in the financing section of the statement of cash flow. The tax effects of the extraordinary loss, a tax savings, also should be removed from operating cash flow.

The effects of discontinued operations on operating cash flow were discussed above. Note that when operating cash flow includes the cash effects of the operating income component of discontinued operations, the after-tax effects of that operating income should be removed from operating cash flow.

Any cash received from the disposal of discontinued operations is considered to be cash generated by investing activities. Accordingly, in computing operating cash flow, any gain or loss on disposal of discontinued operations will be removed from net income. However, the amount of the gain or loss removed will be on a pretax basis, leaving the tax effects within operating cash flow. Accordingly, the tax effects of the gain or loss should be removed.

The statement of cash flow will highlight the cumulative effects of any changes in accounting principles made during the year. If any such changes did occur, resulting cumulative-effect gains will be subtracted while cumulative-effect losses will be added back to net income in computing operating cash flow. Such changes in accounting principle typically involve no current tax payments or savings, and, accordingly, no adjustments to operating cash flow for their tax effects are warranted.[16]

Illustrative Example   To demonstrate the adjustment of operating cash flow to remove the tax effects of transactions classified as investing or financing activities, excerpts from the statement of cash flow for The Standard Register Co. are used. The excerpts are presented in Exhibit 11.3.

The cash-flow statement in the exhibit is presented in the indirect-method format. Standard Register calculates operating cash flow by adjusting net income for noncash expenses and nonoperating gains and losses. Other adjustments also are made for changes in operations-related assets and liabilities. While the company provided detail of these account changes, that detail is omitted from Exhibit 11.3.

Note that in the reconciliation of net income to operating cash flow there are adjustments for a gain on sale of discontinued operations, for a loss on sale of assets, and for a gain in one year and a loss in another on the sale of investments. As discussed previously, these adjustments are for pretax gains and losses, leaving their tax effects within operating cash flow. To obtain a more sustainable measure of operating cash flow, the tax effects should be removed.

Standard Register's income statement reports that the 1999 gain on sale of discontinued operations, net of income taxes of $10,568,000, was $15,670,000. This disclosure indicates that income taxes in the amount of $10,568,000 serve as a reduction in operating cash flow and should be added back.[17]

Unlike the gain on sale of discontinued operations, the income tax effects of the losses on sales of assets and the gains and losses from investments are not disclosed separately in the financial statements or footnotes. Thus the tax effects of these items must be estimated. The company's income tax footnote indicates that a combined federal and state income tax rate of 40.3% is appropriate for use. This rate consists of the federal statutory rate of 35% plus a state rate, net of federal benefit, of 5.3%. The 40.3% rate is multiplied by each of the individual gains and losses to determine the amount of income taxes to remove from operating cash flow. The tax effects of gains would be added to operating cash flow while the tax effects of losses would be subtracted.

Exhibit 11.3   Summarized Excerpts from the Statement of Cash Flow: The Standard Register Co., Years Ending December 28, 1997 (1997), January 3, 1999 (1998), and January 2, 2000 (1999) (thousands of dollars)

	1997	1998	1999
Cash flows from operating activities:			
Net income	$ 66,894	$ 59,583	$ 70,901
Add (deduct) items not affecting cash:			
Depreciation and amortization	36,646	54,112	53,042
(Gain) on sale of discontinued operations	—	—	(26,238)
Loss on sale of assets	346	19	603
(Gain) loss from investments	1,558	(7)	—
Deferred income taxes	3,938	2,494	5,094
Increase (decrease) in cash arising from changes in assets and liabilities, net of acquisition/disposition[a]:	(10,937)	(73,246)	(7,442)
Net cash provided by operating activities	$ 98,445	$ 42,955	$ 95,960

[a]The company provided details of these amounts that are not provided here.

Source: The Standard Register Co. annual report, January 2, 2000, p. 38.

These calculations and adjustments, together with an adjustment for the tax effects of the gain on sale of discontinued operations, are summarized in Exhibit 11.4.

Before adjustments for income taxes, operating cash flow at Standard Register was slightly lower in 1999 than in 1997, although the amount was up from 1998. Operating cash flow in 1999 was $95,960,000, versus $98,445,000 in 1997 and $42,955,000 in 1998. After adjustment, however, operating cash flow shows a marked increase in 1999 over 1997, rising to $106,285,000 in 1999 from $97,678,000 in 1997 and $42,950,000 in 1998. After adjustment, the company is performing better on a cash-flow basis than was the case before adjustment.

Note on Income Taxes and Foreign-Currency Gains and Losses   While not apparent in the Standard Register statement of cash flow, many companies with sales or expenses denominated in foreign currencies will experience foreign-currency gains and losses. These gains and losses will be included in net income and, to the extent they are unrealized, will be removed in calculating operating cash flow. For two important reasons, no adjustments should be made for the income tax effects of these gains and losses.

1. Because they are unrealized, no income taxes would have been paid or received as a result of the gains or losses.
2. Because foreign currency gains and losses are, for the most part, considered to be operating items, their income tax effects are appropriately included with operating cash flow.

Exhibit 11.4 Adjustments to Operating Cash Flow to Remove the Effects of Income Taxes on Nonoperating Items: The Standard Register Co., Years Ending December 28, 1997 (1997), January 3, 1999 (1998), and January 2, 2000 (1999) (thousands of dollars)

	1997	1998	1999
Reported net cash provided by operating activities	$98,445	$42,955	$95,960
Add: tax effects of gain on discontinued operations			10,568
(Deduct): tax effects of loss on sale of assets	(139)	(8)	(243)
	($346 × 40.3%)	(19 × 40.3%)	(603 × 40.3%)
Add/(deduct): tax effects of gain/(loss) from investments	(628)	3	—
	($1,558 × 40.3%)	($7 × 40.3%)	
Adjusted net cash provided by operating activities	$97,678	$42,950	$106,285

Source: The Standard Register Co., Annual Report, January 2, 2000, p. 38, and calculations as noted.

Tax Benefits of Nonqualified Employee Stock Options

When nonqualified employee stock options are granted, the issuing company receives a tax deduction for the difference between the exercise price and market price of the options on the date they are exercised. That deduction times the tax rate results in a tax benefit that accrues to the company, reducing income taxes paid. That benefit is accounted for as an increase in paid-in capital, a shareholders' equity account.

Until recently, there was disagreement on how the tax benefits of nonqualified employee stock options, subsequently referred to as the tax benefits of stock options, should be classified on a statement of cash flow. Some firms viewed the cash flow as a financing item, presumably because the tax benefits are accounted for as increases in shareholders' equity. Others, citing the position of the FASB that all income taxes are operating items, opted to classify the tax benefits as operating cash flow.

The significant run-up in the stock market experienced in recent years resulted in sizable differences between market prices and option exercise prices and generated notable tax benefits for many issuing companies. As a result, the implications for financial analysis of the cash-flow classification of those tax benefits for operating cash flow has become very important.

For example, for the years ended January 29, 1999, January 28, 2000, and February 2, 2001, Dell Computer Corp. reported operating cash flow of $2.4 billion, $3.9 billion, and $4.2 billion, respectively. Included in that operating cash flow were tax benefits related to stock options of $444 million, $1.0 billion, and $929 million, respectively, for the same three-year period. That is, tax benefits generated by employee stock options comprised between 18% and 26% of operating cash flow for the three years ended February 2, 2001.[18]

Also reporting tax benefits from stock options as operating cash flow was Cisco Systems, Inc. For the three years ended July 25, 1998, July 31, 1999, and July 29, 2000, the company reported cash provided by operations of $2.9 billion, $4.3 billion, and $6.1 billion, respectively. During those same three years, the company included in operating cash-flow tax benefits from stock options of $422 million, $837 million, and $2.5 billion, respectively.[19] Thus, like Dell Computer, operating cash flow at Cisco was boosted significantly by the tax benefits of stock options. In the case of Cisco, for the three years ended July 29, 2000, tax benefits from stock options comprised between 15% and 41% of operating cash flow.

During the late 1990s, significant contributions to operating cash flow from the tax benefits of employee stock options were not exclusively the domain of large technology firms. Consider Papa John's International, Inc. For the three years ended December 27, 1998, December 26, 1999, and December 31, 2000, the company reported operating cash flow of $64,998,000, $89,581,000, and $76,718,000, respectively. Included in these amounts for the same three-year period were tax benefits related to stock options of $2,953,000, $3,945,000, and $542,000, respectively.[20] While these amounts were not as significant as the cases of Dell and Cisco, if discontinued, they would be missed.

One company that did not include the tax benefits of employee stock options in operating cash flow was Microsoft Corp. For the three years ended June 30, 1997, 1998, and 1999, the company reported operating cash flow of $4.7 billion, $6.9 billion, and $10.0 billion, respectively. Excluded from these amounts and reported in the financing section of the cash-flow statement were the tax benefits of employee stock options of $796 million, $1.6 billion, and $3.1 billion, respectively.[21] Presumably because they are accounted for as increments to paid-in capital, the company considered the tax benefits to be financing-related items.

Another company that received a very sizable tax benefit from employee stock options, but elected to report it in the financing section of its cash-flow statement, was the Quigley Corp., a provider of natural health products. In its year ended December 31, 1998, the company reported operating cash flow of $8,947,419. That year the company could have boosted its operating cash flow considerably by including $3,512,205 in tax benefits from employee stock options.[22] However, it was probably best that the tax benefits were excluded from operating cash flow because a decline in the company's share price in 1999 and 2000 eliminated any additional tax benefits for those years. Had the benefits been included in operating cash flow in 1998, cash generated by operations that year would have given an overly optimistic view of the company's cash-generating potential.

Guidance from the Emerging Issues Task Force   Aware that users of financial statements could be confused by the disparity found in practice for the reporting of stock option tax benefits, the Emerging Issues Task Force was convened to consider the matter. The EITF, a special task force of the FASB, is a committee established to reach consensus on how to account for new and unusual financial transactions that have the potential for creating differing financial reporting practices. While consensus views of the EITF do not have the same authoritative support as accounting standards promulgated by the FASB, they nonetheless are considered to be part of GAAP. Reporting companies are expected to follow them.

In 2000 the EITF reached consensus on how the tax benefits of stock options are to be classified in cash-flow statements. According to the task force, such tax benefits are to be included with operating cash flow.

In its 2000 annual report, Microsoft noted the consensus opinion of the EITF with this statement:

> As required by Emerging Issues Task Force (EITF) Issue 00-15, Classification in the Statement of Cash Flows of the Income Tax Benefit Received by a Company upon Exercise of a Nonqualified Employee Stock Option, stock option income tax benefits are classified as cash from operations in the cash flows statement. Prior period cash-flows statements have been restated to conform with this presentation.[23]

This change in classification had a dramatic effect on the operating cash flow reported by Microsoft. For the three years ended June 30, 1998, 1999, and 2000, the company reported cash provided by operations of $8.5 billion, $13.1 billion, and $14.0 billion, respectively. The amounts reported included tax benefits of employee stock options for the same three years of $1.6 billion, $3.1 billion, and $5.5 billion, respectively. Recall that in its 1999 annual report, the company had reported operating cash flow for 1998 and 1999 of $6.9 billion and $10.0 billion, respectively. The increases in operating cash flow noted for these years in the 2000 report were due entirely to the reclassification of the stock option tax benefits. The effect was quite dramatic.

Adjusting Operating Cash Flow for the Tax Benefits of Employee Stock Options   We do not disagree with the position taken by the Emerging Issues Task Force that the tax benefits from nonqualified employee stock options should be included with operating cash flow. Such treatment is consistent with current accounting standards that call for the reporting of all income taxes as operating cash-flow items. Our concern, however, is that the tax benefits of stock options, especially at the levels observed in recent years, are inherently nonrecurring. They tend to provide an undue boost to operating cash flow, sending a signal of heightened cash-generating ability that may not be sustainable.

Given its inherent nonrecurring nature, operating cash flow generated by the tax benefits of employee stock options should be removed from operating cash flow before using that measure in analysis. Such a step is tantamount to adjusting net income for nonrecurring items in an effort to get a measure of sustainable earnings.[24]

In order to adjust operating cash flow, the tax benefits of stock options must be identified. Typically, companies will identify the benefit clearly on the statement of cash flow. It will be reported as a separate line within the operating section. On those occasions where the tax benefit is netted with other items in the operating section and not disclosed separately, the amount of the benefit must be located elsewhere. If it is material, it will be reported as an increase in additional paid-in capital on the statement of shareholders' equity.

Cash Flow from the Purchase and Sale of Trading Securities

For the most part, the purchase and sale of investments in debt and equity securities are reported in the investing section of the statement of cash flow. The purchase and sale of debt and equity securities classified as available for sale and debt securities considered to be held to maturity are reported in this manner. Cash income from these investments, including interest and dividends, is reported in the operating section of the cash-flow statement.

In contrast, any cash flow associated with debt and equity investments considered to be trading securities is classified as operating cash flow. This includes not only interest and dividend income from the trading securities, if any, but also cash flow associated with the purchase and sale of those short-term investments.

Because these purchases and sales of trading securities can involve significant amounts, especially relative to operating cash flow, they have the potential to significantly alter any impressions gained from that measure. This is particularly true when there is an imbalance between purchases and sales.

For example, in operating cash flow for the year ended September 30, 1997, Qualcomm, Inc., reported a use of cash in the amount of $9,729,000 for the purchase of trading securities. That same year, the company reported a source of cash of $23,129,000 as the proceeds from the sale of trading securities. For the year, the company consumed $28,623,000 in cash from operations. In the absence of the effects of its investments in and sales of trading securities that year, the company would have consumed a much higher $42,023,000 ($28,623,000) – ($23,129,000 – $9,729,000) in operating cash flow.

It is not difficult to see the potential for managing reported operating cash flow through carefully timed purchases and sales of trading securities. For example, one year might be particularly strong on an operating cash-flow basis. Many factors can lead to this result, including declines in receivables or inventory, or an amount of nonrecurring income that is cash-flow backed. In such a year, the company could purchase more trading securities than it sells, reducing operating cash flow. In a subsequent year, when operating cash flow is below a desired level, more sales than purchases of trading securities could be effected.

Consider Standard Register. In fiscal 1997 the company purchased $15,000,000 in trading securities and reported the purchase as part of operating cash flow.[25] Cash from operations that year, including the purchase of trading securities, was $98,445,000. Then in its fiscal 1998, a year when operating cash flow was $34,184,000 before the effects of trading securities, the company sold $8,771,000 of its investments, boosting operating cash flow to $42,955,000. Additional trading securities were sold in fiscal 1999, generating proceeds of $6,150,000 and helping to boost operating cash flow to $95,960,000 that year.[26] We do not claim that the company used sales of trading securities to artificially inflate operating cash flow in 1998 and 1999. Without question, however, the sales did temporarily boost operating cash flow in those years.

After dipping to $11,677,000 in the year ended February 1999 from $17,631,000 in 1998, operating cash flow at Helen of Troy, Ltd., increased noticeably to $28,630,000 in 2000. Contributing to that increase, however, were $21,530,000 in proceeds from sales of marketable securities that were held for trading purposes. There were no such sales in the two previous years. No purchases of trading securities were noted in any of the years presented.

From a cash-flow standpoint, 2000 appears to have been a very good year for Helen of Troy. However, once the proceeds from sales of trading securities are removed, operating cash flow was actually down in 2000 from 1999 and 1998.

Adjusting Operating Cash Flow for the Effects of Trading Securities   For financial companies that maintain a trading desk and regularly trade securities as part of their business plan, an operating designation for cash flow associated with trading securities seems proper. A regular buying and selling of securities is part of what these companies do. For nonfinancial companies, however, investing in trading securities is a sideline and undertaken only on occasion. Accordingly, operating cash flow used by the purchase or provided by the sale of debt and equity investments considered to be trading securities is inherently nonrecurring in nature. It certainly does not have the same recurring quality as operating cash flow generated by the providing of goods and services.

It is a simple and straightforward step to adjust operating cash flow for cash provided by or used for trading securities. If material, the amounts involved will be disclosed prominently in the operating section of the statement of cash flows. Sources of cash from trading investments should be subtracted from operating cash flow while uses of cash from trading investments should be added.

Other Cash-Flow Issues

Capitalized Expenditures   The effects on net income of capitalized expenditures and creative accounting practices noted in that endeavor were dealt with at length in Chapter 7. While the effects on earnings of cost capitalization can be significant, their impact on operating cash flow can be even greater.

Cost capitalization increases earnings while its subsequent amortization reduces it. The net impact on earnings is the excess of amounts capitalized over amounts amortized. With respect to classifications on the cash-flow statement, capitalized costs typically are accounted for as investing items. The thinking here is that the expenditures were capitalized because they benefit future periods and, accordingly, are considered to be long lived assets—investing items on the statement of cash flows. Thus operating cash flow is not penalized for expenditures on most capitalized costs. Moreover, because amortization is a noncash expense, it does not reduce operating cash flow. Accordingly, unlike earnings, where capitalized costs increase and their subsequent amortization reduce earnings, capitalized costs never reduce operating cash flow. From an operating cash-flow point of view, it is as if the capitalized costs were never incurred.

Cash-flow classification for purchases and additions to most property, plant, and equipment items, including capitalized interest, is very consistent across companies. Financial statement users are aware that such expenditures are treated as investing items while their subsequent depreciation is added back to net income in computing operating cash flow. As such, operating cash flow is reported before such expenditures. Because the accounting and cash-flow treatment for property, plant, and equipment items is consistent across companies, financial statement users are aware that operating cash flow excludes them. What many will do to compensate for the cash-flow effect of purchases and additions to property, plant, and equipment is subtract them or, possibly, subtract what is often referred to as replacement capital expenditures from operating cash flow in determining a more discretionary or free cash-flow amount.

For some capitalized expenditures, however, major differences exist in accounting treatment across companies. Some firms will capitalize significant amounts of certain expenditures while others will capitalize small amounts or none at all. As such, there is not the same general awareness of the issue and no established guidelines for dealing with their cash-flow effects as there are for traditional purchases of property, plant, and equipment.

In particular, the effects of capitalized software development costs warrants special attention. As discussed in Chapter 7, software costs are expensed as incurred until technological feasibility is reached. Capitalization begins at that point and continues until the software product is ready for sale or lease. As noted previously, judgment is used in determining the proportion of incurred software costs to be capitalized. The range across companies in the proportions of amounts capitalized is great. It can be as little as zero, where all software costs are expensed as incurred, or as high as 75% to 80%. It depends on management judgment and its evaluation of the software product in development and assessment of when the specific requirements of technological feasibility have been reached.

Software costs that are expensed as incurred are treated as uses of cash in the operating section of the statement of cash flows. Capitalized software costs typically are treated as investing items and do not impact operating cash flow. Accordingly, companies that capitalize software costs will, all else being equal, report higher operating cash flow than companies that expense software costs as incurred. Moreover, the subsequent amortization of the capitalized costs does not affect operating cash flow. As a result, capitalized software costs can have a dramatic effect on operating cash flow.

In Chapter 7 it was noted that for the three years ended April 30, 1998, 1999, and 2000, American Software, Inc., capitalized $8,827,000, $10,902,000, and $10,446,000 in software development costs, respectively. During those same years, the company amortized software costs that had been previously capitalized in the amounts of $6,706,000, $6,104,000, and $3,632,000, respectively. The net effects of the company's capitalization policy on pretax income were the differences in these amounts, or $2,121,000, $4,798,000, and $6,814,000, respectively, for the years 1998, 1999, and 2000.

For the three years ended April 30, 1998, 1999, and 2000, the company reported net income (loss) of $7,795,000, ($32,817,00), and ($1,242,000), respectively.[27] During those same three years, the company was able to take solace from the fact that operating cash flow remained positive at ample amounts. Operating cash flow generated for 1998, 1999, and 2000 was $18,566,000, $14,179,000, and $13,779,000, respectively. However, if amounts of software costs capitalized during those three years, $8,827,000, $10,902,000, and $10,446,000, respectively, were deducted, the reported amounts of operating cash flow would be reduced to $9,739,000, $3,277,000, and $3,333,000, respectively. This is operating cash flow that the company would report if it were to expense all software development costs as incurred. The amounts are still positive, but much less convincing.

There is the issue of income taxes on capitalized expenditures, including software. For tax purposes, most companies will deduct capitalized costs, including software, in the year incurred, providing a tax benefit that is included in operating cash flow that year.[28] Companies that expense these costs will receive a comparable tax benefit that is also reported in operating cash flow. Given this consistency in the treatment of tax benefits, no adjustment for taxes on capitalized expenditures is needed.

There are many other examples that are similar to that of American Software. For example, consider Dun & Bradstreet Corp. For the three years ended December 31, 1998, 1999, and 2000, the company reported cash flow from continuing operations of $152,800,000, $135,200,000, and $27,900,000, respectively. During those same three years, the company capitalized software development costs of $86,000,000, $70,500,000, and $41,700,000, respectively. After deducting capitalized software development costs, the company's cash flow from continuing operations would have been reduced to $66,800,000, $64,700,000, and ($13,800,000), for the years 1998, 1999, and 2000, respectively[29]—not a particularly promising development.

There are many alternative examples of companies that expense all of the software development costs incurred. As noted, by choosing the expense option, these companies automatically include software costs incurred in the operating section of the cash-flow statement. Example software companies include Advent Software, Inc., Primus Knowledge Solutions, Inc., Web Methods, Inc., and, of course, Microsoft Corp.

During the three years ended December 31, 1997, 1998, and 1999, Advent Software reported net income of $6,713,000, $4,399,000, and $17,443,000, respectively. During that same period, the company reported operating cash flow of $7,682,000, $15,571,000, and $19,046,000, respectively. Software costs expensed as incurred during that period were $9,439,000, $21,022,000, and $16,770,000, respectively.[30] Note that the company's operating cash flow during the period in question is strong even after absorbing significant amounts of software development costs.

We do not advocate the expensing on the books of all software development costs as incurred. Capitalization serves a role and is proper when done in accordance with GAAP. It is our position, however, that such expenditures are more operating than investing, much like research and development, which also are expensed as incurred, and should be classified as such on the cash-flow statement.

When a company capitalizes expenditures that others expense, as in the case of capitalized software, care should be taken to note the classification of the expenditure on the statement of cash flow. If the expenditure has been reported in the investing section, the amount expended should be subtracted from reported operating cash flow and added back to the investing section. This adjustment is necessary to obtain an operating cash-flow amount that is more comparative across companies.

Nonrecurring Income and Expenses　Much has been written about the need to adjust net income for nonrecurring items of income and expense in order to obtain a sustainable measure of earnings. A similar step should be taken with operating cash flow. That is, to the extent that cash received from nonrecurring sources or cash paid for nonrecurring uses is included in operating cash flow, those amounts should be removed.

Most nonrecurring sources of cash are related to the sale of assets or businesses and are classified as investing items on the statement of cash flows. No adjustment would be needed to remove these items from operating cash flow. It is possible, however, that a litigation award might be included in operations and should be removed in computing a more sustainable measure of operating cash flow.

It is more likely that some portion of nonrecurring charges will involve a cash payment that will be classified as an operating item. Certainly the largest component of nonrecurring charges will be noncash. A restructuring charge that includes asset write-downs and accruals for severance pay and plant closings will entail little, if any, current cash payment. However, while the asset write-downs may result in a future cash inflow resulting from a sale that would be classified as an investing item, the liability accruals may involve current or future operating cash payments. These nonrecurring payments should be removed from operating cash flow in computing a more sustainable measure.

In the reconciliation of net income to operating cash flow, either the noncash or non-operating portion of nonrecurring charges will appear as additions to net income. If the items do not appear in the reconciliation, they are considered to be operating items that entail cash payments.

For example, on its income statements for the years ended January 29, 1999, and January 28, 2000, Lands End reported a nonrecurring charge of $12,600,000 and a nonrecurring credit of $1,774,000, respectively.[31] On the statement of cash flow for the same years, the company added the entire nonrecurring charge to net income in 1999 and subtracted the entire nonrecurring credit from net income in 2000. The charge and credit involved no operating cash payment in those years. No further adjustment to operating cash flow is needed.

Nonrecurring charges provide a tax benefit in the year they entail a cash payment. For example, the noncash portion of a restructuring charge recorded for plant closings and severance would provide no cash tax relief in the year recorded. A tax deduction would be received, however, in the year that cash disbursements are made to close the plant and pay the severance amounts. Thus, any adjustments to operating cash flow for nonrecurring cash expenses should be made on an after-tax basis.

Consider the case of The Men's Wearhouse, Inc. In its year ended January 29, 2000, the company recorded combination expenses from its moves to consolidate the operations of Moore's Retail Group, Inc., and K & G Men's Center, Inc. These combination expenses consisted of transaction costs, duplicate facility costs, and litigation costs in the amounts of $7,707,000, $6,070,000, and $930,000, respectively. The expenses were reported on the company's income statement for that year. On the cash-flow statement, in the operating section where net income is reconciled to operating cash flow, only one item appeared. Duplicate facility costs of $4,004,000 were added to net income in computing operating cash flow.[32] Accordingly, nonrecurring cash payments are included in the company's operating cash flow for those years and should be removed, on an after-tax basis, to obtain a more sustainable measure of operating cash flow. The calculations are presented in Exhibit 11.5.

In the exhibit the nonrecurring cash disbursements for transaction costs, duplicate facility costs, and litigation costs related to the company's business combinations in the year ended January 29, 2000, are added back to reported operating cash flow. The adjusted operating cash flow represents a more sustainable operating cash-flow amount.

Exhibit 11.5 Adjustments to Remove Nonrecurring Cash Payments from Operating Cash Flow: The Men's Wearhouse, Inc., Year Ending January 29, 2000 (thousands of dollars)

Reported cash provided by operating activities	$ 101,285
Cash payment for transaction costs ($7,707 nonrecurring charge less noncash portion of $0) × .6[a]	4,624
Cash payment for duplicate facility costs ($6,070 nonrecurring charge less noncash portion of $4,004) × .6	1,240
Cash payment for litigation costs ($930 nonrecurring charge less noncash portion of $0) × .6	558
Adjusted operating cash flow	$ 107,707

[a]The nonrecurring charges were reported on the income statement while the noncash portion of each charge was reported on the statement of cash flow as an adjustment to net income in calculating operating cash flow. A combined federal and state income tax rate of .4 (40%) is used. Thus, to tax effect each item, 1 minus the 40% tax rate is used, or 60%.

Source: The Men's Wearhouse, Inc., annual report, February 3, 2001, pp. 33 and 36.

Managing Cash Flow through Operations-Related Assets and Liabilities   Operating cash flow also can be managed either up or down by effecting nonrecurring changes in operations-related assets and liabilities. For example, inventory may be reduced by temporarily postponing replacement. Accounts payable may be increased by postponing vendor payments. These actions would temporarily boost operating cash flow. However, neither of them would provide cash flow that is sustainable.

It would appear that adjustments to operating cash flow for such nonrecurring changes in operations-related assets and liabilities would be needed to obtain a more sustainable measure. We are hesitant to recommend such adjustments, however, because to do so is tantamount to recommending an adjustment of operating cash flow back toward accrual-based earnings. Moreover, because adjusted operating cash flow can be used to help detect creative accounting practices employed in a company's reported accrual-based earnings, putting these accruals, or parts of them, back into operating cash flow would lessen the effectiveness of that measure.

For these reasons, we do not advocate, except for limited exceptions, adjustments to operating cash flow for nonrecurring changes in operations-related assets and liabilities. Instead, it is recommended that the analyst review carefully the ratios outlined in Chapter 8 and consider the implications for creative accounting practices detailed there.

The limited exceptions where we would advocate adjustments to operating cash flow for changes in operations-related assets and liabilities consist of the cash effects of significant isolated events that affect operations-related assets and liabilities. One example is an arrangement, either through a factoring transaction or securitization, where a material amount of receivables are collected. Another example is the sale of a significant portion of inventory in one or a few large sales that are atypical of a company's normal sales channels. Such isolated events can provide significant amounts of operating cash flow that is nonrecurring.

USING OPERATING CASH FLOW TO DETECT CREATIVE ACCOUNTING PRACTICES

Increases in earnings obtained through creative accounting practices will not generate operating cash flow. Consider, for example, premature or fictitious revenue. As noted in Chapter 6, such actions result in growing receivables but not cash. Also, steps taken to misstate inventory, as outlined in Chapter 8, might boost gross profit and net income but will not provide cash flow. Similar statements can be made about aggressive cost capitalization, as detailed in Chapter 7, and other creative accounting acts outlined throughout this book. Earnings are boosted but operating cash flow is not.

Adjusted Cash Flow–to–Income Ratio

Because earnings altered through creative accounting practices do not change operating cash flow, the relationship between earnings and cash flow can be used to detect creative accounting practices. In particular, the ratio of adjusted cash flow from continuing operations to adjusted income from continuing operations, or the adjusted cash flow–to–income ratio (CFI), is sensitive to earnings changes that are not cash-flow backed.

We speak here of adjusted cash flow provided by continuing operations. This cash-flow measure consists of cash provided by operations adjusted for the items described in this chapter. Income from continuing operations also should be adjusted for nonrecurring items of income or expense. Examples here consist of gains and losses typically reported with income from continuing operations, including gains and losses from the sale of property, plant, and equipment or investments, foreign currency gains and losses, restructuring charges, and litigation-related charges and credits. A full description of all such nonrecurring items that are included in income from continuing operations is beyond the scope of this chapter. However, Chapter 9 highlighted many nonrecurring items in the discussion of the format of the income statement.[33]

To properly use the adjusted cash flow–to–income ratio, a time-series analysis should be performed. That is, the CFI should be calculated for several years and/or several quarters in an effort to detect discernible trends. To eliminate seasonality effects in quarterly amounts, comparisons for quarterly results should be made on a quarter-by-quarter basis, that is, comparing quarterly results for the same quarter in a previous year.

Quarterly cash flow is typically reported in SEC filings on a cumulative year-to-date basis. That is, while operating cash flow for the first quarter consists of cash generated during that period only, operating cash flow for the second quarter will include the first quarter's results. When only cumulative results are available, operating cash flow for an individual quarter can be calculated by subtracting from the current period cumulative cash flow the cash flow accumulated through the most recent prior period.

Quarterly results have the benefit of being available on a more timely basis than annual amounts. Quarterly numbers, however, are inherently more volatile and less reliable than annual results. For this reason, special care should be taken in studying quarterly filings, and confirmation from annual figures should be obtained whenever possible.

For both the quarterly and annual comparisons, declines in the adjusted cash flow–to–income ratio will be an indication that earnings are growing faster than operating cash flow. When such a development occurs, a closer examination should be made, consistent with steps described in earlier chapters, to determine why that is the case. It is possible that creative accounting steps are being taken to boost earnings temporarily.

A sudden increase in the ratio, caused by an increase in operating cash flow in excess of an increase in earnings, while of less concern, also should be examined. Such a development may be the result of a concerted effort to manage earnings downward in an effort to store them for future periods. The analyst should use the steps outlined in this book to ensure that he or she understands the reasons for this development.

Operating cash flow is inherently more volatile than operating earnings. Accordingly, it should be expected that the adjusted cash flow–to–income ratio will vary around its general trend. To discern broad movements, it may be necessary to compare the ratio for a current period with the mean or average ratio calculated over two or three previous periods. The number of periods used depends on the volatility of the company's operating earnings and cash flow and the number of periods of data available.

An alternative approach, when the data are particularly volatile, is to compute the percent change in adjusted operating cash flow over several quarters or years and divide it by the percent change in adjusted income from continuing operations over the same time period. A resulting factor of less than one would indicate that earnings are growing faster than operating cash flow over the period of interest and a closer examination of the company's accounting methods would be in order.

Illustrative Example: Xerox Corp.

Xerox Corp. has been singled out by the SEC for premature revenue recognition. Before filing its financial statements with the Commission for the year ended December 31, 2000, the company was forced to restate results for 1998 and 1999. Xerox conceded that "it had 'misapplied' a range of accepted accounting rules, including some related to its huge copier-leasing business."[34]

Given that Xerox has admitted to premature revenue recognition during 1998 and 1999, the company should provide a good example for demonstrating use of the adjusted cash flow–to–income ratio. That is, there should be a deterioration in the ratio over time as revenue boosted through artificial means is not accompanied by increases in operating cash flow.

Exhibit 11.6 provides data and calculations of the adjusted cash flow–to–income ratio for the years ended December 31, 1994 to 1999. The amounts presented exclude the effects of the company's recent restatement.

In examining the exhibit, the importance of adjustments to reported cash provided by operating activities becomes immediately apparent. Note how the company reported

Exhibit 11.6 Operating Cash Flow, Operating Income, and Calculation of the Adjusted Cash Flow–to–Income Ratio: Xerox Corp., Years Ending December 31, 1994, 1995, 1996, 1997, 1998, and 1999 (thousands of dollars)

	1994	1995	1996	1997	1998	1999
Obtained from statement of cash flows:						
Reported cash flow provided by continuing operations	$479	$599	$324	$472	($1,165)	$1,224
Adjustments:						
Cash payments related to restructuring—net of tax[a]	254	199	118		199	262
	(423 × .6)	(331 × .6)	(197 × .6)		(332 × .6)	(437 × .6)
Proceeds from securitization of finance receivables[b]						(1,495)
Adjusted cash flow provided (used) by continuing operations	$733	$798	$442	$472	($966)	($9)
Obtained from income statement:						
Reported income from continuing operations	$794	$1,174	$1,206	$1,452	$585	$1,424
Adjustments:						
Restructuring charge and asset impairment—net of tax[a]					919	
					(1,531 × .6)	
Inventory charge—net of tax[a]					68	
					(113 × .6)	
Gain on affiliate sales of stock—net of tax[a]			(7)			
			(11 × .6)			
Adjusted income from continuing operations	$794	$1,174	$1,199	$1,452	$1,572	$1,424
Adjusted cash flow–to–income ratio: Adjusted cash flow provided (used) by continuing operations divided by adjusted income from continuing operations	.92	.68	.37	.33	–.61	–.01

[a] A combined federal and state income tax rate of 40% is used. Thus, to tax effect each item, 1 minus the 40% tax rate is used, or 60%.

[b] It is assumed that no gain or loss was recorded on this transaction. Accordingly, the transaction has no income tax implications.

Source: Xerox Corp. Form 10-K Annual Report to the Securities and Exchange Commission, December 31, 1999, pp. 42 and 44, and December 31, 1996, pp. 26 and 42.

more cash provided by operating activities in 1999, $1.2 billion, than in any of the other years presented. That amount is up from a use of operating cash flow of $1.2 billion in 1998. Operating cash flow would not be expected to increase in such a way when revenue is being recognized in a premature fashion.

However, cash provided by operations was temporarily boosted in 1999 by an inflow of $1.5 billion from the securitization of finance receivables. The company sold a large portion of its receivables, effectively borrowing operating cash flow from future years. Other adjustments consist primarily of amounts added back for payments made related to the company's restructuring efforts.

Once adjusted, cash provided by continuing operations is not a particularly pretty sight. It declines virtually every year between 1994 and 1998, rising slightly in 1999, although remaining negative, after a very dismal 1998.

Using reported income from continuing operations as a measure of performance, the company prospered over the 1994 to 1999 time period. After adjusting for nonrecurring items of income, income from continuing operations increased from $794 million in 1994 to as high as $1.6 billion in 1998 and declined somewhat to $1.4 billion in 1999.

The adjusted cash flow–to–income ratio gives a very clear signal of developing problems at the company. The ratio, calculated by dividing adjusted cash flow provided by continuing operations by adjusted income from continuing operations, declined in virtually every year presented. The number became negative in 1998, interestingly in a year when the company's adjusted income from continuing operations was the highest it had been over the entire sample period. It improved slightly in 1999 but was still a negative .01, well down from the .92 reported in 1994.

If one did not know about the problems with revenue recognition at Xerox Corp., the results presented in Exhibit 11.6 would certainly be reason to investigate further. Earnings growth that exceeds the growth in operating cash flow cannot continue for extended periods and should be investigated.

CHECKLIST FOR USING OPERATING CASH FLOW TO DETECT CREATIVE ACCOUNTING PRACTICES

Operating cash flow is useful in detecting creative accounting practices employed in other areas. However, before employing operating cash flow in this manner, it should be adjusted for nonrecurring cash inflows and outflows. A checklist that serves as a guide in this adjustment process and in using operating cash flow to detect creative accounting practices is presented in Exhibit 11.7.

SUMMARY

A complete examination for creative accounting practices requires a careful study of a company's cash-generating ability. This chapter focuses on the use of operating cash flow to identify creative accounting practices. Key points raised in the chapter include the following:

- While less than the flexibility available in the measurement and reporting of earnings, there is flexibility available in the reporting of operating, investing, and financing cash flow without altering the total change in cash.
- Cash-flow statements can be prepared in an indirect-method or direct-method format. The indirect-method format is used more frequently than the direct-method format.

Exhibit 11.7   Checklist for Using Operating Cash Flow to Detect Creative Accounting Practices

---

A. Isolate nonrecurring cash inflows and outflows and adjust reported cash provided by operations, including:
1. Cash flow resulting from the operating income component of discontinued operations
2. Income taxes paid or recovered on transactions classified as investing or financing activities, including:
    a. Gain or loss on sale of assets, investments, or businesses
    b. Gain or loss on disposal of discontinued operations
    c. Extraordinary items, especially early retirement of debt
    d. Changes in accounting principle, if any
    e. Tax benefits of nonqualified employee stock options
3. Cash flow from the purchase and sale of trading securities
4. Capitalized expenditures that other companies expense as incurred
    a. In particular, capitalized software development costs
5. Nonrecurring cash income and expense
    a. Cash receipts arising from nonrecurring income
    b. Cash payments arising from nonrecurring charges
6. Significant isolated events leading to changes in operations-related assets and liabilities, including:
    a. Factoring or securitization of receivables
    b. Special inventory reduction sale outside normal channels
B. Compute adjusted cash flow provided by continuing operations
1. Adjust reported cash flow provided by operating activities for identified nonrecurring cash flow items
C. Compute adjusted income from continuing operations
1. Adjust reported income from continuing operations for nonrecurring items of income and expense
D. Compute the adjusted cash flow–to–income ratio
1. Adjusted cash flow provided by operating activities divided by adjusted income from continuing operations.
    a. Compute for several years and quarters
    b. Examine results for discernible trend

- Cash flow provided by operating activities includes the cash-flow effects of items related to a company's generation of income. Because cash provided by operating activities is cash available for shareholders, interest paid is included with operating activities.

- Cash flow from investing activities consists of purchases and sales of property, plant, and equipment, investments, and other assets.

- Cash flow from financing activities consists of cash provided from the issue of, and cash used for, the repayment or repurchase of debt and equity. Cash used in the payment of dividends also is included with financing activities.

- Cash provided by operating activities may include many nonrecurring items and, accordingly, is not necessarily a sustainable source of cash. Nonrecurring inflows and outflows of cash that may be reported as part of operating cash flow include: cash inflows resulting from the operating income component of discontinued operations, income taxes on items classified as investing or financing activities, cash flow arising from the purchase and sale of trading securities, certain capitalized expenditures, and cash payments associated with restructuring charges.

- To enhance its effectiveness in the detection of creative accounting practices, operating cash flow should be adjusted for nonrecurring cash inflow and outflow.

- A useful ratio in the detection of creative accounting practices is the adjusted cash flow–to–income ratio, which is calculated by dividing adjusted cash provided by continuing operations by adjusted income from continuing operations.

GLOSSARY

Adjusted Cash Flow Provided by Continuing Operations   Cash flow provided by operating activities adjusted to provide a more recurring, sustainable measure. Adjustments to reported cash provided by operating activities are made to remove such nonrecurring cash items as: the operating component of discontinued operations, income taxes on items classified as investing or financing activities, income tax benefits from nonqualified employee stock options, the cash effects of purchases and sales of trading securities for nonfinancial firms, capitalized expenditures, and other nonrecurring cash inflows and outflows.

Adjusted Income from Continuing Operations   Reported income from continuing operations adjusted to remove nonrecurring items.

Available-for-Sale Security   A debt or equity security not classified as a held-to-maturity security or a trading security. Can be classified as a current or noncurrent investment depending on the intended holding period.

Capital Expenditures   Purchases of productive long-lived assets, in particular, items of property, plant, and equipment.

Capitalized Expenditures   Expenditures that are accounted for as assets to be amortized against income in future periods as opposed to current-period expenses.

Cash   Currency, coin, and funds on deposit that are available for immediate withdrawal without restriction. Money orders, certified checks, cashier's checks, personal checks, and bank drafts are also considered cash.

Cash Equivalents   Highly liquid, fixed-income investments with original maturities of three months or less.

Cash Flow Provided by Operating Activities   With some exceptions, the cash effects of transactions that enter into the determination of net income, such as cash receipts from sales of goods and services and cash payments to suppliers and employees for acquisitions of inventory and expenses.

Cash Flow Provided or Used from Financing Activities   Cash receipts and payments involving liability and stockholders' equity items, including obtaining cash from creditors and repaying the amounts borrowed and obtaining capital from owners and providing them with a return on, and a return of, their investments.

Cash Flow Provided or Used from Investing Activities   Cash receipts and payments involving long-term assets, including making and collecting loans and acquiring and disposing of investments and productive long-lived assets.

Cash Flow–to–Income Ratio (CFI)   Adjusted cash flow provided by continuing operations divided by adjusted income from continuing operations.

Cumulative Effect of a Change in Accounting Principle The change in earnings of previous years based on the assumption that a newly adopted accounting principle had previously been in use.

Direct-Method Format   A format for the operating section of the cash-flow statement that reports actual cash receipts and cash disbursements from operating activities.

Discontinued Operations   Net income and the gain or loss on disposal of a business segment whose assets and operations are clearly distinguishable from the other assets and operations of an entity.

Earning Power   A company's ability to generate a sustainable, and likely growing, stream of earnings that provides cash flow.

Earnings Before Interest, Taxes, Depreciation, and Amortization (EBITDA)   An earnings-based measure that, for many, serves as a surrogate for cash flow. Actually consists of working capital provided by operations before interest and taxes.

Emerging Issues Task Force (EITF)   A special committee of the Financial Accounting Standards Board established to reach consensus of how to account for new and unusual financial transactions that have the potential for creating differing financial reporting practices.

Extraordinary Gain or Loss   Gain or loss that is judged to be both unusual and nonrecurring.

Factoring   The discounting, or sale at a discount, of receivables on a nonrecourse, notification basis. The purchaser of the accounts receivable, the factor, assumes full risk of collection and credit losses, without recourse to the firms discounting the receivables. Customers are notified to remit directly to the factor.

Free Cash Flow   Discretionary cash flow that is available for equity claims while maintaining a company's productive capacity. Generally calculated by subtracting dividends and replacement capital expenditures from cash provided by operating activities.

Generally Accepted Accounting Principles (GAAP)   A common set of standards and procedures for the preparation of general-purpose financial statements that either have been established by an authoritative accounting rule-making body, such as the Financial Accounting Standards Board (FASB), or have over time become accepted practice because of their universal application.

Held-to-Maturity Security   A debt security for which the investing entity has both the positive intent and the ability to hold until maturity.

Income from Continuing Operations   After-tax net income before discontinued operations, extraordinary items, and the cumulative effect of changes in accounting principle.

Indirect-Method Format   A format for the operating section of the cash-flow statement that presents the derivation of cash flow provided by operating activities. The format starts with net income and adjusts for all nonoperating items and all noncash expenses and changes in working capital accounts.

Net Cash after Operations   Cash flow available for debt service—the payment of interest and principal on loans. Generally calculated as cash provided by operating activities before interest expense.

Replacement Capital Expenditures   Capital expenditures required to replace productive capacity consumed during a reporting period.

Securitization   The pooling and repackaging of similar items into marketable securities that can be sold to investors.

Trading Security   A debt or equity security bought and held for sale in the near term to generate income on short-term price changes.

Working Capital   Current assets minus current liabilities.

NOTES

1. *The Wall Street Journal,* July 21, 1998, p. B5.
2. *CFO Magazine,* online article, "Charting the Disconnect between Earnings and Cash Flow," November 10, 2000.
3. Accounting and Auditing Enforcement Release No. 723, *In the Matter of Donald A. VandenBerg, CPA* (Washington, DC: Securities and Exchange Commission, September 29, 1995), §III.
4. *CFO Magazine*, "Charting the Disconnect between Earnings and Cash Flow."
5. Ibid., para. 43.
6. Statement of Financial Accounting Standards No. 95, *Statement of Cash Flows* (Norwalk, CT: Financial Accounting Standards Board, November 1987).
7. The company uses the term *net* cash provided by operating activities to make note of the fact that cash provided by operating activities consists of the net of cash inflows and outflows.
8. Statement of Financial Accounting Standards No. 102, *Statement of Cash Flows—Exemption of Certain Enterprises and Classification of Cash Flows from Certain Securities Acquired for Resale* (Norwalk, CT: Financial Accounting Standards Board, February 1989).
9. An accompanying change in accounting practice for tax purposes may entail a tax effect that would be included with cash provided by operating activities. A change from the LIFO method to FIFO method for tax purposes would be an example.
10. CytRx Corp., annual report, December 2000, p. 19.
11. Dean Foods Co., Form 10-K annual report to the Securities and Exchange Commission, May 30, 1999, p. 31.
12. Statement of Financial Accounting Standards No. 95, *Statement of Cash Flows.*
13. Lands End, Inc., annual report, January 28, 2000, p. 26.
14. IBM Corp. annual report, December 1999, pp. 68 and 72.
15. Federal Mogul Corp., annual report, December 1999, pp. 12 and 15.
16. In the unlikely event that a change in accounting principle is accompanied by a change in accounting for tax purposes and an immediate tax payment or receipt, an adjustment for taxes

would be warranted, but only if the accounting change is considered to be other than an operating item. That likelihood is very remote.

17. The Standard Register Co., annual report, January 2, 2000, p. 40.

18. Dell Computer Corp., Form 10-K annual report to the Securities and Exchange Commission, February 2, 2001, p. 29.

19. Cisco Systems, Inc., annual report, July 29, 2000, p. 27.

20. Papa John's International, Inc., annual report, December 31, 2000, p. 39.

21. Microsoft Corp., Form 10-K annual report to the Securities and Exchange Commission, June 30, 1999, Exhibit 13.4, p. 3.

22. The Quigley Corp., annual report, December 31, 2000, p. 23.

23. Microsoft Corp., Form 10-K, June 30, 2000, Exhibit 13.4, p. 6.

24. Payroll taxes on benefits earned by employees from stock options would reduce operating cash flow and marginally reduce any operating cash inflow related to income tax benefits. Given the immateriality of these items relative to the income tax benefits, no adjustment was proposed for them.

25. This was a reclassification from the original 1997 report where the $15,000,000 investment in trading securities was initially classified in the investing section. Refer to The Standard Register Co., Form 10-K annual report to the Securities and Exchange Commission, December 28, 1997, p. 20.

26. Standard Register Co., annual report, p. 38.

27. American Software, Inc., Form 10-K annual report to the Securities and Exchange Commission, April 30, 2000, p. 43.

28. If a company deducted for tax purposes costs that were capitalized for book purposes, a deferred tax liability for the tax effects of the item, as reported in the income tax footnote, will increase.

29. Dun & Bradstreet Corp., Form 10-K annual report to the Securities and Exchange Commission, December 31, 2000, pp. 37 and 59. Information also obtained from *Accounting Trends & Techniques: Annual Survey of Accounting Practices Followed in 600 Stockholders' Reports* (New York: American Institute of CPAs, 2000), p. 238.

30. Advent Software, Inc., annual report, December 1999. Information obtained from Disclosure, Inc., *Compact D/SEC: Corporate Information on Public Companies Filing with the SEC* (Bethesda, MD: Disclosure, Inc., March 2001).

31. Lands End, annual report, pp. 18 and 21.

32. The Men's Wearhouse, Inc., annual report, February 3, 2001, pp. 33 and 36.

33. Note that these adjustments are not designed to remove the effects of creative accounting practices from income but rather to adjust income only for reported nonrecurring items. The adjustments made are comparable to those made by analysts before reported earnings are compared with a forecast in deciding whether the forecast had been met. For a more careful delineation of nonrecurring items included in income and the calculation of what is referred to as a company's sustainable earnings base, the reader is referred to C. Mulford and E. Comiskey, *Financial Warnings* (New York: John Wiley & Sons, 1996) and E. Comiskey and C. Mulford, *Guide to Financial Reporting and Analysis* (New York: John Wiley & Sons, 2000).

34. *The Wall Street Journal,* June 1, 2001, p. C1.

Subject Index

Company Index

Company Index